Effective Groups

Effective Groups

Concepts and Skills to Meet Leadership Challenges

MARK D. CANNON

Peabody College at Vanderbilt University

BRIAN A. GRIFFITH

Peabody College at Vanderbilt University

JAMES W. GUTHRIE
Series Editor

Peabody College at Vanderbilt University

Boston   New York   San Francisco
Mexico City   Montreal   Toronto   London   Madrid   Munich   Paris
Hong Kong   Singapore   Tokyo   Cape Town   Sydney

Senior Series Editor: Arnis Burvikovs
Development Editor: Christien Shangraw
Series Editorial Assistant: Erin Reilly
Marketing Manager: Erica DeLuca
Series Production Editor: Gregory Erb
Editorial Production Service: Nesbitt Graphics, Inc.
Composition Buyer: Linda Cox
Manufacturing Buyer: Linda Morris
Electronic Composition: Nesbitt Graphics, Inc.
Interior Design: Nesbitt Graphics, Inc.
Cover Designer: Joel Gendron

For related titles and support materials, visit our online catalog at www.ablongman.com.

Between the time website information is gathered and then published, it is not unusual for some sites to have closed. Also, the transcription of URLs can result in typographical errors. The publisher would appreciate notification where these errors occur so that they may be corrected in subsequent editions.

Library of Congress Cataloging-in-Publication Data

Cannon, Mark.
    Effective groups: concepts and skills to meet leadership challenges / Mark D. Cannon, Brian A. Griffith.
        p. cm.—(The Peabody education leadership series)
    Includes bibliographical references and index.
    ISBN 0-205-48291-0
    1. Teams in the workplace. 2. Leadership. I. Griffith, Brian. II. Title.
    HD66.C344 2007
    658.4'022—dc22

                                                              2006050684

Printed in the United States of America

10 9 8 7 6 5 4 3 2 1 RRD-VA 10 09 08 07 06

To Emma Pingree Cannon,
my greatest source of inspiration,
joy, and learning.

—Mark D. Cannon

To Alan and Maureen Griffith,
the first ones to teach me the importance
of both education and teamwork.

—Brian A. Griffith

Please look for these other titles in The Peabody Education Leadership Series:

Modern Education Finance and Policy
James W. Guthrie, Matthew G. Springer, R. Anthony Rolle,
Eric A. Houck
ISBN: 0-205-47001-7

Successful Schools and Educational Accountability: Concepts and Skills to Meet Leadership Challenges
Kenneth K. Wong, Anna Nicotera
ISBN: 0-205-47478-0

Strategic Leadership for 21st-Century Schools
James W. Guthrie, Patrick J. Schuermann
To publish © 2008

The Dynamics of Modern School-Community Relations
Robert Crowson, Ellen Goldring, Katherine Taylor-Haynes
To publish © 2008

Brief Contents

Contents

CHAPTER TWO

Group Goals and Shared Vision   24

CHAPTER THREE

Group Structure and Strategy   44

CHAPTER SIX

Power and Influence 112

Decision Making   129

CHAPTER ELEVEN
Team Learning   221

Series Preface

▓ THE PEABODY EDUCATION LEADERSHIP SERIES

Vanderbilt University's Peabody College is one of the world's foremost schools of education and human development. The Peabody faculty is in the vanguard of research and knowledge creation, while a long tradition of collaboration "on the ground" with learners, educators, policymakers and organizations ensures that, at Peabody, theory and practice inform each other. In addition to conferring a full range of graduate, professional, and undergraduate degrees, the College is committed to strengthening current educators and organizational leaders in their efforts to propel greater achievement and enhance human development.

This book and others in the Allyn & Bacon Peabody Education Leadership Series are published to facilitate wider understanding of the means by which human learning takes place and how greater learning can be fostered. Much of the nation's most forward thinking regarding learning and instruction emanates from Peabody. For example, the National Research Council's famous research synthesis, *How People Learn*, was undertaken with the leadership of Peabody faculty. Current faculty members are generating research and constructing the paradigms that will influence the teaching of reading, mathematics, and science well into the future.

Consistent with its mission and its own research, Peabody strives to model good instruction. In that spirit, each book in the Educational Leadership Series has a number of instructional aids. These include full outlines of the volume's substantive material, complete tables of contents, indexes filled with significant concepts and citations, chapter previews with summaries of what has been and is to be covered, extensive use of topical case studies, clearly understandable graphics, and discussion questions. These aids will enable readers to grasp the complexities associated with what 21st-century leaders need to know about such topics as leadership, finance, accountability, community relations, organizational dynamics, or education law.

▓ TEXT SUPPLEMENTS

Each text in this series is accompanied by a **Companion Website**. Students and Instructors should visit www.ablongman.com/Peabody for test cases, simulation exercises, sample data for end-of-chapter exercises, URLs for further research and interest, added bibliographies, and other up-to-date information.

Students can find help with research projects using **Research Navigator**, which provides access to three exclusive databases of credible and reliable source material, including EBSCO's ContentSelect Academic Journal Database, the *New York Times* Search by Subject Archive, and the "Best of the Web" Link Library. Research Navigator is available through

Allyn & Bacon's **MyLabSchool**, located at www.mylabschool.com. MyLabSchool needs to be requested by the instructor with a separate ISBN that is free with new books.

An **Instructor's Manual** with teaching resources and test items is also available to adopting instructors through their local Allyn & Bacon representative.

■ THE PEABODY EDUCATION LEADERSHIP SERIES AND EDUCATION'S EVOLVING CONTEXT

Education today must respond as never before to a set of global economic and cultural conditions. These rapidly changing conditions, and the competition they are creating, serve as a subtext for virtually every concept covered by books in this textbook series.

For most of the nation's history, it was possible for an individual to forego formal schooling and still own land, acquire relatively well-paying employment, participate in civic life as an informed citizen, and achieve a substantial degree of personal fulfillment. For many, probably most, individuals, these comfortable circumstances have changed. Modern economies render formal education crucial for individual success, social mobility, and engagement with the demands of the workforce, the environment, and government. The eventual outcome of these relatively new challenges now matters as much for a child being raised on a family farm in South Dakota as to one from a farm family in South Africa.

What has become true for individuals also applies to nations. A people once flourished or floundered based on what they could extract from the ground. Today, a nation is more likely to survive and prosper based on what it can extract from the minds of its citizens.

Readers of this series also will have to grapple with the challenges posed by global changes. Many of the divisive questions facing society as a whole have powerful implications for the conduct of education, as well.

- How can immigrants be fully integrated into American society?
- How many languages can schools reasonably be expected to offer or to use for instruction?
- How much testing is too much?
- How much should be spent on schools to ensure that all students have an opportunity to achieve the learning standards that governments set?
- How should teachers be trained and licensed?
- Should private providers be permitted to offer public schooling?
- Should the public pay for preschool and interschool programs?
- Should high school exit examinations determine graduation?
- What should class sizes be to maximize the positive effects of instruction?

These questions illustrate the complicated and interconnected policy and practical dilemmas upon which books in this series will attempt to shed light. The goal is not so much to provide direct answers to such questions as it is to arm readers with the tools that will enable them to keep pace with and contribute solutions to these and future problems. Specifically, this series will:

- Harness useful concepts and evidenced-based practical understandings applicable to understanding and solving emerging policy challenges and to managing and reforming modern organizations.

- Provide readers with technical understanding of important components of education resource deployment, policy development, organizational development, and institutional governance and operation.
- Suggest research-based means by which education institutions and practices can be undertaken to greater effect and with greater efficiency.
- Enable educators to participate better in policy-related and professional debates regarding best practice.

We welcome your comments and suggestions as a reader, researcher, or other user of this book, or other books in the series.

James W. Guthrie
Series Editor
Professor of Public Policy and Education

Camilla P. Benbow
Patricia and Rodes Hart
Dean of Education and Human Development

Peabody College
Vanderbilt University
Nashville, Tennessee

Preface

This text provides a practical, research-based approach to building effective groups that accomplish meaningful goals in various settings. The value of groups is recognized by a wide variety of organizations as evidenced by their increased popularity. But despite the frequency with which groups are implemented to perform various tasks, their performance potential often remains elusive. Getting the most out of groups requires that organizational leaders and group members understand enough about groups to staff, structure, and manage them appropriately. Unfortunately, organizational leaders often assume that everyone knows how to work in a group. In contrast, research demonstrates that the knowledge, skills, and ability to operate effectively in groups needs to be learned; education and training in group dynamics are often essential for establishing effective work groups (Salas & Cannon-Bowers, 2001). This text provides the key knowledge that students need to operate effectively within—and even lead—groups in organizations. Rather than cover every possible topic in great detail, we have selected those areas that we believe are most beneficial for professionals to understand.

We address all the topics that are traditionally covered by texts on group dynamics: goals and shared vision, structure and strategy, communication, leadership, power and influence, decision making, diversity, conflict, and training and development. Also, because there is a great deal of interest among academics and practitioners on both **team learning and virtual teams**, this text dedicates a full chapter to each.

The topic of organizational learning was popularized in the late 1980s as many organizations recognized the need to become more agile and make greater use of their employees' potential. At the heart of this movement was the realization that groups and organizations can learn more effective ways to achieve their goals. Interestingly, groups will repeat mistakes without learning from them at a higher rate than individuals. Groups tend to settle into routinized, mechanistic patterns of operation rather than creating synergy to innovate and adapt creatively to changing circumstances. As a result, some groups are simply not able to learn and adapt (Cannon & Edmonsdon, 2001). Chapter 11 describes the barriers that inhibit team learning and what can be done to overcome them.

In an increasingly global and dynamic economy, virtual teams have become commonplace in organizations. Advances in technology have enabled individuals in any variety of locations to work together in real time. Yet despite the advances in technology that enable members to communicate and collaborate in cyberspace, these types of teams are not without distinctive challenges. Chapter 12 examines the unique challenges virtual teams engender, along with methods for increasing their odds of success.

In addition to the chapters on virtual teams and team learning, **another feature that distinguishes this text from other leading texts is the use of real-world cases.** Each chapter begins with an introductory case that presents students with a workplace dilemma that is relevant to the chapter. Each introductory case is based on an actual situation within an organization, though most of them have been adapted to protect anonymity. At the end of each chapter the outcome of the particular case is discussed. These cases are engaging to students and provide interesting illustrations of how to resolve a variety of issues particular to group work.

In addition to these introductory cases, **each chapter also concludes with an open-ended case study.** These cases provide opportunities for students to analyze a variety of group situations and leadership challenges. We find these types of cases helpful both for engaging students in the course material as well as for assisting them in applying the concepts and theories to real-world situations. Each chapter also includes at least one exercise to engage students and deepen the learning process. Exercises are designed to give readers the skills needed to become effective group leaders.

TEXT SUPPLEMENTS

Each text in this series is accompanied by a **Companion Website**. Students and Instructors should visit www.ablongman.com/Peabody for test cases, simulation exercises, sample data for end-of-chapter exercises, URLs for further research and interest, added bibliographies, and other up-to-date information.

Students can find help with research projects using **Research Navigator**, which provides access to three exclusive databases of credible and reliable source material, including EBSCO's ContentSelect Academic Journal Database, the *New York Times* Search by Subject Archive, and the "Best of the Web" Link Library. Research Navigator is available through Allyn & Bacon's **MyLabSchool**, located at www.mylabschool.com. MyLabSchool needs to be requested by the instructor with a separate ISBN that is free with new books.

An **Instructor's Manual** with teaching resources and test items is also available to adopting instructors through their local Allyn & Bacon representative.

ACKNOWLEDGMENTS

First, we would like to thank our editors, Arnis Burvikovs and Christien Shangraw, for their wise editorial guidance and enduring patience. They are experts in their field and a joy to work with. The following people were also instrumental in commenting on early drafts of this book: Mark W. Cannon, Betty Schoeman Cannon, Lucy Cannon, and Kristen Snuck. More specifically, Chapter 8, Diversity in Groups, is indebted to the work of one of our students, Debangshu Roychoudhury. His insight and research made a significant contribution to this challenging topic in group work. Finally, a number of highly qualified academic reviewers gave excellent feedback that helped make this book more readable and more empirically grounded. They are: Amy Aldridge, Northeastern State University; Angela Humphrey Brown, Piedmont College; Michael Jazzar, University of North Carolina, Charlotte; David N. Rapp, University of Minnesota; Agnes Smith, University of South

Alabama; Angela Spaulding, West Texas A&M. We are grateful for their thoughtful observations and suggestions.

A number of other people gave of their time and energy by helping with research, editing, or providing suggestions for improvement. They include (in alphabetical order) L. K. Browning, Cindy Franco, Melissa Holley, Brandelyn Klein, Laura Minteer, Leah Morgan, Tatiana Peredo, Sally Santen, Avi Spielman, and Dana Wolf. A special thank you goes to Jacqueline Whelan for her editorial expertise and responsiveness. In addition, a portion of this book was written while the second author was teaching an internship class in London, England during the subway bombings of 2006. The way in which a group of eleven Vanderbilt students organized a communications structure, rallied together, and cared for each other was inspiring. Many of them have gone on to successful careers as competent leaders of groups and teams.

Finally, we would like to thank our colleagues in the Department of Human and Organizational Development at Peabody College of Vanderbilt University. We are the beneficiaries of their encouragement and generous mentoring. Brian A. Griffith is especially grateful to Bob Innes and Pat Arnold, from whom he has learned much about groups, both theoretically and experientially.

■ REFERENCES

Cannon, M. D., & Edmondson, A. C. (2001). Confronting failure: Antecedents and consequences of shared beliefs about failure in organizational work groups. *Journal of Organizational Behavior 22,* 161–177.

Salas, E., & Cannon-Bowers, J. (2001). The science of training: A decade of progress. *Annual Review of Psychology, 52,* 471–499.

About the Authors

Mark D. Cannon is an assistant professor of educational leadership at Peabody College of Vanderbilt University. He earned a BS and MS from Brigham Young University, and an AM and PhD from Harvard University.

Professor Cannon studies barriers to learning in organizations. He has published on giving effective interpersonal feedback, how organizations can learn from failure, and how coaching can help leaders transition more quickly and effectively to new positions. He is co-editor of Dartmouth Publishing Company's *Organizational Psychology* (Volumes 1–3). He teaches courses in organizational theory and behavior, executive coaching, work team management, strategic human resource management, and learning organizations.

Brian A. Griffith is an assistant clinical professor in the Department of Human and Organizational Development at Peabody College of Vanderbilt University. Professor Griffith, who earned a BS from Miami University, an MDiv from Columbia International University, and a PhD from the University of South Carolina, teaches courses in applied human development, small group behavior, and organizational theory. In 2003, he was the recipient of the Peabody Award for Excellence in Classroom Teaching, a teaching award given every three years to a Peabody College faculty member who has demonstrated the highest caliber of teaching. In the Spring of 2006, he was awarded the Madison Sarratt Prize for Excellence in Undergraduate Teaching, one of two annual teaching awards given to Vanderbilt faculty.

Effective Groups

CHAPTER ONE

Introduction to Effective Groups

▋ INTRODUCTION

This chapter explains why groups have become popular and illustrates many significant benefits achieved through groups in various settings such as education, commerce, the military, and not-for-profit agencies. However, groups often fail to reach their performance potential. Understanding what makes groups successful is essential for constructing effective groups. Group performance is influenced by multiple factors that are explored in more detail in later chapters.

LEARNING OBJECTIVES

After reading this chapter, you should be able to

- Recognize the assets associated with group performance.
- Understand why groups do not always achieve their potential.
- Describe the difference between a group and a team.
- Identify the key areas of knowledge for establishing and maintaining effective groups.
- Describe how groups influence their members and how individual members can influence the group.
- Recognize the advantages of understanding group dynamics.

OPENING CASE

The Case of the Possible Wrong-Site Surgery

Everyone on the surgical team was at their appointed post, and all seemed to be in order. The surgeon, Dr. Johnson, was about to cut when Nurse Rainey suddenly had a very sick feeling in the pit of her stomach. For some reason, she had the powerful impression that Dr. Johnson was about to remove the wrong kidney. Could she be correct? Hadn't the team followed all the procedures that should keep this kind of mistake from happening? Was there any good reason to think her concern had any real validity, or was she just being influenced by the powerful episode she saw on the television show *ER* in which this kind of error was made?

Without any hard evidence, it seemed unlikely that she was right about this. In addition, she was new to the hospital and the surgical team, so she had good reason to doubt her gut feeling. To compound the matter, surgeons hate to be questioned, and Dr. Johnson seemed like the type who would hold a grudge against anyone he did not like. As a single mother, she desperately needed this job and this shift. Dr. Johnson was very influential and could easily have her assigned to the midnight shift which would make her child-care situation disastrous and turn her life upside down. The negative consequences of speaking up and being wrong were clear. But what if she spoke up and ended up being right? What would happen then? Probably the embarrassing error would be swept under the rug and there would not likely be any reward or gratitude. This hospital had a reputation for "shooting the messenger"—punishing the deliverer of bad news whether he or she had anything to do with the cause of the problem. And if she were going to bring it up, how could she do so diplomatically to minimize the risk of a backlash?

Discussion Questions

1. Would you speak up if you were in Nurse Rainey's shoes?
2. If so, what exactly would you say?
3. How do you think the surgical team would respond if she spoke up?

▨ INTRODUCTION TO EFFECTIVE GROUPS

The case above illustrates several important points about groups. First, our society regularly depends on groups to provide all kinds of goods and services, and a surgical group is just one example of the many ways people rely on groups to meet important needs. Second, the effectiveness with which groups perform their work can have a significant impact on our well-being. Effective surgical groups save lives and increase the quality of life for numerous people every day. When groups are effective, they can be immensely productive, creative, entertaining, and enjoyable. Finally, as is illustrated by the case, groups are not without complications and tensions that can limit their effectiveness in significant ways if group members and leaders do not handle them productively.

Groups have played an impressive role in our history. Three inventions of the twentieth century which helped make globalization possible were initiated by very small groups—the airplane, the personal computer, and the Internet. The airplane was the invention of the Wright Brothers, who owned a bicycle shop but worked intrepidly in their garage until they had a working model which was able to fly for 300 feet.

In 1938, Bill Hewlett and Dave Packard dreamed up Hewlett-Packard while they warmed the bench at a Stanford football game. Bill Gates and his friend, Paul Allen, wrote their first marketable program for an Atari in Bill's parents' garage. Steve Jobs and Steve Wozniak developed user-friendly personal computers and started Apple Computer in a parent's garage. Larry Page and Sergey Brin started Google while they were graduate students at Stanford and used Larry's dorm room as Google's first data center. The early standards of the fledgling Internet were implemented by small groups of people collaborating together long before it was of any interest to governments, businesses, or educators. Their standards of openness and consensus showcase group work at its finest and enabled information and knowledge to be developed and disseminated at an incredible pace. Larger groups are responsible for goods, services, government, laws, religion, electronics, education, health care, disaster response, and a host of other duties.

In short, groups have had and will continue to have a major impact on our daily lives. The use of groups as work units in organizations became popular in the 1980s and '90s, and organizations continue to be sold on the group concept. Cohen and Bailey (1997) reported that 80 percent of companies with more than 100 employees were using teams regularly to accomplish their work. A survey of Fortune 1,000 companies revealed that approximately 68 to 70 percent are using teams to achieve organizational goals (Tata & Prasad, 2004).

In addition, group membership marks many transitions of our lives and can be very rewarding personally. Most babies in the industrialized world are born with the help of a medical group. Groups of people celebrate birthdays, parties, graduations, and weddings, and mourn together at funerals. The energy and excitement of a startup company are hard to match and fondly remembered. Religious groups join together for worship and spiritual sustenance. Work groups can achieve remarkable designs, products, and innovations. Political groups work toward a candidate's election and the chance to mold a new government. The Declaration of Independence, a founding document of America's government, was written by a relatively small group of five main authors. Most of us grow up in some kind of family group and then tend to form new groups of our own. We also go to school in groups.

Unfortunately, group membership can also be a source of unhappiness. In particular, work groups can be a source of daily unpleasantness. Nurse Rainey's tense situation is just one of the many possible predicaments in which teams members can sometimes find themselves. In addition, people at work often dislike each other, and the enforced proximity of membership in the same work group can exacerbate the conflict or irritation (Tindale, Dykema-Engblade, & Wittkowski, 2005). When groups start off on the wrong foot, they can spiral downward, deteriorating over time and becoming very uncomfortable and hazardous for their members (Ericksen & Dyer, 2004). In addition, even pleasant, cohesive groups can pressure members to do things that are morally wrong and even illegal.

This book describes the dynamics of how groups function, what factors help them excel, what keeps them from achieving their potential, and what can be done to make them more successful.

▓ GROUPS AND TEAMS DEFINED

The terms *group* and *team* are often used somewhat synonymously, but the term *group* actually refers to a general category of which a *team* is a subset. Thus, all teams are groups, but not all groups should be considered teams. A group is a defined set of individuals who interact with each other for a common purpose. Teams are groups, and a group might become a team, but teams have particular characteristics and are defined somewhat more narrowly.

One general difference is that teams typically have more specific, demanding performance expectations. Teams have the following four characteristics (Alderfer, 1977; Hackman, 1987): First, they are designed with the purpose of accomplishing at least one *specific goal* or *objective*. Second, at least some degree of *interdependence* must exist such that team members depend on each other in order to accomplish the outcome. Third, for the purpose of accomplishing the task, team members adopt or are assigned one or more *specific roles* that they are responsible to enact. Fourth, teams are *bounded* social systems with a relatively stable, intact structure. Membership may vary over time, but team members need clarity as to who is or is not on the team and what their roles are in order to function effectively as a team.

Groups are used regularly even for very minor tasks, whereas teams are somewhat less common and tend to be assigned to work together for longer periods of time. Rather than focusing only on teams, this text focuses more broadly on groups so as to make this text relevant to the widest range of types of situations in which people work toward some common purpose.

▓ WHY HAVE GROUPS BECOME SO POPULAR?

Some Tasks Are Too Large for a Single Individual

Historically, a key reason for organizing groups to accomplish work has been that many tasks are just too big for one person to handle alone. Throughout history, people have needed to collaborate with each other to accomplish large tasks. In jungle regions, members of the village have teamed together to hunt dangerous animals. Settlers have worked together to raise barns. Larger communities have had to work together to build a bridge, build a dam, construct a ship, establish an army, and so on.

One dramatic but tragic example of the rapid formation of a group for a common purpose was the incident aboard United flight 93 on September 11, 2001. Most passengers expected a routine flight and would not have considered their fellow fliers to be a group. Unfortunately for these passengers, this flight turned out to be anything but routine. They soon learned that their plane had been hijacked.

Initially there was confusion during which passengers tried to make sense of what was happening. As they gathered information through their cell phones, they collectively realized that the hijackers would likely crash their plane into some predetermined landmark building. The fliers recognized that they would have to work as a group. The passengers took a vote on what to do, and the majority wanted to mobilize to thwart the hijackers and, if possible, take control of the aircraft.

They quickly organized and formed a plan of attack. Many of them made last minute phone calls to loved ones and then took their assigned places. They rushed through the first class seating area to the cockpit with makeshift weaponry they found and made a determined attack. When the hijacker who was piloting the plane realized that they were under attack, he threw the plane into violent gyrations to throw the passengers off balance. The passengers recovered their balance and made another assault on the cockpit. Finally, realizing that the passengers were about to prevail, the pilot threw the plane into a nosedive and crashed it into a field in order to avoid having the passengers prevail.

Sadly, all passengers perished in the crash. Nonetheless, they had succeeded in saving unnumbered innocent lives of those who would have perished had the plane reached its intended destination. They may also have saved the United States Capitol or the White House from utter destruction along with some of our political leadership. Human beings often show a natural propensity toward collaboration as a group. In this case, strangers formed as a group, shared information, voted, mobilized, and took action all in very short order. It also shows what can be accomplished by a determined group without traditional weapons against a trained and armed group of hijackers.

Group Synergy

The pursuit of synergy has been a key driver of the explosive growth of groups in the workplace in recent decades. Synergy occurs when the productivity of the unit as a whole is greater than the sum of its parts. Specifically, individuals find ways of working together that enable the group to perform better than their aggregated individual contributions (Tindale & Sheffey, 2002).

An interesting example of synergy can be found in the distinctive "V" flying formation that geese use when migrating. By flying in this formation, geese reportedly can travel about 70 percent farther than they would without using this formation. Each individual goose benefits from the updraft and wind breaking that is produced by the goose in front of it. Naturally, the lead goose must exert more energy than the others and thus tires more quickly. However, geese have learned to work as a team, rotating through the leadership position as the lead goose gets tired. This structure also facilitates the ability to see the entire flock and to know whether each goose is accounted for. Military planes have copied this formation for similar reasons.

Workplace implementation of group structures has often resulted in synergies with handsome rewards for organizations. Consider the examples of Globe Metallurgical, Inc., which has grown to be one of the world's largest suppliers to foundries with the help of self-directed work groups. After implementing these teams, the company achieved a 550% increase in market share (for ductile iron), a 380% rise in productivity, and a perfect zero in product returns for two years (Zuidema & Kleiner, 1994). They even became the first small company to win the prestigious Malcolm Baldrige quality award.

Likewise, Honeywell achieved impressive results after implementing teams. The use of teams in their Building Controls Division enabled them to cut their product development time by an estimated 50 to 60%. In the Industrial Automation Systems Division, teams enabled them to cut their cycle times by 30% and save 11.1 million dollars in one year with a near perfect (99.6%) record of on-time shipments (Larson, 1998). Similarly, Johnsonville Foods, a leading producer of sausage, reportedly achieved a 50% increase in productivity after implementing a team structure. And teams at Federal Express were credited with locating errors that eventually saved the company millions of dollars.

Even work that has traditionally been considered highly individualistic, such as financial and brokerage services, has benefited from the implementation of teams. Specifically, Investor Diversified Services (IDS), a subsidiary of American Express, has had great success experimenting with teams. One objective measure of their success occurred during the 1989 stock market crash. One of the problems that concerns investors during violent market corrections is the potential inability to reach their investment representatives to place orders quickly. Many thousands of dollars can be wiped out in a matter of seconds as stocks plunge. Thus, a key measure of effectiveness is the ability to respond to customer calls with immediacy even during crises. The stock market crash of 1987 was similar and provides a benchmark against which to make a comparison. During the 1987 crash, the average time it took IDS representatives to field calls was 7.5 minutes. Just two years later, IDS was able to handle a greater number of calls with an average response time of an astounding 13 seconds (Manz & Sims, 1995). It took over 34 times longer to answer calls before the implementation of teams.

▓ OTHER BENEFITS OF GROUPS

Another factor that may account for the popularity of teams is that they provide a number of psychological benefits. Human beings are social creatures, and groups provide an opportunity for them to meet social needs. People often report that working in a group makes the work more enjoyable. Groups appear to help people have more positive attitudes and affect (Allen & Hecht, 2004). Groups can also reduce uncertainty and anxiety (West, 2001). People working in a mine or other potentially hazardous environments find that being part of a group gives them a greater sense of security. Groups also act as an anchor in social situations, providing a reference point and enabling people to gauge and test what might be appropriate or inappropriate social behavior.

▓ IS UNDERSTANDING GROUPS IMPORTANT?

Dramatic growth in use of groups in organizations, coupled with the fact that groups are often credited with great success might suggest that the cure for organizational ineffectiveness is to implement a group structure. Indeed, groups have achieved incredible feats. However, a more critical look is in order. Let us examine some of the assertions about groups that are widely held among leaders who favor groups:

- Groups outperform sets of isolated individuals doing similar work.
- Groups make better decisions because they draw on more information.
- Groups are more creative because they can brainstorm.
- Groups are more productive because synergies develop.
- Group cohesiveness makes groups more productive.

These propositions are assumed by many practitioners, teachers, consultants, and trainers to be true. The answer is "It depends." In fact, there are at least some conditions under which each of these statements is false (Allen & Hecht, 2004). Group effectiveness is not automatic. It is enhanced when both group leaders and group members have sufficient understanding of group dynamics that they can take the appropriate actions to work through performance challenges and to build on group strengths (Hirschfeld, Jordan, Field, Giles, & Armenakis, 2006). The purpose of this text is to explain the key factors that influence group effectiveness and provide information on how group leaders and members can use this information to develop and maintain successful groups. Each of the assertions noted above will be examined in more detail.

Groups Outperform Sets of Isolated Individuals Doing Similar Work

Although groups often outperform individuals doing similar work, this is not always the case. A more accurate statement would be that groups have the potential to outperform individuals doing similar work, but they frequently fail to achieve that potential. The findings are somewhat inconclusive and depend somewhat on the task, but teams are not guaranteed to regularly outperform individuals doing similar work (Allen & Hecht, 2004). Evidence for this has been established both from laboratory and field settings (Guzzo & Dickinson, 1996).

Groups do not consistently outperform individuals doing the same work. Yet leading researchers have argued that, under appropriate circumstances, groups can and should outperform individuals. What may account for the current findings is that groups tend to have a wider range of performance outcomes (Hackman, 2002). Some groups perform really well, while others do very poorly. In other words, some groups are managed effectively and excel by achieving more of their potential, while others are poorly managed and achieve a poor outcome. Groups can either experience virtuous cycles of performance in which they grow stronger, or downward cycles in which they grow worse (Ericksen & Dyer, 2004). Also, because groups have become so popular, sometimes they have been applied to tasks that are better suited for individuals, so it is only natural that they would not perform as well (Wageman, 1997).

Groups do indeed have a potential to far outperform individuals doing similar work under the right circumstances and when managed effectively (West, Brobeck, & Richter, 2004). If low-performing groups had been more appropriately organized and better managed the outcome could have been different. A better understanding of the nature of groups and how to manage them is the key to achieving greater performance.

Groups Make Better Decisions Because They Draw on More Information

Groups can be a great asset in decision making (Kerr & Tindale, 2004). Each person in a group has different life and professional experiences and perspectives and thus brings a unique perspective to the decision-making process. By drawing on the diverse strengths within the group, better decisions can be made (Patton & Downs, 2003). The question, then, is whether groups effectively draw on the information held by its members. In any group, members have some knowledge and other information that only one or a few individuals within the group know. Often the key to making a good decision is getting this information on the table so that it enriches the knowledge base of the entire group. Thus, individuals who have key bits of knowledge need either to speak up proactively or to be drawn into the discussion. Unfortunately, this does not often happen (Medvec, Berger, Liljenquist, & Neale, 2004). Stasser and Titus (1985) manipulated the information given to group members working on a decision-making task such that some of the crucial information was given to all group members and some crucial information was given to only a few group members (Stasser & Titus, 1985). In other words, some information was common (held by all group members), and some was unique (held by only one individual). When the group attempted to make decisions, the discussion was dominated by the common information that was held by all group members. The unique information (held by only one individual) either did not get into the discussion at all or was underutilized in the decision-making process. The result was that groups made poor decisions because they did not obtain and take into account all the information that was available within the group.

The Case of the Possible Wrong-Site Surgery at the beginning of this chapter is an illustration of the kind of problem that is common in groups—one person has an idea, information, or a question that others do not have but is reluctant to share it with the rest of the group. Thus, the group never accesses useful information contained within the group, and, therefore, does not make the quality decisions that it potentially could.

In addition to failing to identify and use all the information available to them, groups have sometimes been known to suppress the open sharing of information and the use of critical thinking and analytical skills that are essential for effective decision making. Janis (1972) identified this tendency which resulted in disastrous decisions at high levels in government as a phenomenon that he labeled "groupthink." Janis believed that under certain circumstances, the desire of group members to maintain their relationships and feeling of cohesiveness with each other would override their commitment to the open debates, challenges, and confrontations that are critical to making good decisions.

Groups Are More Creative Because They Can Brainstorm

The idea behind brainstorming is to develop group synergy in generating creative ideas. When groups are given problems such as "Develop some good ideas about how we might increase recycling in the community" or "Develop ideas for a TV commercial to introduce a new product," members should be encouraged to take risks and come up with innovative ideas. Effective brainstorming requires that a group adhere to a set of rules that have been designed to facilitate group synergy around this creative process (Osborn, 1957). Group members are instructed to:

1. Generate as many ideas as they can
2. Share wild, eccentric, off-the-wall ideas
3. Build on each other's ideas
4. Avoid evaluating the ideas being shared, and do not make any public commentary on the ideas being shared
5. Share one idea at a time and do not interrupt each other

Once the group has generated as many ideas as possible, it can then go back and start evaluating the quality of the ideas and sort out what ideas are potentially useful. In addition, creative but impractical ideas might be used to enhance the quality of the final idea. One benefit of brainstorming is that exposing each member of the group to the ideas of others will assist them in developing their own higher-quality ideas. Another key feature is that wild, impractical ideas can be helpful because they may act as a catalyst for someone else's idea. Thus, members are encouraged to share ideas, no matter how bizarre or impractical.

Does it work? Unfortunately, the track record is not good (Diehl & Stroebe, 1987). Apprehension and criticism both interfere. Members often worry that others will consider them stupid or strange if they share bizarre, weird, or impractical ideas (Mullen, Johnson, & Salas, 1991). This discourages them from sharing and hinders the nature of the process (Paulus, Larey, Putman, Leggett, & Roland, 1996). Second, the tendency to be critical is a natural human response that is difficult to resist; and public criticism quickly squelches the airing of the more unusual ideas. Even at IDEO, the world's leading design firm where creativity is the key component of daily work, facilitators have a bell that they ring anytime they hear criticism during a brainstorming session to remind participants not to evaluate (Kelly & Littman, 2001). Thus, even skilled design people who brainstorm regularly have a hard time not succumbing to the temptation to prematurely criticize or discount ideas. Evaluation apprehension and other conditions that hinder brainstorming will be discussed later (Diehl & Stroebe, 1991).

Once again, the fact that brainstorming does not work well all the time does not mean that it should not be used. The problem is that group members usually do not follow established ground rules and proven strategies for success. Also, optimistically, technology appears to be a useful intervention here. When group members were able to participate in electronic brainstorming where their responses were anonymous, they were able to achieve the promised benefits of brainstorming especially when the groups were large (Kerr & Tindale, 2004).

Groups Are More Productive Because Synergies Develop

As demonstrated in some of the examples already mentioned, groups can produce synergies that accomplish incredible feats. However, synergies do not always develop, and can be offset by productivity or process losses associated with group work. Steiner (1972), one of the earliest group researchers, developed the following formula for group productivity: the actual productivity (AP) of a group would equal the sum of the individual contributions of each member plus process gains (PG) minus process losses (PL).

$$AP = \text{Individual productivity} + PG - PL$$

In other words, the actual performance of the group and whether that is greater than the sum of the individual performances will depend on the extent to which process gains (synergies) emerge and the extent to which the group is able to minimize process losses. Synergies do not develop automatically, they require the right conditions. Process losses include conditions such as free riding (when individuals within the group realize that they can work less and still enjoy the overall performance of the group), coordination problems, communication problems, conflict, and so on. Because process losses occur fairly regularly and synergies are more difficult to create, the losses tend to outweigh the gains which make the group achieve below its potential (Hill, 1982).

Group Cohesiveness Makes Groups More Productive

Cohesiveness is present when members feel a bond or connection with each other and value being members of the group. Cohesiveness has been argued to enhance the productivity of the group, and some believe that increasing group cohesiveness is the best way to make a group more productive. Research suggests that there is generally a relationship between cohesiveness and productivity, with more-cohesive groups tending to be more productive than less-cohesive groups (Gully, Devine, & Whitney, 1995).

In fact, group norms mediate the effects of group cohesiveness on productivity, and the preservation of that cohesiveness can also preempt good ideas and lead to groupthink. *Groupthink* is the tendency within a cohesive group to let pressure for building or maintaining consensus block critical thinking and analysis. Cohesiveness increases the extent to which group members adhere to specific norms (expectations within the group as to what behavior is and is not desirable). Some norms lead to an increase in productivity while others decrease productivity. So, whether cohesiveness enhances productivity or not is significantly affected by the direction of the norms as is illustrated in Figure 1.1 (Guzzo & Dickson, 1996). Groups that have high-productivity norms (norms that foster hard work, investing time, and taking initiative to make sure the job is done right) and that are cohesive are likely to be productive. By contrast, groups with low-productivity norms that are cohesive are likely to be relatively unproductive.

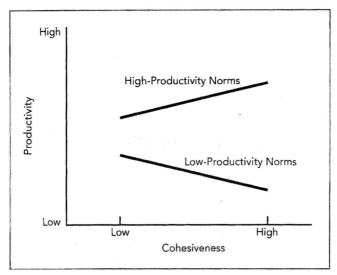

FIGURE 1.1   **The Relationship Between Productivity and Cohesion**

A group with low-productivity norms that is not cohesive will be unlikely to enforce those norms to the extent that a highly cohesive group would. So, some individuals may behave in a productive manner for personal reasons. By contrast, cohesive groups have been known to enforce low-productivity norms. Consider the practice of "binging" that early management scientists discovered on the factory floor. Cohesive factory workers who were mistrustful of management and disliked their working conditions would intentionally keep productivity low by hitting or "binging" workers who violated the low-productivity norms. For example, a new employee might come in and start working at a rapid pace. Upon noticing this, other workers would give this worker a punch or "bing" in the arm as they walked by. After a few hundred "bings," the worker would get the idea that it was not advantageous to violate the norms of low productivity.

Rivethead: Tales from the Assembly Line, (Hamper, 1991) a best selling book by Ben Hamper, provides a vivid account of how factory workers at General Motors would act cohesively in ways that were counter to the company's interests. For example, irritated workers retaliated against management by putting a nut in the hubcap of cars so that they made a clanking noise as they rolled off the assembly line. Workers did not fear being reported by their peers because they were a cohesive unit and adhered to a code of silence. Similar problems of rate setting or norm imposition can be present in school settings. Teachers who dislike an administrator can withhold information, refuse to fill out central office–requested forms, or drag their feet in volunteering for out-of-class activities such as directing dramas and other events that are highly visible to the community. In this way they can resist authority and socialize a principal or other administrator to their norms.

Another potential problem with cohesiveness has already been pointed out. Janis (1972) asserted that members of cohesive groups often want to protect that cohesiveness and do not want to risk being disenfranchised from the group for being combative or argumentative. Therefore, when decisions need to be made, rather than get all the different perspectives on the table and then vigorously debating their merits and liabilities, group members prematurely seek consensus for the sake of preserving the group's cohesiveness. Thus, Janis identified cohesiveness as a potential culprit in contributing to poor decision making.

In sum, teams have tremendous potential that often goes unrealized. Sometimes this is due to problems within the groups, and other times it is untapped potential that is never developed. The key to avoiding problems and maximizing potential is learning enough about group dynamics to diagnose what is happening and intervene effectively. The goal of this text is to assist students in this process by discussing the relevant facets of group dynamics and their impact on group performance.

◼ KEY AREAS OF KNOWLEDGE FOR ESTABLISHING AND MAINTAINING EFFECTIVE GROUPS

This section introduces the key areas of knowledge that employees should understand in order to develop effective groups. The text dedicates one chapter to exploring each of these areas (see Figure 1.2). What follows is a brief introduction to some of the important issues in these key areas.

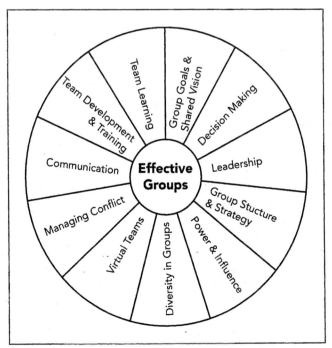

FIGURE 1.2   Components of Effective Groups

Group Goals and a Shared Vision

A compelling vision and a set of clear, challenging goals facilitate group performance (Collins & Porras, 1991). They have both motivational and informational benefits. A vision that inspires, and goals that challenge group members to stretch themselves, are helpful in motivating the team. They also provide the information that enables group members to understand their responsibilities and stay on task. Alternatively, when groups do not have a clear vision and set of goals, they may drift or even spend unproductive time quarreling about what they should be doing.

Unfortunately, goals and vision are often lacking in work groups. Furthermore, group and organizational leaders often overestimate the extent to which group members understand and are guided by a clear and compelling vision (Daft, 2005). Thus, leaders are often unaware of what they should be doing to facilitate performance because they are unaware of the gap between what they have in their own heads and what the group really needs in terms of clarity and specificity. They do not realize that they have not sufficiently conveyed the vision or specific the group. In other cases, leaders do not have a clear vision or goals themselves, and do not know how to develop them in a group context.

Group Structure and Strategy

Once groups have a clear vision and specific set of goals, they need to determine an effective strategy for achieving those goals. However, groups have a tendency to act quickly and take action rather than take the time to develop options and thoughtfully consider which option is most sensible to pursue (Kerr & Tindale, 2004).

Carrying out the strategy often requires creating a distinct set of roles and responsibilities. Sometimes roles are not clearly defined or the team may find that they do not have sufficient talent to fill all the roles adequately. Or, they may find that people are in the wrong roles, such that there is a mismatch between the skills needed for a particular role and person who occupies that role. Finally, the norms that develop can have a large impact on performance, so developing high-productivity norms is crucially important for effectiveness.

Communication

To function effectively, communication must be maintained within the group and with the outside constituencies that the group serves. Without effective communication, groups are vulnerable to mishaps. The Case of the Possible Wrong-Site Surgery at the beginning of this chapter illustrates potential communication problems in groups. Groups tend to do a poor job of identifying and using relevant information held by individual group members. This is just one of the many potential communication problems to which groups are vulnerable (Nielsen, Sundstrom, & Halfhill, 2005).

In fact, statistics on medical error and airplane accidents due to pilot error reveal that communication is the primary cause of wrong-site surgeries, medication errors, delays in treatment, and airplane accidents (Hackman, 2002).

People have a tendency to be overconfident in how well and how much they have communicated to other group members, and we overestimate how well others understand the message. Effective groups develop norms of openness and procedures for ensuring that information is clearly communicated and understood (Sunwolf & Frey, 2005).

Leadership

Teams have tremendous potential, but that potential is not always realized. Instead, groups can misstep and trigger a downward spiral. The actions of the leader are often a critical determinant of whether the group moves toward its potential, stagnates, or drifts into a dysfunctional spiral. However, leading a group is not an easy process. It requires finding the right balance between facilitating and directing. Traditional managers often find adjusting to the role of leading a team, especially a self-managing team, a difficult transition. If they are to enable a group to move toward achieving its potential, they need to take a different approach from the "command and control" posture that has been popular in the past. They must provide enough structure so that the group is not in chaos, but not so much that they keep the group from evolving through mutual adjustment toward greater performance (Daft, 2005).

Group initiatives in organizations often struggle because first-line supervisors or managers feel their authority is threatened by empowering groups and who are uncomfortable with the role of facilitator (Hackman, 2002). The prospects for group success are greatly enhanced when leadership functions are handled effectively.

Power and Influence

Group members, both leaders and non-leaders alike, have various degrees of power and influence over other group members. Power is awarded to individuals based on a number of variables including their ability to reward or punish others, special knowledge, experience or expertise they possess, and certain perceived personality characteristics. Group members can sometimes give too much power to others which can then disrupt the collective functioning of the group. Other times, too little power is given to individuals within the group who need power in order to play their roles effectively (Kanter, 1977). To run properly, group members should understand the dynamics of power and influence and use this understanding to more effectively influence others (Pfeffer, 1994).

Decision Making

Groups have the potential to be a tremendous asset in problem solving and decision making. Despite this great potential, history suggests that groups have often made horrendous decisions despite the great intelligence, hard work, and good intentions of their members. Unfortunately, groups are vulnerable to a variety of biases and complications that can lead to bad decisions (Beach & Connolly, 2005). Awareness of these tendencies can enable group members to enact a process that allows them to utilize its full range of resources in addressing a problem or decision (Bazerman, 2006).

Diversity in Groups

Groups produced many of our greatest innovations and ideas; yet there are various conditions and actions that can stifle creative processes in groups. Group diversity can be immensely helpful in generating creativity and innovation (De Drue & West, 2001). At the same time, diversity can be uncomfortable at times and can lead to conflict. Consequently, groups sometimes struggle with managing diversity. To be effective, groups need to learn how to leverage the strengths of unique perspectives and experiences for the benefit of the group.

Managing Conflict

Some degree of conflict is inevitable in groups, but conflict can be constructive or destructive. The ability to deal constructively with conflict is not a skill that most people develop naturally (De Drue & Van Vianen, 2001). Understanding the nature of conflict and having the ability to negotiate or work through differences is essential for keeping conflict constructive.

Team Development and Training

A frequent mistake in organizations is to develop a group structure without making sufficient investment into training members and developing the team. Organizations also struggle with knowing what kind of training to provide or how to intervene to make sure that groups develop over time (Stewart, Manz, & Sims, 1999). Making the right kind of initial investment in training and providing the right kind of support for continued development are important for effective groups.

Team Learning

Although learning may seem like a natural and sensible thing to do, people in the workplace often do not take the initiative to be continual learners. Mistakes and failures are a fundamental source of new learning and growth. Yet, many individuals and groups prefer to avoid their mistakes and, thus, miss out on opportunities to learn and become more productive. Making sure that a group learns and develops over time requires that a proactive process be put in place (Cannon & Edmondson, 2005).

Virtual Teams

Increasingly, employees are participating in virtual teams. As a matter of fact, employees can work together on projects for years without ever meeting their colleagues face to face. Fortunately, technology has evolved in ways that support these long-distance collaborations. However, the lack of face-to-face contact can present unique problems and challenges that must be addressed (Furst, Reeves, Rosen, & Blackburn, 2004). Understanding the impact of distance and technology on groups is essential for making the most of virtual teams (Poole & Zhang, 2005).

▓ HOW GROUPS IMPACT THEIR MEMBERS

The fact that group structures have become so popular in organizations means that most jobs will involve some degree of group membership and work. Thus, an understanding of group dynamics, how they affect members, and how individuals can best lead groups is key knowledge for work satisfaction and career effectiveness. Groups can have a significant impact on the feelings, beliefs, and actions of their members.

As an example of how groups affect their members, you might reflect back for a moment on your high school or junior high school days and the different social groups that formed. Consider the way each group shaped members' attitudes, feelings, and behavior—body piercings or lack of body piercings, for example. As you, or people you knew, affiliated with various social groups, you may have noticed significant changes in clothing,

In the News

SANTA MARIA, Calif.—Like many American teenagers, Julissa Vargas, 17, has a minimum-wage job in the fast-food industry—but hers has an unusual geographic reach.

"Would you like your Coke and orange juice medium or large?" Ms. Vargas said into her headset to an unseen woman who was ordering breakfast from a drive-through line. She did not neglect the small details—"You Must Ask for Condiments," a sign next to her computer terminal instructs—and wished the woman a wonderful day.

What made the $12.08 transaction remarkable was that the customer was not just outside Ms. Vargas's workplace here on California's central coast. She was at a McDonald's in Honolulu. And within a two-minute span Ms. Vargas had also taken orders from drive-through windows in Gulfport, Miss., and Gillette, Wyo.

Ms. Vargas works not in a restaurant but in a busy call center in this town, 150 miles from Los Angeles. She and as many as 35 others take orders remotely from 40 McDonald's outlets around the country. The orders are then sent back to the restaurants by Internet, to be filled a few yards from where they were placed.

The people behind this setup expect it to save just a few seconds on each order. But that can add up to extra sales over the course of a busy day at the drive-through.

While the call-center idea has received some attention since a scattered sampling of McDonald's franchises began testing it 18 months ago, most customers are still in the dark. For Meredith Mejia, a regular at a McDonald's in Pleasant Hill, Calif., near San Francisco, it meant that her lunch came with a small helping of the surreal. When told that she had just ordered her double cheeseburger and small fries from a call center 250 miles away, she said the concept was "bizarre."

The call-center workers do have some advantages over their on-the-scene counterparts. Ms. Vargas said it was strange to be so far from the actual food. But after work, she said, "I don't smell like hamburgers."

---

social interaction, and choices about how to spend spare time. In the working world, the impact of groups on their members may be less obvious, but it is potent nonetheless.

Although people, especially in the western world, like to think of themselves as independent thinkers and masters of their own destiny, we may be affected by our group memberships far more than we realize. In an early study of organizational functioning, researchers observed attitude changes as employees cycled through different jobs and became associated with different peer groups. One particular individual started as a line worker on the factory floor and was later promoted to management. However, when the organization fell on hard times, he had to return to being a line worker. Interestingly, his attitudes reflected those of the group of which he was a member at any particular time. At first, he had attitudes of a typical line worker with pro-labor sentiments and skepticism about management. After becoming a manager, his attitudes turned pro-management, and he was skeptical of the line workers' contribution. After rejoining the line workers, he returned to his original attitudes.

Groups have a powerful effect on shaping the beliefs and attitudes of their members. Numerous experiments in laboratory settings support this fact. When asked to estimate the length of a line, or the apparent movement of a light on a wall, or even something as objective as identifying a color, the behavior of participants was strongly affected by the responses of others in their group. Of course, these others were confederates who were actually giving false judgments as prescribed by the experimenter.

Sometimes groups influence us for the better. People often refer to athletic teams, wilderness adventures, ropes courses, and so on, in which they achieve physical feats they never thought possible. Working in a successful group that effectively functions as a team can be an exquisitely satisfying experience and a highlight of one's career. Software developers and inventors of new technologies have often been known to go days without sleep or with only an occasional nap in a sleeping bag under their desks. They nonetheless describe the collaborative effort of birthing a new product as an almost euphoric experience despite the enormous effort and lack of sleep.

On the other hand, participating in a group that contains destructive working relationships can lead to daily frustration and dissatisfaction on the job. Otherwise mild-mannered people entertain homicidal thoughts on occasion as their frustration with group members mount. Groups can also put pressure on their members to agree with inappropriate decisions. For example, people can feel pressured into illegal behavior. Consider many of the corporate scandals toward the end of the 1990s (e.g. Enron, Worldcom, Healthsouth, Adelphia Communications, and Tyco International). Many top management teams had apparently been committing fraud for years. Few, if any, started their careers thinking that someday they would "cook the books" and be tried as a criminal. However, the pressures on them and the norms that developed among senior management led people to think that such behavior was the most reasonable, or perhaps even the only, alternative available. Cheating scandals in schools, institutions where teachers and administrators sometimes collude inappropriately to alter student scores, can stem from group pressures and distortions of institutional norms.

▪ OUR OWN IMPACT ON THE GROUP

For better or worse, a single individual either as the leader or a member has limited influence in the way a group operates. Organizations often replace leaders of ineffective groups with the hopes that doing so will turn performance around. This is difficult to accomplish because group norms, once established, are powerful and groups often co-opt new members, socializing them to accept the group norms, beliefs, and attitudes rather than the other way around.

Given that groups can be ineffective, veer in the wrong direction, or make bad decisions, someone, either member or leader, may need to influence the group in a positive or corrective direction. Understanding groups is essential to increasing the chances that our interventions will be effective (West, Brobeck, & Richter, 2004). Our goal in this text is to introduce readers to knowledge areas critical to effective groups. We will show both the problematic factors that can cause groups to fail and how to avoid them, as well as the positive things that help support group success.

▨ CAREER ADVANTAGE OF UNDERSTANDING GROUPS

As the use of groups in organizations has grown, the importance of having an understanding of group dynamics and skills for working in teams has become more important (Stevens & Campion, 1999). Increasingly, organizations are seeking applicants who have the ability to work effectively in teams (Chen, Donahue, & Klimoski, 2004). Southwest Airlines is known for being team oriented, and apparently is quick to screen out job candidates who might not be team players. For example, job candidates who say "I" too much (suggesting that they are not team oriented) in the job interview are eliminated (O'Reilly & Pfeffer, 2000).

▨ TEAM PERFORMANCE

Although this text focuses primarily on groups rather than teams, the later chapters will address team performance. Katzenbach and Smith (1993) illustrate that the wide variation in group performance is due to whether there is a "significant incremental performance need" and whether individuals really come together and learn to work as a true team. Figure 1.3 provides an illustration of Katzenbach and Smith's categories of team performance (1993, pp. 91–92).

1. **Working group:** This is a group for which there is *no significant incremental performance need* or opportunity that would require it to become a team.
2. **Pseudo-team:** This is a group for which there could be a significant, incremental performance need or opportunity, but is has *not focused on collective performance and is not really trying to achieve it.*
3. **Potential team:** This is a group for which there is a significant, incremental performance need, and *which is trying to improve its performance.*
4. **Real team:** This is a small number of people with complementary skills who *are equally committed to a common purpose, goals, and working approach for which they hold themselves mutually accountable.*
5. **High-performance team:** This is a group that meets all the conditions of real teams, and has members who are also *deeply committed to one another's personal growth and success.*

Incremental performance need addresses whether or not group tasks are enhanced through teamwork. Some tasks are not conducive to teams. When teamwork does little to augment performance, there is little need for real teamwork, and a working group is sufficient. By contrast, when there is a significant incremental need, performance varies widely depending on how well individuals work collaboratively and cohesively as a team. Performance can be relatively poor, as in the case of the pseudo-team, or exceptional, as in the case of the high-performance team. The ability to work as a real team or high-performance team rarely happens automatically; instead, it must be cultivated with care.

Each chapter in this textbook contains opening and concluding case studies for discussion. Some of the cases describe situations that the authors have personally observed or experienced, and others are based on published reports. In every case, names and details have been changed in order to protect the identities of those involved. In each chapter we will return to the case that began the chapter and provide additional information and insight about the case. We now revisit the case of the possible wrong-site surgery.

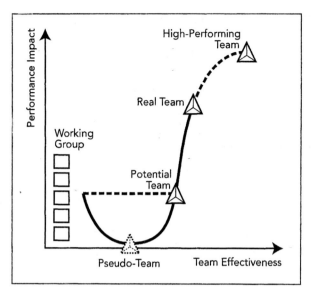

FIGURE 1.3   The Team Performance Curve

🗁 OPENING CASE REVISITED ————————————————

The Case of the Possible Wrong-Site Surgery

Despite the continually rising costs of medical care, medical errors continue to occur at an alarming rate. Drawing on existing research, Rosenthal and Sutcliffe (2002) offer the following estimate on the frequency of fatal medical errors:

> The committee combined the percentage of patients admitted to hospitals who had an adverse event (3–6 percent), the proportion of those who died (7–14 percent), the proportion of deaths judged to have been preventable (50 percent), and the number of admissions in 1997 (34 million) to generate an estimate of 44,000 to 98,000 deaths from medical care error in that year. That figure is greater than the number of deaths from motor vehicle injuries (43,000), breast cancer (42,000), or AIDS (16,000) in that year. And that figure does not include deaths from preventable adverse events in outpatient care, home care, or self-care. (p. x)

Physicians are encouraged to do "root cause" analyses after documented errors have occurred in order to isolate the cause of the error. Medical care associations have categorized medical errors into different types such as wrong-site surgery, medication errors, and delays in treatment. Root cause analyses of each of these types of errors indicated that communication was the most frequently sited cause of error. Whether in medicine or other areas, research demonstrates that groups frequently fail to effectively use the valuable information available to them within the team.

Historically, hospital staff who have low status often do not speak up and share their perceptions or information. This is generally true in nursing where nurses fear irritating high-status physicians with their observations or suggestions. In some cases, nurses have spoken up and were overruled by the physician. In other cases nurses just keep their thoughts to themselves. Frequently, nurses "hint and hope." In other words, rather than state their concern directly, they hint that there might be something wrong and hope that the physician will pick up on what they are trying to communicate. We will address this issue further in Chapter 4 on communication.

Because medical errors can be so hazardous, a great deal of effort is being placed into prevention. As an example of being extra cautious, Vanderbilt Medical Center works to build redundancy into its system. Prior to surgery, the surgical resident is responsible for re-checking for potential errors. If possible, the resident not only confirms with the medical records but also speaks with the patient and has the patient both describe and touch the area of the body which is to be operated on. The resident then uses a marker to mark the spot. Finally, the resident is supposed to sign his or her name on the body part for the sake of accountability that he or she personally checked everything out and that the operation can proceed.

The medical arena is just one area in which interpersonal dynamics lead groups to make insufficient use of the information available to them. Communication is a key area to which groups need to attend in order to be effective.

Summary

In modern society, groups affect the quality of our lives on a daily basis. We rely on groups to design, produce, and deliver the goods and services we consume. As citizens, we are affected by the actions of groups that work in the local, state, and federal governments and in the legal system. Finally, our membership in groups inside and outside of work also has a significant impact on the quality of our lives.

As we have seen from the examples early in the chapter, groups have incredible potential for performance. They can also be a source of personal satisfaction and improve the work lives of their members. At the same time, groups also have the potential to produce disastrous results and make the work lives of their members miserable.

Groups are regularly credited with the following characteristics:

- Groups outperform sets of individuals doing similar work.
- Groups make better decisions because they draw on more information.
- Groups are more creative because they can collectively brainstorm.
- Groups are more productive because synergies develop.
- Group cohesiveness makes teams more productive and improves member satisfaction.

However, we have seen from research that each of these statements should be qualified to some degree (Allen & Hecht, 2004). Achieving effective group performance starts with the recognition that groups do not guarantee superior results. The purpose of this text is to provide insight into the nature of groups and the factors that influence their performance so that you will be in a better position to take advantage of their potential benefits.

📁 CONCLUDING CASE ───

Creating a Team to Evaluate Science Education

Cora Johnson recently graduated with a master's degree in educational administration and was hired as an assistant superintendent. She works in a rural school district that had recently come under criticism for poor standardized test scores in science. The superintendent was especially concerned about the middle school science curriculum and asked Johnson to set up a task force to evaluate the curriculum and make recommendations for improvement. She had complete autonomy to create the task force in whatever way she thought would be effective. The superintendent gave her a small budget for travel and promised to "strongly encourage" those whom she thought would be good candidates for the group.

Ms. Johnson had always been impressed by the power of groups in graduate school. She worked on some exciting group projects and learned about the benefits of groups in her coursework. She thought the district could benefit from a more-collaborative and team-oriented culture. Johnson had observed that most of the administrators at the school level did a competent job, but had little sense of camaraderie and little knowledge or real interest in how their peers in other parts of the district were functioning.

Johnson had to decide what kind of task force to form and who should be on it. She thought that by working in a team environment, members would start to collaborate more, innovate and be more proactive in observing student needs and district goals. Instead of thinking just about their particular school, they would have a holistic perspective on student achievement and be empowered to achieve excellence. Yet, she wondered if she was ready to lead her own team.

Discussion Questions

1. What are the strengths and weaknesses associated with teams?
2. What specific steps should Johnson take to set up the task force?
3. Who should be on the team and how will the team go about its mission?
4. What are some possible problems or challenges Johnson might face?

Group Exercise

This exercise is designed to increase your awareness of the frequency and variety of your participation in groups. It will also provide you with an opportunity to identify and compare the characteristics that are associated with effective and ineffective group experiences.

Part I: Make a list of every group of which you consider yourself a member.
Part II: Make a list of the least effective and/or least pleasant group experiences you have had. What characteristics of these groups made them ineffective or unpleasant?

Part III: Make a list of the most effective and/or most pleasant group experiences you have had. What characteristics of these groups made them effective or pleasant? What observations and conclusions can you make from this exercise?

References

Alderfer, C. P. (1977). Group and intergroup relations. In J. R. Hackman, J. L. Suttle (Ed.) *Improving Life at Work* (pp. 227–296). Santa Monica, CA: Goodyear.

Allen, N. J., & Hecht, T. D. (2004). The "romance of teams": Toward an understanding of its psychological underpinnings and implications. *Journal of Occupational and Organizational Psychology*, 77, 439–461.

Bazerman, M. (2006). *Judgment in managerial decision making* (6th ed.). Hoboken, NJ: John Wiley & Sons.

Beach, L. R., & Connolly, T. (2005). *The psychology of decision making*. Thousand Oaks, CA: Sage Publications.

Cannon, M. D., & Edmondson, A. C. (2005). Failing to learn and learning to fail (intelligently): How great organizations put failure to work to innovate and improve. *Long-Range Planning, 38,* 299–319.

Chen, G., Donahue, L. M., & Klimoski, R. J. (2004). Training undergraduates to work in organizational teams. *Academy of Management Learning and Education, 3*(1), 27–40.

Cohen, S. G., & Bailey, D. E. (1997). What makes teams work: Group effectiveness research from the shop floor to the executive suite. *Journal of Management, 23,* 239–290.

Collins, J. C., & Porras, J. I. (1991). Organizational vision and visionary organizations. *California Management Review*, Fall, 30–52.

Daft, R. (2005). *The leadership experience* (3rd ed.). Cincinnati, OH: Thompson Southwestern.

De Drue, C., & Van Vianen, A. (2001). Managing relationship conflict and the effectiveness of organizational teams. *Journal of Organizational Behavior, 22,* 309–328.

De Drue, C., & West, M. (2001). Minority dissent and team innovation: The importance of participation in decision making. *Journal of Applied Psychology, 86*(6), 1191–1201.

Diehl, M., & Stroebe, W. (1987). Productivity loss in brainstorming groups: Toward the solution of a riddle. *Journal of Personality and Social Psychology, 53,* 497–509.

Ericksen, J., & Dyer, L. (2004). Right from the start: Exploring the effect of early team events on subsequent project team development and performance. *Administrative Science Quarterly, 49,* 438–471.

Furst, S. A., Reeves, M., Rosen, B., & Blackburn, R. S. (2004). Managing the life cycle of virtual teams. *Academy of Management Executive, 18*(2), 6–20.

Gully, S., Devine, D., & Whitney, D. (1995). A meta-analysis of cohesion and performance: Effects of level of analysis and task interdependence. *Small Group Research, 26,* 497–520.

Guzzo, R. A., & Dickson, M. W. (1996). Teams in organizations: Recent research on performance and effectiveness. *Annual Review Psychology, 47,* 307–338.

Hackman, J. R. (1987). The design of work teams. In J. W. Lorsch (Ed.), *Handbook of Organizational Behavior*. Upper Saddle River, NJ: Prentice Hall.

Hackman, J. R. (2002). *Leading teams: Setting the stage for great performances*. Boston: Harvard Business School Press.

Hamper, B. (1991). *Rivethead: Tales from the assembly line*. New York: Time Warner Book Group.

Hill, G. W. (1982). Group versus individual performance: Are N + 1 heads better than one? *Psychological Bulletin, 91,* 517–539.

Hirschfeld, R. R., Jordan, M. H., Field, H. S., Giles, W. F., & Armenakis, A. A. (2006). Becoming team players: Team members' mastery of teamwork knowledge as a predictor of team task proficiency and observed teamwork effectiveness. *Journal of Applied Psychology, 91*(2), 467–474. Retrieved June 7, 2006, from the Journal of Applied Psychology database.

Janis, I. L. (1972). *Victims of groupthink: A psychological study of foreign-policy decisions and fiascoes.* Boston: Houghton Mifflin.

Janis, I. L. (1982*). Victims of groupthink.* Boston: Houghton Mifflin.

Kanter, R. (1977). *Men and women of the corporation.* New York: Basic Books.

Katzenback, J. R., & Smith, D. K. (1993). *The wisdom of teams.* Cambridge, MA: Harvard Business School Press. 111–120.

Kelley, T., & Littman, J. (2001). *The art of innovation: Lessons in creativity from IDEO, America's leading design firm.* New York: Currency Books.

Kerr, N. L., & Tindale, S. R. (2004). Group performance and decision making. *Annual Reviews, 55,* 623–655.

Larson, C. (1988). Team tactics can cut product development costs. *The Journal of Business Strategy,* Sept./Oct., 22–25.

Lee, F. (1993). Being polite and keeping MUM: How bad news is communicated in organizational hierarchies. *Journal of Applied Social Psychology, 23*(14), 1124–1149.

Manz, C. C., & Sims, H. P. (1995). *Business without bosses: How self-managing teams are building high performing companies.* New York: John Wiley & Sons.

Medvec, V. H., Berger, G., Liljenquist, K., & Neale, M. A. (2004). Is a meeting worth the time? Barriers to effective group decision making in organizations. In S. Blount (Ed.), *Research on managing groups and teams volume 6: Time in groups* (pp. 213–233). Oxford, UK: Elsevier.

Mullen, B., Johnson, D., & Salas, E. (1991). Productivity loss in brainstorming groups: A meta-analytic integration. *Basic Applied Social Psychology, 12*(1), 1–23.

Nielsen, T. M., Sundstrom, E. D., & Halfhill, T. R. (2005). Group dynamics and effectiveness: Five years of applied research. In S. A. Wheelan (Ed.), *The handbook of group research and practice* (pp. 285–312). Thousand Oaks, CA: Sage Publications.

O'Reilly, III, C. A., & Pfeffer, J. (2000). *Hidden value: How great companies achieve extraordinary results with ordinary people.* Boston: Harvard Business School Press.

Osborn, A. F. (1957). *Applied imagination.* New York: Scribner.

Patton, B. R., & Downs, T. M. (2003). *Decision-making group interaction: Achieving quality* (4th ed.). Boston: Pearson Education.

Paulus, P. B., Larey, T. S., Putman, V. L., Leggett, K. L., & Roland, E. J. (1996). Social influence process in computer brainstorming. *Basic and Applied Social Psychology, 18,* 3–14.

Pfeffer, J. (1994). *Managing with power: Politics and influence in organizations.* Boston: Harvard Business School Press.

Poole, M. S., & Zhang, H. (2005). Virtual teams. In S. A. Wheelan (Ed.), *The handbook of group research and practice* (pp. 363–384). Thousand Oaks, CA: Sage.

Rosenthal, M. M., & Sutcliffe, K. M. (2002). *Medical error: What do we know? What do we do?* San Francisco: Jossey-Bass.

Roy, M. C., Gauvin, S., & Limayem, M. (1996). Electronic group brainstorming: The role of feedback on productivity. *Small Group Research, 27,* 215–247.

Steiner, I. D. (1972). *Group process and productivity.* New York: Academic.

Stevens, M., & Campion, M. (1999). Staffing work teams: Development and validation of a selection test for teamwork settings. *Journal of Management, 25*(2), 207–228.

Stevens, M., & Campion, M. (1994). The knowledge, skill, and ability requirements for teamwork: Implications for human resource management. *Journal of Management, 20*(2), 503–530.

Stewart, G., Manz, C., & Sims, H. (1999). *Team work and group dynamics.* New York: John Wiley & Sons.

Stasser, G., & Titus, W. (1985). Pooling of unshared information in group decision making: Biased information sampling during discussion. *Journal of Personality and Social Psychology, 48,* 1467–1478.

Sunwolf, & Frey, L. R. (2005). Facilitating group communications. In S. A. Wheelan (Ed.) *The handbook of group research and practice* (pp. 485–510). Thousand Oaks, CA: Sage Publications.

Tata, J., & Prasad, S. (2004). Team self-management, organizational structure, and judgments of team effectiveness. *Journal of Managerial Issues, 16*(2), 248. Retrieved May 9, 2005, from the Vanderbilt University Library database.

Tindale, R. S., Dykema-Engblade, A., & Wittkowski, E. (2005). Conflict within and between groups. In S. A. Wheelan (Ed.) *The handbook of group research and practice* (pp. 313–328). Thousand Oaks, CA: Sage Publications.

Tindale, R. S., & Sheffey, S. (2002). Shared information, cognitive load, and group memory. *Group Processes and Intergroup Relations, 5*, 5–18.

Wageman, R. (1997). Critical success factors for creating superb self-managing teams. *Organizational dynamics, 26*(1). Retrieved February 4, 2006, from the Business Source Premier database.

West, M. A. (2001). The human team: Basic motivations and innovations. In N. Anderson, D. S. Ones, H. K. Sinangil, & C. Viswesvaran (Eds). *Handbook of industrial, work and organizational psychology: Volume 2, organizational psychology* (pp. 270–288). London: Sage Publications.

West, M. A., Brodbeck, F. C., & Richter, A. W. (2004). Does the 'romance of teams' exist? The effectiveness of teams in experimental and field settings. *Journal of Occupational and Organizational Psychology, 77*, 467–473.

Zuidema, K. R., & Kleiner, B. H. (1994). New developments in developing self-directed work groups. *Management Decision, 32*(8), 57–63.

CHAPTER TWO

Group Goals and Shared Vision

▓ INTRODUCTION

Individuals are drawn to groups for many reasons. Group membership not only meets social needs for belonging, but may also increase chances for personal success, however defined. Maximum effectiveness of groups depends, in part, on the ability of members to cooperate with each other and work toward a common goal. This chapter describes the development of group cohesion and a commitment to shared goals.

LEARNING OBJECTIVES

After reading this chapter, you should be able to

- Understand the importance of setting clear and meaningful group goals.
- Recognize how individual goals interact with group goals.
- Describe how a shared vision and member commitment affects goal attainment.
- Describe the importance of ongoing assessment and evaluation in group performance.

 OPENING CASE

Superintendent Durone's Cabinet Meeting

Superintendent Laval Durone was an impressive fellow, having once played guard on his state university's championship basketball team. He was smart, tough, ambitious, and committed to elevating student achievement. He was a perfect model for No Child Left Behind leadership. Or was he? During one of his weekly cabinet meetings, his newly employed Director of Testing and Measurement, Paul Laffwell, was reporting on recent state standardized tests results.

Contrary to what Laval thought, his school district's lowest-scoring students were not recently arrived immigrants from Latin America, but rather the low-income

African American children. If Laffwell were right, then Durone would have to shift substantial resources from one set of students, a set to whom he had promised his Latino school board he would pay particular attention, to another set. Could not Laffwell see the political consequences of what he was saying, wondered Durone? Couldn't he be a better team player?

Laffwell was equally committed to the goals of No Child Left Behind. But he wanted resources to be allocated by need not by a political agenda. He was new to the team so he didn't feel it was his place to challenge the direction set by Superintendent Durone. But he was surprised that nobody else on the team spoke up after he presented some of the data on student achievement. Most members were cynical about the goals of No Child Left Behind and the bureaucracy that supported the policy. Laffwell was quite concerned about the lack of commitment and a shared understanding of the importance of working toward clear, data-driven goals. He wasn't sure how long he could last before speaking up.

Discussion Questions

1. How should Laffwell approach this situation?
2. How can he express his concerns without being seen as a threat to the superintendent?
3. How can the cabinet really work together as a team to accomplish its goals?
4. How can Durone make more data-driven decisions and policies?
5. How can Durone handle group members with different goals and interpretations of those goals?
6. How can he build consensus and a shared vision of excellence for the schools with such competing goals and commitment levels?

Effective groups require a clear, goal-oriented vision of where they are going as well as a shared commitment from members to pursue that vision (Hackman, 2002; Huszczo, 2004; Kline, 1999; Locke & Latham, 1990; O'Leary-Kelly, Martocchio, & Frink, 1994; Senge, 1990; Thompson, 2004). Group members must know why the group exists and what they are trying to accomplish. Goal ambiguity can produce frustration, apathy, cynicism and even hostility toward the leader. Leaders have the challenging task of not only helping their groups define clear, measurable goals but also to instill a shared commitment to achieve those goals.

Well defined and manageable goals keep groups on task and focused. Without a clear sense of mission and direction, group members tend to lose interest and commitment to the group (Lee, Sheldon, & Turban, 2003). When this happens, leaders may assume that poor performance is related to lack of motivation and effort. This can lead to a power struggle where managers or administrators try to force team members into working harder and performing at higher levels. In addition, managers may feel resentful and angry that group members are not as committed to the group goals as they are. For example, a team of sixth-grade teachers may have performed well in the past as measured by annual increases in standardized test scores but can become stagnant. Annual increases in test scores have been level for two years with no prospects for significant increases. Because the principal is receiving pressure from her district office, she may be inclined to push certain individuals to work harder. But if team members are comfortable with their current level of performance, they may not be interested in working harder for the principal's sake. They may, however, be persuaded to work harder for the children.

To begin, it is useful to define the following terms: mission, goals, and tasks or strategies. The **mission** of a group is the overall purpose for which that group exists. For example, the cafeteria at a local school exists to efficiently prepare and serve healthy as well as tasty meals for faculty, staff, and students. Within the scope of that larger mission, the cafeteria staff will have more specific goals related to efficiency, healthiness, and tastiness of the meals. Quarterly or annual performance evaluations that define excellence in those areas provide formal feedback to workers about how well they are doing. **Goals**, then, refer to the desired outcome or end result of a group's work. They are different from the mission (which is broader) and from the strategies or tasks (which are narrower). Goals are the specific results that the group desires to attain. **Tasks** or **strategies** (we will use these terms interchangeably) are the means to accomplishing the goals of the group. They are the various actions the group will take to accomplish its goals. For example, specific strategies for improving food services might include improving the quality of food, reducing waste, reducing the time it takes children to go through the lunch line, or reducing the number of non-nutritious deserts or drinks available to children.

Groups have various levels of freedom to define their own goals. Of course, most groups don't have complete autonomy. In education, mission, goals, and tasks or strategies often translate as follows. A district might well have as its mission the well-rounded education of all students within its charge and the maximum of parent satisfaction preferences in the process. The district's goals might well be raising graduation rates, state mathematics scores, or college admissions. Finally, the tasks or strategies could involve successful implementation of specific curricular efforts intended to achieve these goals.

Groups are established to perform certain functions to contribute to organizational goals. For example, task groups might look for ways to improve organizational efficiency or elevate reading scores. Project groups might be called on to accomplish certain tasks, such as producing an annual corporate or school district report. The annual budgeting process might require department heads to assemble to create budgets for the following year. A technology group might be involved in the redesigning of a school or business website. For most of these groups, whether ongoing or time-limited, the task is assigned by superiors. But, for example, the task of "redesigning the school website" is very vague and requires quite a bit of clarification and definition before productive work can begin. As a general rule, when groups are able to define their own goals, individual members will be more committed to those goals (Cohen & Bailey, 1997).

Talented and competent people respond more favorably when they have some influence in defining goals and strategies (Porter, Hollenbeck, Ilgen, Ellis, West, & Moon, 2003). The technology group mentioned above might not respond positively to the charge: "The school board wants a new website, and they want it to look like this." The group is more likely to be invested in the project if they are given a slightly different charge: "The school board wants a new school website, and they suggest that it look like this, but they would like you to present a few alternatives for them to consider." In the first charge, the goal of a new website was well defined by the prototype given to the project group. In the second charge, the group was given some structure and direction but also an opportunity to define for themselves what a new and improved school website might look like. In addition to greater levels of commitment, the creative potential of the group is released.

Assume that most work groups have a general understanding of their purpose, but that the group itself must further define its own goals (what they are doing) and strategies (how they will do it). This goal clarification process is not only needed for new groups but also for existing groups which, over time, tend to become complacent and unfocused (Arrow, Poole, Henry, Wheelan, & Moreland, 2004). A group leader might call a meeting or set aside a day for goal-setting and future direction. The following example demonstrates how to facilitate this process:

> As the group facilitator, ask every member of the group to write a mission or goal statement about what they perceive to be the main goal or purpose of the group. Collect those statements, write them on a white board or easel and have the group make observations about the similarities and differences between goal statements. See if the group can modify, combine, or create an entirely new goal statement for the overall goal/purpose of the group. After the group has come to consensus on a goal statement, lead them through the next step of making sure the goal or goals are clear and well-defined as described below.

The **SMART** acronym is a good way to evaluate the quality and clarity of goal statements. Goals must be Specific, Measurable, Attainable, Relevant, and Time-bounded. **Specific** goals are clear and unambiguous. The goal of "increasing test scores" is too vague to provide meaningful direction and motivation. "Increasing math scores by a third of a standard deviation" is more specific but still lacks criteria against which it can be measured. **Measurable** goals are defined in such a way that allows concrete and objective assessment as to whether or not the goal has been attained. For example, "raise math scores by more than 10% from last year's level" allows for direct and ongoing evaluation of the goal. **Attainable** goals are those that require a stretch from group members, but are still within the group's reach. Goals that are too ambitious risk not being taken seriously. Insufficiently ambitious goals may fail to challenge and engage a group. As a general rule, organizational theorists suggest a good challenge offers a 50% chance of success (Hackman, 2002). **Relevant** goals are perceived to be within the ability and responsibility of the group. For example, a character-education team would not be given a profit goal because they aren't responsible for budgets and expenses. However, a reduction in absenteeism is a goal they do have some control over. Finally, goals need to be **time-bounded**. Goals need to be linked to a schedule and have time limits. In the case of the character-education team, the goal might be that "during the fall semester of the current year, attendance will improve by 10% over the fall attendance of the previous year."

The opening case study describes how a superintendent might approach the goals of No Child Left Behind (NCLB). NCLB seems to meet most or all of the criteria of **SMART** goals. There are ten specific objectives measured by annual standardized tests. The objectives are attainable in that they require a minimum criterion of achievement or, in the very least, improvement over the previous year. Groups such as the National Education Association (NEA) have been critical about the relevance of the framework. The NEA argues that No Child Left Behind neglects meaningful student learning in the classroom and relies too heavily on standardized tests. The achievement objectives defined by NCLB have strict timelines whereby schools that don't meet standards lose more and more of their autonomy if progress is not made.

▓ MEMBERSHIP SELECTION

Collin's (2001) well-researched and popular book, *From Good to Great: Why Some Companies Make the Leap . . . and Others Don't*, stresses the importance of having the right people on your team. Metaphorically speaking, he suggests that "getting the right people on the bus" is even more important than deciding where the bus is going. If you have the right people, they can figure out where the bus needs to go and determine the best route to get there. In addition to having the specific skills related to the tasks of the group, groups that have members who are both conscientious and socially mature have a greater chance of success (Neuman & Wright, 1999).

Selecting members for a group requires an understanding of the type of group being built. Potential group members need to possess or acquire the necessary skills for the specific tasks of the group. In addition, they need adequate motivation and a strong work ethic. While there are many different ways to define groups, the following categories will guide our thinking.

- **Strategic groups** are primarily involved in decision making and setting strategic direction. They create policies, operational procedures, and plans. Group members need to have a broad understanding of the organizational setting and system within which they operate. In the opening case study, Superintendent Durone's cabinet is an example of a strategic group that makes policy, sets goals, and allocates resources for the district.
- **Problem-solving groups** are called on during specific times to solve specific problems and tend to be short lived. Group members need to be able to think clearly during a crisis and construct solutions that are well thought out and don't create unintended negative consequences. For example, if a school district realized its student database and financial records had been infiltrated by computer hackers, a special group might be formed to assess damage and generate tighter security measures.
- **Task-management groups** are the most popular types of groups in organizations because they are involved with the day-to-day functioning of the organization. These groups include the ability to solve problems that are part of the challenges within every organizational context. Grade-level teaching teams are a good example of this type of group.
- **Creative groups** are groups designed to think beyond current organizational practices and to create new ideas for various purposes. A classic example would be a product-development group trying to come up with dozens of new product ideas and possibilities. Similarly, a district about to construct a new high school might want a particularly creative group of teachers and other professionals and parents to work as a design team. These members need to be divergent thinkers who are able to step outside of the mainstream of traditional thought.

In addition to potential members having the right technical and cognitive skill set for the group in question, they must also have the capacity for respectful and positive interpersonal relationships with others (Halfhill, Sundstrom, Lahner, Calderone, & Nielsen, 2005).

Hollenbeck, DeRue, and Guzzo (2004) suggest that when recruiting members, team leaders should look for individuals who have teamwork skills in addition to individual-level technical skills. For example, teamwork requires the ability to give and receive feedback. Communication skills such as active listening and assertiveness can be used to support, as well as challenge, others. Members must also be able to hear potentially negative feedback from others and respond in a non-defensive manner. Furthermore, well-suited members will have a measure of team spirit or commitment to the success of the group. They are able to balance their own needs and goals with those of the group. In addition, they are enthusiastic and bring optimism to the group. They are able to cooperate and coordinate with others. And, finally, they are flexible and able to adapt to other ways of doing things.

Team leaders are not always fortunate enough to choose their own members. In that case, an assessment of members' skills is in order and, if deemed necessary, training can be utilized to raise the collaborative abilities of members. Stevens and Campion (1999) have developed *The Teamwork-KSA Test* to measure team skills. After a review of research, they determined that five specific skill categories are needed for effective participation in groups:

1. Conflict resolution skills
2. Collaborative problem-solving skills
3. Communication skills
4. Goal setting and performance-management skills
5. Planning and task-coordination skills

This test is commercially available and can be used to assess potential and current members. Results can be used for recruitment purposes and staff development.

Another variable to consider in group composition is group size. Groups larger than eight or so members can become bulky or cumbersome. Coordination losses become pronounced as more people are involved in the distribution, status reporting, and synthesis of subtasks. As group size grows, individual members can become passive due to a diffusion of responsibility, a lack of accountability, and a reduction in commitment (Wagner, 1995). In a study of 54 groups working on a decision-making task, 3-person groups significantly outperformed 7-person groups (Seijts & Latham, 2000). Not only did the extra four people not contribute anything to the 7-person groups, those dynamics actually took away from the group's ability to perform up to a level of a 3-person group. To avoid this, large groups are often divided into smaller subgroups. For example, the faculty of a high school is responsible for certain decisions and tasks, but is too large to effectively perform specific functions. As a result, grade-level teams (ninth grade teachers), subject teams (math teachers), and functional teams (guidance counselors) are formed to accomplish more specific tasks.

Groups with fewer than three members may lack the energy and synergy that comes from multiple perspectives. Laughlin, Hatch, Silver, and Boh (2006) found that 3-, 4-, or 5-member groups outperformed individuals and dyads on a problem-solving task but did not differ from each other. Smaller groups tend to have higher levels of cooperation and commitment. Fewer members engage in social loafing or the practice of allowing other members to do the bulk of the work. Smaller groups cannot afford for someone not to contribute. They may already be understaffed and overwhelmed. Frustration can build quickly and lead to a confrontation and mutual accountability. Therefore, an optimal size for most groups will be four to eight members, depending on the complexity and breadth of the task.

Deliberate selection of members will go a long way toward group success, but having the right people on the bus will not guarantee a smooth and trouble-free ride. Ideally, group leaders will meet individually with members for preparation on the initial structure and purpose of the group. Expectations and attitudes about group work, including past experiences, could also be discussed. It is important to identify any potential problems up front and to give members some basic training on effective group functioning.

▪ UNDERSTANDING GROUP MEMBERS

Human beings are complex and multidimensional. We often fail to fully understand our own behavior, much less another person, and even less so a group of people. Effective group leaders are students of human nature, always learning how their own blind spots prevent them from accurately seeing others. Leaders are constantly trying to make sense of their own beliefs, goals, and behavior while at the same time trying to make sense of group members. Behavior can often be understood in relation to an individual's goals and beliefs. Goal-oriented behaviors are attempts to meet human needs and fulfill various desires (Griffith & Graham, 2004). When leaders understand the goal or needs that members are attempting to meet, their behavior will make sense even if the strategy is largely ineffective.

A survey of psychological, philosophical, and theological literature consistently identifies four basic human needs: physical well-being, personal competence, relational closeness, and self-transcendence (Griffith, 2004). Because its definition may not be as intuitively obvious as the others, the need for self-transcendence refers to the need to be involved with something greater than oneself. Sometimes that comes in the form of religion, spirituality, service to humankind, or commitment to a collective goal. Human beings have always affiliated in groups to increase their chances of meeting these basic needs. Families, neighborhoods, communities, work teams, organizations, societies, and nations are all attempts to increase collective stability in ways that meet core individual needs. Working for the benefit of the group or team can be one way to experience a sense of self-transcendence and can provide personal satisfaction.

Related to goals and needs are the core beliefs people have about themselves, others, and the world, in general. They are formed through personal experiences within a larger sociocultural environment (Griffith, 2004). Core beliefs about one's self include self-concept (how I see myself), self-esteem (how I judge myself), and self-efficacy (the confidence I have in myself to accomplish various tasks). Beliefs about others include (a) the degree to which people can be trusted, (b) stereotypes about various categories of people based on such things as gender, race, ethnicity, and role, and (c) assessments of individual personalities. Finally, beliefs about the world include a basic understanding of cause-and-effect relationships. We all have to explain our experiences and make sense of why things happen in life. These beliefs help us make sense of the past, give stability in the present, and help predict the future.

Based on beliefs about self, others, and the world, people construct strategies to meet needs and achieve goals. These strategies become the behaviors that are observed by others. Even unusual behavior will make sense when an individual's internal processing and past experiences are understood. This combination of beliefs, goals, and strategies that are grounded in past experiences and contained within a sociocultural context is referred to in the social science literature by many names, including *mental models, personal constructs*, and *identity*. We will refer to this concept as the *internal working model* as graphically portrayed in Figure 2.1.

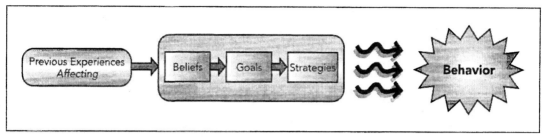

FIGURE 2.1   Internal Working Model and Behavior

Emerging from internal working models are interpersonal styles based on how people view themselves and others as well as the relative weight they give to each of the four goal domains. A wealth of theory and research has consistently confirmed the importance of attachment style as it relates to interpersonal relationships and group experiences (Rom & Mikulincer, 2003; Smith, Murphy, & Coats, 1999; West & Sheldon-Keller, 1994). Attachment theory (Bowlby, 1969) suggests that past relationships with parents or caretakers, peers, and romantic partners creates an orientation and pattern of behavior toward current relationships. Based on those experiences individuals develop relatively stable patterns of interpersonal behavior that can be categorized as *secure, avoidant,* or *anxious-ambivalent.* A securely attached person is able to pursue task goals while maintaining positive relationships with others. Securely attached group members are able to resist groupthink (pressure to conform) because they are confident enough in themselves to take risks and offer divergent perspectives.

Insecure attachment styles are classified as either avoidant or anxious-ambivalent. An avoidant attachment style is one in which people tend to be aloof, self-sufficient, and overly rational. They have learned not to trust others and resist letting down their guard. In contrast, those with an anxious-ambivalent attachment style tend to be overly concerned with obtaining approval from others and can be relationally needy and attention-seeking. Research has found that roughly half of all adults are securely attached with the remaining 50% closely divided between avoidant and anxious-ambivalent (Hazan & Shaver, 1987; Rholes & Simpson, 2004). For group leaders this means that there will be a significant proportion of their groups interested in focusing solely on tasks and a significant proportion overly concerned with acceptance and belonging. This might be one reason why groups can be so challenging. Leaders must continually balance the task and relationship dimensions while recognizing that there will often be members who want more of a task focus and other members who want more relational focus.

Group goals are often held in tension with individual goals. While each member can be committed to the self-transcendent goal of collective success, he or she is also motivated in various degrees to expend minimal effort and conserve energy (physical well-being), to advance personal interests and success (personal competence), or to build friendships and have fun (relational closeness). Group leaders are in the precarious position of helping members meet their own individual needs while at the same time contributing to the collective goals of the group. Group members have higher levels of satisfaction and will contribute more when the goals of the group are congruent with their own personal goals

(Kristof-Brown & Stevens, 2001). Helping members align their personal goals with the group's goals is a leader's principal challenge.

Unfortunately, some members are much more interested in their own needs then those of the group. Researchers have long noted the frequent occurrence of *social loafing*: one or more members of a group exert less than 100% effort relying on others to pick up the slack (George, 1992; Karau & Williams, 1993). Because this is so common, group members are often sensitive to the issues of workload and fairness. Members frequently evaluate the contributions of others relative to their own. When someone perceives they are doing more than their share of the work, they can become frustrated and angry with other members, with the team leader, and with the group in general.

Another challenge for group leaders is working with member resistance. People are drawn to groups for collective benefits but, at the same time, want to preserve personal and private interests. The result of this is a tension between conforming to the will of the group and the desire to preserve individuality and autonomy. Not all members will be committed to the group's goals; some will resist. This resistance can come in many forms including a passive response (do nothing to help the group), an aggressive response (actively resist the leader or other members), or a passive-aggressive response (resist indirectly while appearing to be supportive of the group's goals). Leaders can overcome member resistance by creating a shared vision around which members can rally.

▨ SHARED VISION AND COMMITMENT

In the movie *Braveheart*, William Wallace (played by Mel Gibson) rides to the battlefield at Stirling, Scotland to confront a group of Scottish peasants fleeing before a superior British army. Wallace is faced with the daunting task of communicating a vision for a free Scotland. He asks the peasants to consider giving up physical well-being (they could die in the battle), personal competence (they are certainly outmatched), and relational closeness (they may lose love ones) for the transcendent and collective goal of freedom. The peasants, who have heretofore been nothing more than pawns with which the Scottish nobles bargained for their own personal gain, begin to embrace Wallace's vision and are willing to fight. They envision the possibilities for their children and future generations, and become willing to make great personal sacrifices. According to the Hollywood version of this historical event that happened in 1297, Wallace with the help of the peasants, nobles, and some clever strategy, managed to defeat the British in battle, against all odds.

Unfortunately, motivational speeches rarely generate the long-term commitment required for group success. Eventually, motivation must come from within the group itself, not outside of it. The vision might start in the mind of one or more members of the group and through their influence spread to the rest of the group. History suggests that this was not a one-time speech for Wallace. It was his passion, his core purpose, and he was willing to pay the ultimate price for it, which he eventually did. There was no coercion and few extrinsic rewards, but Wallace offered the possibility of a better life for future generations. According to Senge (1990), an effective leader must (a) be committed him- or herself, (b) be honest by not over promising rewards or minimizing costs, and (c) let others voluntarily choose to participate. All three characteristics are portrayed in the movie and demonstrate how Wallace motivated others through modeling techniques and voluntary enlistment.

A shared vision stimulates the interest, enthusiasm, and creativity of group members (Cohen & Bailey, 1997). Personal goals are put aside as members work for the common good of the group and the ultimate mission of the organization. This can happen when the work of the group is perceived as meaningful and part of a larger, greater good. If a group of maintenance workers in a school only see their work as cleaning bathrooms and classrooms, they might not be engaged or motivated. But if they can connect their job to the overall mission of educating children and preparing them for a better life, then sweeping hallways and emptying trash cans takes on a whole new meaning. This transformation of thinking can be a wonderful benefit of working in teams or groups. Work groups can help reinforce the mission and remind members why they do the things they do. In addition, a loyalty to the group also provides motivation for excellence. Monitoring a study hall is not much fun for a teacher or teacher's aide. However, if the duty is attached to a larger district goal of elevated achievement, it takes on the probability of a loftier task.

Defining and clarifying goals may be the single most important condition for group success, but getting a majority of group members to embrace the vision and commit to the goal is a close second (Aubé & Rousseau, 2005; Klein, Wesson, Hollenbeck, & Alge, 1999). Successful groups have a clear understanding of their purpose, even if that understanding is unstated. Even so, it is usually helpful to verbalize goals and gain collective agreement and commitment. As previously discussed, sometimes goals are defined outside of the group and handed down for execution. Other times they are defined within and by the group. Groups that have the freedom to define or partially define their own goals, or at least have the ability to create the strategies to achieve those goals, tend to have the greatest number of committed members (Cohen & Bailey, 1997). Group members can have any of the following attitudes toward the group's goals:

- **Commitment:** These members are committed to the goal and motivated to achieve it. There is also a commitment to the group and interest and concern for the other group members.
- **Compliance:** Members who are compliant will do what they are asked but haven't yet embraced the importance of the group's mission. While they rarely volunteer or go above and beyond what is expected, they will do their part.
- **Resistance:** Group members who are resistant are working against the group. They are actively trying to sabotage the group, or certain members of the group, for personal reasons. If the leadership of the group is fairly authoritarian, resistant members tend to be passive-aggressive and secretly try to enlist other members to work against the group.
- **Disengagement:** These members are "present" but not "accounted for." They are apathetic toward the work of the group, having neither positive nor negative feelings. They are not very interested or engaged and, as a result, are undependable.

Each member's commitment level determines the collective strength of the group. Compliant members are loosely connected to the group while resistant or disengaged members are negative forces that weaken the group. Effective leaders pay attention to group interactions to assess the commitment level of each member and appropriately address those members whose commitment is lacking.

The initial challenge for any group with well-defined goals is to create cohesion within the group and foster commitment to those goals. Cohesion is the force that brings the group together and creates a sense of commitment to other members of the group and to the success of the group as a whole. Groups that are cohesive can do things well beyond the aggregate skills and abilities of each member. Sporting examples provide excellent evidence of what can happen when individuals believe in a goal and are committed to each other and to the team's success. For example, in the 1980 Olympics, the U.S. hockey team defeated a more talented and experienced Soviet team to go on to win a gold medal. Each member of the team was relatively unknown, but together, they were an extremely cohesive and effective unit. In 2002, the New England Patriots took the concept of cohesion to new levels when they refused to be introduced as individuals before Super Bowl XXXVI. They got to the Super Bowl as a team and would be introduced as a team. They went on to beat an arguably superior St. Louis Rams. Cohesion is also the reason All-Star teams don't fare well in competition. Superior talent without cohesion will not produce desired results. The Ryder Cup is a biennial golf tournament that pits the United States against Europe in a team competition. In the last 20 years, the U.S. Ryder Cup golf teams with superior talent have lost more often than they have beaten the European/Great Britain team. And in the 2004 Winter Olympics, the U.S. men's basketball team which included some of the world's best players from the NBA suffered defeats by Puerto Rico, Lithuania, and Argentina, and had to settle for a bronze medal.

Cohesion acts as a lever to strengthen groups and propel them to greater levels of goal achievement (Cohen & Bailey, 1997). Additionally, when cohesion is high, group members have greater levels of enjoyment and satisfaction. Creating cohesion or building "team spirit" requires deliberate attention. Leaders who are primarily task oriented may be tempted to neglect this important aspect of group work. Cohesion is built on trust which emerges when members are valued and respected. Allowing members to participate in defining the goals and structure of the group will help create both cohesion and commitment. The following suggestions are other ways that may facilitate cohesion.

- **Information Sharing:** Spend some time during group meetings sharing background information about each member. Members can do this by answering general questions or they can be paired together to gather some information and report back to the rest of the group about what they learned.
- **Build Group Identity:** Encourage the team to create their own group identity. Simple exercises like coming up with a team name or creating a collective description of the group will get members thinking along these lines.
- **Tying Together:** Cohesion is enhanced when group leaders make connections between member's similar experiences, backgrounds, ideas, or opinions. Sharing those observations allows members to see themselves as connected to other members of the group. For example, the leader might say "Bob, you and Suzy both have a strong background in curriculum improvement. That will be helpful to this group."
- **Create Competition:** Competition can be a catalyst to motivate members and help them focus on a common task. Leaders can challenge another group or use a previous performance achievement to stimulate motivation and cohesion.

▮ ASSESSMENT AND EVALUATION

High-performing groups undergo continual assessment and evaluation (Meyer, 1994). Group members will often ask the following questions: What are we working toward? and Are we making any progress? To answer those questions, goals need to have been clearly defined and measurable. Instead of something to be feared, assessment can be a tool to strengthen and support the group instead of something that will be used to punish or criticize. Ongoing assessment helps keep groups continually striving for excellence. Even the most productive groups lose their edge. Over time, groups can become diffused and complacent both in the immediate sense (meetings become unproductive) as well as in the general sense (no clear direction or purpose). Assessment and evaluation can help keep groups, both new and old, on the cutting edge of performance.

Ongoing assessment can be done in the two primary areas of group functioning described in this chapter: productivity or goal attainment (tasks) and cohesion (relationships). Assessing group productivity is fairly straightforward when goals that are clear and measurable have been defined from the beginning. A more difficult task may be assessing group cohesion and attitudes between members. Interpersonal problems can be the most challenging and potentially destructive aspect of group work, so accurate assessment is crucial.

■ PRODUCTIVITY ASSESSMENT

The goal-setting process should include a plan for assessment. SMART goals, by definition, are specific and measurable; so performance can be measured by specific criteria and deadlines that are ultimately related to the mission of the group. NCLB, for example, has very specific criteria for assessment. Each school must meet criteria and timelines set by the Department of Education in order to remain in good standing. Figure 2.2 illustrates how goals emerge from a group mission and are defined by specific criteria and deadlines.

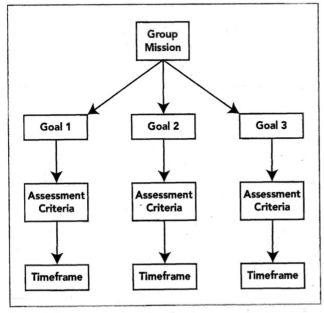

FIGURE 2.2 Assessing Goals

Productivity can be measured not only on the group level (How is the group doing?) but also on the individual level (What is each member contributing to the group's goals?). When the group is in danger of failing to achieve performance goals, adjustments need to be made. Mutual accountability is necessary for groups to identify poorly performing individuals and assignments.

Ongoing collection, analysis, and reporting of data relative to the assessment criteria helps groups know where they stand in relation to their goals. Regular feedback and reporting not only assess progress, but also keep the goals front and center in the group's awareness. For example, a group of school psychologists might have a monthly goal related to the number of children they have tested. One goal for a hypothetical team of four itinerant psychologists might be to test 400 students every month (approximately 25 students per week per psychologist). At the end of each week within the 30-day time frame, the district manager can email or report the group's progress relative to the monthly goal. In addition, there might be added benefit to post individual performances as well. Although this can detract from the collective identity of the team, it may produce some healthy internal competition.

Many people resist setting goals because they do not like to experience failure or be seen as a failure by others. In the absence of clear, measurable goals, people generally overrate their own performance and contribution to the group (Savitsky, van Boven, Epley, & Wight, 2005). This is a well-researched concept called *self-serving bias* (Rosenfeld, 1990; Urban & Witt, 1990). These core beliefs that overestimate our efforts are embedded in internal working models and are fairly resistant to change. When faced with negative feedback from the environment, people tend to be defensive and shift the blame for the failure to someone or something else. While this might prevent a drop in self-esteem in the short-term, in the long-term, it keeps people from assuming responsibility, learning from experience, and improving performance. Group and individual assessment, then, can be seen not as a threat but an opportunity to learn and grow.

Peer feedback can be a challenge both to give and receive. Members resist giving negative feedback to other members even when those members are performing poorly (Argyris, 1994). Groups and organizations can become accustomed to poor performance and unwilling to hold each other accountable. Some members, in contrast, can give an overly negative assessment due to personal reasons or a personality conflict. In either case, group members might be reluctant to let others within the organization see the evaluations they give or receive. For these reasons, many organizations prefer to have outside consultants facilitate comprehensive peer reviews. In this way, the very powerful but delicate process of peer review can be handled by those with experience and objectivity.

While group productivity can be easily evaluated if goals are clearly defined and measurable, assessing the individual contribution of each member is a bit trickier. Managers don't see everything that goes on inside and outside the group and, thus, are limited in their perspective. Consequently, 360-degree reviews have become quite popular for a number of reasons. A *360-degree assessment* is one that collects data from supervisors, peers, customers, associates, and subordinates in order to get a more complete picture of a person's performance. Multiple perspectives lead to a more accurate assessment. In addition, consistent feedback from multiple sources is more difficult to discount or ignore.

When hiring an outside consultant is not possible, group leaders can still facilitate peer reviews that are nonthreatening, informal, and positive. For example, the group may decide to give out monthly or quarterly awards for the "most valuable player," the "most creative contribution," or the "person who saved the day." Group members might even be given the option of awarding certain members of the group with various rewards such as gift certificates, lunches, or tickets to concerts or sporting events. These awards indirectly create performance norms and allow group members to positively reinforce each other. Exercise 2.1 is an example of another way for members to give feedback to each other in a fairly benign and nonthreatening way.

Exercise 2.1   Metaphors

Instructions: This exercise is intended to be a creative way to give each other positive feedback. You are to describe each member of your group with one or two metaphors and explain your choices with the appropriate adjectives or description.

Write your metaphors on the large labels you have been given. At the feedback session each member will pass around a sheet of paper with his or her name on it. You will verbally describe your metaphors and stick the written label on their sheet. When everyone has shared their metaphors with that person, another person will send his or her feedback sheet around the circle until all members have gone.

Examples:

- "You remind me of a jeep—practical, dependable, and able to navigate rugged terrain."
- "I picture you as a sailboat—sleek, quick, and bound for peaceful waters."
- "I see you as a terrier puppy—full of life, adventuresome, and sometimes so full of energy that she falls over her own feet as she tumbles to her next destination."

This exercise tends to meet with some initial resistance (it's not that easy coming up with good metaphors) but in the end provides meaningful feedback and creates positive feelings.

Relationships can be the most rewarding and, yet, most frustrating facet of being part of a group. The camaraderie and stimulation can be quite engaging when a group of people pursue a meaningful goal together. Various assessments such as the Team Player Inventory, the Group Attitude Scale, or the Harvard Group Cohesiveness Scale are established instruments that researchers use to measure levels of group cohesion. These evaluation tools provide a general understanding of how people are feeling toward the group as a whole. They can be administered anonymously with the results being tallied and reported back to the group. This feedback can be used to encourage a dialog that allows members to discuss their feelings about the group, both positive and negative. The conversation, itself, can be helpful in improving cohesion. If cohesion is lacking, the facilitator can ask for suggestions to improve the group climate.

There will inevitably be times when group members are at odds with each other. This has the potential to impact the group experience for all members. While cohesion is a force that pulls members into the group, interpersonal conflict is a force that pushes people away. The smallest comment, whether accidental or deliberate, can be misunderstood and has the potential to threaten the relational climate of the group. Periodic frustration with others is quite common as group members challenge each other and banter ideas, goals, and strategies. There is, however, a tipping point when too much interpersonal tension can limit the effectiveness of the group. Unfortunately, unresolved conflict and frustration can go underground and be expressed outside of group meetings. Coalitions will often develop as tension in the group increases. When people feel threatened or frustrated, they tend to find others who feel the same way to commiserate and to validate their own perspective. Furthermore, there is strength in numbers. A minority position can be strengthened within the group by enlisting others to be part of the coalition.

Apart from asking them directly, leaders can use other means to assess the strength and quality of interpersonal relationships. Yet their own internal working models filter out certain pieces of data and incorrectly interpret others. We tend to see only that which confirms our pre-existing beliefs and filter out disconfirming evidence. In general, people see what they already believe and expect to see. Thus, evaluators must be diligent to separate out their own opinions and to continually question their judgments. The following reflection questions might provide data that can be used to assess group cohesion:

- Do members seem to enjoy working together?
- What do you see when you observe members as they enter and exit meetings?
- Is there an atmosphere of lightheartedness and laughter in the meetings?
- Is everyone participating equally?
- What nonverbal messages do people seem to be projecting?
- Do members express frustration directly or indirectly?
- Are members assertive, passive, passive-aggressive, or aggressive?

In addition to the evaluator asking and answering these questions, they can also be posed to the group for further discussion and assessment.

The questionnaire in Figure 2.3 is another way of collecting data to assess interpersonal relationships within the group.

Guidelines for Scoring the Group Attitude Questionnaire

Evaluators can analyze the participant responses to Figure 2.3 by totaling the circled numbers for each of the ten questions for each member of the group. The scores can range from 10 to 50 with 30 representing neutral attitudes toward cohesion. Individual scores of all group members can then be averaged to arrive at a group cohesion score. Average responses in the 35 to 50 range indicate generally healthy levels of cohesion. Averages ranging from 25 to 35 reflect neutral attitudes about others in the group. Finally, average scores of less than 25 indicate a lack of adequate cohesion. In addition, average scores for each of the individual questions can identify strengths as well as areas for potential improvement. The open-ended questions are also a rich source of information for assessment.

Average responses for the individual questions, as well as the total group cohesion score, could be reported back to the group for further discussion. Group members could then reflect on both of these results. Asking the group for specific suggestions on how to improve the group climate might also yield rich data and recommendations for improvement. The process itself is conducive to creating higher levels of group cohesion. Once again, the purpose of ongoing assessment is to improve the functioning of groups, both in terms of productivity and cohesion.

Group Attitude Questionnaire

For each question, please circle the number that best corresponds to your own opinion. Then please answer the open-ended questions at the bottom. Your answers are confidential and will be used to improve the functioning of this group. Thank you for your thoughtful responses.

	Strongly Disagree	Disagree	Neutral	Agree	Strongly Agree
I enjoy working with this group	1	2	3	4	5
People in this group seem to like each other	1	2	3	4	5
Everyone does an equal share of the work	1	2	3	4	5
Everyone is free to express their ideas	1	2	3	4	5
People are respectful of others	1	2	3	4	5
This group works well together	1	2	3	4	5
I feel appreciated in this group	1	2	3	4	5
People are committed to this group	1	2	3	4	5
This group understands its goals and purpose	1	2	3	4	5
Relationships are an important part of this group	1	2	3	4	5

Strengths of the group:

Suggestions for improvement:

FIGURE 2.3   Group Attitude Questionnaire

◢▱ OPENING CASE REVISITED

Superintendent Durone's Cabinet Meeting

Dr. Durone has very clear achievement goals for his schools. No Child Left Behind has specific and measurable objectives that must be met. But he also has made a political promise to Latino constituents to provide services to their children. And this group is a powerful force from which any successful superintendent must have support to survive in the district. So he has competing goals: academic, political, and personal. And the teachers are fairly resistant to NCLB so he's in danger of pleasing nobody.

Mr. Laffwell is obviously concerned about the use of district resources and strongly believes that decisions should be made on the basis of concrete data and student achievement standards. He feels the need to confront Dr. Durone; and a week after the cabinet meeting, he has his chance. He set up an appointment to see the superintendent and share his concerns. Mr. Laffwell was well prepared to defend his concerns with research and measurement data. Although the meeting was uncomfortable, Dr. Durone began to see a way out of his predicament. He didn't want to alienate his new director of research and knew that if he disregarded Laffwell's concerns, his credibility would be compromised and the cabinet possibly fractured. He wanted to create a team atmosphere where cabinet members felt free to challenge each other and critique decisions. This allows the best ideas to surface and for members to create a shared vision for the goals of the group.

At the next meeting, Durone announced that he and Laffwell met to evaluate the most recent standardized test data. He told his board that this new information presented a challenge to his former assumptions and required a reallocation of resources. Members of the group appeared relieved and seemed energized by the decision. Laffwell was validated for his commitment and concern for student achievement. Using the data from Laffwell's research, Durone prepared a presentation for his Hispanic constituents that highlighted the need for all students to succeed. He renewed his commitment to them and their children and asked for their continued support. While the community was not happy about the reallocation of resources, they admired Durone's integrity and felt like they were part of a larger collaborative effort to improve the school system through regular and ongoing evaluation of student achievement.

Summary

Group research and literature is consistent and emphatic about the importance of setting clear and measurable goals. Effective groups have a clear sense of where they are going. Group cohesion operates like a lever to propel groups toward their goals. Groups are most effective when members share a common vision and work together to accomplish those goals. An evaluation plan provides groups and group leaders with the necessary data to make corrections and keep the group on course.

Once a group has a clear understanding of its goals and a moderate level of trust and cohesion, it is ready to construct specific strategies and structures to achieve those goals. In addition, groups go through predictable stages as they develop and learn more effective ways to work together. These strategies, structures, and stages are the topics of the next chapter.

 CONCLUDING CASE ————————————————————————

Building a Math Team

Mary Lowe is a math teacher in a large high school in a growing school district in the Midwest. She has been at the school for two years but has been disappointed by the isolation and lack of collaboration in her school. Lowe is convinced that teachers must become part of a cohesive team to maximize their efforts. In the earlier part of her career, she worked on an innovative teaching team and experienced, first hand, that high-performing teams have synergy and can really deliver. But she also knows that faculty departments have to be deliberate in creating a shared vision and cohesion; it just doesn't happen by itself. A number of the teachers in the school have years of experience and prefer to be left alone to do their jobs.

Lowe has garnered the reluctant support of her principal, Mr. Dickerson, who is willing to try a team-based approach in the math department. He knows they cannot continue with their current structure as achievement scores have leveled off and morale is in decline. For the most part, teachers operate independently of each other. While a few of the newer teachers have gone to lunch together periodically, most have little interest in spending time together outside of work. The teachers are diverse in terms of age, length of employment, stage of life, and interests, and so have little in common with each other. Consequently, they do not have a sense of camaraderie or cohesion.

Lowe wants to help this group of loosely affiliated individuals develop collective goals and a sense of commitment to each other. She has been informally building relationships with each of the faculty members in the department with the hope of bringing them together. Through these contacts, she has gotten to know each member, their agendas, what motivates them, and the potential problems they might have in working with a team. Lowe has even gotten the teachers to have more contact with each other and work on small projects together. After a few months of this, Lowe plans a department retreat. She has received approval and funding to conduct a two-day meeting at a local retreat center. Her goals are to build commitment to a shared set of goals and to each other as team members.

Discussion Questions

1. If you were planning this retreat, how would you structure it?
2. What kinds of activities would you use?
3. Come up with a two-day schedule.
4. How would you measure the program's success?
5. Do you agree with Lowe's approach to implementing teams into her department?

References

Argyris, C. (1994). Good communication that blocks learning. *Harvard Business Review*, July–Aug., 77–85.

Arrow, H., Poole, M. S., Henry, K. B., Wheelan, S., & Moreland, R. (2004). Time, change, and development: The temporal perspective on groups. *Small Group Research, 35,* 73–105.

Aubé, C., & Rousseau, V. (2005). Team goal commitment and team effectiveness: The role of task interdependence and supportive behaviors. *Group Dynamics: Theory, Research, and Practice, 9,* 189–204.

Bowlby, J. (1969). *Attachment and loss: Vol. 1. Attachment.* New York: Basic Books.

Cohen, S. G., & Bailey, D. E. (1997). What makes teams work: Group effectiveness research from the shop floor to the executive suite. *Journal of Management, 23,* 239–290.

Collins, J. (2001). *From good to great: Why some companies make the leap . . . and others don't.* New York: HarperCollins.

George, J. M. (1992). Extrinsic and intrinsic origins of perceived social loafing in organizations. *Academy of Management Journal, 35,* 191–203.

Griffith, B. A. (2004). The structure and development of internal working models: An integrated framework for understanding clients and promoting wellness. *Journal of Humanistic Counseling, Education, and Development, 43,* 163–177.

Griffith, B. A., & Graham, C. C. (2004). Meeting needs and making meaning: The pursuit of goals. *The Journal of Individual Psychology, 60,* 25–41.

Hackman, R. J. (2002). *Leading teams: Setting the stage for great performances.* Boston: Harvard Business School Press.

Halfhill, T., Sundstrom, E., Lahner, J., Calderone, W., & Nielsen, T. M. (2005). Group Personality Composition and Group Effectiveness: An Integrative Review of Empirical Research. *Small Group Research, 36,* 83–105.

Hazan, C., & Shaver, P. (1987). Romantic love conceptualized as an attachment process. *Journal of Personality and Social Psychology, 52,* 511–524.

Hollenbeck, J. R., DeRue, D. S., & Guzzo, R. (2004). Bridging the gap between I/O research and HR practice: Improving team composition, team training, and team task design. *Human Resource Management, 43,* 353–366.

Huszczo, G. E. (2004). *Tools for team leadership: Delivering the X-factor in team eXcellence.* Palo Alto, CA: Davies-Black Publishing.

Karau, S. J., & Williams, K. D. (1993). Social loafing: A meta-analytic review and theoretical integration. *Journal of Personality and Social Psychology, 65,* 681–706.

Klein, H. J., Wesson, M. J., Hollenbeck, J. R., & Alge, B. J. (1999). Goal commitment and the goal-setting process: Conceptual clarification and empirical synthesis. *Journal of Applied Psychology, 84,* 885–896.

Kline, T. (1999). *Remaking teams: The revolutionary research-based guide that puts theory in practice.* San Francisco: Jossey-Bass/Pfeiffer.

Kristof-Brown, A. L., & Stevens, C. K. (2001). Goal congruence in project teams: Does the fit between members' personal mastery and performance goals matter? *Journal of Applied Psychology, 86,* 1083–1095.

Laughlin, P. R., Hatch, E. C., Silver, J. S., & Boh, L. (2006). Groups perform better than the best individuals on letters-to-numbers problems: Effects of group size. *Journal of Personality and Social Psychology, 90,* 644–651.

Lee, F. K., Sheldon, K. M., & Turban, D. B. (2003). Personality and the goal-striving process: The influence of achievement goal patterns, goal level, and mental focus on performance and enjoyment. *Journal of Applied Psychology, 88,* 256–265.

Locke, E. A., & Latham, G. P. (1990). *A theory of goal setting and task performance.* Englewood Cliffs, NJ: Prentice Hall.

Meyer, C. (1994). How the right measures help teams excel. *Harvard Business Review*, May–June, 95–103.

Neuman, G. A., & Wright, J. (1999). Team effectiveness: Beyond skills and cognitive ability. *Journal of Applied Psychology, 84,* 376–389.

O'Leary-Kelly, A. M., Martocchio, J. J., & Frink, D. D. (1994). A review of the influence of group goals on group performance. *Academy of Management Journal, 37,* 1285–1301.

Porter, C. O. L. H., Hollenbeck, J. R., Ilgen, J. R., Ellis, A. P. J., West, B. J., & Moon, H. (2003). Backing up behaviors in teams: The role of personality and legitimacy of need. *Journal of Applied Psychology, 88,* 391–403.

Rholes, W. S., & Simpson, J. A. (Eds.). (2004). *Adult attachment: Theory, research, and clinical implications.* New York: Guilford Press.

Rom, E., & Mikulincer, M. (2003). Attachment theory and group processes: The association between attachment style and group-related representations, goals, memories, and functioning. *Journal of Personality and Social Psychology, 84,* 1220–1235.

Rosenfeld, P. (1990). Self-Esteem and impression management explanations for self-serving biases. *The Journal of Social Psychology, 130,* 495–500.

Savitsky, K., van Boven, L., Epley, N., & Wight, W. M. (2005). The unpacking effect in allocations of responsibility for group tasks. *Journal of Experimental Social Psychology, 41,* 447–457.

Seijts, G. H., & Latham, G. P. (2000). The effects of goal setting and group size on performance in a social dilemma. *Canadian Journal of Behavioural Science, 32,* 104–116.

Senge, P. M. (1990). *The fifth discipline: The art and practice of the learning organization.* New York: Doubleday.

Smith, E. R., Murphy, J., & Coats, S. (1999). Attachment to groups: Theory and measurement. *Journal of Personality and Social Psychology, 77,* 94–110.

Stevens, M. J., & Campion, M. A. (1999). Staffing work teams: Development and validation of a selection test for teamwork settings. *Journal of Management, 25,* 207–228.

Thompson, L. L. (2004). *Making the team: A guide for managers.* Upper Saddle River, NJ: Pearson Prentice Hall.

Urban, M. S., & Witt, L. A. (1990). Self-serving bias in group member attributions of success and failure. *The Journal of Social Psychology, 130,* 417–418.

Wagner, J. A., III. (1995). Studies of individualism-collectivism: Effects on cooperation in groups. *Academy of Management Journal, 38,* 152–172.

West, M. L., & Sheldon-Keller, A. E. (1994). *Patterns of relating: An adult attachment perspective.* New York: Guilford Press.

CHAPTER THREE

Group Structure and Strategy

■ INTRODUCTION

All social systems have structure and operate from certain explicit and implicit norms that regulate member behavior. Once goals are defined, groups must decide how to achieve those goals. Members negotiate their roles and various tasks are assigned. Structure and norms may be imposed externally, they may be defined by a strong leader, or they may emerge over time from within the group itself. This chapter describes the components of group structure and presents a strategy for solving problems, managing projects, and achieving goals.

LEARNING OBJECTIVES

After reading this chapter, you should be able to

- Describe the components of group structure.
- Understand the dynamics of group roles and relationships in groups.
- Describe two theories of group development.
- Describe a five-step model for group problem solving and project management.

◢ OPENING CASE

Top Management Meetings at Kotch Industries

The top management team meeting had just ended, and Taylor Felton was wondering how Kotch Industries had become so successful. She had been the chief financial officer of privately owned Kotch Industries for just over six months. These meetings seemed boring, and she felt that the other members were consistently closed minded when she brought up good ideas, and they did not want to face up to the possible disadvantages associated with their proposals. She felt that her talents were going underutilized and unappreciated.

By contrast, the president, Peter Kotch, and most of the others felt that Felton was abrasive and uncooperative. They wondered how she had gotten so far in her career given her deficiencies. She just did not seem to get it. Frankly, they sometimes had doubts about whether they should have hired her. They had all worked together as a group rather smoothly until she came along.

The main point of contention in this meeting had to do with the acquisition of a mine in Texas. The sum of money being put at risk was not large enough to be of great concern to the company, but as the discussion seemed to be closing with unanimous support for the acquisition, it occurred to Felton that she had read about a similar acquisition that a competitor had made. She recalled that while the mine was productive, it was not in full compliance with Environmental Protection Agency standards. As a result, the competitor ended up with a costly mess on its hands, and bad publicity as a polluter and violator of EPA standards.

When Felton raised this concern, the group did not even consider the question of whether they had done sufficient investigation. They simply moved on and approved the acquisition. Felton felt ignored and discouraged about the meetings since members were not interested in considering the perspectives and talent within the group to make high-quality decisions. By contrast, others gave her the impression that she was a problem and slowing down progress. As a result, she felt more and more resistant and found herself taking on the role of devil's advocate in group meetings.

Discussion Questions

1. What are some possible explanations for what is going on at Kotch Industries?
2. What do you think should be done to correct this situation?
3. How will your solution solve the problem?

It is one thing to know where you are going, but quite another to know how to get there. A well-designed strategy provides the direction and specific task assignments for goal attainment. As the strategy is formulated and executed, a unique group structure will develop, defining group norms, roles, and intermember relationships. This chapter presents a model for building an effective strategy to accomplish group objectives and describes the underlying structural components that support those efforts.

Work groups, as opposed to social groups, are designed to accomplish some goal, task, or project. After the mission of the group is understood and there is some measure of cohesion or a foundation for reasonable working relationships, a group can go about devising a strategy for accomplishing its mission. For example, assume a group has been formed to work on a certain project or solve a specific problem. How does it go about its work? The members have been selected, introductions have been made, and the goal or task has been initially presented. The leader may have even had the opportunity (hopefully) to meet with each member and prepare them for the work of the group. Now what? The team leader plays a critical role in setting the initial pattern (structure and strategy) for the work of the group.

The first few meetings will establish patterns of interaction or norms that define and govern group behavior. Yet those norms can and do change over time. The first meeting of a new group is obviously very different than the 20th meeting of a group (Arrow, Poole, Henry, Wheelan, & Moreland, 2004). Group-development models attempt to explain those differences and identify typical stages through which groups evolve. Knowledge of these stages can help leaders and members understand those changes and manage expectations. Virtual teams, those groups that use computer-mediated technology to interact and work with each other, also establish norms and develop over time. But they have a unique challenge in developing trust and cohesion as described in Chapter 12.

▦ GROUP STRUCTURE

As groups create strategies to solve problems and accomplish goals, certain structures emerge to support the process. In the same way that individuals construct internal working models that include beliefs, goals, and strategies for daily functioning, groups create a shared working model (also known as shared mental model) to define the life of the group (Ilgen, Hollenbeck, Johnson, & Jundt, 2005). While an initial structure is provided by the group leader (either loosely or rigidly defined), group structure will change over time due to the unique makeup and general stages of group development (Wheelan, Davidson, & Tilin, 2003). Groups are strongly influenced by the larger organizational context within which they operate, but within those limits they will define their own structure. This structure includes the norms of group behavior, roles of each of the members, and patterns of relating between members (Forsyth, 2006). To borrow an analogy from the sports world, players need to know the rules of the game, their function or role on the team, and how to interact with other members. Football teams, for example, have very explicit rules for play, specialized roles for each player, and fairly complex interactions between players (e.g., a running back getting a hand-off from the quarterback).

Structure provides stability for groups by defining the rules of social interaction and task functions. Initial structure provides security and stability for the group and reduces anxiety. But social systems don't remain stable very long. They frequently oscillate from stability (order) to instability (chaos) and back again (order), as depicted in Figure 3.1. This fluid dynamic makes groups unpredictable yet provides the potential for creativity and growth. Because of the diversity of opinion in groups, members will have different perspectives on how they should operate and will push against the existing structure. This pushing and pulling is what defines the boundaries of group life and forges group identity. In this way, ongoing reorganization and restructuring can be seen as a creative force that has the potential to maximize group effectiveness.

Norms

Norms are implicit and explicit rules that tell us how to behave in various contexts and also create order and stability. They make social settings more predictable by acknowledging what is expected and thereby reduce anxiety. Norms are often defined initially by the leader or facilitator, but are later adjusted over time by the group itself. They can be stated explicitly as ground rules, mission statements, or organizational values, but are also communicated implicitly by the types of behaviors that are rewarded or reprimanded (Horne, 2001). For example, when a team leader says in a somewhat frustrated manner, "I really wish we could start this meeting on time but we're still waiting for Bob," she is stating an expectation about punctuality. Norms can describe many parts of group life, including

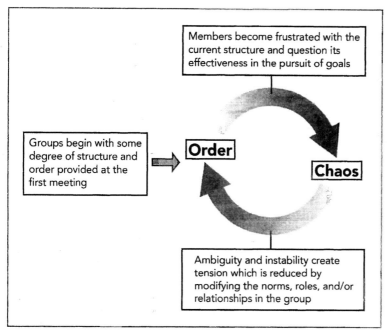

FIGURE 3.1   The Oscillation between Order and Chaos

seating arrangements, communication patterns, language, attire, humor, respect for the leader, and so on. Norms not only describe "what is" (descriptive norms), but also "what should be" (prescriptive norms). Norms form a group identity within which members define themselves (Hogg & Reid, 2006).

Hackman (2002) identifies two primary norms for effective group functioning: ongoing self-evaluation and ethical standards of behavior. First, effective groups are proactive and self-critical as they develop project management and problem-solving strategies (Postmes, Spears, & Cihangir, 2001). They continually scan the environment to determine the best course of action for any given situation and point in time. These groups are willing to discard outdated or poorly conceived strategies when they are no longer effective. This norm is important because the general human tendency is to respond to problems and demands with automatic and habitual responses (Cannon & Witherspoon, 2005). Groups and organizations have a tendency to take a strategy or solution that worked in a given situation and apply it to other situations until it becomes an unquestioned operating procedure, even though it may be less than optimal.

The second norm that Hackman (2002) sees as crucial for effective group performance is the commitment to ethical guidelines and operational responsibility. Groups exist within organizational contexts which have rules about proper behavior. When challenges and pressures confront a group, they must act ethically and responsibly according to organizational guidelines and general ethical principles such as honesty and integrity. Without this explicitly stated norm, it is all too easy to compromise when clients, bosses, or influential peers are demanding results, or when there is great incentive for personal gain. Hackman acknowledges that secondary norms involving issues such as punctuality and conflict can help groups function more efficiently but are best determined by members of the group instead of some outside entity. Effective facilitators, then, are aware of the norms in operation and can address those secondary issues for discussion when needed.

Families and work groups share many similarities. Indeed, the families we grew up in are our first experiences with a group. Just like work groups, families have rules and values (descriptive and prescriptive norms, respectively). Parents or primary caretakers establish rules to provide stability for the family and so children know what is expected of them. Every family develops a structure that includes norms, roles, and patterns of relating. Over time, family members tend to develop certain roles. One parent might be known as the disciplinarian, or one child might become the hero. In the same way, group members adopt familiar patterns of behavior and roles that give the group predictability and structure. And just as every family is different, groups also develop a unique identity with idiosyncratic norms.

Roles

Complex group tasks require members to fill various roles as strategies are defined and executed. Members volunteer for those tasks that they feel most comfortable, confident, and competent to do. And because social groups attempt to establish homeostasis and stability, members tend to take on similar functions over time and come to expect others to behave in similar ways as well. Thus, group members that demonstrate consistent patterns of behavior become associated with that role. Forsyth (2006) describes three categories of group roles: task roles, relational roles, and individual roles.

Task roles contribute to the ultimate goal of the group. Members who fill these roles provide critical thinking and strong organizational skills. They are able to analyze problems and overcome obstacles to success. These roles include the ability to make plans and create accountability structures. Sometimes perceived as driven, those in task roles are goal oriented and keep the group focused and on track. They may become frustrated if the group wastes time or becomes inefficient. Productivity and movement toward success are important values.

Relationship roles, on the other hand, build cohesion in the group. They fulfill important functions such as creating trust and increasing member satisfaction (Ilgen, Hollenbeck, Johnson, & Jundt, 2005). Those in relationship roles are aware of the interpersonal dynamics of the group and strive to encourage and validate others. While some may perceive these roles as overly concerned with non-task related issues, both task and relationship roles work together to balance the group and increase the chances for group success.

In contrast, individual roles work against the group's goals and distract the group from its work. People who are playing individual roles can be quite frustrating to other members of the group as they passively or actively resist the work of the group. While they may serve a function by challenging and thereby establishing boundaries, individual roles are generally seen as more of a hindrance then a help. Table 3.1 is adapted from a much larger list of functional group roles originally identified by Benne and Sheats (1948).

At times, roles can become overly rigid to the point where members get stuck in less-than-optimal roles or become stagnant in their role. This not only hinders their own development, but it can also prevent others from having an opportunity to experience that role. Family systems theory suggests that the healthiest families allow members to try different

TABLE 3.1 Types of Group Roles

Task Roles	Function
Information seeker	Asks for facts, opinions, and ideas from the group. Seeks clarification and elaboration about existing concepts.
Information giver	Contributes facts, opinions, and novel ideas to the group.
Discussion facilitator	Facilitates the discussion by engaging the group.
Task manager	Keeps the group on task and focuses on practical details.
Evaluator/critic	Challenges the ideas of others and evaluates potential solutions.
Recorder	Takes notes and records the decisions of the group.

Relationship Roles	Function
Encourager	Encourages and supports others.
Harmonizer	Mediates conflict between group members.
Process observer	Observes and periodically comments on the groups progress.
Advocate	Helps quieter members to speak up and be heard in the group.

Individual Roles	Function
Resister	Opposes the group by being negative and passive aggressive.
Dominator	Dominates discussions and intimidates others.
Avoider	Tries to do as little work as possible.
Attention seeker	Calls attention to self to meet personal needs,

roles at different times. In that way, the rebel of the family doesn't always have to be in that role. Or the family hero no longer has to be perfect. Applied to groups, the person who has played the role of recorder does not always need to be the one to take notes. He or she might want a break or somebody else might want to adopt that role. Also, those members who previously played a negative role in the group are able to move to more productive roles. Interestingly, groups can actually make it difficult even for members playing negative roles to change. Later chapters will discuss in greater detail how to work with challenging members, and how to help groups stay open and adaptable in terms of roles.

Patterns of Relating

As group members begin to work together, certain relational patterns will emerge. First, members will acquire various degrees of status and influence in the group. When some members speak, everyone listens. Conversely, when others speak, nobody listens. Second, group members will be drawn to some and repelled by others. Friendships and alliances will develop as members associate with each other. Sometimes these relationships are formed in reaction to other members and subgroups in order to create a power base that provides security and influence in the group. Third, members will begin to position themselves anywhere from the center of group activity to the outer areas of member disengagement. In larger groups, it is easier to be on the periphery and become only marginally involved. In smaller groups, however, it is harder to be anonymous and members may confront those who are not doing their share of the work.

Again, these dynamics are often present in our family experiences. Certain family members, such as parents, have more status and influence over the rules and operation of the family. And while some family members get along great, others have ongoing conflict and disagreement. Finally, some family members like being the center of activity and attention, while others prefer to be on the periphery. These patterns may be obvious in families, but are present in work groups as well.

When members enter a new group, they will often assess the competency of others. This is done partly out of insecurity to see how they compare to others, but it is also done to take inventory of the group's resources. Those people who are perceived as competent and skilled are allotted greater amounts of influence over the decisions, direction, and dynamics of the group. Status is also assigned based on general characteristics such as age, race, gender, educational level, and occupation (Forsyth, 2006) even though these characteristics might have little or nothing to do with the work of the group. Group facilitators are well advised to identify high-status members and understand how they might influence the group. Influential members can be a great asset if they embrace the goals of the group and encourage cohesion among members.

Relationships with fellow members can be one of the most enjoyable aspects of group work. Because relational closeness is a core human need, it can be the source of extreme frustration when blocked. Conflicts and personality clashes can make group experiences exhausting. Certain members will really hit it off, while others will be at odds. When high levels of anxiety, uncertainty, and conflict exist, group members form alliances with each other for their own safety and security. Effective leaders are aware of these relational patterns and use that knowledge to the group's advantage in terms of subgroup assignments and dealing with potential interpersonal conflicts.

Finally, groups develop communication patterns that regulate the flow of information. Obviously, not every member can speak at the same time. As a result, a communication structure emerges with some members taking a more active role in discussions. Those active members with high status can become a communications hub where others direct their comments for validation (Horne, 2001). Communication is a vital component of group life and will be taken up in greater detail in the next chapter. For now, we focus on the level of verbal participation and the direction of members' comments.

Figure 3.2 shows a sample of how leaders can conceptualize the patterns of relating in groups. The concentric circles represent levels of verbal activity from a high level of interaction at the center to low levels on the outermost layer. Members can be placed on the diagram to indicate their relative level of interaction. In addition, members with high status can be identified with a box around their name. Lastly, those members who are especially close can be grouped together and identified with a dotted line around those alliances.

▣ STAGES OF DEVELOPMENT

Groups are complex social systems that change and progress over time (Arrow, Poole, Henry, Wheelan, & Moreland, 2004). Tuckman (1965) suggests that groups go through the predictable stages of forming, storming, norming, and performing. Wheelan (1999) constructs a similar linear model that includes many of the same concepts. During the first few meetings when a group is **forming**, members are sizing each other up and self-consciously assessing their own competence. They have an over-reliance on the leader and are generally cautious and tentative because of a lack of role clarity and understanding of the rules of

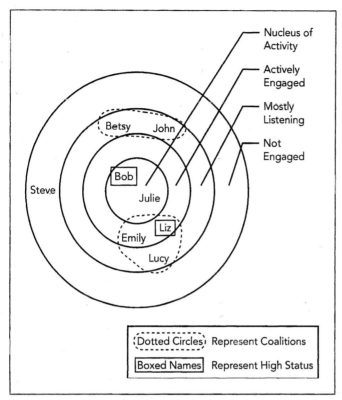

FIGURE 3.2   A Sample Relational Structure Diagram

operation (norms). At this stage, members are often concerned with acceptance and belonging. Coincidentally, when existing groups add new members or change the composition of the group, they will often return to the forming stage. In this way, stagnant groups can be shaken up to encourage an examination of the existing strategy and structure.

Storming is the stage of group life when members become increasingly impatient with the existing structure and directly or indirectly challenge the group's leader or leaders. Members get frustrated with how things are working and become critical of the existing leadership. Again, it is the nature of social groups that not everyone will be happy. There will be disagreement over procedures, role assignments, and any number of details related to group life. As the newness of the group wears off, members are bolder in questioning and challenging each other. *Individual roles* emerge at this time as members take a passive, passive-aggressive, or aggressive stance against the group (avoider, resister, and dominator roles, respectively). Groups will often become polarized as members form alliances as they jockey for status and power. Although uncomfortable for some, this stage is necessary for optimal cohesion and group functioning.

The **norming** stage is an attempt by the group to restore stability and cohesion and to develop a more effective strategy to achieve goals. Having gone through some conflict, the group has tested the boundaries and, hopefully, developed trust. At this stage, groups not only become more unified but also better organized. Relationships deepen at the same time that task efficiency increases. The storming period has given way to a renewed commitment to the goals and purpose of the group resulting in an examination and redefinition of norms, roles, and relationships.

In the **performing** stage, groups are focused on getting the work done. Relationships and cohesion have been built, optimal strategies have been constructed, and the underlying group structure has solidified. The group is now positioned for maximum effectiveness and productivity. With the group infrastructure in place, members are able to focus more specifically on work tasks. During this stage, effective groups spend 80 to 85% of their time on task completion (Wheelan, 1999; Wheelan, Davidson, & Tilin, 2003). Unfortunately, not all groups make it to this productive stage. Many groups remain stuck in one of the earlier stages. In terms of timeframe, Wheelan (2004) suggests it will take approximately six months for a group to get to this level of functioning.

On the other hand, an in-depth study by Gersick (1988, 1989) of eight work groups finds little support for the sequenced Tuckman and Wheelan models. Instead, she asserts that by the end of the first meeting, groups had an initial structure that remained fairly stable until the middle of the project or life of the group. At the midpoint, Gersick observed a burst of energy and transition. Consistent across various types of groups, the chronological midpoint was a time when members critically examined their progress and reorganized themselves for more effective functioning. Interestingly, whether the groups she studied met four times or 25 times, over seven days or six months, they all had a major transition at exactly the chronological midpoint of the project. So, instead of stages, she postulates phases.

According to Gersick, the first phase of group development starts with a stable structure that gets established by the end of the first meeting. Thus, the first meeting is extremely important in setting the climate, culture, and direction of the group. Then at the midpoint, the group goes through a period of instability and transition before entering the second phase with a newly defined stable structure that can guide the project through to the end. She also noted a flurry of activity and effort toward the end of the project as the deadline approached.

Research partially supports both the Tuckman/Wheelan and Gersick models (Chang, Bordia, & Duck, 2003). Table 3.2 summarizes the different models. One way to reconcile them is that the Tuckman and Wheelan models have more to do with the relationship dimension of group work, while the Gersick model has more to do with the task dimension. Again, these two dimensions of group dynamics (task and relationship) are separate yet related. Some groups might be very effective in terms of task completion but might neglect the relational aspect of the group which provides member satisfaction and, thus, long-term sustainability. Conversely, some groups might be very close relationally but ineffective

TABLE 3.2 Models of Group Development

Tuckman (1965)	Wheelan (1999)	Gersick (1988)
Forming	Dependency and Inclusion	Phase 1 (Stability)
Storming	Counterdependency and Fight	Transition (Instability)
Norming	Trust and Structure	
Performing	Work and Productivity	Phase 2 (Stability)

in accomplishing its goals or mission. Both dimensions are important for long-term group success. The forming and storming stages set the relational stage for the later, more task-oriented stages of norming and performing. Tuckman and Wheelan help us understand the development of group structure while Gersick helps us understand the development of an effective strategy for task completion. In addition, groups that have concrete deadlines may, indeed, undergo more of an identifiable midpoint transition as the deadline looms.

■ SOLVING PROBLEMS AND MANAGING PROJECTS (DAPEE)

Many of the project management and group problem-solving strategies in the literature contain similar components. Effective groups are able to gather information, evaluate that information, and devise a strategy to accomplish its mission (Ilgen, Hollenbeck, Johnson, & Jundt, 2005). More specifically, groups need an accurate understanding of the goal or problem to be solved, a comprehensive plan for achieving the desired results, efficient execution of that plan, and then a systematic evaluation of the results. Thus, the following components describe the basic structure of a task management or problem-solving strategy and will be referred to by the acronym **DAPEE**.

- **Define** the problem, project, or task
- **Analyze** the problem, project, or task
- **Plan** the solution or strategy
- **Execute** the plan
- **Evaluate** the outcome

This model describes how groups can systematically and effectively work toward long-term solutions. Yet, this is not a purely linear model. Real-world problems are often complex, messy, and ill structured. While the general flow of the project moves from top to bottom, there are often times when the group will need to circle back to a previous stage, as illustrated in Figure 3.3.

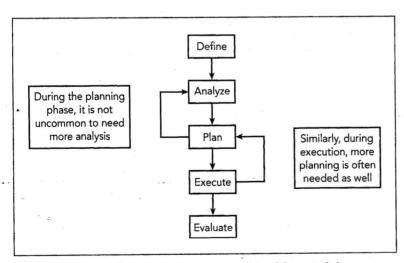

FIGURE 3.3   Project Management and Problem-Solving Model (DAPEE)

Define the Problem, Project, or Goal

The first part of strategic planning relates directly to the previous chapter. Effective groups are guided by SMART goals that are specific, measurable, attainable, relevant, and time bounded. Groups must know where they are going before they can figure out the best way to get there. Because this has been covered at length, we can move to application.

The concepts of strategy and structure can be illustrated by a project given to undergraduate students at Vanderbilt University, shown in the box below. In a group behavior class, students are divided into groups of 12 or 13 students and assigned various tasks or challenges about which they reflect and apply group theory. The teams become their own case studies that they analyze and from which they learn by experiencing the concepts. A recent project had students propose programming for a new dining center being built on the Peabody campus. This new center is designed to be a residential and integrated community for all incoming freshman. Students had to research the problem, construct a solution, and make a presentation with their findings. This project is presented as an example of the challenges and pitfalls that occur when teams attempt to develop a strategy that solves an assigned problem.

Request for Proposal

Vanderbilt University is currently designing a freshman commons on the Peabody College campus. According to a university spokesperson, "The Freshman Commons will be a one-year living learning environment that includes all the features of a residential college, such as resident faculty and staff, music rooms, study rooms, and a dining hall. New construction will add five new residence halls to the five existing dormitories at Peabody to form a community of ten houses. A new dining facility will replace the current Hill Center and provide additional spaces for social and academic programming."

The new dining center will be a centerpiece of student life at Peabody. Your task is to construct a proposal for mealtimes, special programs, and general operations that will accomplish the following goals: (a) create a cohesive community for incoming students, (b) facilitate the transition to college, and (c) facilitate academic development. The proposal should draw from empirical research that supports your recommendations. In addition, you will need to conduct interviews and focus groups with current Vanderbilt University students to find out what might be helpful to them and to get feedback for your proposed programs. The proposal should include a one-year programming calendar that takes into consideration the stages of group development.

Two weeks from today, your group will make a 25-minute PowerPoint presentation that outlines your proposal. Please include graphs or charts of empirical research and collected data that support your recommendations. Also, you will be expected to submit a two-page executive briefing of your proposal.

Presentations will be evaluated by faculty members, graduate assistants, and the director of dining services using the following criteria:

- Persuasiveness of the presentation
- Effective use of empirical research and collected data
- Level of preparation and professionalism

Typical of the kind of project or tasks given to groups, some external entity has defined the work to be completed which, in this case, comes from the course instructor. After the assignment is presented to the students, they ask quite a number of questions about what the proposal should include and how it will be evaluated (e.g., "What does it take to get an A?"). They seek further clarification of the project until they are reasonably sure they understood what is expected. An assignment like this leaves much room for interpretation but is typical of the ill-structured problems with which most work groups are faced.

Students receive a group grade on the project which everyone shares equally. High achievers will settle for nothing less than an A. Other students are quite content to get a B or C. So, from the start there is a potential conflict over personal goals as they relate to the overall group goal. Member motivation and effort is directly related to the relative importance of the grade. The groups must find a way to establish a shared commitment to the task. One way group members have engaged their colleagues is to frame the project as a competition against other groups. This creates **in group/out group bias:** overly positive attitudes about one's own group in conjunction with overly negative attitudes about other groups, and can lead to hostility toward other groups. Another way for leaders and high achievers to improve group performance is to do most of the work themselves. This encourages less-motivated members to become even more passive in the group. In the end, high-achieving members often experience resentment and bitterness for having done most of the work.

Some groups clarify their performance goal by having an open discussion about standards and commitment. Members discuss their expectations and what they are willing and able to contribute to achieve the goal. This kind of open dialogue requires mature communication skills (discussed in the next chapter) to help members verbalize unspoken assumptions and understand other perspectives. The dialogue, itself, is helpful in engaging all members and building cohesion as the group works toward its goal. In addition, expectations and roles can be negotiated and clarified.

Analyze

Problems and projects do not exist in a vacuum. There is, most assuredly, a context, history, and system within which they operate. As Senge (1990) suggests, today's problems are yesterday's solutions. Current problems are often the results of past attempts to solve problems that had unintended consequences. For example, when Nissan Motor Company needed to improve cash flow in the early 1990s, they cut back on product development. Money was saved in the short term, but the decision created a situation less than a decade later where they were losing market share and revenue due to an outdated product line (Ghosn, 2002). At that point, instead of relying on short-term cost cutting measures, Nissan decided to implement cross-functional teams to solve their cash-flow problem. When problems or projects aren't understood in a larger systemic context, solutions have a tendency to generate short-term gains that can turn into long-term liabilities. Before an effective plan of action can be created and executed, groups must thoroughly understand the issues involved in their project. Group members are prone to jump too quickly to solution planning before completely understanding the problems, potential hazards, and unintended consequences of well-meaning solutions.

Comprehensive analysis requires an accurate assessment of the current situation in relation to the group's goal. Senge (1990) describes this creative tension between the current reality and ideal state as a catalyst for innovative problem-solving and planning.

A well-formulated action plan is built on concrete information and critical dialogue (Postmes, Spears, & Cihangir, 2001). While past experiences and personal opinions can influence group discussions, groups benefit when they have actual data on which to design, execute, and evaluate plans. A colleague at Vanderbilt is fond of saying that when confronted with tasks and problems, we want our students to have an automatic response of asking Where's the data? concerning the problem or issue and What's the evidence? regarding potential solutions.

An analytic tool that can help groups create an effective plan is known as **force field analysis.** It identifies the forces working toward goal attainment as well as those forces working against it (Kayser, 1994; Robson, 2002). First, the group must have a clear understanding of the goal or ideal state. Then, members define the current reality in relation to that goal. For every goal or ideal state, there are forces and resources that support success and forces that hinder it. Here are the four questions associated with a force field analysis:

1. Where are we now (current reality)?
2. Where are we going (goal)?
3. What will help us reach the goal?
4. What is hindering us from making progress and reaching the goal?

Figure 3.4 shows the force field analysis and gives a visual representation of the goal and those forces working for and against the group.

Once the supporting and hindering forces have been identified, the group can decide which of the forces to focus on. In theory, if supporting forces are strengthened and hindering forces are removed, the current reality will move closer toward the goal. Some of the hindering forces are hard realities and cannot be changed; others are not significant enough to address. For example, limited financial resources are often a reality within which groups must work. But the group can create a plan to eliminate as many of the hindering forces as is possible. As the hindering forces are neutralized, the supporting forces will move the current reality toward the ideal state.

In the student project example, a thorough analysis of the present dining situation will help students understand whether the three goals in the request for proposal are currently

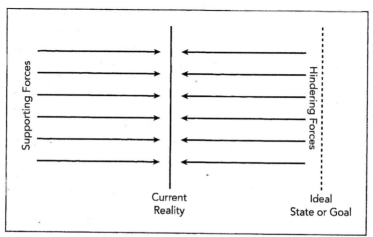

FIGURE 3.4   Force Field Analysis

being met and to what degree. They can get an idea of what is working, what isn't, and why. In addition, students might want to acquire information on the concept of residential colleges within which the new dining center is embedded. Dining centers are important components of residential colleges and should contribute to the overall goal of what they are trying to accomplish. Large projects like the creation of a new campus culture will have political forces working for and against it. A good proposal needs to be aware of the concerns and political issues related to the project. And since other universities presumably are interested in these same issues, examples of best practices would be informative. Teams need to understand how the three goals of the dining center (to create a cohesive community for incoming students, to facilitate the transition to college, and to facilitate academic development) are defined, measured, and facilitated in the lives of college students. Before the students can proceed with a specific proposal, they need to collect and analyze quite a bit of data.

The request for proposal specifically asks groups to conduct interviews and focus groups with current students to assess existing attitudes and suggestions for improvement. This requires planning to (a) identify the information they want to collect from their peers, (b) design structured or semi-structured interview questions to get it, (c) determine how to choose participants in order to achieve a representative sample, and (d) create a process to document, store, and analyze the data. From those interviews, a force field analysis can be constructed that identifies those driving and hindering forces that are related to a successful dining center. Once the group has collected and analyzed the data, they can divide up the remaining research tasks and set up a future meeting to share their findings. When the project and obstacles are thoroughly understood, they are ready to create a proposal and plan the presentation.

Plan

The creative tension between the existing reality and the ideal state has the potential to unleash the power of collective problem-solving. During the planning stage, high-performing groups avoid typical mistakes such as not spending enough time brainstorming various options (choosing premature solutions) and judging, critiquing and discounting ideas as they are shared (Kramer, Fleming, & Mannis, 2001). A good brainstorming session is first measured by the quantity not quality of ideas that are generated. Evaluating the quality of various options comes next. The first goal of brainstorming is to generate as many ideas as possible. Group members should be encouraged to participate without screening or censuring their thoughts. The most creative ideas can be withheld out of fear of what others might think.

Often a group scribe will volunteer or be assigned the task of recording all the ideas. Members can shout out ideas spontaneously or go around the room sequentially in an orderly manner to give everyone an opportunity to contribute. Another method is the index card technique where members write one idea per card for as many ideas that they can generate. Cards are then collected and a master list is created (Kayser, 1999). Once a list of possible ideas has been generated, discussion can commence.

The next step after brainstorming is to evaluate the ideas that have been generated. Each of the possibilities are discussed and critiqued. For larger lists, ideas can be grouped together and combined. With shorter lists (less than 15 or so items), ideas can be examined sequentially (Kayser, 1999). Members might ask for clarification, give opinions, or evaluate the quality and viability of each of the options. At this point, some ideas might need more analysis to determine their relative worth in solving the problem or advancing the project. Another meeting might be needed to give time for members to do additional research and report their findings. When the group has sufficiently discussed the various ideas and has enough supporting evidence to make an informed decision, they are ready to choose the best course of action.

Some problems require a single solution, but more often groups will use a combination of ideas. Decisions are often made by consensus, group vote, or by leader proclamation. Alternate approaches to group decision making will be discussed in Chapter 7. In our dining center example, students often settle on an idea before thoroughly brainstorming all of their options. Typically, a few ideas are shared (and critiqued as they are proposed) until an influential group member suggests that the group choose a particular idea. Other members validate the idea, momentum increases, and the group accepts this direction. Unless someone slows down the process, the group has defaulted into a premature solution and starts dividing up the tasks and creating a work plan.

A work plan identifies, defines, and assigns the tasks that need to be completed by group members or sub-groups. Since certain tasks are dependent on the completion of other tasks, due dates and completion schedules are formulated. After the tasks are defined, sequenced, and scheduled, group members either volunteer or are assigned to those tasks. Having the right people assigned to the right tasks is an important step in successfully completing the project. Issues of availability, motivation, and competence will influence those assignments. One particularly difficult issue is when a group member volunteers for an important assignment that he or she is not qualified for. In this case, leaders can simply ask the group if the tasks are assigned to the right people. If there is trust and good communication in the group, the wisdom of the collective will prevail. Otherwise, the leader may need to intervene and make an executive decision.

In our example, students identify the key work processes of the project and the specific tasks that need to be completed. Some groups draw the work plan out on the classroom white board; others just verbalize it and rely on loose commitments. Of course, the more detailed and thorough the work plan, the better the outcome. Figure 3.5 shows a partial work plan created by one of the groups with only the first key process (student interviews) described in detail. After the tasks were identified, students volunteered to be on one or more of the sub-groups based on interest, ability, and experience.

In Figure 3.5, the sequencing of tasks moves from left to right. The information gathered from student interviews, including analyzed data in the form of charts and tables and an edited video tape, is needed by the research team to complete their task. The research team then gives their information to the group assigned to create PowerPoint slides, and so on. Working backwards from the date of the presentation, the group is able to create a work schedule that includes due dates for each individual task. Interdependencies are accounted for as groups identify what they need from others to complete their own task. Of course this all looks fine on paper, but turns out to be quite complicated and ill-conceived in practice.

Execute

Once work tasks have been assigned to members and everyone is aware of the deadlines, the group is ready to disperse. Some tasks will be done by solitary members; others will be done in subgroups. Tasks are often underestimated in terms of difficulty and time required. As a result, sequential tasks get backed up and members get frustrated. Groups

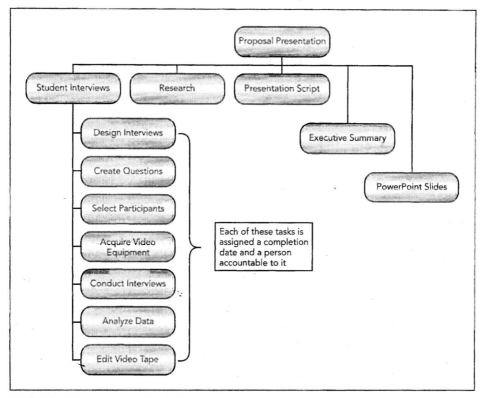

FIGURE 3.5   Sample Work Plan

that are most effective closely monitor their progress and manage the interdependencies of tasks and subgroups.

During the execution phase, a well-defined communication structure that reports on both progress and problems is invaluable. Status meetings allow all members to update the group and to hear how the project is developing. In general, individuals and task groups report (a) the progress they've made on specific tasks, (b) any problems or obstacles they may have encountered, and (c) whether or not they are still on schedule. The answers to these questions will determine whether resources need to be reallocated to meet deadlines, whether deadlines need to be adjusted, or whether more planning or analysis is needed. Group members may be tempted to minimize their difficulties and report their progress in overly positive terms to save face. The reporting of problems need not be a source of failure or embarrassment or else they will go underground only to resurface later (often at the most inopportune times). When problems are openly acknowledged and discussed, they can be effectively resolved through the collective wisdom of the group.

Members of cohesive groups feel loyalty toward their colleagues and are motivated to do their part for the team. Reporting structures that reinforce accountability to the group as opposed to accountability to the leader encourage members to work toward the self-transcendent goal of group success. The most effective groups learn to monitor their own progress and confront group members who are not fulfilling their responsibilities

(Lencioni, 2002; 2005). Otherwise, social loafing is likely to occur. **Social loafing** occurs when certain members rely on the efforts of others and minimize their own contribution. Social loafing not only diminishes group satisfaction but it also has a negative impact on group performance (Mulvey & Klein, 1998).

For the dining center project, the concept of mutual accountability is fairly difficult for students to embrace. After a plan is constructed, students volunteer for various tasks and commit to target dates. Unfortunately, most groups neglect to set up an adequate reporting structure to keep everyone on task and aware of the group's progress. A few high-performing student groups will have regular status meetings or regular email updates. It is not unusual for individuals or subgroups to fail to meet deadlines which leave other groups impatiently waiting for the information they need to complete their task. When these bottlenecks occur, tempers can flare.

For example, the PowerPoint group is dependent on the student interview and research groups for the content that will be used in their slide show. Similarly, the presentation group is not able to write the presentation script until they know what content is covered in the PowerPoint slides. Each missed deadline creates a bigger and bigger backlog. Inevitably, a few of the members are stuck at the eleventh hour throwing the last minute details together. This can create quite a bit of frustration and resentment which could have been avoided with more open communication and regular status updates.

Evaluate

The final step in the DAPEE model is evaluation. After defining project goals and analyzing relevant data, creating plans and executing those plans, the group is ready to evaluate the results. As previously stated, a well-defined project goal or problem statement will have clear and measurable criteria from which to evaluate success.

In the case of our student project, criteria for evaluation were given to the students when they got the assignment. After the project is completed, students receive multiple evaluation sheets from instructors and teaching assistants with feedback on their presentations and a grade for the project. The criteria for evaluation, though specified in the assignment, are still somewhat subjective. Evaluators try to provide as much concrete evidence as possible to support their judgments. For example, they might observe that charts and graphs were not clearly labeled in the PowerPoint slides or that the method of sampling was not clearly communicated. While students are often dissatisfied with their grade (especially the overachievers who did most of the work), they can still learn from the feedback.

Students are also asked to fill out an internal assessment of the group's preparation and presentation of the project. This helps members identify the strengths and weaknesses of the team. Here is a sample of some of those questions:

1. What part of the group's presentation process are you most proud of?
2. How did the group go about making decisions?
3. What part of the preparation process created "unfinished business" (i.e., tension which hasn't been resolved)? What needs to happen about that issue?
4. Who were the unsung heroes for this presentation?
5. Who seemed to work the hardest?
6. Who demonstrated new positive behaviors or increased commitment to the group?
7. How well did the group include the quieter members of the group?
8. Who were the most influential members in the process?

9. If you were giving awards which individuals might be (and you can have more than one person):
   a. The most encouraging of others?
   b. The most creative?
   c. The most fun to work with?
   d. The most reliable?
   e. The most helpful standard setters?
   f. The best presenters of information?
   g. The best technical experts?
10. What could have been done to improve the presentation?

During a post-presentation debriefing session, both the external feedback and internal assessments are shared and discussed. As Argyris (1994) suggests, most workers have sophisticated defense mechanisms that prevent them from learning meaningful lessons. A competent facilitator can help students move past their tendency to blame others, encourage them to take responsibility for their own shortcomings, and to hold each other accountable to standards of excellence (Cannon & Witherspoon, 2005).

 OPENING CASE REVISITED

Top Management Meetings at Kotch Industries

Although Felton did not feel appreciated, she did not realize until receiving the results of her 360-degree feedback report just how negatively she was viewed. Fortunately, the company had invested in a capable executive coach to conduct the 360-degree feedback assessment and discussion. The president viewed her as uncooperative and not a team player and was frustrated with her. Rather than just accept this explanation, the executive coach pressed for a better understanding of what specifically she did that led him to see her this way. The coach discovered that the source of the trouble had to do with very different understandings about the group norms for management meetings.

Kotch Industries had developed a norm of using these team meetings in a very ceremonial way. The critique and debate were to have happened before the meeting. If an issue got to the meeting, it was to have been decided already. The purpose of the meeting was to give a blessing to the new initiatives and celebrate them. However, no one had ever explained that to Felton. When she did not follow the group norm, they assumed that she was just combative and resistant.

In the organizations where Felton had worked previously, the norms supported a much more open critique and debate of ideas and concerns. Neither she nor the others had understood each other, but it became much clearer after Felton discussed her 360-degree feedback with the coach. This understanding reduced the tensions between Felton and the others. At the same time, Felton simply did not like this norm and found the meetings unproductive. Rather than adapt to the norms of this group or try to change the norms, she opted to leave the company for another organization with more open give and take.

This case illustrates just how different group norms can be across organizations. Unfortunately for Felton, she did not recognize these differences prior to taking a job at Kotch Industries and the experience proved unnecessarily frustrating for her. It also illustrates how easy it is for people to be unaware of group norms, especially those who are new to the group. Rather than recognizing that Felton might be operating under a different set of norms, they simply concluded that there was something wrong with her.

Summary

Work groups are formed to serve a purpose. The mission and related goals must always be kept in mind as groups develop effective strategies to achieve those goals. Group structure which includes norms, roles, and relational patterns support those strategies and, hopefully, lead to goal attainment. Furthermore, groups change over time. They require an initial structure established by the leader or organizational context to lower anxiety and ambiguity but will eventually develop their own structure and unique identity. This developmental process creates group cohesion which then releases the creativity and commitment needed to generate effective strategies for success. The next chapter will take a closer look at the process of communication and how it affects group functioning and success.

 CONCLUDING CASE ───────────────────────────────

Finding the Next Superintendent for Washington County

Jennifer Stone had worked hard as a school board member for Washington county schools for many years, and she had recently been elected chair of the board. She was proud of the work that they had done for underprivileged children in the community. Standardized test scores were on the rise, and she felt that they were moving to the next level as a school district. The superintendent had recently retired and Stone believed this was somewhat of a blessing. The district was experiencing tremendous growth and was beginning to outstrip the former superintendent's skills as an administrator.

One of the things she loved about the board was that it collaborated with community partners and developed successful programs such as tutoring after school, community education for parents, and a quality day care at a reasonable cost so that children would have a safe place to go while their parent or parents were at work. They just launched a program to combat teen pregnancy and had a successful mentoring program in place. Most of the board members were mentors and felt that they grew personally from playing a significant role in the lives of children. This attitude was prevalent in the district staff as well. None was there just for the money. In fact the former superintendent had been paid a relatively low salary. It was understood that wages were kept modest in order for district resources to go toward the children. But, something was now threatening that spirit.

Paul Krantz, the vice chairperson of the board had his own idea about who should replace the superintendent. He wanted to hire Krandal Thurston, formerly a high-powered and highly paid lobbyist. The Thurston family were a powerful group in the community, but they were not without controversy. Krandal Thurston's brother Terrence had been convicted of taking bribes as a high-level government official. Also, the family's wealth had come from running an illegal brewery during prohibition. Although Krandal Thurston had never been accused of any crime, he was known for cutting corners and seemed to be in the grey area of ethics as he managed his dealings with politicians. At the same time, Krandal Thurston knew all the influential people in the community and he had a charismatic personality and a terrific ability to navigate the state financial system. That was the only reason Krantz wanted to hire him.

Thurston was interested in the job but demanded a hefty salary. Although Thurston's motives were unknown, Krantz thought he would be an excellent investment because of his connections with political leaders. Krantz thought, *Who cares how much it costs. If he increases funding, he can pay his salary plus give us more operating funds than we have ever seen before. We will be able to do vastly more for students than if we paid a considerably smaller salary for someone who did not have the contacts or political skills.*

Stone was sickened by the idea. She could imagine raising the superintendent's salary a modest amount, but was disgusted by the thought of paying Thurston his asking price. She felt it would send the wrong message, and she thought that Krantz was betraying the mission to which they were all committed. She felt that the very goals, norms, and culture of the district were being challenged.

Discussion Questions

1. What do you think of their predicament?
2. What are the norms of this school board?
3. How will a new superintendent affect school board and district norms?
4. What is a reasonable strategy to use in hiring a new president? (Use the DAPEE model.)
5. Why do you suggest these choices?

References

Argyris, C. (1994). Good communication that blocks learning. *Harvard Business Review*, July–Aug., 77–85.

Arrow, H., Poole, M. S., Henry, K. B., Wheelan, S., & Moreland, R. (2004). Time, change, and development: The temporal perspective on groups. *Small Group Research, 35*, 73–105.

Benne, K. D., & Sheats, P. (1948). Functional roles of group members. *Journal of Social Issues, 4*, 41–49.

Cannon, M. D., & Witherspoon, R. (2005). Actionable feedback: Unlocking the power of learning and performance improvement. *Academy of Management Executive, 19*, 120–134.

Chang, A., Bordia, P., & Duck, J. (2003). Punctuated equilibrium and linear progression: Toward a new understanding of group development. *Academy of Management Journal, 46*, 106–117.

Forsyth, D. R. (2006). *Group dynamics* (4th ed.). Belmont, CA: Thompson Wadsworth.

Gersick, C. J. G. (1988). Time and transition in work teams: Toward a new model of group development. *Academy of Management Journal, 31*, 9–41.

Gersick, C. J. G. (1989). Marking time: Predictable transitions in task groups. *Academy of Management Journal, 32*, 274–309.

Ghosn, C. (2002). Saving the business without losing the company. *Harvard Business Review, 80*, 37–45.

Hackman, J. R. (2002). *Leading teams: Setting the stage for great performances.* Boston: Harvard Business School Press.

Hogg, M. A., & Reid, S. A. (2006). Social identity, self-categorization, and the communication of group norms. *Communication Theory, 16*, 7–30.

Horne, C. (2001). The enforcement of norms: Group cohesion and meta-norms. *Social Psychology Quarterly, 64*, 253–266.

Ilgen, D. R., Hollenbeck, J. R., Johnson, M., & Jundt, D. (2005). Teams in organizations: From input-process-output models to IMOI models. *Annual Review of Psychology, 56*, 517–543.

Kayser, T. A. (1994). *Building team power: How to unleash the collaborative genius of work teams.* New York: Irwin Professional Publishing.

Kramer, T. J., Fleming, G. P., & Mannis, S. M. (2001). Improving face-to-face brainstorming through modeling and facilitation. *Small Group Research, 32*, 533–557.

Lencioni, P. (2002). *The five dysfunctions of a team: A leadership fable.* San Franscisco: Jossey-Bass.

Lencioni, P. (2005). *Overcoming the five dysfunctions of a team: A field guide for leaders, managers, and facilitators.* San Francisco: Jossey-Bass.

Mulvey, P. W., & Klein, H. J. (1998). The impact of perceived loafing and collective efficacy on group goal processes and group performance. *Organizational Behavior and Human Decision Processes, 74*, 62–87.

Postmes, T., Spears, R., & Cihangir, S. (2001). Quality of decision making and group norms. *Journal of Personality and Social Psychology, 80*, 918–930.

Robson, M. (2002). *Problem-solving in groups* (3rd ed.). Hampshire, England: Gower Publishing.

Senge, P. M. (1990). *The fifth discipline: The art and practice of the learning organization.* New York: Doubleday.

Tuckman, B. (1965). Developmental sequence in small groups. *Psychological Bulletin, 63*, 384–399

Wheelan, S. A. (1999). *Creating effective teams: A guide for members and leaders.* Thousand Oaks, CA: Sage Publications.

Wheelan, S. A. (2004). *Group processes: A developmental perspective* (2nd ed.). Boston: Allyn and Bacon.

Wheelan, S. A., Davidson, B., & Tilin, F. (2003). Group development across time: Reality or illusion? *Small Group Research, 34*, 223–245.

CHAPTER FOUR

Communication

■ INTRODUCTION

Group and individual goals, structure, and norms are evident in communication patterns between members. Verbal and nonverbal interaction between group members defines much of group life. Yet, not all interpersonal communication is positive, and some members are reluctant to enter into a group dialogue. This chapter describes communication skills and patterns that lead to efficient and effective group functioning.

LEARNING OBJECTIVES

After reading this chapter, you should be able to

- Describe the process of interpersonal communication.
- Detail the components and importance of active listening.
- Describe various types of messages individuals communicate to each other.
- Understand the importance of clear and assertive statements.
- Describe four social styles that individuals use to relate to others.

 OPENING CASE

The Contentious School Board

Kevin Humphrey was a successful management consultant. He specialized in assisting school boards and high-level school administrators improve communication and governance skills. The superintendent of a large southern California district in which school board members and the superintendent were having rocky experiences had engaged him. The board did not want to fire the superintendent, having run through four chief executives in the past seven years. The superintendent did not want to leave. Still, they were just not getting along.

Humphrey entered the conversation at an executive session and gained agreement on some ground rules for what was to follow. He tried to clarify the roles of the administration and the school board when it happened. One board member asked why it was so important for the board to make policy only to leave policy implementation to the administration. In attempting to respond to this question, Humphrey said, "You," meaning the board members, "cannot teach all of the children yourselves. Therefore, you must depend on others to instruct. You can make rules, but you cannot yourself act to ensure successful implementation in every classroom."

To Humphrey this statement seemed obvious. However, to two of the assembled five board members, what they heard was "He is saying that not all of our children can learn. He must be prejudiced." They tuned him out from then on. He was not able to have any positive effect for the remainder of the evening's executive session. What they heard is not what he meant.

Discussion Questions

1. If you were Humphrey and sensed the tension in the room, what would you do?
2. How would you handle misunderstandings in this group?
3. Two of the board members are angry. How would you handle that?
4. What communication skills are needed in this group?

Communication is the engine that drives the work and life of groups. In contrast to working alone where thinking and processing occurs internally, group work requires the sharing of ideas and concerns through discussion and dialogue. The free exchange of ideas, the courage to make innovative suggestions, and the ability to really listen to others are characteristics that create synergy. In a study of 280 people who had previously participated in 522 work groups, communication was cited as one of the seven main reasons that those groups either succeeded or failed (Hirokawa, DeGooyer, & Valde, 2000). Communication is a crucial component of group success.

Most of us have been part of group discussions that were energizing and thought provoking. Stimulating conversations prompt new ideas and learning. They help teams create effective strategies and form the basis for the underlying group structure. Meaningful group dialogue occurs when members thoughtfully interact with the topic of discussion, accurately transmit an understood message, listen to what others are saying, and contribute their own ideas in a clear and concise manner. Community life is enriched when people are active participants, and progress is made toward collective goals and tasks. Strongly related to member satisfaction and group success, these types of discussions are not guaranteed. They must be facilitated and require some basic competence in communication skills and interpersonal maturity on the part of group members.

▓ THE PROCESS OF COMMUNICATION

While interpersonal communication can be exhilarating, it can also be boring, cantankerous, insensitive, argumentative, and unproductive. Communication can be extremely challenging and prone to misunderstandings and potential disaster. An engaging conversation can quickly turn negative and relationally damaging. Having more people involved in a given discussion increases the possibility of synergic brilliance, but also increases the possibility for misunderstanding and frustration. Communication can be the demise of many social arrangements, from marriages to teams to whole organizations. So much can go wrong and, thus, there are tremendous challenges to effective communication.

We are prone to misinterpret others' messages due to the way we process information. Words and visual cues are perceived through the senses and ascribed meaning. Raw data are interpreted and evaluated based on idiosyncratic and unique internal working models. People bring all their past experiences with them into each new interpersonal context. Argyris (1994) describes this process as the *ladder of inference*. Incoming messages are interpreted based on inference, using past experiences and existing assumptions to interpret current messages. Figure 4.1 shows the steps, or ladder rungs, that describe how information is perceived and processed. At the lower rungs of the ladder, perception and information processing occurs unconsciously. Moving up the ladder, more of the processing occurs on a conscious level. However, over time, repetitive patterns of processing become ingrained and less conscious. For example, learning to drive a

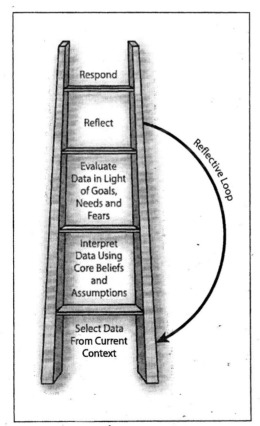

FIGURE 4.1   Ladder of Inference

car, especially a car with a manual transmission, requires great concentration and effort. But after driving for a while, the process becomes automatic and conscious thought is no longer needed.

These steps happen instantaneously. It would be inefficient and ineffective for people to be a blank slate and experience all new data as if it were their first time seeing, hearing, smelling, tasting, or touching that phenomenon. The benefit of this process is that we can respond quickly to stimulus without much conscious thought. The downside is that not all new experiences fit neatly into our database of previous experiences. We make assumptions and inferences based on how close we think the new data resembles past experiences. Deliberate, conscious reflection may not always take place, in which case, a preprogrammed response is made without much thought. Reflection is a practice that can help reevaluate old patterns of thinking and assumptions that are either outdated or limited in perspective.

Each of the steps of this information-processing model is related to specific components within the internal working model. Once data are selected from our current context, core beliefs and assumptions about ourselves, others, and the world are used to interpret that data. Interpretation includes paraphrasing and naming what we perceive as described more completely in Chapter 11. Then, goals and needs are used to evaluate whether that information is friend or foe, whether it can move one toward goal achievement, or is perceived as a threat. Strategies are learned responses that help us pursue goals and avoid fears. The discipline of reflection allows people to assess the accuracy of their interpretation and evaluation and to consider their options in terms of how to respond.

Select Data

People have the capacity to process and pay attention to only a limited number of pieces of incoming data. While some may have a greater capacity to multitask, there is still a limit to what we can pay attention to at one time. For example, we might be in a large meeting with literally hundreds of pieces of information bombarding our senses including such variables as lighting, room temperature, nonverbal messages from all the members present, various verbal messages, and so on. We can only attend to a limited number of these variables.

We are more likely to attend to information that is perceived as either important to us personally or important to the group. For example, if a group is having a discussion about whether or not to request a deadline extension for an existing project, some members might have strong feelings about the issue that lead them to sit up and pay close attention. Other members who are ambivalent about the topic might not engage in the discussion, and only partially listen. Some topics will hold little or no interest to members. Subsequently, members may be fairly disengaged from the discussion on that topic.

In addition to the perceived level of interest in any given topic, we tend to notice the things that confirm our existing beliefs. Data that are at odds with core beliefs are often screened out. In general, we see what we expect to see and what we want to see. We experience a certain level of comfort and security when our experiences are predictable and understandable. Unfortunately, this can limit our ability to discover new ideas and novel solutions to problems. So we must continually ask ourselves what we are missing, both individually and collectively as a group. Realizing that our perception is limited and potentially flawed is the first step toward opening up to new perspectives and seeing things that have yet to be discovered. But increased awareness is only the first step; that information must then be interpreted.

Interpret the Data

Past experiences have been summarized and cataloged into core beliefs and assumptions called *schemas* (Griffith, 2004). **Schemas** are the internal dictionaries or rule books that help us make sense of incoming data quickly and efficiently. For example, a red light at an intersection is automatically interpreted as a symbol for "stop" which then triggers a response on our part. To proceed could mean danger to physical well being so a driver will automatically start braking (response) without giving much thought. The interpreted stimulus and resulting response is deeply ingrained as a habit and requires little or no awareness (i.e., reflection). Similarly, group members might hear a certain word or interpret a certain nonverbal gesture as a "red light" (danger) and disengage from the conversation. Under duress, people have the tendency to revert to the deeply embedded primal responses of fight or flight, both of which can be counterproductive to meaningful communication.

Different people see things differently based on how data are interpreted. Core beliefs and assumptions based on past experiences are used to identify and understand new streams of information. Core beliefs include generalizations about other groups of people. We may have certain stereotypes based on any number of variables such as gender, age, race, and geographic background. The following exercise helps to identify some of those generalizations.

Exercise 4.1   **Individual Perception**

What do you think is going on in this group setting? Be creative and speculate on the dynamics that are taking place. How do you perceive each member of the group? How do you think each member is feeling about the situation and about the other members?

If you compared your answers in Exercise 4.1 to others, you would likely find out that your perception is somewhat different. What makes one person "see" one thing, and another person "see" another? First, each notices different things and interprets that information based on idiosyncratic assumptions and past experiences.

When messages are vague and group members don't ask for clarification, inferences are based on fewer data points and, consequently, more prone to misunderstanding. For example, if a male team leader told a female member that she wasn't pulling her weight in the group, she could internally respond to that statement from a variety of interpretive grids including those related to:

- Her assumptions about her own competence ("I know I am competent")
- Her assumptions about management ("Managers are never satisfied")
- Her assumptions about men ("This is a typical male power play")
- Her assumptions about the organization ("Women can't get ahead in this organization")
- Her assumptions about other members of the group ("They're all threatened by me")
- Her assumptions about groups in general ("I knew this would happen, I wish I could work by myself")

Obviously, her interpretation may have very little to do with the intended message from the team leader. Voicing thoughts that are based on incorrect interpretations and assumptions can cause interpersonal problems and hinder group functioning. Paraphrasing and the use of probing questions, discussed later in this chapter, are tools that can help avoid misinterpretation and gain a more accurate understanding of what another person is saying.

Since messages are prone to individual interpretation and are inherently ambiguous, we look to the accompanying nonverbal cues to help interpret them. Mehrabian's (1981) classic research suggests that messages, especially those that express feelings, are overwhelmingly understood through nonverbal cues. The following percentages represent relative contributions of verbal and nonverbal components of communication that are used to interpret messages.

- 7 percent from verbal cues (words)
- 38 percent from vocal cues (volume, pitch, rhythm, etc.)
- 55 percent from facial expressions (smiling, frowning, etc.) and other body movements (arms crossed, eye contact, etc.)

Facial expressions, especially, give meaning to words that are spoken. Yet, if words can be misinterpreted, then nonverbal cues are even more open to individual interpretation.

Evaluate the Data

Once a message has been interpreted, correctly or incorrectly, it must then be evaluated. Incoming messages are evaluated by comparing them against individual and collective goals which are related to the needs and fears in the four goal domains described in Chapter 2. In a very rudimentary way, our brains evaluate interpreted messages against the ideals defined in our individual goal system. Messages will be evaluated as either moving toward goal attainment, as an obstacle to goal attainment, or as being insignificant to goal attainment.

Necessary for the effective evaluation of ideas and plans is the ability to determine cause-and-effect relationships. This is no small task. A strategic planning group might be evaluating whether or not to open a new school in a new residential development. After looking at demographic data and proposed operating costs, the group must evaluate whether or not a decision to proceed is warranted. They use the best available information to make a data-based, informed decision based on what will most likely happen if they take a certain action. The more data they have, the better informed their decision. Groups are most effective when they have a clear understanding of where they are going and are able to use concrete and accurate information to get them there.

Senge (1990) warns against overly simplistic causal evaluations without considering the large, complex systems within which organizations exist. Systems thinking is a discipline that encourages group members to consider unintended consequences of decisions and to resist a reductionistic view of problems and challenges. Ideas, decisions, and plans must be considered in light of the context within which they will be implemented. Today's problems are often the result of yesterday's well-meaning solutions.

Finally, we are once again confronted with the tension between personal, group, and organizational goals. Some discussions, ideas, and plans may be conducive to the success of the group but, at the same time, may hinder personal goals. For example, a group leader might emphatically state that the organization must embark on an aggressive marketing strategy to regain lost market share. A public school superintendent may be reacting to the proposed opening of a new independent school in the district and desirous of stifling a trend toward private schooling in the community. Members of the group will interpret a message in idiosyncratic ways and then evaluate whether or not the suggestion is a viable strategy. That evaluation includes the costs and benefits not only to the organization and work group but also to the individual. Within this mixed-motive environment, it can be helpful to ask whose interests are best served by any given group decision. The larger goals and mission of the organization can be used as guiding principles for the evaluation of ideas and comments.

Reflection

Many of our responses are automatic and do not require much thinking or processing. This allows for efficiency and speed of processing but also creates patterns of thinking that resist adaptation and change. Reflection, in contrast, is the deliberate and proactive discipline of processing incoming information and determining the best response. Developing the skills of reflection is an important component of individual and group effectiveness (Griffith & Frieden, 2000). Reflection links theory and practice and can occur before some particular action, during that action, and after. According to Schon (1983; 1987), reflective practitioners think through and plan their actions to determine the best way to proceed on any given decision. Furthermore, when individuals are able to reflect while they are engaged in a particular action or experience, they are able to think on their feet, evaluate the process, and determine midcourse corrections. Finally, the practice of reflection increases awareness and learning from previous experiences.

Individuals who are not reflective may not understand how their behavior affects the group. For example, in many groups a small number of members dominate discussions. There is no shortage of people who speak without listening and offer opinions without understanding what is being discussed. But there are also group members who overanalyze and cautiously rehearse their responses before contributing to discussions. By the time they are ready to speak, the discussion has moved on, and they have missed their opportunity. Until group members become aware of their patterns of processing and participation, they will not likely change. As a result, groups hear too much from some and not enough from others, a common problem in groups.

Psychologist Carl Jung, the theoretical father of the Myers-Briggs Type Indicator, categorizes people as either introverts or extroverts. Introverts gain energy from being alone and process information internally. Extroverts, in contrast, gain energy from being with people and process information out loud. This means that introverts will tend to analyze and wait for the right moment in the conversation to contribute. They will have reflected on their response and will come out with a fairly complete thought. Extroverts do their reflecting verbally. They will offer ideas that may not have been thought out and, subsequently, may be incomplete. Extroverts prefer fast-moving and active discussions while introverts prefer more time for thoughtful reflection. Group leaders who are aware of the preferences of their members will seek to facilitate a conversational pace suited to all. In addition, they will monitor the amount of talk time ensuring that all members, especially the introverts, are contributing to the discussions.

Exercise 4.2   High Talkers and Low Talkers

Divide into two groups, those who talk more than an average amount in class and those who talk less than an average amount in class. Join the group that you think most accurately fits your level of participation. Adjust groups accordingly and form a circle with low talkers in the middle of the room and high talkers along the outside.

The goal of this exercise is for low talkers and high talkers to gain an understanding of what it is like to experience a different role. When one group is talking (the group in the middle) the other group (the group on the outside of the circle) is to remain quiet.

The low talkers should answer the following questions:

- What is it like to be a low-talking member of this class?
- What do the high talkers need to know about what it is like to be a low talker in this class?
- What would you like for the high talkers to do to help you be more included in class discussions?

The low talkers should then switch places with the high talkers and remain quiet while the high talkers answer the following questions:

- What was it like for you to not be able to speak?
- What did you hear the low talkers say about what it is like to be a low talker in this class?
- What did you hear the low talkers asking for?
- What do the low talkers need to know about what it is like to be a high talker in this class?
- What would you like for the low talkers to do in future discussions?

Switch positions once again so the low talkers are back in the middle. The high talkers should listen and not speak as the low talkers answer the following questions:

- What did you hear the high talkers say about what it was like to be a high talker in this class?

- What did you hear the high talkers ask for?
- What are the low talkers willing to do?

Finally, the high talkers describe what they are willing to do to help make class discussions more balanced. This exercise is likely to make you feel uncomfortable as you examine your own level of participation in class and get feedback from others. While this process may challenge you, it also has the potential to stimulate reflection, self-awareness, and growth.

Reflection is especially helpful when members of a group are experiencing strong emotions (anger, anxiety/fear, joy, or sadness). We feel anxiety when our goals are threatened, sadness when we have failed or lost something important, anger and frustration when our goals are blocked, and joy when we have accomplished success, either individually or collectively. Emotion is a feedback loop that indicates the activation of issues within the internal working model. Those emotions can be traced back to goals (physical well being, personal competence, relational closeness, or self-transcendence) and core beliefs about self, others, and the world. Active reflection can be used to (a) identify more effective problem-solving and task-management strategies, (b) construct more concrete and attainable goals, and (c) evaluate the accuracy of deeply held beliefs and assumptions about self, others, and the world.

Reflective thinking involves identifying the facts, formulas, and theories that are relevant for supporting existing positions and for solving complex and ill-defined problems (King & Kitchener, 1994). A theoretical framework for this approach stems from the reflective judgment model developed by King & Kitchener (1994) which is a developmental model of critical thinking that describes various epistemological assumptions inherent in the reasoning process. The seven stages of development are grouped into three levels: pre-reflective thinking, quasi-reflective thinking, and reflective thinking. Pre-reflective reasoning assumes that knowledge is either gained by direct observation or from an authority figure, and is absolutely correct and certain. This type of thinking sees problems in very concrete and simplistic ways. People at this level tend to see things as "black and white." Reasoning at the quasi-reflective level recognizes that understanding ill-structured problems can be complicated and that knowledge is uncertain. People at this level have difficulty processing the ambiguity of such problems and, therefore, are tenuous in responding to them. Knowledge is typically based on personal opinion with the inability to make critical evaluations about how the problem is framed and about potential solutions.

The highest level of reflective thinking assumes that knowledge is gained from a variety of sources and is understood in relationship to a specific context. While it may be impossible to arrive at a perfect understanding of certain problems, some judgments may be more accurate than others. Evaluation criteria might include "conceptual soundness, coherence, degree of fit with the data, meaningfulness, usefulness, and parsimony" (King & Kitchener, 1994, p. 17). At this level, individuals and groups draw reasonable conclusions and know the criteria on which those conclusions are based. Effective groups are receptive to the multitude of options and perspectives, but are clear about the criteria upon which they base their decisions and actions.

Respond

Group members receive verbal messages, focus on certain parts of the message, interpret and evaluate that data, and then finally respond to it. No two people process information in exactly the same way. Leaders can make sure that everyone is in agreement by regularly summarizing what has been said. Another strategy is to ask other group members to reflect on the content of a discussion. Many groups record minutes to document what has been discussed; those minutes then serve as a starting point for shared understanding and to reduce the ever-present potential for misunderstanding.

The following hypothetical situation highlights how different people might interpret the same message. Sue is a project director of an after-school program with a staff of three people (Bob, Mary, and Sharon) who administer the program and submit weekly attendance reports to the district office. At their weekly staff meeting, Sue announces that the district office is concerned about the quality and timeliness of the reports being done for them. Each of the three workers might interpret this message differently and respond accordingly. Bob might think, *They are all a bunch of overpaid spoiled brats*, whereas Mary might think, *I called in sick last week. I bet my job is on the line*. And Sharon might be thinking, *Here we go again, same old story, it will blow over.* They may have heard the same message but processed it in entirely different ways resulting in either anger, fear, or indifference.

Based on those interpretations, a subsequent dialogue might go something like this:

Dialogue

Sue: The district office is concerned with the quality and timeliness of the weekly attendance reports.

Bob: I can't believe they're complaining. We work very hard for them.

Mary: Did they say anything about me specifically?

Sharon: Bob, don't get too upset. This comes up every three to four months. It's no big deal.

Sue: I think there might be ways to improve our work. What can we do differently?

Mary: Well, I just couldn't make it to work last Wednesday. It wasn't my fault. My child was sick. I knew they would hold it against me.

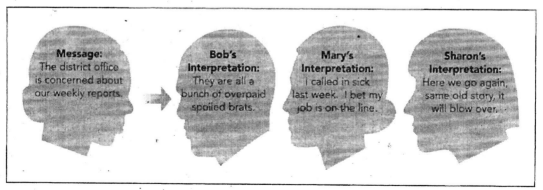

FIGURE 4.2   Multiple Interpretations of the Same Message

Bob: That's what I mean. We're barely making it and have to struggle to make our lives work while they drive around in their expensive cars, coming and going as they please.

Sue: Ok, let's just keep doing what we're doing. I know you're all trying to do the best you can.

In this example, we see that an attempt by the manager to improve the quality of work done by the staff is met with resistance and defensiveness. Sue was unable to engage the group in meaningful problem solving that might have generated more effective strategies to meet the goals and mission of the organization. Instead, each member's beliefs and assumptions about the organization are left intact and probably strengthened. Sue is left feeling torn between what she hears from the brokers and what she hears from her staff members. The two groups are likely to become more frustrated with each other and communication between and within the groups can become even more polarized and contentions.

Common Cognitive Distortions

As seen in the example above, different people can interpret the same message or experience in very different ways. Given the ambiguous process of communication, it is easy to see why members can misunderstand comments made by other group members. Arriving at an accurate understanding requires listening skills and awareness in order to minimize possible distortions. Beck (1995) has found that people make remarkably similar mistakes in processing information. The following list describes those common mistakes when receiving and responding to messages.

- *Overgeneralization:* Conclusions are based on a limited number of past experiences. Example: "Employee health programs don't work. We tried that before."
- *All-or-nothing thinking* (also called dichotomous or black-and-white thinking): Viewing a situation as all-or-nothing without considering other possibilities or recognizing that most issues exist on a continuum. Example: "Either we engage with the new instructional strategy immediately or we should abandon it."
- *Catastrophizing:* This occurs when a current negative experience is speculated to produce a larger, more lasting, longer-term catastrophe. Example: "We missed our deadline. Our bosses won't like us. We'll lose our jobs."
- *Personalization:* Speculating that the comments or behavior of others is related to you in some way. Example: "The group leader didn't recognize my contribution in the meeting today because she doesn't like me."
- *Emotional reasoning:* Strong feelings about an issue or a person may cloud one's ability to hear other perspectives. Example: "She may have a good argument for the policy change, but I still feel like it's the wrong direction for our organization."
- *Mind reading:* When a person attributes motives to others and speculates on what they are thinking. Example: "He thinks I don't have enough experience for this project."

The practice of reflection can help group members monitor the interpretation and evaluation of messages and avoid these common mistakes.

▓ THE ART OF LISTENING

Listening for accurate understanding is hard work and requires discipline. Group members are often preoccupied and distracted from hearing the messages spoken by others (McKay, Davis, & Fanning, 1995). For example, listeners can be comparing themselves with others, mentally rehearsing what they want to say next, day dreaming of being somewhere else, or recalling a past experience. Additional obstacles to listening include speculating on what is going on in the mind of the speaker (mind reading), filtering out parts of the message, judging the speaker, or jumping to conclusions and offering premature advice. Finally, some listeners are more focused on debating and critiquing than listening. This argumentative style of communication will often elicit either a defensive response from the speaker or passive detachment. In either case, meaningful dialogue and the opportunity to learn from others is diminished.

In order to respond to the comments of others adequately, we must first understand what is being said. Effective listeners suspend judgment in order to first understand the perspective of the speaker. The speed at which we process and interpret information can make it difficult to capture the essence of another's message before responding. A premature response can short circuit communication and shut down authentic dialogue.

Perspective taking is an advanced developmental skill (Kegan, 1994) where listeners try to "walk in the shoes" of another person. Group members can move beyond a potentially limited and ego-centric predisposition by being open to other perspectives. The viewpoints of others will make more sense if they are understood within a context and if the past experiences, beliefs, goals, and strategies of the speaker are known. The listener can ask for clarification using phrases such as "help me understand how you came to believe that," or "what experiences have led you to that conclusion." Listening skills can help the listener understand the message more accurately in addition to helping the speaker feel heard and validated.

Listening Skills: Paying Attention, Paraphrasing, and Probing

Listening is a set of skills anyone can learn. The first step is simply to pay attention. Active listening requires mental discipline and effort. Certain behaviors can be helpful both to the listener and the speaker. The acronym **SOLER** describes characteristics that communicate to the speaker that one is paying attention to what he or she is saying.

S—**Square:** Face the person squarely.
O—**Open:** Keep an open posture without crossed arms or legs.
L—**Lean** slightly forward to communicate interest and engagement. Head nods and verbal encouragers like "uh-huh" and "go on" are also effective.
E—**Eye Contact:** Maintain direct eye contact according to appropriate social norms.
R—**Relax:** Stay relaxed. Listeners should be comfortable with silence if appropriate and let the conversation unfold without being forced.

These characteristics suggest that the listener is paying attention and is interested in what is being said. In this way, the speaker will be more likely to feel valued and share more information.

Exercise 4.3   Conversation Killers

Name at least five things that people do that communicate they may not be listening or interested in what you are saying. Experiment with these roadblocks in conversations and see how they affect the person you are talking to. Then try using the **SOLER** characteristics and see if those behaviors elicit a different response.

Paraphrasing is a powerful listening skill that validates others, builds trust, and often leads to deeper levels of communication. Paraphrases restate the message one is hearing in order to clarify and confirm an accurate understanding of that message. For example, a curriculum designer who is frustrated with missed ship dates of evaluation textbooks might complain to the publisher's representative assigned to that school. If the account manager responds with defensiveness or discounts what the customer says, the school employee might escalate the conversation in anger or detach in passive resignation. Either response can potentially hurt the working relationship. The following dialogue uses paraphrasing without necessarily endorsing the customer complaint or discounting it.

Dialogue ____

Curriculum Specialist: The textbooks should have arrived here last week. One of my teachers told me you said they would be here by last Wednesday at the latest. We just can't work like this. I've got a number of teachers that are waiting to evaluate your book. If you can't get it to us by next Monday, we won't consider adopting it for next year.

Account Manager: OK, it sounds like you're getting quite frustrated with our company. I'm sure it puts you in a bad position when we don't deliver on time. For one thing, the delays can hinder your own timeline and goals. This is serious enough that it might force you to not consider our text. Am I reading the situation correctly?

This paraphrase invites the customer to talk more about some of the core issues that are involved with this situation. The account manager has not gotten defensive nor has she discounted the customer's concern. At this point, the account manager is just listening and trying to understand what the issues are. An accurate understanding of the situation is necessary before an appropriate response can be made.

In a group context, it can be helpful for the facilitator or group members to paraphrase what individuals have said or what the group has discussed in general. It gets everyone on board with the conversation and refocuses the discussion. Paraphrasing that links multiple people and perspectives also has the added benefit of building cohesion in the group.

Probing is the third skill that leads to more effective listening. In order to understand the ideas, opinions, or perspectives of others, the listener may need more information beyond that which has already been presented by the speaker. In many ways a good question is a precursor to a good response. Open-ended questions that lead to a deeper understanding help not only the speaker and the listener, but the group as a whole. A good open-ended question can stimulate reflective thinking and identify underlying assumptions. In the example of delayed ship dates above, here are some possible probing questions:

How does this impact the evaluation process?
How does this affect the teachers?

Where do you think the breakdown is?
How can we be more helpful in the future?
What do you need from us now?

These questions can be used in an individual customer meeting or in a group meeting. Instead of avoiding difficult issues, probing questions deal directly with them.

Receiving Feedback

There are times when the messages we are trying to understand are about our own performance. If the information is perceived as negative or potentially negative, we may be tempted to discount it in order to preserve positive feelings about ourselves. Another potential pitfall occurs when we receive an abundance of positive feedback in conjunction with some negative information, and all we can focus on is the negative. We totally discount the positive and obsess exclusively on the negative.

Most of us do not like to be confronted and easily respond with defensiveness. The tension between work and family life can be an ongoing challenge that creates tension in relationships. Most of us have feverishly worked to finish that last task of the day before racing home to be with loved ones. In the following example, the clock has won again and Marsha, a real estate agent, is late coming home to a family that is less than welcoming.

Dialogue

Bill (husband): You're late again. That's three times this week. The kids and I are sick and tired of waiting for you. This is just not working out.

John (son): Yeah, Mom, we don't like the way Dad cooks. We're tired of eating spaghetti and hot dogs all time.

Sara (daughter): Don't you want to be with us anymore? You're never home.

Instead of discounting, ignoring, or defensively reacting to the concerns of family members, Marsha could stop what she is doing and sit down with them to really listen to their concerns. She can use some of the skills described above such as maintaining eye contact with the person who is speaking and squarely facing her family members. Even though she may have been racing to get home, she can take a deep breath and relax so she can really listen to their concerns.

After hearing their concerns, Marsha has to avoid the instinctive responses of fight or flight. A fight response goes on the attack and might sound like this: "Look, I work hard all day. It would be nice if you were a little more supportive. I've been there for all of you!" This response will likely elicit a counter argument and power struggle from her family. Even if it elicits guilt and sympathy, it shuts down any meaningful dialogue and problem solving. A flight response might be a quick apology and promise not to be late again in order to diffuse the confrontation and avoid further discussion. This might work if it hasn't been overused, but still does not encourage further dialogue and discussion. A third response might be to list all the reasons and excuses why she is late. The family is not asking for that information so her response misses the mark of their actual concerns. If you take away those three typical responses, Marsha might not know what to say!

Paraphrasing is an all-purpose skill that can be used whenever a listener doesn't know exactly what to say. It is a safe response that begins with understanding others and buys time until it is clear what is being communicated to you and how you may want to respond. Here is a paraphrase Marsha could state to her family:

> *Marsha:* OK, we obviously have a problem here. I've been late quite a bit this week and you are all getting frustrated. My work causes a lot of extra work for you and you're getting concerned that I'm not as available as I have been in the past. You seem to feel neglected and might even think that I don't care about you anymore. Is that what I'm hearing?

This response will likely diffuse some of the anger and frustration of the family by validating their concerns. Next, they can discuss what might be done to resolve the issues. Before Marsha responds to her family's concerns, she gathers more information by using probing questions.

> *Marsha:* Tell me more about what is so frustrating when I don't come home for dinner? What is the worst part about this situation for you? Besides being here every night for dinner, what are some other possible solutions to this problem?

Marsha is beginning to get a better understanding of her family's concerns and expectations. And yet, she has professional goals that are important to her as well. New roles, responsibilities and expectations might need to be negotiated between Marsha and her family. Once she has listened and gotten a better understanding of their concerns, she is now ready to express her own perspective.

■ EXPRESSION

Effective expression begins with paying attention, paraphrasing, and probing to gain an accurate understanding the perspectives of other group members. Members who make statements in a group meeting without understanding what is really going on not only hurt their own status but also hinder the group's progress. When group members do not understand each other or, worse yet, misunderstand each other, the potential for group success is compromised. Understanding what others are saying, however, is not enough. Group effectiveness is enhanced when members learn to express their ideas and concerns in a way that is clear and direct.

Communication experts McKay, Davis, and Fanning (1995) suggest four kinds of expression: observations, thoughts, feelings, and needs. Each type of expression is loosely related to the specific steps of the information-processing model described at the beginning of this chapter. Observations, for example, describe a situation or idea without interpretation or evaluation. They are the objective facts and data visible to all and may be introduced by sentence stems such as "this is what we know" or "this is where we are now." The following statements, at face value, are examples of observations:

- "The website had an average of 2,000 hits per day last month."
- "We've been talking for two hours and still haven't come to a decision."
- "This is the third meeting in a row that Bob has missed."

These comments are expressed as observations but may include embedded interpretations or evaluations within them. Those who receive these messages do not know for sure. Listeners might interpret the messages from their own perspectives or speculate on the potential hidden message of the speaker. But the messages, as stated above, may only be observations.

Thoughts, on the other hand, include interpretations and evaluations based on one's internal working model. Thoughts may be expressed as beliefs about self ("I can't lead this team effectively"), others ("New teachers need at least two years' experience before they really know what's going on in the classroom"), or some aspect of the world or organization ("If we invest money in professional development, morale will improve"). While some group members are comfortable contributing their thoughts to the discussion, others may need a bit of prompting. Leaders can ask low talkers what their thoughts are on any given topic to get a broader range of perspectives. It can also be helpful to ask people to provide the data (observations) on which they base their thoughts.

Feelings can be difficult to discuss in any relational setting, but especially so in organizational contexts. Norms regarding the appropriate expression of emotion vary from culture to culture (Trompenaars & Hampden-Turner, 1998). While feelings are often present in meetings and group discussions, they may not be directly acknowledged or communicated. As a result, feelings may not be expressed until after the meeting when subgroups and coalitions assemble to discuss and debrief. When this happens, the larger group is not able to benefit from private discussions and frustrations remain unresolved.

The feelings of fear, frustration, and anger are especially powerful in influencing the atmosphere of a group either in a positive or negative direction. Group work can trigger deep feelings toward others as various opinions and personalities emerge. Positive emotional expressions such as "I'm glad I'm a part of this team" can go a long way in fostering cohesion and commitment. Negative emotions can be expressed in a positive way that respects the opinions and feelings of others. For example, a group member might say "I understand the group's decision on this issue, but I'm very anxious that we may be making a serious error" or "I'm extremely angry right now. I feel unheard in this discussion." While these may sound like risky statements to make, the alternative is that feelings which are not expressed directly may emerge later in hostile or passive-aggressive ways.

Needs and desires can be another challenging type of communication to express. Some have difficulty directly asking for what they want or need. To make a direct request of others can put one at risk of being rejected. Furthermore, asking for help on a task may be perceived as incompetence, lack of commitment, or weakness. But members can overcome this fear and be willing to express their concerns as demonstrated in the following statements:

- "I need more time to think about this decision. Can we vote at the next meeting?"
- "Would anyone have some time to take a look at the press release I wrote? I'd like to get another perspective."
- "Jane, could you describe the evidence from which you base your conclusion? I'm not sure I completely understand your thinking."

These are all reasonable requests assuming they are genuine and not contaminated by mixed messages or hidden agendas.

Mixed messages are comments that include more than one type of expression. For example, a comment expressed as an observation or thought might be embedded with other types of expression such as a feeling or need. A group member might say that she thinks a certain decision is wrong with intense emotion that includes an implied request for reconsideration. In this case, multiple types of expression are being used. Paraphrasing and probing become even more important as listeners seek to sort out what is being said; the speakers, themselves, might not even be aware of the messages they are communicating.

Assertive Communication

Assertive communication occurs when group members are direct and open about what they think and feel while simultaneously respecting the perspectives of others. They make requests in nonhostile or nonaggressive ways. In order to remove ambiguity and encourage understanding, assertive statements include all four of the types of expression: observations, thoughts, feelings, and needs or desires. For example, the following is an assertive statement that might occur in a meeting that is discussing the hiring of a new employee:

> Based on this candidate's experience in mathematics software sales and the very positive reference by her former employer [observation], I think Jane would be a great addition to our department [thought]. She is a likable person and I feel she would fit well with our team philosophy [feeling]. I would like to extend her an offer [desire] but I'm open to other perspectives.

Assertiveness is a style of communication that expresses one's view directly and respectfully. Those who are assertive value other perspectives but are also willing to enter into constructive conflict and work through differences. The alternatives to assertiveness are communication styles that are passive, aggressive, or passive-aggressive.

Passive communication avoids confrontation and disagreement to the degree that passive members are reluctant to share their perspective. They are comfortable letting others lead and defer to the decisions of the group. This pattern is tied to core beliefs that devalue self and overestimate the competence of others. Those with passive interpersonal styles tend to subordinate their needs to the needs of others. They can often carry more than their fair share of the load because they are unable to speak up for themselves and say "no." As a result, they can become resentful and detach from the group over the long term.

Aggressive patterns of communication tend to be confrontational to the point of intimidation and even bullying. Aggressive members tend to see their own ideas as overly important and devalue the contributions of others. They are comfortable defending their position and seek to win arguments at the expense of interpersonal relationships. Aggressive behavior can be detrimental to the group as it can compromise feelings of safety and trust. While a spirited discussion can be helpful in generating energy and passion, it can also create an atmosphere of guardedness and defensiveness.

Passive-aggressive communication is an indirect attempt on the part of members who wish to retaliate against other members and impede the progress of the group. This type of communication may use humor and indirect attempts to criticize others and slow the group down. Passive-aggressive behavior usually indicates that one or more members of the group are angry, but are not able to express their anger directly in a way that can be resolved. Leaders can call attention to passive-aggressive behavior (comments, deep sighs, eyes rolling) without putting people on the spot by asking members how they feel about the meeting and whether or not they would like to make requests concerning the way members are communicating with each other.

▧ SOCIAL STYLES

Group members express themselves in a multitude of ways within the range of productive communication and group dialogue. Because we are social creatures and live in social contexts, we develop interpersonal strategies that move us toward goals and protect us from fears. Those interpersonal strategies exhibit certain characteristics and patterns that can be categorized into various "styles" of verbal and nonverbal interaction. Baney (2004) describes a four-quadrant model of interpersonal expression that is based on two variables: degree of assertiveness and expression of emotion. Based on these two variables, group members can be classified as one of four social styles: analytical, driving, expressive, and amiable (see Figure 4.3). Understanding the social styles of members can help leaders know how to better relate to and communicate with those who have a different social style (Wicks & Parish, 1990).

Assertiveness is plotted on the horizontal axis and ranges from *asking* to *telling*. Those with an *asking* orientation are less interested in influencing others as compared to those with a *telling* orientation. People interact differently depending on the social context but will have a predominant style. The following descriptions of asking and telling can help identify a person's prevailing orientation:

- *Asking:* States opinions more carefully without a call for action from others. Speaks in a softer voice and uses less animated nonverbal gestures.
- *Telling:* States opinions more authoritatively with a stronger call for action from others. Speaks in a louder voice with more forceful gestures.

Again, people are complex and do not fit neatly into categories. But theoretical models can still help us gain a clearer picture of ourselves and others.

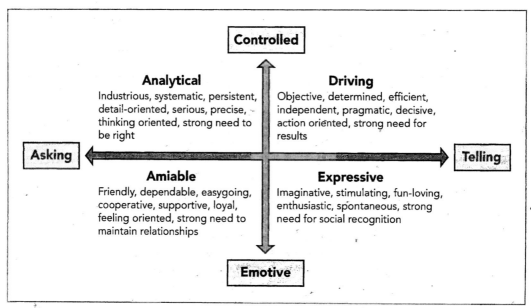

FIGURE 4.3   Social Styles

Next, the expression of emotion is plotted on the vertical axis and ranges from *controlled* (very little expression of emotion) to *emotive* (lots of emotion and energy).

- *Controlled:* Prefers facts and details to feelings. Limits small talk and speaks with a limited range of vocal inflection and facial expression.
- *Emotive:* Prefers stories and jokes. Enjoys small talk and the expression of feelings. Speaks with more animated vocal inflection and facial expression.

Based on these two variables, individuals can be classified as one of four social styles as seen in Figure 4.3.

As a general rule, driving and expressive styles need to learn to be better listeners while the analytical and amiable styles need to learn to be more assertive. Since the driving and expressive styles have a telling orientation, they can benefit from the active listing skills of asking probing questions and using paraphrases to draw out the opinions of others. Those skills also slow down the dialogue so they can gain a better understanding of what others think and feel. In contrast, analytical and amiable styles need to learn to express themselves more directly. They can learn to confidently communicate their observations, thoughts, feelings, and desires. In addition, they can learn to engage in conflict directly and effectively.

Group members with an identical style will typically communicate well together. They speak in a similar way and have an easier time understanding each other. Those with bordering styles (quadrants that are touching each other) are compatible and will also have a relatively easy time working together. Those with a diagonally opposite style (amiable–driving and analytical–expressive) will typically have the most difficulty communicating with each other. Leaders who understand the social styles of their members can adapt their own style in order to communicate in the predominant style of others. For example, an expressive leader can periodically slow down the group discussion and focus on facts in order to engage the analytical members in the group.

 OPENING CASE REVISITED

The Contentious School Board

In the California school district case, the management consultant was never able to help the board and superintendent communicate effectively. Each was earnest, but no matter what he said, they heard something else, and vice versa. This was indicative of the lack of communication, in general. The board was full of individuals, mostly driving styles, who liked to express opinions but were not very good listeners. The superintendent, on the other hand, had an analytical social style and was frustrated that board members were making uninformed suggestions. Their decisions were not well thought out or supported by data.

The superintendent got so frustrated with the school board that he began to dread their monthly meetings. The hostility and contentiousness grew until he finally offered to resign. While he was highly qualified and competent to do the job, he was never able to establish a good working relationship with the board. Misunderstandings, the lack of listening skills, and frequent cognitive distortions made it difficult for the school board to fulfill its mission to provide a quality education for children.

Summary

The process of communication is complex and highly idiosyncratic. Different people can hear the same message and have completely different interpretations. The practice of reflection can help group members slow down the interpretation and evaluation of messages so that understanding is more accurate and responses are more thoughtful. In addition, certain listening skills (paying attention, paraphrasing, and probing) can increase the likelihood that accurate understanding is taking place.

Group members can also learn to express themselves more intentionally by becoming aware of when they are communicating observations, thoughts, feelings, or needs. Members can come down the ladder of inference and provide the data that lead to their conclusions. In addition, members can avoid mixed messages and become more assertive. Assertiveness is a form of communication that respects the opinions of others while valuing one's own thoughts and needs enough to communicate them directly. Group discussions in organizational contexts will primarily contain observations and thoughts with periodic expressions of feelings and needs.

 CONCLUDING CASE ————————————————————————————

Speaking Up at a Disciplinary Hearing

Jorge Ramirez stood in Assistant Principal Calhoun's office of Corado del Boca High School. He was shaking with anxiety. A fight had taken place in the men's room on the third floor. A school security officer discovered it, joined the turmoil of flailing bodies, and pulled the major actors apart. He quickly recognized one of the boys as Jorge, a wiry sharp-eyed young man who had once given him a dirty look. The guard gripped Jorge by the arm and ushered him out into the hallway when he spotted a switchblade knife lying on the floor. The guard picked up the knife and marched Jorge down to Mr. Calhoun's office and told him that Jorge was the instigator of the fight and had been found with a contraband weapon. The school had a zero tolerance policy, and Jorge was at risk of being expelled.

Mr. Calhoun assembled his three assistant principals the next day to discuss what to do about Jorge. One of the other assistants, Rita Mize, felt sorry for Jorge. He had once loaded her car with supplies without her even having to ask. She questioned the guard's report as it didn't seem consistent with her experience with Jorge. The other assistant principals were outraged that a weapon was found on school property and felt the need for swift and decisive action. They wanted to communicate a specific message to the school. Mr. Calhoun agreed with the majority.

Discussion Questions

1. What assumptions about Jorge were made by the security guard?
2. What assumptions about Jorge were made by Assistant Principal Mize?
3. How should the group proceed?
4. How can Rita Mize assertively communicate her thoughts to her peers?

References

Argyris, C. (1994). Good communication that blocks learning. *Harvard Business Review*, July–Aug. 77–85.

Baney, J. (2004). *Guide to interpersonal communication*. Upper Saddle River, NJ: Pearson Education.

Beck, J. S. (1995). *Cognitive therapy: Basics and beyond*. New York: Guilford Press.

Griffith, B. A. (2004). The structure and development of internal working models: An integrated framework for understanding clients and promoting wellness. *Journal of Humanistic Counseling, Education, and Development, 43*, 163–177.

Griffith, B. A., & Frieden, G. (2000). Facilitating reflective thinking in counselor education. *Counselor Education and Supervision, 40*, 82–93.

Hirokawa, R. Y., DeGooyer, D., & Valde, K. (2000). Using narratives to study task group effectiveness. *Small Group Research, 31*, 573–591.

Kegan, R. (1994). *In over our heads: The mental demands of modern life*. Cambridge, MA: Harvard University Press.

King, P. M., & Kitchener, K. S. (1994). *Developing reflective judgment: Understanding and promoting growth and critical thinking in adolescents and adults*. San Francisco: Jossey-Bass.

McKay, M., Davis, M., & Fanning, P. (1995). *Messages: The communication skills book* (2nd ed.). Oakland, CA: New Harbinger Publications.

Mehrabian, A. (1981). *Silent messages: Implicit communication of emotions and attitudes* (2nd ed.). Belmont, CA: Wadsworth Publishing.

Schon, D. A. (1983). *The reflective practitioner*. New York: Basic Books.

Schon, D. A. (1987). *Educating the reflective practitioner*. San Francisco: Jossey-Bass.

Senge, P. M. (1990). *The fifth discipline: The art and practice of the learning organization*. New York: Doubleday.

Trompenaars, F., & Hampden-Turner, C. (1998). *Riding the waves of culture: Understanding cultural diversity in global business* (2nd ed.). New York: McGraw-Hill.

Wicks, T. G., & Parish, T. S. (1990). Enhancing communication through the use of control theory applied to social styles. *College Student Journal, 23*, 294–295.

CHAPTER FIVE

Leadership

▓ INTRODUCTION

Although groups have the potential to outperform separate or co-acting individuals, their actual performance may range from exceptional to poor. Leadership is a key factor in determining group performance. This chapter describes both traditional and contemporary theories of group leadership and illustrates mechanisms through which leadership affects performance.

LEARNING OBJECTIVES

After reading this chapter, you should be able to

- Understand the historical evolution of leadership theories.
- Recognize the differences among behavioral theories and contingency theories.
- Identify the key features of the various leadership theories.
- Understand the distinctive leadership needs of groups.
- Identify the criteria associated with leading effective groups: a real team, a compelling direction, an enabling structure, core performance norms, and expert coaching.
- Recognize the elements of workplace strength.

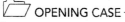 OPENING CASE

Maps and Globes for Edmonton Public Schools

In addition to supplementing his income by running a hog farm and constructing homes, Mike Stembritsky was a young principal in the city of Edmonton in Alberta, Canada. He was popular in the community, and he was selected as district director of social studies. As part of this job, he was given $50,000 to use for buying maps and globes for the public schools in his district. When he inquired as to how to go about using the money, he was told that he should hire a consultant who would do interviews and then make recommendations. He could then make purchases based on the consultant's recommendations and rent a storage facility to store the goods until they were needed by the schools. Somehow, this did not seem like the smartest method of going about this, and he wondered about better options.

Discussion Questions

1. In what other ways might this task be handled?
2. Can you think of better alternatives than the one Mike was given?

▓ INTRODUCTION TO LEADERSHIP

The subject of leadership has fascinated people for centuries and has been the topic of much discussion and debate. A great deal of attention has been given to the formal study of leadership in recent decades. This chapter traces the history of the formal study of leadership and describes a number of influential theories before examining leadership in groups. Leading a group has its own set of unique challenges. Consider the term *self-managing group* and you might ask, Where does leadership fit in? In some ways, the concept of leadership for self-managing groups sounds like an oxymoron. Nonetheless, leadership plays an important role in group effectiveness, even for self-managing groups. However, as you will see, what would be considered effective leadership can vary significantly depending on the distinctive nature of the particular situation or group. We will address the idiosyncratic needs of leadership in groups after examining traditional leadership research and theories.

Leadership has been defined in many different ways. This book defines leadership as "the ability to influence others toward a desired end."

▓ TRAIT THEORIES—WHAT MAKES A GREAT LEADER?

Initial efforts to understand leadership focused on identifying traits or attributes of great leaders. Early researchers identified great leaders and examined their personal characteristics and attributes. Their goal was to determine what characteristics great leaders shared, thereby enabling them to understand what characteristics are needed to make a great leader (Bass, 1985). They could then evaluate people who aspire to lead through the use of these "great leader" characteristics and get a sense of which individuals would be likely to succeed as leaders and which would not. They might also get a sense of what qualities aspiring leaders would need to cultivate in order to enhance their chances of becoming effective leaders.

Literally hundreds of studies have been conducted over several decades under this paradigm's assumptions in order to discover these key traits that make great leaders (Yukl, 2006). Unfortunately, despite this great investment of time and effort, this paradigm has produced little useful information.

The traits of numerous great leaders have been identified and subjected to rigorous analysis. Despite decades of study and analysis, researchers were unable to identify a distinctive set of traits that were consistently associated with great leadership across any variety of contexts. Each great leader seems to have been able to find a way to use his or her own unique traits effectively to address the issues he or she faced at the time. Each leadership situation is somewhat different and apparently calls for a somewhat distinctive approach (Yukl, Gordon, & Tabor, 2002).

Although trait researchers have failed consistently to differentiate between effective and ineffective leaders across situations, they have identified some characteristics that tend commonly to exist among leaders. These include intelligence, initiative, interpersonal skills, self-confidence, drive for responsibility, personal integrity, aggressiveness, independence, and tolerance for stress (Stodghill, 1948; 1974). Stodghill notes that the relevance of any one of these traits in predicting effective leadership will vary from situation to situation.

▓ BEHAVIORAL THEORIES—WHAT DO EFFECTIVE LEADERS DO?

The study of leadership traits was not conclusive in explaining effective versus ineffective leadership. Other scholars at Ohio State and University of Michigan began to examine leader behavior—what leaders actually do. These scholars observed two key orientations or areas in which leaders focused their attention—tasks and relationships (Fleishman & Harris, 1962; Katz & Kahn, 1952; Stogdill, Goode, & Day, 1962). Task-oriented leaders' main focus is accomplishing the work in an efficient manner. Their attention is on whether employees are doing what needs to be done to get the task done. They may or may not be concerned with how employees feel about the task they are doing, or about each other, as long as they are getting the job done. By contrast, relationship-orientated leaders tend to be concerned with employees' feelings and psychological needs. Such leaders are usually sensitive to their relationships with their subordinates and what can be done to strengthen relational bonds.

Ohio State and University of Michigan Studies

In the 1950s, a group of researchers at Ohio State began studying leaders. They designed questionnaires and used factor analyses in an effort to condense the multiple possible behaviors of leaders into a few robust categories (Shartle, 1979). Their research uncovered two key dimensions that they labeled *initiating structure* and *consideration* (Schriesheim & Bird, 1979). These behaviors appear to be relatively independent of each other, meaning that a leader does not have to choose one over the other but can also be high or low in both. *Initiating structure* is a kind of task orientation and is associated with organizing, planning, scheduling, directing efforts, giving instructions, checking up on progress, assessing gaps between budget and actual spending, and between goals and actual performance. *Consideration* is a relationship-oriented approach that is characterized by taking an interest in employees' opinions, perceptions, feelings, home lives, and making an effort to see that employees are satisfied and the relationships are good.

Close to the same time of the Ohio State studies, scholars at Michigan State were also studying leadership within the context of supervision. They also came up with two distinctive categories of leader behavior that they referred to as *job-centered* and *employee-centered* (Likert, 1979). These categories bear resemblance to the initiating structure and consideration categories of leader behavior that were developed in the Ohio State studies.

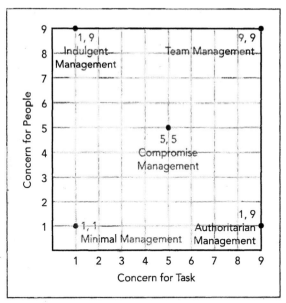

FIGURE 5.1   Blake and Mouton's Managerial Grid

Source: Blake, R., & McCanse, A. (1991). *Leadership dilemma—Grid solutions* (p. 29). Houston: Gulf Publishing.

Managerial Grid

Blake and Mouton (1964) continued working within the broad themes of the Ohio State and University of Michigan studies, but referred to these two dimensions as *concern for people* and *concern for production*. Using these two dimensions, they developed a managerial grid theory that could be used to categorize leaders according to the extent to which their behavior corresponds to varying levels of these two dimensions (see Figure 5.1). Their theory also has a prescriptive orientation; they take a stand on what is the best approach to leadership. Specifically, they hypothesized that the ideal leader would be a 9,9 leader who was very high in both concern for people and concern for production. They identified five categories of leadership according to the corners of the grid and a middle area. They termed the 1,1 position *minimal management* in which the manager exhibits neither concern for production nor concern for people. This is the least effective approach to leadership. The 1,9 area is referred to *indulgent management* in which there is a great concern for people but virtually no concern for production. The leader is concerned about issues such as how people are feeling, how morale is, what is new in employees' lives, and how well are they relating. This is the high school principal who desires that all teachers and others at a school, including parents, get along well with one another. At 9,1, the opposite corner of the grid, is *authoritarian management* in which the concern is almost completely for the task with essentially no concern for the people. This is the principal for whom elevating math and reading test scores is at the heart of the job. The center of the Grid is 5,5 which is labeled *compromise management*. This approach combines the benefits of concern for people and concern for production, but at moderate levels of each. Finally, what Blake and

Mouton proposed as the most effective approach is to be very high on both dimensions (9,9)—*team management*. Thus, Blake and Mouton identified "one best way" to lead that they believed would be useful in any variety of situations. However, later research demonstrated that situations can be highly variable and can require different approaches.

▓ CONTINGENCY THEORIES—HOW SHOULD LEADERS BEHAVE IN DIFFERENT SITUATIONS?

As scholars continued to grapple with the topic of leadership, they came to realize the limitations of the "one best way" of thinking and began to recognize how significant the differences across situations are in predicting leadership effectiveness (Yukl, 2006). Consider, for example, Winston Churchill, who was perceived as highly effective while England struggled through the crisis of World War II. However, after the war was over and the circumstances had changed, he did not have the same appeal as a leader, and he was voted out of office. A growing sense of the importance of the context or situation led leadership theorists to begin developing contingency theories about leadership. In other words, they recognized that the appropriate style or behavior was contingent on (would depend on) the distinctive nature of a particular situation.

Fiedler's Contingency Theory

One of the best-known contingency theories was developed by Fred Fiedler (1964; 1967). Fiedler categorized situations as favorable, moderate, and unfavorable. He developed three key variables for predicting favorability, which are: leader-member relations, position power, and task structure.

Leader-member relationship has to do with the extent to which trust and good feelings are present between the leader and the subordinates. If we consider the factory floor at General Motors that Ben Hamper describes in *Rivethead* (1991), there was a history of mistrust and hostility between union members and their supervisors which would mean low leader-membership relationship favorability. By contrast, leader-member relations would be more favorable in a start-up firm in which the company is a small, fast growing, exciting place to work, and the employees are valued as being a part of the organization and working together toward a common goal.

Position power refers to the leader's formal authority within the organization. High position power would be exemplified by the military in which leaders have the formal authority to give orders, and subordinates are expected to carry them out or face undesirable consequences. An example of low position power might be found in a task force made up of people at the same level from diverse functions within the organization. The individual who is selected to lead the task force may be at the same level within the organizational hierarchy and might not even work in the same part of the organization. Each of the members of the task force has his or her own boss to report to, and the task force leader does not have formal authority over them.

Task structure refers to the extent to which there is clarity about the end goal and what methods will lead to success. Favorable task structure would exist in a factory in which the procedures for doing the work have been clearly articulated in manuals, and all the employees have to do in order to achieve success is to follow the procedures that have been laid out for them. A less-favorable task structure would exist in a country that is fighting against an insurgency. The insurgents may blend in with the population and are thus difficult to detect. They may change tactics regularly, making the development of a reliable plan for working against them very difficult to formulate.

Fiedler developed what he called the *least preferred coworker* (LPC) scale for differentiating leadership styles. Completing the scale requires that an individual identify the person whom he or she found least pleasant to work with and to rate that person on a bipolar scale with various adjectives. Individuals tend to vary in how negatively they rate this individual. A negative rating results in a low LPC score, and a relatively positive rating results in a high LPC score. The LPC score as a way of categorizing leadership orientations has a degree of similarity with previous research and theory. Fiedler has argued that a positive LPC score indicates a relational orientation which signifies the importance of developing and maintaining friendly relationships at work. The logic appears to go something like this: Although this person is the least preferred coworker, the rater has still found positive qualities in the individual and maintained a relational orientation. By contrast, a highly negative rating of the least preferred coworker suggests that the rater is less relationally oriented and more task-oriented. This rater is more concerned with production than with people and cannot find the good in someone who he or she feels has not lived up to the task.

By combining leader-member relationship, formal authority, and task structure variables, Fiedler developed a way of classifying situations according to their level of favorability. He hypothesized that the appropriate leadership styles would be determined by whether the situation was unfavorable, moderately favorable, or favorable. He believed that in an unfavorable setting the low LPC (task-oriented) leader would be most effective. These tough leadership situations would require a task-oriented leader who could push for results and be strict in holding people accountable. He also believed that the low LPC leader would be more successful in the favorable condition, but for different reasons. In the unfavorable condition, the leader would need to push for success despite the poor leader-member relations. By contrast, in the favorable situation, there would be little need to spend a lot of time on developing relationships because things are already going smoothly and relations are already favorable. It is the middle ground (moderate favorability) where Fiedler thought that the high LPC leader would perform best. This is the area in which conditions are neither so good that little need for relationship building exists, nor so bad that building relationships may be insufficient to enhance performance. Under moderately favorable conditions, there is room for improvement, and building relationships and motivating people may be just what is needed to raise the level of performance. Figure 5.2 illustrates how the model works by combining the favorability or unfavorability of the leader-member relationship, position power, and task structure.

Hersey and Blanchard's Situational Theory of Leadership

Like Fiedler, Hersey and Blanchard (1977) believed that the most effective way for a leader to behave would depend on the situation (Figure 5.3). Their approach to understanding the situation placed a significant emphasis on the characteristics of subordinates or followers and their level of maturity or readiness—the extent to which they are willing and able to perform successfully on their own. Hersey and Blanchard argue that the leader should adapt his or her style to followers' readiness levels. The followers' readiness is a function of both willingness and ability. Subordinates at a high level of readiness have both the ability and the willingness to perform the task effectively. Subordinates at the

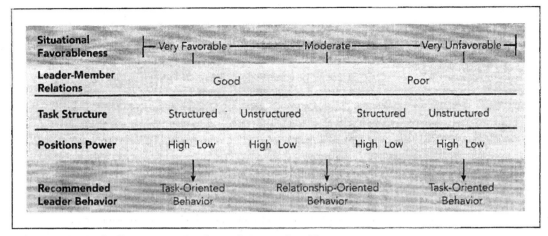

FIGURE 5.2   Fiedler's Least Preferred Coworker Theory

Source: Adapted from Fiedler, F. (1972). The effects of leadership training and experience: A contingency model interpretation. *Administrative Science Quarterly 17*, 455.

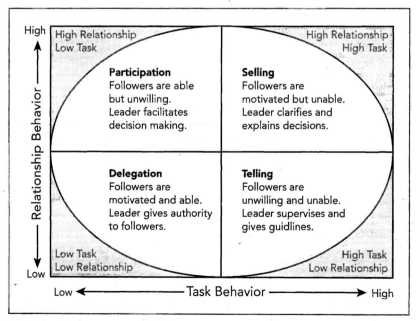

FIGURE 5.3   Hersey and Blanchard's Situational Theory

Source: Hersey, P., & Blanchard, K. H. (1977). *The management of organizational behavior* (3rd ed.). Englewood Cliffs, NJ: Prentice Hall.

lowest level of maturity have neither the willingness nor the ability to perform the task effectively. As subordinates evolve, Hersey and Blanchard argue that the leader should adapt his or her style. At the lowest level of readiness, they argue that the leader should adopt a *telling* style. This is a directive approach with a focus on task-oriented behavior with little emphasis on building relationships. As subordinates evolve toward greater readiness by being more willing but still lacking somewhat in ability, the leader should shift to a *selling* style. This style combines a high relational orientation with a high task orientation. If subordinates are able but unwilling, the leader should adopt a *participating* style. In this style, the leader drops the task focus in favor of a relational focus and effort is placed on building a relationship that will motivate subordinates to use the ability that they have attained. At the highest level of readiness, subordinates are both willing and able to perform, and the leader can switch into a *delegating* style. Because the leader is now able to delegate responsibility to the subordinates, the leader does not need to engage in either task-oriented or relationship-oriented behavior because the subordinates are capable of doing the job on their own. Research has not been particularly supportive of this theory.

Path-Goal Theory

Robert House (1971) and colleagues (Evans, 1970, 1974; House & Dessler, 1974; House & Mitchell, 1974) developed and refined the path-goal theory of leadership. They theorized that the job of the leader is to facilitate subordinates' movements toward goals. Effective leaders assess subordinates' characteristics and the work environment and use that information to determine how they can best propel subordinates toward goals. House described four basic leadership styles as *directive, achievement-oriented, supportive,* and *participative*. If the task is ambiguous or the means of achieving the goal are unclear, the leader should take a *directive* approach to give instructions and clarify what subordinates should do. If subordinates are not motivated, lack challenging goals and high performance standards, a leader should take an *achievement-oriented* approach. In this case, the leader works with subordinates to develop specific, challenging goals and to raise achievement orientation. If subordinates lack confidence, a leader should use a *supportive* approach in order to encourage subordinates and build their confidence and morale. Finally, if joint decision-making activities are called for and subordinates have valuable input or would benefit from higher levels of participation, a *participative* approach is most appropriate.

■ RECENT THEORIES

Charismatic Leadership

Scholars have also observed that some leaders seem to have a special ability to ignite the spirit and imagination of others to dedicate themselves to the leader's particular cause (Conger & Kanungo, 1987, 1998; House, 1977). These leaders have been labeled charismatic leaders. Something about their personal charisma drives others to special feats of performance. Charisma is understood more in terms of its potency than in terms of producing either desirable or undesirable consequences. Charismatic leaders may serve the needs of followers and the broader organization or community, but they may also be primarily serving their own personal interests.

In addition to having a personality that activates others, charismatic leaders often achieve their ends by articulating a vision that captivates the attention of followers and galvanizes their support. Vision also tends to be a key component of transformational leadership.

Transformational Leadership

Transformational leadership shares some characteristics with charismatic leadership, but the focus is more on the ability to transform the way people think or act than on the charisma itself (Bass, 1985, 1996). The term *transformational* stands in contrast to the term *transactional*. The term *transactional* suggests something along the line of "a fair day's work for a fair day's pay" (Burns, 1978). The leader and subordinate are merely making an economic transaction. By contrast, *transformational* leadership refers to the ability of the leader to transcend the normal transactional approach. The leader activates higher-order motivations of the subordinates such that their desire, inspiration, and commitment go beyond the ordinary; they are committed to the work for its own sake rather than merely for financial remuneration.

▓ A THEORY OF GROUP LEADERSHIP

Richard Hackman spent decades doing critical research in lab and field settings on how groups function and what makes them effective or ineffective (Hackman, 2002). He observed that leaders come in all shapes and sizes, some effective and some ineffective. On its own, this was not very useful; however, he also recognized that effective leaders were those who were able to do the right thing at the right time for the group. In order to provide clarity as to what a group would need, he identified a set of conditions that, if put in place, would increase the chances that the group would perform effectively. According to Hackman (2002), the job of a group leader is to work toward putting these conditions in place so that the group can function effectively. What follows is a description of his theory of leading groups, and a set of guidelines for group leaders.

Throughout his decades of research (Hackman, 2002), he identified the following criteria that are associated with group effectiveness:

- A real team
- A compelling direction
- An enabling structure
- A supportive organizational context
- Expert coaching

Hackman argued that these conditions will significantly increase the chances that teams will be effective. Thus, a leader's job is to understand these conditions, assess their presence or absence, and do whatever is necessary to produce or enhance any of these that are missing or low. Next, we describe each of these conditions in more detail.

▓ A REAL TEAM

Key features of *real teams* include the following: Having a team task, being bounded, having delimited authority, and showing stability over time.

A Team Task

Because teams are in vogue, organizations often put together teams without much thought as to whether the task that they are assigned to is one that necessitates a group or is one that is better suited to individuals. Sometimes employees are called a team primarily because they share the same workspace or because they do the same type of work rather than because they actually have any need to operate as a real team. For example, a small company might call the people who do data processing a data-processing team even though the only thing they really share as a team is their workspace. Similarly, teachers in a school may be labeled a "team." However, factually, they may have little interaction. In addition, tasks that one teacher undertakes may be completely unrelated to the work or success of another. Getting the real value out of a team means providing it with a task that is better performed by a team and that requires each member to use his or her particular talents and coordinate efforts toward producing a desired outcome.

Bounded

In order for a team to take shape as an effective performing unit, it needs to be sufficiently bounded. *Boundedness* refers to the extent to which the team has a clear and knowable membership; in other words, who is on the team and who is not. Teams with an unclear sense of who is a member and who is not a member are too loosely bounded. Consider a school committee that is developed with an understanding that it needs representation from each of the academic departments but does not require that the representation be consistent. So, the head of the English department may attend meetings, but might just as well send any of the other teachers of the department instead, depending on how busy each person is. Because group members who show up to the meeting vary in each meeting, acting as a coherent unit becomes difficult. New members may raise issues that have already been discussed and ruled out by the group's former constituents. New members may not have sufficient knowledge of what the group has already discussed in order to be effective participants in building from previous discussions toward some constructive end.

On the other side of the spectrum, teams can also be too tightly bounded and suffer from a different set of problems. When the boundary of the team is not permeable, the group can become isolated from the rest of the organization and have too much insularity. It may become disconnected from the organizational environment that surrounds it and not pick up on issues that it should be addressing. Imagine a school discipline committee that involved only counselors and no teachers, or all subject matter teachers and no PE or remedial teachers.

Delimited Authority

As mentioned in Chapter 1, multiple options exist for delegating authority to groups. Either delegating too much or too little authority to the group can cause serious problems. If too much authority is delegated, the group may make decisions or take actions that are inappropriate for them or for the organization. If too little authority is delegated, a group is likely to be frustrated and may fail because they do not have the freedom to act and take initiative to effectively accomplish the work. For groups to be effective, organizational leaders must address what the group is being asked to do, and what level of authority it requires (see Figure 5.4).

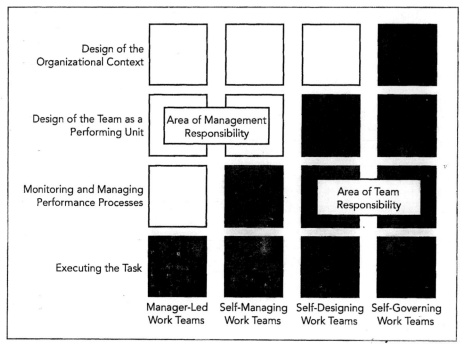

FIGURE 5.4   Division of Responsibility

Source: Hackman, J. R. (2002). *Leading teams: Setting the stage for great performances.* Boston: Harvard Business School Press.

Figure 5.4 illustrates several ways of dividing responsibility between the team and management. In a manager-led team, the team is only responsible for executing the task. In a self-managing team, the team has more responsibility and autonomy and is more proactive in deciding how the team should go about accomplishing its work and monitoring its progress. A self-designing team has the additional responsibility of making decisions about who will be on the team and who will not be on the team and for structuring its task. Finally, self-governing teams tend to exist at the tops of organizations such as a top management team or a board of directors. These teams have the additional responsibility of setting their own direction and deciding their own priorities.

Stability over Time

Assuming the task has longevity, then having a sense that the team will be relatively stable over time is important for several reasons. Members will be more likely to invest in building constructive working relationships if they expect to work with each other over a long period of time. When members do not expect to work together for long, they are likely to take a short-term perspective and to make less effort to improve the group's functioning. Hackman described palpable differences in the operation of flight crews depending on whether they were just starting out on the first leg of their journey together, or whether they had had a day or so to form cohesion and get used to each other's ways of doing things. He noted that his qualitative observations were also backed up by data from the

National Transportation Safety Board (NTSB). They track the performance of flight crews and the frequency with which they run into significant problems. Their records reveal that 73% of significant problems are experienced in a flight crew's first day working together (Hackman, 2002, p. 55). Furthermore, 44% of those incidents happened on their very first flight together. Additional research confirms that a reasonably stable membership over time is associated with team effectiveness in other environments as well (Argote, et al., 1995).

■ A COMPELLING DIRECTION

Chapter 2 discussed the importance of an inspiring vision and compelling direction, but Hackman's view of the benefits of a compelling direction are worth summarizing. He asserted that in order for direction to be effective, it should be *challenging, clear,* and *consequential.* These characteristics in turn *energize, orient,* and *engage* (see Figure 5.5). Research demonstrates that challenging goals generate more motivation than goals that are not particularly challenging (Locke & Latham, 1990). Thus, a direction that is challenging energizes team members and produces a higher level of motivation than a direction that does not challenge them to stretch themselves.

Sufficient clarity of direction is important for enabling a team to orient itself to a task. Orienting has to do with sorting out performance strategies for achieving a task and making choices about how group members should invest time. When direction is clear, team members have a more informed perspective and are thus better able to select strategies most appropriate for accomplishing a task efficiently and effectively.

In addition to being challenging and clear, being consequential has the impact of engaging team members more completely such that they do a better job of fully utilizing the knowledge, skill, and talent within the team. When the direction is consequential, team members have the feeling that "our performance really matters," and they are more thoughtful about making sure that the job gets done and gets done right. Compare the two different orientations toward a job. One group might be involved in delivering supplies, and consider it just a job. By contrast, if the team is aware that these supplies are going to an intensive care unit for premature babies who are fighting for survival, their work

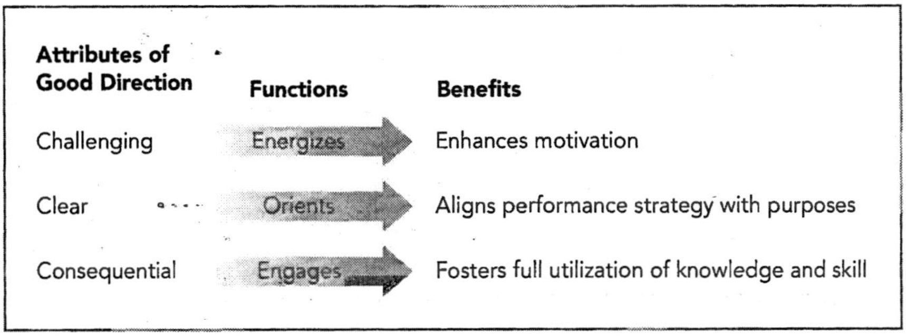

Attributes of Good Direction	Functions	Benefits
Challenging	Energizes	Enhances motivation
Clear	Orients	Aligns performance strategy with purposes
Consequential	Engages	Fosters full utilization of knowledge and skill

FIGURE 5.5   The Functions and Benefits of Good Direction

Source: Hackman, J. R. (2002). *Leading Teams: Setting the stage for great performances.* Boston: Harvard Business School Press.

may seem more consequential and engage the best of their efforts. They are more likely to do whatever it takes to get the supplies to their destination in a timely manner and act conscientiously to make sure that the supplies are handled with care.

Ends and Means

In addition to being challenging, clear, and consequential, Hackman also noted that recognizing differences between ends and means and constructing an appropriate amount of clarity and specificity for each is crucial for the effectiveness of teams. As Figure 5.6 illustrates, both ends and means may be defined very specifically, neither may be made specific, or one but not the other may be specified, and each of these possible combinations is likely to lead to a different performance outcome. Hackman contended that the combination that has the greatest potential for drawing out the full talents of the team and leading to the highest level of performance is having the ends clearly specified while giving the team the freedom to figure out the best means. With specificity regarding the desired end, the team will not waste time bickering about what direction it should head. Instead, that will be clear; and the team can focus on the best way fully to utilize their unique knowledge, skills, and abilities in achieving that end. Each team is made up of a unique set of individuals, each with somewhat different capabilities and interests. If the means are specified by some authority figure from above who does not know the particular abilities within the team, then the means may be poorly matched with employee capabilities. In addition, when procedures are specified from above and workers have no ability to influence the work process, they tend to become disengaged and find the work tedious. The organization fails to draw on their creative abilities to solve problems and to innovate to make the product or service better. For example, at Disney resorts, the housekeepers may have a clear direction of delighting each guest with the "magic of Disney" whenever possible. If management developed a list of procedures dictating exactly how to clean a room and the exact, uniform way to leave it,

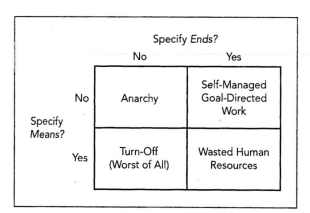

FIGURE 5.6   Setting Direction about Ends versus Means

Source: Hackman, J. R. (2002). *Leading Teams: Setting the stage for great performances.* Boston: Harvard Business School Press.

there would be no opportunity for employees to use their creative freedom in achieving the end of delighting guests with the "magic of Disney." By contrast, if management does not specify the means, employees can unleash their own creativity. So, if house-keepers find the children's stuffed animals strewn about the room, rather than lining them up in an orderly fashion, they might configure them in an exotic way that gives the appearance that stuffed animals have had their own playful adventure in the hotel room while kids were out enjoying the park.

Schools and school districts provide a special illustration of the means and ends point being made here. The larger in size (enrollment) a district is, the greater the tendency of central office officials to operate the system by rules. A regulation-bound district dictates how to spend money, how to teach, what texts to order, and how to arrange the daily schedule of instruction. Some school districts mimic authoritarian bureaucracies in the degree to which they specify subordinate behaviors. For example, at one point in its seeming endless efforts to reform itself, the Chicago public schools began to "script" teachers, providing them with detailed scenarios of how to instruct particular subject matter modules. Bel Kaufman (1964), a former New York City teacher, and a gifted writer, wrote a best seller entitled *Up the Down Staircase*, in which she portrayed poignantly, and rendered hapless and hopeless, the rule-bound mentality of the New York City public school system.

If management specifies both ends and means, the outcome may not be unfavorable, but the organization fails to utilize the knowledge and talent of the team members resulting in wasted human resources. The two other possibilities are less desirable. When neither ends nor means are specified, there is a complete lack of clarity both about what is supposed to be accomplished and about how to go about making it happen. Each team member may head in a different direction and the result may be chaos or anarchy. Finally, the worst condition is to have the means specified but not the ends. In this case, there is no compelling direction about where the group should be headed, what it is trying to accomplish, or why. So there is little motivational drive, yet the means are specified in detail. Thus, team members may have a prescribed, routinized set of procedures to follow that may be tedious or monotonous; and there is no compensating benefit of knowing that their efforts are at least going toward a good cause or achieving something of value for the organization or customer. This tends to result in disengagement and turn-off. It is not difficult to identify schools that operate in such a manner.

■ AN ENABLING STRUCTURE

Structure is a key issue in organizational and team effectiveness. Traditional organizational structures have been criticized for being too tight and bureaucratic. Sometimes teams have been proposed as the antidote for organizational structures that have become overly rigid. At the same time, too little structure can be just as damaging for a team. So, getting the appropriate structure in place is crucial for team effectiveness. But what are the key structural elements related to team effectiveness?

Hackman identified three structural elements that seem to have a significant effect on team performance: (1) the design of the task or work that the team performs, (2) the composition of the team, and (3) the core performance norms of the team that guide team behavior. Each of these should be managed effectively in order to enhance team performance.

Work That Is Designed to Produce Internal Motivation

A number of years ago, Hackman and Oldham (1980) noted that the way work is designed can have a significant effect on the level of internal motivation and commitment that workers experience. They identified variables they believed would significantly affect the psychological state of workers in a way that would produce internal work motivation. This should give organizational leaders a sense of how to design work such that it would naturally contribute to employee motivation and thus lead to good performance. They identified *skill variety*, *task identity*, and *task significance* as variables that would affect how workers experienced the meaningfulness of their work and would thus affect their internal work motivation.

Skill variety has to do with the range of skills that a worker uses. Presumably workers would experience the job as more meaningful if they were able to use a wider variety of skills on a regular basis. A worker whose job is restricted to tightening one bolt all day long is less likely to experience the work as meaningful than if he or she were able to do that for part of the day, but also use the lathe, drill press, and saw for variety.

Task identity is influenced by the amount of the entire task a worker completes. Workers are more likely to experience their work as meaningful and thus have greater task identity if they complete the whole task or at least a significant part of it. The worker who merely tightens one bolt can easily feel disconnected from the product that he or she is working to construct. By doing a larger portion of the project, the worker has a better feel for the whole of what is being produced. Volvo, the Swedish automobile manufacturer, was among the first to discover this principle and implemented it by reforming assembly lines into task groups, which produced a larger section of an automobile to see something closer to the finished product.

Task significance has to do with the extent to which the employees perceive their work as significant or important in some way. Workers who think of themselves doing masonry have less task significance than corresponding laborers who imagine the possible grandeur of their construction and the significance that it might have to them or to others. By contrast, these masons could be thinking of themselves as building a school and thus contributing to education of young people. The workers who are responsible for delivering supplies to an intensive care unit for premature babies have a sense of task significance because they know that their work contributes to sustaining the lives of tiny, struggling newborns.

Providing workers with autonomy is likely to affect the level of responsibility that they feel for their work. When workers do not have sufficient autonomy to influence the process through which they do their work, they often become disengaged and do not feel responsible. For example, a worker on an assembly line might have no ability to influence the process or communicate concerns to anyone who is overseeing the system. If a product that appears faulty comes down the assembly line, his or her job continues to be conducting the same procedure he or she has always done. He or she can simply let the faulty product go down the line thinking, "It is not my problem, and even if it were, I could not do anything about it." By contrast, on some assembly lines, every worker has the autonomy to stop the assembly line for any reason. These workers feel more invested in the process because they know that they are trusted to stop the line if they see something that appears to be out of order. Thus, they experience more responsibility for their work. It is interesting to ponder the degree to which those employed in public schools, such as teachers, can stop the assembly line if something faulty occurs.

Finally, feedback is also important so that a worker can know the results of what he or she is producing. If people do not know if their performance is effective, they have a hard time knowing what they might need to improve and how to go about making improvement. If they decide nonetheless to make improvements, they do not have the feedback to tell them whether their improvements are successful or not, and thus have little incentive or encouragement.

The implications of this are that team leaders should do what they can to ensure they influence the design of work such that it naturally contributes to internal work motivation. They can do this by increasing task variety, skill identity, task significance, autonomy, and feedback.

Team Composition

In addition to having employment designed to enhance motivation, appropriate team composition is essential for work to be accomplished effectively. As discussed in Chapter 2, different types of teams are formed for various reasons and might be strategic, problem solving, task management, or creative. Each of these has a different purpose, and its composition should be guided by the reason for which the group was formed or the task that it was designed to accomplish. No two employees in any organization are exactly alike. Each has a different personality, set of life experiences, and range of knowledge, skills, and abilities. One dilemma that leaders sometimes face is that they have a limited pool of employees from which to select in order to form teams. There is often pressure to take anyone who is not fully occupied with other obligations to staff the team. However, availability and appropriate fit for any particular team may not be correlated at all. Thus, leaders need to identify what the essential knowledge, skills, and abilities are for the particular team and make sure that the membership reflects an adequate level of each of these.

Hackman observed that one of the most common mistakes of leaders regarding team composition is to assume that everyone already knows how to work on a team. Thus, they pay insufficient attention to getting enough people with interpersonal skills that are necessary to keep teams functioning effectively.

For example, a team with a diverse membership that is operating in an unpleasant environment and under pressure may have all the needed technical knowledge and cognitive ability, but may still get bogged down if it does not have at least one person with sufficient interpersonal skills to build relationships among diverse individuals and knowledge of how to relieve group tensions. Without such an individual, tempers may flare, and conflicts within the group could escalate until they impede the group's progress.

Two other common errors that leaders often make are putting too many people on the team and making the team too homogeneous. First, leaders often seem to think that they can assist a team by providing more human assets, given that each individual may have something unique to contribute. Unfortunately, they tend to overlook the fact that teams become increasingly difficult to manage and coordinate as they become larger. Thus, leaders tend to make teams too large.

Second, in constructing teams, leaders often err on the side of making them too homogeneous. Leaders recognize that homogeneous team members are more likely to get along with each other. However, this harmony often comes at the expense of creativity and innovation that often result from diversity that sparks conflict but also fosters novel thinking.

▧ CORE PERFORMANCE NORMS

The norms that develop to govern team member behavior are also powerful predictors of performance. As explained earlier, cohesiveness tends to affect team performance, and may contribute to great or poor performance depending on whether a group has developed norms that foster high or low productivity. Norms can address just about anything that the team wants them to address. They can be about punctuality, freedom to interrupt others in the office, attire, whether conflict is aired openly or submerged, socializing in the office, office romance, and so on. For teams to be effective, the norms should address issues key to their performance, and norms should be in the proper direction.

For example, productive performance of software developers is significantly hindered by interruption. It takes time to work through long strings of code, and when interrupted they can lose their train of thought and have to start again from scratch—a significant loss. So, having norms that limit the number of times that they interrupt each other or limiting interruptions to particular times of the day can greatly enhance the productivity of a software-development team. Norms for appropriate attire may be important for sales teams who need to call on high-level business clients. Conversely, teachers and administrators in a school may compromise their authority by dressing in attire that is too casual.

In the area of core-performance norms, leaders should identify the target area and type of norms that will be more important in contributing to team performance, and the leader should foster the development of those norms.

▧ A SUPPORTIVE ORGANIZATIONAL CONTEXT

The fourth element in Hackman's theory, a supportive organizational context, consists of the following four elements:

- Reward system
- Information system
- Education system
- Contextual supports and intergroup relations

Reward System

Few would argue that desirable behavior should not be rewarded, but designing effective reward systems for teams is easier said than done. Leaders should keep the following points in mind. Appropriate forms of recognition and nonfinancial rewards should be fully utilized to encourage constructive behavior, but Hackman argues that these alone may not be sufficient. Some kind of financial incentive may also be important, though it will need to be administered effectively in order to avoid the potential pitfalls that can accompany pay-for-performance systems (Beer & Cannon, 2004).

Hackman suggests that the following are characteristics of effective team-reward systems:

1. Rewards should be something that the team values ·
2. Rewards should be connected to measurable, visible outcomes that are true indicators of team effectiveness
3. The team should have the power to influence these outcomes through their behavior
4. Rewards should be team rewards, not individual rewards in order to reinforce cooperation and a team focus rather than intrateam competition.

The leader's job is to design rewards that meet these conditions. This can be challenging for several reasons. The leader needs to determine what the team values, determine what measurable outcomes are good indicators of team effectiveness, make sure that the team can influence these outcomes, and make sure that the rewards target the team rather than individuals. One additional challenge is that leaders who are first-line supervisors often do not have automatic influence over how money for rewards is allocated within the organization. Thus, they may need to take initiative to acquire the resources by finding a way to influence someone who does have control over them.

Information System

Teams need accurate and timely information in order to function effectively. The information that is most crucial for a team will depend somewhat on the work that team does, and the leader's job is to understand the team's key information needs and ensure that this information is provided in as timely and accurate a method as possible.

Key information needs for the team might include available inventory so that it can make accurate promises to a customer, or raw-material costs in order to correctly price a product. They may need a system that provides them with immediate feedback about how their work is being received so that they can make adjustments quickly should there be any problems.

Education System

An education system is essential for making sure that team members have knowledge, skills, and abilities to perform effectively. New hires may need to learn how to work in a team, how to perform technical functions of their job, and how to get things done within the organization. Employees may need to have their skills upgraded in order to keep up with new developments in their field or with changing technologies. We will examine training in much greater detail in Chapter 10 on team development and training.

Hackman also included technical assistance under the education system. Timely technical assistance that is aligned with the team's way of working can enable a team to keep up a high level of productivity. Consider, for example, an information system. If a new information system is developed for a team, they may need training in how to operate the system. In addition, they may need technical assistance in order to ascertain how to perform a complicated information query or to address glitches in the system. Any effective education system provides whatever training or technical assistance is necessary for effective performance.

Contextual Supports and Intergroup Relations (Adequate Material Resources)

While the importance of providing adequate material resources may seem obvious, organizations often fail in this regard. When all other conditions are in place for effective performance and the team is set to go but the whole operation comes to a grinding halt because the team is missing a resource necessary to perform its job, immense frustration can arise. The lack of material resources can also have a negative impact on intergroup relations. If there is a sense of scarcity, teams may compete and hoard needed resources rather than cooperate and support each other. This can poison the atmosphere. Thus, leaders should ensure that teams have the material resources necessary for their work.

▓ EXPERT COACHING

The final element in Hackman's theory of team leadership is expert coaching. The topic of coaching has received much attention in recent years, and it has grown explosively. Leaders recognize that traditional training provides limited growth and development in employees. Coaching may be conducted on its own or in conjunction with training. Coaching helps employees develop skills and put conceptual knowledge to work in practice. The three key areas to target for coaching are: *effort, performance strategies,* and *knowledge and skill* (Hackman & Wageman, 2005). When employees have necessary knowledge and skills to do their work, select appropriate performance strategies, and apply appropriate effort, the ingredients for a successful performance are in place. Leaders should observe where team members are lacking in these areas and use coaching to fill in the gaps. We will explore coaching in more depth in Chapter 11 on team development and training.

In sum, Hackman identified a number of conditions that can maximize chances that teams will succeed. Rather than attempting to specify the particular behavior that a leader should implement, he asserts that leaders should know the conditions that lead to team effectiveness, assess those conditions, and take whatever action is necessary to produce favorable conditions. Having these conditions in place should lead to effective teamwork. In addition, the leader should constantly assess how things are going and what adjustments are needed as the organization and the team evolve and change.

The final topic in this chapter is the criteria for strong workplaces that was developed by the Gallup polling organization. Leaders can use these criteria to help clarify what type of workplace they need to cultivate in order to build productive teams.

▓ ELEMENTS OF WORKPLACE STRENGTH

In addition to the criteria identified by Hackman, leaders may benefit by drawing on other sources of data to get a sense of the practices that enhance performance at work. For example, the Gallup organization (Buckingham & Coffman, 1999) has collected an immense amount of data in an effort to determine what predicts productivity, profitability, employee retention, and customer satisfaction. Over a period of 25 years, they surveyed over a million employees and found that these criteria for success were associated with positive employee responses to the following twelve questions (Buckingham & Coffman, 1999):

Gallup's 12 Core Elements of Workplace Strength
1. Do I know what is expected of me at work?
2. Do I have the materials and equipment I need to do my work right?
3. At work, do I have the opportunity to do what I do best every day?
4. In the last seven days, have I received recognition or praise for doing good work?
5. Does my supervisor, or someone at work, seem to care about me as a person?
6. Is there someone at work who encourages my development?
7. At work, do my opinions seem to count?
8. Does the mission/purpose of my company make me feel my job is important?
9. Are my co-workers committed to doing quality work?
10. Do I have a best friend at work?

11. In the last six months, has someone at work talked to me about my progress?
12. This last year, have I had opportunities at work to learn and grow?

Examining these questions provides us with a sense of what matters to employees, brings out their best effort at work, and keeps them working where they are rather than seeking employment with competitors. An awareness of what is represented by these questions should enable leaders to see what kind of environment they should be building at work.

📁 OPENING CASE REVISITED

Maps and Globes for Edmonton Public Schools

Stembritsky thought that each local school probably had a better idea of what maps and globes would be most useful for their particular needs. So, he decided to divide the money up across schools according to the number of students in each school and let the schools make their own decisions. This move toward decentralization and empowerment was so unconventional that he was almost fired for taking this action. However, a few years later, he was selected as superintendent of the Edmonton schools, and he launched a bold effort to turn decision-making authority and resources over to the schools. He believed that the local school leaders had the best understanding of their own school's needs and would be very conscientious in using the money. The result was that school performance jumped dramatically. Graduation rates and student achievement rose significantly. Eventually, principals in Edmonton controlled about 92% of their budgets. By sharp contrast, principals in New York City and Los Angeles control approximately 6 to 7% of their budgets.

The public schools became so good that today there are no more private schools in Edmonton and no more charter schools. The public schools improved so much that private schools were no longer a competitive alternative, and charter schools simply decided to join the rest of the public system. For more information on this case, see *Making Schools Work: A Revolutionary Plan to Get Your Children the Education They Need* (2003) by William G. Ouchi.

Summary

Both scholars and practitioners have wrestled with the topic of leadership for many years. Early researchers sought to identify effective leaders' traits. However, analysis of data they collected indicated that we have been unable to identify any set of traits that consistently predicts effective leadership. Later researchers focused more on behavior and discovered that many leaders vary in the degree to which they attend to issues related to task and issues related to relationships. Blake and Mouton hypothesized that the best leadership style is one that is high in both task and relationship orientation. Later theorists recognized that situations vary and demand different characteristics in order for leaders to be effective.

Fiedler developed criteria for assessing situational favorableness or unfavorableness and argued that low-LPC (task-oriented) leaders would perform best under conditions of high and lower favorableness, and that high-LPC (relationship-oriented) leaders would perform best under moderately favorable conditions. Hersey and Blanchard also developed a contingency theory that focused on the maturity of the subordinates. The path-goal theory specifies that the leader's job is building incentives and clarity for goal achievement.

Richard Hackman developed a theory specifically for group leaders that clarified the importance of putting conditions in place that would naturally facilitate group effectiveness. He specified the following as important variables: a real team, a compelling direction, an enabling structure, a supportive organizational context, and expert coaching.

◻️ CONCLUDING CASE ─────────────────────────────

Principal Edwards and No Child Left Behind

Jonathan Edwards was the principal of a grade 6–8 middle school in a large Midwestern city. He had been a principal for 20 years, having previously been an assistant principal for five years, and a high school mathematics teacher for six years. He was jovial, outgoing, and absolutely committed to public school success. He was confident in his abilities to operate an absolutely first-rate school, one where parents were satisfied, students motivated to learn, and district superiors and city officials were proud.

In Jonathan's 19th year as a principal, the U.S. Congress enacted the No Child Left Behind Act. Most of Jonathan's 100 classroom teachers and 20 or so other employees were opposed to this piece of federal legislation. They feared it would distort the purposes of education, and many of them claimed that they would end up testing and not teaching.

District and state officials had initially discussed refusing to comply with the federal statute. They later gave up this notion. The flow of federal funds accompanying the act was too large a part of the district's discretionary operating budget to forego. The state teachers' association was still planning on suing the federal department of education claiming that the federal funds were insufficient to accomplish the goals. Jonathan was pretty sure this legal effort would fail. Most informed individuals knew that money was not the state's nor the district's major problem when it came to elevating student performance.

Jonathan was ambivalent regarding the act. It had some tough goals attached to it. Within 12 years, all students in his school had to demonstrate that they were "proficient" in reading, mathematics, and science. He knew that given the low-income and immigrant backgrounds of many of his students, such levels of proficiency were daunting challenges.

On the other hand, while Jonathan admired his teachers, most of whom were handpicked by him over his career as principal, he knew he had a few who had been beyond his ability to motivate. They were coasting, and students in their charge often suffered as a consequence. Because they taught low-income and immigrant students, parents seldom complained. It still bothered Jonathan.

Jonathan knew some children were being left behind, and it nagged at him. Further, he not only knew he had some weak teachers, but he thought it was possible to strengthen the performance of even his best teachers and, along the way, reclaim some of his low-performing teachers. To do all of this, however, was going to take a lot of effort on his part. It had crossed his mind that the ultimate NCLB accountability for student performance was several years downstream, and he was eligible for retirement in just two years from now. What to do? As he reflected, he was fairly certain that he wanted to give it his best shot.

Discussion Questions

1. What options are available to Edwards for leading his organization forward?
2. How do you think he should proceed?

Exercises

First Activity: Tower Building Management Simulation Using a Traditional Bureaucracy Organization Structure (45 Minutes)

Explain the traditional organizational structure being used in this activity (management team of four, one supervisor, and workers) and explain how the first activity will work.

Each lab's task is to build the tallest tower (as measured from the floor) from building materials supplied by the instructor. Towers will be measured, and members of the team with the tallest tower will receive five bonus-quiz points.

- Role assignment should be random. Identify four managers, one supervisor, and seven to ten workers in each of the four labs.
- Managers will leave the room and meet for ten minutes to develop a plan for building the tallest tower. They will be able to view (but not touch) the materials. They may or may not choose to provide anything in writing to the supervisor. (During this time, three lab facilitators will assist the four management teams in finding meeting space and ensuring that the managers do not touch the materials, while the other lab facilitator leads a discussion with all workers and supervisors). The three lab leaders need to ensure that materials are given and that the clock begins for all labs at the same time. Lab leaders (or a manager designated by a lab leader) should dump all the contents of the materials folder onto the floor and remind the managers that they cannot touch them.
- Then the supervisors will meet with their management team for two minutes to be told about the plan. The supervisor can view (but not touch) the materials. Supervisors should take notes and prepare to assign the task to the workers. The three lab leaders will take the supervisors to meet with the managers and again ensure that the materials are not being touched.
- A lab leader, or a supervisor or manager directed to do so, should pick up the materials and deliver them to the workers.

Supervisors and Workers—While managers are meeting, process the characteristics and feelings of each role with the remaining students, i.e. ask for a show of hands of people in the room of those who have had a job or worked in a volunteer organization. What is it like for people at various levels of a hierarchical organization structure? It may help to point out that families are hierarchical structures, wherein the parents are the managers, sometimes older siblings are supervisors, and younger siblings can feel as if they take on the role of worker (from a power and influence standpoint). In the case of Cinderella, she was actually a worker. Another example is in a classroom setting where the teacher is the supervisor and the students are the workers.

The goal here is to discuss strengths and weaknesses of traditional versus team organizational structures. **Explain** that in the traditional bureaucracy, the management team makes decisions and tells the supervisors to get the workers to do the work. Generally, they expect the work to be done according to plan. **Ask:**

- Who holds most of the power and influence in traditional bureaucracies?
- What is it like to be told not only what to do, but exactly how to do it?
- Do people enjoy work when they have no say in what they are expected to do (when they cannot use their own creativity)?

  How might the workers feel in this situation? *(Unmotivated, stifled, frustrated with management for not understanding the realities of doing the work.)*
  How might the supervisors feel? *(Stuck in the middle, resentful of managers and workers.)*
  The managers? *(Frustrated with workers for not doing work the way they think it should be done, guilty.)*

Ask: What can you do to prepare for this task?

Allow:
- Ten minutes for managers to meet.
- Two minutes for the managers to meet with their supervisor.
- Two minutes for the supervisors to brief their team on the plan. The team can look at the materials but cannot touch them yet. Workers may ask questions. The supervisor must implement the manager's design.
- Five minutes for the workers to build the tower. Workers cannot talk with each other.
  Supervisors can talk (direct the workers), but they cannot touch the materials.
  Managers can observe but cannot talk or touch the materials.
  Workers must use the supervisor's plan.

Performance Measure #1
Measure the height of each tower. Declare the winning lab and award five bonus quiz points for each lab member.

Performance Measure #2
Managers check their workers' product (the tower). Determine how closely the product matches the design plan.

Explain that if this were a real situation of this nature, and your product did not match the design, there would be consequences (perhaps even if your team built the tallest tower), people could be fired because the management team's plan was not implemented to spec (specifications). Also, the reward (the money in business, the bonus points in our case) would not be divided equally. They would be divided somewhere along the lines of ten points for managers, five points for the supervisor, and two points for each worker.

Activity 1 Debrief
- What went well with your group process?
- How clear were the instructions for each role?
- Did any supervisors or workers feel they had a better plan?
- What was frustrating about each role?

Transition
Now that you have experienced a traditional bureaucracy let's try the team approach.

Second Activity: Tower Building Management Simulation Using Self-Managed Work Teams (50 Minutes)

Explain that each group will build a tower with the same goal as before (to build the tallest tower, as measured from the floor).

Allow: Ten minutes for groups to make plans for the tower construction. They can talk and touch the materials. Allow five minutes more to build the tower.

Measure towers, declare winning lab, and award five bonus quiz points to each member of that lab.

Activity 2 Debrief
- How would you compare the two situations? Compare and contrast the experiences of having prescribed roles in the first activity to having the group determine roles in the second activity.
- What role did power and influence play in each simulation? Did involvement affect your sense of commitment? We've discussed some of the pros of working in teams, what are some of the cons?
- What are your pet peeves about working in groups, in this class or in your other courses?

Third Activity: Group Process (15 Minutes)
Stay in the room, but huddle with your lab and debrief their group process (offer feedback on what you observed and solicit their feedback).

Tower Building Exercise Role Assignments
Each lab should have one supervisor, four managers, and the rest are workers. You are a **Supervisor**. The goal for your team is to build the tallest tower. The height of the tower will be measured from the floor. Your team will use the Tinker Toys provided to construct the tower. Your team will have five minutes to build it. The *managers* will design the plan for the tower. Your job is to explain this plan to the workers. You can only talk with the workers—you cannot touch the materials while the tower is being built.

You are a **Manager**. The goal for your team is to build the tallest tower. The height of the tower will be measured from the floor. Your team will use the Tinker Toys provided to construct the tower. Your team will have five minutes to build it. Your job is to plan the design of your tower. During the time allocated for design, you and the other managers will create a plan. The plan will be relayed to your team through your supervisor. You cannot talk with your workers, nor touch the materials while the tower is being built.

You are a **Worker**. The goal for your team is to build the tallest tower. The height of the tower will be measured from the floor. The materials which your team will use are Tinker Toys which will be provided. Your team will have five minutes to construct the tower. Your *managers* have designed the plan for the tower. You will receive instructions from your *supervisor*. You may only ask your *supervisor* questions to clarify the instructions. You may not offer any suggestions relating to the plan, nor talk with any of your coworkers.

References

Argote, L., Insko, C. A., Yovetich, N., & Romero, A. A. (1995). Group learning curves: The effects of turnover and task complexity on group performance. *Journal of Applied Social Psychology, 25*, 512–529.

Bass, B. M. (1985). *Leadership and performance beyond expectations*. New York: Free Press.

Bass, B. M. (1996). *A new paradigm of leadership: An inquiry into transformational leadership*. Alexandria, VA: U.S. Army Research Institute for the Behavioral and Social Sciences.

Beer, M., & Cannon, M. D. (2004). Promise and peril in implementing pay-for-performance. *Human Resource Management, 43*(1), 3–20.

Blake, R. R., & Mouton, J. S. (1964). *The managerial grid*. Houston: Gulf Publishing.

Buckingham, M., & Coffman, C. (1999). *First, break all the rules: What the world's greatest managers do differently*. New York: Simon & Schuster.

Burns, J. M. (1978). *Leadership*. New York: Harper & Row.

Conger, J. A., & Kanungo, R. (1987). Toward a behavioral theory of charismatic leadership in organizational settings. *Academy of Management Review, 12*, 637–647.

Conger, J. A., & Kanungo, R. (1998). *Charismatic leadership in organizations*. Thousand Oaks, CA: Sage Publications.

Evans, M. G. (1970). The effects of supervisory behavior on the path-goal relationship. *Organizational Behavior and Human Performanc, 5*, 277–298.

Evans, M. G. (1974). Extensions of a path-goal theory of motivation. *Journal of Applied Psychology, 59*, 172–178.

Fiedler F. E. (1964). A contingency model of leadership effectiveness. In L. Berkowitz (Ed.), *Advances in experimental social psychology*. New York: Academic Press.

Fiedler, F. E. (1967). *A theory of leadership effectiveness*. New York: McGraw Hill.

Fleishman, E. A., & Harris, E. F. (1962). Patterns of leadership behavior related to employee grievances and turnover. *Personnel Psychology, 15*, 43–56.

Hackman, J. R. (2002). *Leading Teams: Setting the stage for great performances*. Boston: Harvard Business School Press.

Hackman, J. R., & Oldham, G. R. (1980). *Work redesign*. Reading, MA: Addison-Wesley.

Hackman, J. R., & Wageman, R. (2005). A theory of team coaching. *Academy of Management Review, 30*(2), 269–287.

Hamper, B. (1991). *Rivethead: Tales from the assembly line*. New York: Time Warner Book Group.

Hersey, P., & Blanchard, K. H. (1977). *The management of organizational behavior* (3rd ed.). Englewood Cliffs, NJ: Prentice Hall.

House, R. J. (1971). A path-goal theory of leader effectiveness. *Administrative Science Quarterly, 16*, 321–339.

House, R. J. (1977). A 1976 theory of charismatic leadership. In J. G. Hunt & L. L. Larson (Eds.), *Leadership: The cutting edge* (pp. 189–207). Carbondale: Southern Illinois University Press.

House, R. J. (1996). Path-goal theory of leadership: Lessons, legacy, and a reformed theory. *Leadership Quarterly, 7*, 323–352.

House, R. J., & Dessler, G. (1974). The path-goal theory of leadership: Some post hoc and priori tests. In J. Hunt & L. Larson (Eds.), *Contingency approaches to leadership*. (pp. 29–55). Carbondale: Southern Illinois University Press.

House, R. J., & Mitchell, T. R. (1974). Path-goal theory of leadership. *Contemporary Business*, 3(Fall), 18–98.

Katz, D., & Kahn, R. L. (1952). Some recent findings in human-relations research in industry. In W. Swanson, T. Newcomb, & E. Hartley (Eds.), *Readings in social psychology* (pp. 650–665). New York: Holt.

Kaufman, B. (1964). *Up the down staircase*. Englewood Cliffs, NJ: Prentice Hall.

Likert, R. (1979). From production- and employee-centeredness to systems 1-4. *Journal of Management*, 5, 147–156.

Locke, E. A., & Latham, G. P. (1990). *A theory of goal setting and task performance*. Englewood Cliffs, NJ: Prentice Hall.

Ouchi, W. (2003). *Making schools work: A revolutionary plan to get your children the education they need*. New York: Simon & Schuster.

Ouchi, W., Riordan, R., Lingle, L., & Porter, L. (2005). Making public schools work: Management reform as the key. *Academy of Management Journal*, 48(6), 929–940.

Schriesheim, C. A., & Bird, B. J. (1979). Contributions of the Ohio State studies to the field of leadership. *Journal of Management*, 5, 135–145.

Shartle, C. L., (1979). Early years of the Ohio State University leadership studies. *Journal of Management*, 5, 126–134.

Stogdill, R. M. (1948). Personal factors associated with leadership: A survey of the literature. *Journal of Psychology*, 25, 35–71

Stogdill, R. M. (1974). *Handbook of leadership: A survey of the literature*. New York: Free Press.

Stogdill, R. M., Goode, O. S., & Day, D. R. (1962). New leader behavior description subscales. *Journal of Psychology*, 54, 259–269.

Yukl, G. (2006). *Leadership in organizations*. Upper Saddle River, NJ: Pearson Prentice Hall.

Yukl, G., Gordon, A., & Taber, T. (2002). A hierarchical taxonomy of leadership behavior: Integrating a half century of behavior research. *Journal of Leadership and Organizational Studies*, 9(1), 13–32.

CHAPTER SIX

Power and Influence

■ INTRODUCTION

Group members, both leaders and non-leaders, have varying degrees of power and influence over other group members. Power is awarded to individuals based on a number of conditions and characteristics including ability to reward or punish others, special knowledge, experience or expertise, and certain perceived personality characteristics. Group members can give too much power to others which can then disrupt the collective functioning of the group. This chapter will describe the dynamics of power and influence in groups and help members become more aware of their own power base and ability to influence others.

LEARNING OBJECTIVES

After reading this chapter, you should be able to

- Describe how power influences group dynamics.
- Describe the factors related to the use of power in groups.
- Identify the source of members' power.
- Describe five different tactics used to influence others.
- Demonstrate the four components of persuasion.

 OPENING CASE

Laval Diego's Dilemma

Laval Diego was an elected school board member in New Orleans. He had first been elected in 2004, two years before the devastation caused by Hurricane Katrina. His parents, who had arrived from Cuba after the Castro revolution with no money and few possessions, had raised him in New Orleans.

Laval had been reared as a devout Catholic. He had done well at the public school he attended, and had received a scholarship to a local Catholic university. He obtained a law degree by studying at night. He was a successful, but far from wealthy, lawyer. His clients could not afford to pay him much, and sometimes could not pay him at all.

Laval had been elected in his parish ward on a school-reform platform. His constituents, mostly poor working-class Hispanic families, knew public schools did not function effectively for their children as students. Laval was committed to making New Orleans's public schools among the best in the nation. He wanted the same success for all other students that he had had himself.

Once elected to the board, Laval was surprised to see that not all fellow members shared his aspirations. Some seemed more interested in a political future or material well-being than in the success of children. Too many times he had come, after the fact, to learn of dishonest relationships with vendors. He saw too many school board votes cast consistent with the rantings of a demagogic mayor, an individual Laval was coming to see as putting political ambition ahead of pedagogy. In contrast, Laval was greatly respected by the other members on the board. He seemed genuinely concerned about the welfare of the education system and was a man of deep principles and integrity.

Then it all fell apart. Katrina hit, and all schools were closed. Destruction and desolation was everywhere. Many of Laval's constituents lost their homes, their jobs, and their hope. Many moved, and some said they would never come back. Laval was committed to rebuilding the public schools and felt that he might be the person to lead the effort. He just wasn't sure how to proceed.

Discussion Questions

1. How should Laval proceed?
2. How should he deal with board members who are not committed to the best interests of the students?
3. How should he deal with the mayor?
4. What specific actions need to be taken in both the short term and the long term to rebuild the schools?
5. How can Laval build consensus and move the board forward?

In previous generations of bureaucratic organizations, managers and supervisors used their positional power to issue commands and control subordinates' behavior. Command and control hierarchies used the promise of rewards and the threat of punishment to manage and motivate employees. This business model was designed in the early 1900s by powerful men such as J. P. Morgan, Andrew Carnegie, and John D. Rockefeller, Sr. to run their growing organizations (Kayser, 1994). But today's competitive and fast-paced, global environment requires a different organizational model that shares power and is built on collaborative work groups (Guillen, 1994; Senge, 1990).

Power is an important construct studied by a number of academic disciplines including sociology, philosophy, psychology, and political science. All individuals and social systems are influenced by the desire for power and control (Friedman & Lackey, 1991). Organizations and work groups are no different. Bolman and Deal (2003) assert that power dynamics are always a part of organizational life because individuals and groups are constantly competing for limited resources. According to Osland, Kolb, and Rubin (2001), power is defined as "the capacity to influence the behavior of others, while influence is the process by which people successfully persuade others to follow their advice, suggestions, or orders" (p. 450). In other words, *power* is the ability to direct others while *influence* is the means by which power is exercised.

Work groups in organizations exist to accomplish goals or tasks. Sometimes those goals are specifically determined by forces outside the group; sometimes those goals and the strategies used to accomplish them are defined within the group. Groups with more power are able to determine their own goals and strategies. Thus, power is related to the concept of autonomy, in that people or groups with power have the freedom to direct their own behavior and the behavior of others. Those without power are dependent on others and are restricted from making their own choices and choosing their own behavior.

Group membership often requires individuals to surrender a certain amount of autonomy or pay dues to gain entrance and acquire the benefits associated with membership. Some groups, such as the military, exert a lot of pressure to conform to certain standards of behavior, while others require very little. Groups have various degrees of collective power to influence both its members and the larger organizations within which they exist. For example, labor unions gained prominence in the early 20th century to exert pressure on organizations to improve working conditions. Individually, members had very little power to raise concerns or demand ethical treatment but, collectively, they could make an impact. However, those who joined unions had to give up freedoms as they were required to pay membership dues and strike if called on. Thus, group membership may reduce personal power but increase collective power.

The concept of power often has a negative connotation because it has been used against people. The 19th-century historian Lord Acton stated that "Power corrupts and absolute power corrupts, absolutely." Power differentials toward others forms a familiar pattern as seen in a multitude of contexts including parenting style (authoritarian, authoritative, permissive), communication style (aggressive, assertive, submissive), leadership style (autocratic, democratic, laissez-faire), and interpersonal style (independent, interdependent, dependent) to name a few. One extreme is the use of power against others in a competitive or self-serving fashion. At the other end of the spectrum is the surrender of personal power to allow oneself to be used by others. The *mediating position* is to avoid the use of control and manipulation by collaborating in genuine and respectful ways to achieve common goals and interests (Craig & Craig, 1979; Griffith & Duesterhaus, 2000). This creates synergy and allows power to be used to achieve the goals of the group. *Directive power*, or power that is used primarily to advance individual goals, dilutes the strength of the group and is likely to create power struggles and provoke resistance.

Synergy occurs when individual resources, strengths, and power are collectively maximized and used toward the success of the group, as shown in Figure 6.1.

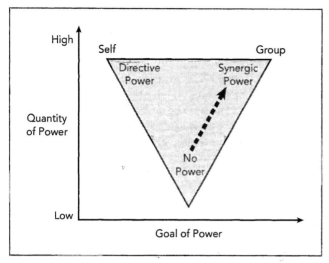

High

Self   Group

Directive   Synergic
Power   Power

Quantity
of Power

No
Power

Low

Goal of Power

FIGURE 6.1   Synergic Power

■ USES OF POWER AND INFLUENCE

Alfred Adler (Ansbacher & Ansbacher, 1956) a contemporary of Sigmund Freud, was convinced that power is the primary drive of human beings. Because people feel vulnerable and insecure, they strive for power and superiority over others to compensate for that condition and to protect themselves. For Adler, the most significant measure of human development was the use of personal power for the good of the community, a concept he called *social interest*. Other researchers and social theorists have identified power as one of three core social needs (McClellan, 1975; Schutz, 1958). Power provides control over one's environment to ensure safety and protect personal interests. At the core of internal working models are fears that must be managed (Griffith, 2004). Power allows people to gain some measure of control to protect against fears and to accomplish goals in the areas of physical well-being, personal competence, relational closeness, and self-transcendence. Thus, individuals use power in various contexts and ways to avoid pain and accomplish goals. These goals include advancement of personal interests, advancement of group goals, or to effect organizational change.

Power is often used to advance personal interests and meet personal needs. Group members can have personal agendas, hidden agendas, and mixed-motive agendas. In competitive cultures like that of the United States, individuals can be more concerned about their own well-being as opposed to the well-being of the group (Trompenaars & Hampden-Turner, 1998). Furthermore, personal goals may be conscious or unconscious (Barker, Wahlers, & Watson, 2001). Most people have mixed motives when working in groups. They want to experience personal benefits while, at the same time, contribute to the overall success of the group. When members use power exclusively for personal gain, this creates mistrust and threatens cohesion.

The accumulation of personal power can also be an end in itself. History suggests that certain individuals enjoy having power over others. Zimbardo's (Haney & Zimbardo, 1998) prison guard experiment at Stanford University in 1971 exemplifies the dangers of how power can be misused. Students who volunteered to participate in the experiment were assigned to be either prisoners or guards in a mock prison constructed in the basement of one of the university buildings. The guards became so abusive and intoxicated with their own arbitrarily assigned power that the experiment had to be stopped prematurely to protect the prisoners. Apparently, power over others can be rewarding to some and meets a personal need that can easily go awry. Certainly, some individuals have a greater need or desire for power over others.

Persons can also use their power to influence group behavior in a positive way to improve performance. When individuals cooperate on tasks or projects, different perspectives arise as to the best way to accomplish goals. Power, then, allows individual members to exert their opinions and positively influence group decisions and actions. As Johnson and Johnson (2006) suggest, "The effectiveness of any group is improved when power is relatively mutual among its members and power is based on competence, expertise, and information" (p. 240). Shared power based on competence gives all members an opportunity to contribute to group success. When power is shared, members tend to be more cooperative and committed to group goals. Synergy is created when members use personal power to advance group goals (Craig & Craig, 1979).

Thus, while power can be used to advance personal interests and accomplish group goals, it can also be used to influence the larger organization and facilitate change. After an initial period of structuring and defining norms, social systems establish homeostasis. Predictability and stability provide security for members. Once groups and organizations have achieved stability, they resist attempts to change (Valley & Thompson, 1998). Thus, old outdated ways of doing things can become norms, creating blind spots and resistance to new ideas and perspectives. Today's competitive marketplace requires adaptability and a constant evaluation of efficiency and quality. For organizational change to take place, influential members understand that organizations are inherently political and are aware of the political terrain. Change agents have an ability to network and form coalitions to affect change at an organizational level (Bolman & Deal, 2003).

Organizations must regularly evaluate and reinvent themselves to avoid complacency and to stay abreast with a changing, competitive marketplace. Kotter (1998) studied change initiatives in more than 100 companies and found that fewer than 15 had success with programs such as total-quality management, reengineering efforts, or restructuring. He identified eight crucial steps in changing the culture of an organization. If any of the steps are missing, he found that lasting change will not take place.

1. Establish a sense of urgency
2. Form a powerful guiding coalition
3. Create a vision
4. Communicate the vision
5. Empower others to act on the vision
6. Plan for and create short-term wins
7. Consolidate improvements and produce still more change
8. Institutionalize new approaches

Organizational leaders who successfully bring about change know how to use their power and influence to accomplish these eight steps. Furthermore, Kotter (1998) found that top-level executives and middle managers are willing to commit to change initiatives but second tier executives such as vice presidents and directors often resist. Those in the second tier of the management hierarchy can be heavily invested in the existing structure and receive too many benefits to want to change.

Sometimes in a school, teachers of long standing are reluctant to do anything different. They have relied on decade-old lesson plans and are reluctant to alter them because of the added effort involved. To persuade them to change requires a substantial effort on the part of a principal or other leader.

■ FACTORS AFFECTING POWER AND INFLUENCE

As organizations become less hierarchical, and decentralize authority, power struggles emerge. For example, self-directed or self-managed work teams are empowered to take responsibility for their own goals and strategies. This can potentially create ownership and motivation but it also leaves a group open to struggles about who is going to be in charge. Although issues of power and control are a normal stage of group development, they can be a significant distraction to group functioning (Shannon, 1996). A number of factors affect the allocation and exercise of power including status differentiation, group conformity, and member resistance.

Status Hierarchies

Even before members meet for the first time, they can be allocated varying degrees of status based on a number of variables including reputation, hearsay of past performance, personality type, education level, or position in the organization. And even if members have equal status initially, over time status differentiation takes place and status hierarchies develop in which certain people acquire more status than others. High status translates into opinions that carry more weight, greater influence over group decisions, and a central role in group communication.

Diffuse status characteristics are individual characteristics that are not directly related to the specific tasks of the group. For example, an older, male, Caucasian physician who is on a school task force might be given status in a group that is charged with evaluation of a school bus maintenance program designed to save money. This person may know nothing about vehicles or saving money, but he will likely be given respect by other group members simply because he is white, male, and a doctor. In contrast, specific status characteristics are those qualities that are directly relevant to the purpose and goals of the group. For example, a fleet maintenance manager for a rental car company should be given status on that task force because of her specific status, even though her diffuse status of being a Hispanic woman who is a single mom in her mid 20s is low.

Not only is status awarded in different degrees, it is also pursued in varying degrees. Some group members might have expertise or information about a certain topic but prefer to stay quiet and in the background. Without this knowledge being available to the group, members make assumptions and assign low status to them. In contrast, some aggressively pursue the status and respect from others. These status seekers will purposely attempt to position themselves in a favorable light to gain power and influence. They can also engage in interpersonal behaviors such as telling others what to do, validating certain viewpoints, and summarizing discussions (Stiles, Lyall, Knight, Ickes, Waung, Hall, & Primeau, 1997). Thus, status is awarded based on diffuse and specific characteristics, but is also influenced by the efforts of group members to acquire it. The result of this interaction is that certain members obtain a greater amount of power and influence over their group.

Group Conformity

Groups and organizations exert various degrees of pressure to encourage conformity to norms and expectations (Cialdini & Goldstein, 2004). While diversity gives groups an advantage in problem solving and creativity, conformity creates cohesion, predictability and structure. In a series of well-known experiments in the 1950s, Solomon Asch asked groups of eight to ten college students to compare the length of three lines on a card to a standard length line on another card. The answer was very obvious as to which of the three lines matched the length of the comparison line. All but one student in the group, the real subject, were confederates instructed to give erroneous answers a majority of the time. The experimenters were interested in understanding to what degree peer pressure affects individuals. Asch and his colleagues were quite surprised to find that 37 out of 50 subjects conformed to the majority at least once. Subsequent studies have confirmed this general principle and, as one would expect, the pressure to conform is even stronger in collectivist cultures (Bond & Smith, 1996).

Not only are members influenced by the majority, but they can also be strongly influenced by a single member of a group. One person who is perceived as an authority can have tremendous sway over the decisions and dynamics of a group. In the well-known Milgram studies in the early 1960s, researchers asked subjects to administer electric shocks to people who answered incorrectly on a verbal test of memory. Milgram's experimenters who were dressed in lab coats and carried clipboards required subjects to administer what they thought were from 15 to 450 volts in increments of 15 volts. In reality, there were no charges administered to the test taker. The real test was to see if subjects would obey the authority who was telling them to continue in spite of their own reluctance. The person taking the fake memory test was a trained actor and exhibited increasing levels of distress as the experiment continued. At 150 volts, he cried out "Experimenter, get me out of here! I won't be in the experiment anymore! I refuse to go on!" (Milgram, 1974, p. 23). All of the subjects continued to administer shocks up to 300 volts and 62.5% obeyed until the 450 volt level which was labeled "XXX" on the fake console. When results of the study were published, social scientists were shocked themselves at the level of obedience carried out by the subjects. Similarly, individuals in groups are susceptible to conforming to the will of a strong leader or group majority. When this happens, groups lose the advantage of multiple perspectives and diverse opinions.

In organizations and work groups, *groupthink* is a condition that occurs when groups are overly cohesive or when one or more members have too much power and influence over the group. For example, the Senate Intelligence Committee (2004) that assessed the U.S. intelligence failure in falsely identifying Iraq's weapons of mass destruction concluded that groupthink was one of the contributing factors. Apparently, there was such a general presumption that Iraq had such weapons that individual group members were reluctant to question what they perceived as the majority position. In a similar way, a dominant member can pronounce judgments for a group that others are reluctant to question. In either case, the checks and balances of group decision making are compromised.

Member Resistance

While there is a general tendency toward conformity in groups, there is also a desire for maintaining individual identity and autonomy (Ashforth & Mael, 1998). Members have different responses to attempts at influencing them from commitment to compliance to resistance (Falbe & Yukl, 1992). Those responses create a group atmosphere that will determine norms that affect future attempts for power and control. Some groups develop a highly cohesive atmosphere that is very conducive to influence while others can be stubborn and resistant. Resistant members can passively avoid doing their duties or aggressively resist the group by refusing, arguing, or delaying. These possible responses can be demonstrated by just one member or a majority of members.

If a member or coalition acquires too much power or control over a group, others will often resist and engage in a power struggle (Shannon, 1996). The wisdom of the U.S. Constitution is that it creates a balance of power with the three branches of government. A series of checks and balances helps to ensure that no one party or coalition can assume complete control of the government. Without structured rules like those set out in the Constitution, groups must struggle and negotiate its own balance of power. As one person rises to power, others will soon become wary and suspicious. Most adults do not like to be told what to do. If group members feel pressured or coerced, they will resist more often than not (Falbe & Yukl, 1992).

When group members resist the direction or requests of the group, influential members and leaders will often respond with control measures. The power struggle can easily escalate as power holders attempt to enforce compliance. If counter-control measures are punitive or coercive, more resistance is likely (Ashforth & Mael, 1998). Groups can bog down in a struggle between individuals and coalitions over control of the group. When powerful members assert particular decisions or strategies without support from a majority of group members, effectiveness of the group will suffer (Wageman & Mannix, 1998). Resistant members can refuse to contribute to group efforts and, in some cases, deliberately attempt to sabotage the group.

SOURCES OF POWER

Power is the capacity to influence one's environment and the people in it. Certain group members have a greater capacity for power and control over others. Power comes from various sources and, in organizational settings, can either be acquired through personal characteristics or derived from a title or position (Pfeffer, 1992; Yukl & Falbe, 1991). Personal power is derived from characteristics such as intellect or charisma, while positional power comes from a person's professional role or position, such as CEO, police officer, or superintendent. A further distinction of power sources comes from French and Raven's (1959) five bases of power: reward, coercive, legitimate, expert, and referent.

Reward power is when a group member possesses sufficient means to reward other members for various behaviors. Rewards can take many forms from verbal encouragement to financial compensation. If the reward is perceived as valuable and the request is reasonably attainable, individuals will comply. But member behavior may only be sustained as long as the rewards are offered. The tasks or vision of the group may never be completely internalized and only dependent on certain rewards. If rewards are promised but not delivered, resentment and distrust can result. For example, if groups are promised a weekend vacation as an incentive for meeting a certain goal, but never receive their reward, motivation will be compromised for future tasks.

Coercive power is the power to punish others. The power holder has the capacity to issue negative consequences when requests are not followed or rules are broken. For example, if a group member continuously fails to show up for meetings, a leader may send a negative email that threatens to report him or her to a superior. Individuals and groups with this type of power can threaten, constrain, block, or interfere with others. Coercive power uses fear to control the behavior of others.

Legitimate power is associated with certain roles and positions in a group or organization. For example, team leaders might be given a certain amount of authority in a group. Members are then obligated to comply with reasonable requests that are within the job description of the leader. If the manager of a sales team requests weekly expense reports, team members will most likely comply if they perceive it as a reasonable request. Members obey legitimate requests out of a sense of duty, loyalty, or moral obligation. Leaders who explain the reasons behind their requests will enhance member compliance and commitment.

Expert power is awarded to members who are perceived as having special knowledge that is of use to the group. Peter Drucker speculated more than thirty years ago that modern employees will need to be "knowledge workers." Their benefit to organizations is the knowledge, intellect, and ability they have to solve complex problems. Group members with these traits are seen as smart and, therefore, powerful. These members are extremely important to group success. While they may be reluctant to volunteer their expertise, the group must discern how to access the knowledge, experience, and skills they possess.

Referent power is a source of power established by people who are well liked by others. Members can be influenced by those with referent power because members want to please them and gain their approval. They tend to be charismatic people who are admired by others. They may not have the best ideas or suggestions, but garner a lot of support because they are very likeable. People with referent power can be quite influential over individual members and the group process in general.

Group members respond differently to different sources of power. Coercive power can generate resistance or reluctant compliance whereas reward or legitimate power will result in positive, compliant behavior. It is referent and expert power, though, that engenders commitment (Yukl & Falbe, 1991). When members are forced into some specific choice or behavior, they can become resentful. In contrast, when members are voluntarily enlisted through rational persuasion and inspirational appeals based on personal versus positional power, they are more likely to be committed to the task or job.

People with multiple sources of power have a greater capacity to influence the behavior of others. For example, after successfully overseeing the merger of Compaq Computer and Hewlett-Packard, Michael Capellas joined MCI/WorldCom in December 2002 as president and CEO. Although MCI/WorldCom was the world's largest telecommunications company at the time, it was embroiled in accounting scandals and forced into bankruptcy. Capellas brought the company out of bankruptcy in early 2004 and successfully negotiated its sale to Verizon Business in late 2005, a feat nothing short of miraculous. One of the reasons Capellas was so successful is that he possesses all five bases of power. He had the power to *reward* competent and highly motivated employees and the *coercive power* to remove those who were not. His *position* at the top of the organizational chart gave him *legitimate power* which garnered respect and obedience. But Capellas was more than a typical high-level executive who understands balance sheets and reporting structures.

TABLE 6.1   Definitions of Influence Tactics

Influence Tactic	Definition
Rational persuasion	Uses logical arguments and factual evidence to persuade others that a proposal or request is viable and likely to result in the attainment of task objectives
Inspirational appeal	Makes a request or proposal that arouses enthusiasm by appealing to values, ideals, and aspirations or by instilling confidence that the other person can do it
Consultation	Seeks others' participation in planning a strategy, activity, or change and is willing to modify a proposal to deal with concerns and suggestions
Ingratiation	Seeks to get others in a good mood or to think favorably of him or her before asking for something
Exchange	Offers an exchange of favors, indicates willingness to reciprocate at a later time, or promises a share of the benefits if help is given to accomplish a task
Personal appeal	Appeals to feelings of loyalty and friendship before asking others to do something
Coalition	Seeks the aid and support of others to help persuade someone else
Legitimating	Seeks to establish the legitimacy of a request by claiming the authority or right to make it, or by verifying that it is consistent with organizational, policies, rules, practices, or traditions
Pressure	Uses demands, threats, or persistent reminders to influence the attitudes or behavior of others
Collaboration	Offers to provide relevant resources or assistance if others will carry out a request or approve a proposed change
Apprising	Explains how others will benefit by complying with the request

He is an *expert* in the field of information technology and an avid reader. Furthermore, he is *likeable* and very relational. His *referent power* inspired hundreds of thousands of discouraged MCI employees to commit to a vision for turning the company around and reasserting its global presence.

■ INFLUENCE TACTICS

While group members have different sources of power, they also have choices as to how they will exercise their power. Influence tactics are the means by which people influence the attitudes and behavior of others. Yukl and associates have thoroughly studied various proactive tactics of influence and their outcomes (Yukl & Falbe, 1990; 1991; Yukl, Kim, & Falbe, 1996; Yukl & Tracey, 1992). In their original work, they uncovered nine ways people try to influence others. Their most recent research has identified two additional tactics (Yukl, Chavez, & Seifert, 2005). Table 6.1 describes each of the eleven tactics.

Exercise 6.1

Imagine you are a member of a task force of mid-level managers that is evaluating the health-insurance plan your school district offers its employees. Costs have increased substantially over the last five years, and the school board feels that it can no longer bear the burden of fully insuring all of its employees. The district is relatively small, with approximately 50 teachers, administrators, and staff employees. The task force has decided to recommend to the superintendent that he drop the insurance coverage of hourly workers and only cover salaried employees. (Note: All the members of the task force are salaried administrators and teachers.) You know staff members, who are hourly employees, in your department who will be seriously affected by this decision, and you think it will be an absolutely disastrous mistake for the school district overall. Thus, you feel strongly that you need to convince task-force members not to make this recommendation. Craft a statement using each of the influence tactics mentioned above that could be used to influence your colleagues.

Various influence tactics produce different outcomes. The Influence Behavior Questionnaire (IBQ) is an instrument designed to evaluate influence tactics and their outcomes. Group members can assess themselves or others. Since collaboration and apprising have only recently been added to their inventory, the majority of Yukl's research did not include those tactics. Three core tactics (rational persuasion, inspirational appeals, and consultation) were found to be the most successful at gaining task commitment and were strongly related to leader effectiveness as evaluated by their superiors (Yukl & Tracey, 1992). Committed members agree internally with the action or decision about which they are being influenced, and will carry out their tasks with enthusiasm, initiative, and persistence.

The most ineffective influence tactics are pressure, coalition, and legitimating (Yukl & Tracey, 1992). While these strategies might bring about compliance, overuse will produce resistance. Compliant members carry out their duties but are not enthusiastic and put forth only minimal or average effort. Ingratiation and exchange were found to be moderately effective at influencing peers and subordinates. Falbe & Yukl (1992) asked 95 managers and nonmanagerial professionals in a variety of private companies and public agencies to evaluate their reaction to 504 influence attempts made on them. Each attempt was categorized as one of the nine original influence tactics and associated with a resulting response of resistance, compliance, or commitment. Table 6.2 describes the results.

TABLE 6.2   Outcomes of Influence Tactics

Influence Tactics	Outcomes		
	Resistance	Compliance	Commitment
Inspirational appeal	0 %	10 %	90 %
Consultation	18	27	55
Personal appeal	25	33	42
Exchange	24	41	35
Ingratiation	41	28	31
Rational persuasion	47	30	23
Legitimating	44	56	0
Coalition	53	44	3
Pressure	56	41	3

Hard tactics such as legitimating, coalition, and pressure often produce resistance and rarely engender commitment. Hard tactics such as these will have significantly better outcomes if paired with a softer tactic such as consultation, inspirational appeals, or ingratiation (Falbe & Yukl, 1992). Feedback and skills training can certainly be effective at helping team leaders develop influence tactics that are most effective. Seifert, Yukl, and McDonald (2003) found that multisource feedback and the use of a feedback facilitator can help leaders and managers become more aware of their own strategies and develop more effective ways to motivate subordinates and peers.

PERSUADING OTHERS

The effectiveness of groups is dependent, in part, on the ability of group members to banter and vigorously discuss various ideas and strategies. When members hold back or avoid sharing their perspective, the synergic power of the group is compromised. If a group member has an opinion on an issue, he or she should be able to offer it to the group with confidence. In terms of frequency of use in organizational settings, rational persuasion is the tactic most often used to persuade others (Falbe & Yukl, 1992; Yukl & Falbe, 1990). Conger (1998) has identified four components of persuasion that his research has shown to be most effective: (1) establishing credibility, (2) finding common ground, (3) providing compelling evidence, and (4) making an emotional connection. The best and most persuasive arguments include all four components.

Establish Credibility

In order to be persuasive, group members must have credibility and respect from their peers. A low-status or resistant member of the group is not going to be heard when he or she contributes an idea or plan, even if the idea is brilliant. It takes some measure of status and personal power to be taken seriously. According to Conger (1998), credibility comes from intellectual competence, interpersonal cooperation, and personal character. Intellectual competence is demonstrated by a track record of significant contributions to the group. When a competent member speaks, others trust that what is said is worth being heard. Competence is one of the characteristics that engenders trust and is established when members have proven themselves to have sound judgment and knowledge.

Credibility is also established through the quality of relationships that one has with other members. Specifically, a commitment to the common goals of the group and an ability to work collaboratively with others will go a long way at building relational trust. When members are seen as team players they are given credibility in the group. An additional source of relational credibility comes from personal character and integrity. Members are valued for honesty, consistency, and reliability. Members who consistently follow through on their commitments are regarded as credible and worthy of respect.

Regardless of the tactic, influence attempts are more likely to result in commitment if the agent has referent power (Yukl, Kim, & Falbe, 1996). Thus, those who seek to influence others will be more successful if they are likeable, agreeable, and enjoyable to work with. These are characteristics that members can adopt in order to be better integrated and influential in their group. Similarly, personal appeal is a successful influence tactic related to the feelings of loyalty and friendship that members have for each other. These relationally oriented bonds can be very effective when attempting to influence others.

Find Common Ground

In addition to having credibility, effective persuasion requires the ability to frame suggestions in terms of their benefit to the whole group. Unfortunately, when people are overly attached to a certain perspective or position, they can lose sight of the group's best interest, make debates personal, become competitive, and feel compelled to win at any cost. When the group resists, some members go on the attack and increase the pressure to convince others to agree with them. Members can easily slip into the negative behavior of threats and demands when others refuse to do what they want. The best arguments should be tied to the ultimate goals and success of the group.

According to Conger (1998), knowing the audience is a prerequisite for finding common ground. The most effective persuaders are students of human nature and understand the concerns and interests of others before advocating an agenda. They are active listeners and collect data through conversations and meetings. Knowing what is important to others allows members to construct arguments that take those issues into account.

Finding common ground also allows for compromise and collaboration. Those who wish to influence the group will be more successful if they stay open to the concerns and perspectives of others and are willing to adapt and modify their position. When met with resistance, they listen, paraphrase, and ask probing questions to better understand the issues of concern. Influence tactics such as consultation, collaboration, and apprising can be effective in identifying shared benefits and building a common framework from which to work.

Provide Compelling Evidence

Data-based decision making is a practice by which groups make decisions and create plans based on the best data available to them. Goals that are measurable and problems that are correctly analyzed can help groups uncover the necessary data to guide group efforts. Powerful and influential members can sway attitudes and behaviors, but solid numerical data provides the reasoning and justification for group decisions and direction. Before putting forth an argument, a member should anticipate the question: "What is the evidence for your position?" Argyris (1994) describes this process as coming down the ladder of inference, whereby members provide the data and reasoning on which a decision, conclusion, or argument has been made.

When a person has credibility and is working within a common framework, strong empirical data makes a compelling argument. Data is always incomplete and ever-changing, but sharing what one knows creates understanding and trust. Knowledge is a source of power and sharing it empowers the rest of the group. The more knowledge and information that is accessible to the group, the greater the likelihood of good decisions and effective group functioning. For example, the best predictor of the future is the past. Trend data, while not perfect, gives approximate projections of what is likely to occur in the future. If a marketing team responsible for selling nutrition bars is trying to estimate growth projections and define goals for the next five years, data from the last five years and information on the changing marketplace are crucial.

But numbers alone do not tell the whole story. Numbers and graphs are most effective when they are presented with vivid language and concrete examples. Stories can be powerful tools that bring numbers to life and persuade members to come to certain conclusions. Examples, analogies, anecdotes, and metaphors can be used to make data more concrete and tangible. Instead of just making an argument based on past performance and current market trends, a customer testimonial might be used to describe how their quality of life improved after buying the company's product. This might make a stronger case for more aggressive growth. Subway, the fast-food sandwich firm, for example, has designed a marketing campaign around Jared, a man who lost over 200 pounds in one year by eating Subway subs. His compelling story has influenced a lot of people. Today there are more Subway stores than McDonald's franchises.

Connect Emotionally

While rational arguments can bring members to compliance, an emotional connection is often needed for commitment. Inspirational appeal is the most effective tactic at generating commitment because it engages people at the heart level. When this is done effectively, people rarely resist. Falbe and Yukl's (1992) found that inspirational appeals resulted in commitment 90% of the time, compliance 10% of the time, and never generated resistance. Connecting emotionally requires that members demonstrate their own emotional commitment to a position they are advocating. In addition, they must be able to accurately read the emotional state of those they are trying to influence and adjust accordingly.

With credibility and common ground, strong data and relevant examples, effective persuaders can passionately advocate their position. If group members cannot tell that the agent is thoroughly convinced, they will likewise be unconvinced. But too much emotion might create the impression that a person has lost objectivity or is too invested in a certain decision. Thus, an appropriate amount of conviction is needed as one champions a certain position. Each group environment will dictate what that optimal level of emotional expression will be.

Conger (1998) believes it is even more important to be able to assess the emotional state of the audience. Presenters must be able to judge whether they are being understood and well received. This can be achieved by observing nonverbal messages or by reading between the lines of questions and comments. In spite of the stated importance of rationality in organizational settings, emotions also play a strong role. Thus, those who are effective at persuading others can judge the emotional reactions of others and adjust their comments accordingly.

The four components of a persuasive argument utilize many of the most effective influence tactics and draw on power sources such as referent power and expert power. If members want to be active and influential in their groups, they can utilize these methods to increase their effect on group functioning and help achieve success.

 OPENING CASE REVISITED ────────────────────────────

Laval Diego's Dilemma

Laval was dedicated to rebuilding New Orleans. However, he was not quite sure what that meant when it came to schools. The teachers' union was adamant in its assertion that pre-Katrina public schools had to be rebuilt. Many Catholic officials had approached him regarding the utility of publicly funded voucher plans and the expansion of private and Catholic schools. He had frequent visits from entrepreneurs who wanted to form publicly supported charter schools. And he was part of a school board that was divided and where individuals had mixed motives for serving.

Whereas public schools had been good for Laval, he could see they did not work well for all other children. What was the right solution for rebuilding education in the "Big Easy"? He decided to empower all the various stakeholders: public schools should be restored and made better, private providers should be supported, and charter schools given a chance. His constituents, as they drifted back to town, were dependent on his decisions, and he was mindful of his personal commitments. He was committed to reforming and building a school system that would be in the best interests of the children. He spent time meeting with the teachers' union, the school board, his constituents, the Catholic Church and charter school backers to work together toward that end. There were limited resources and some groups would just not get everything they wanted. However he had enough respect from all groups that they were willing to come together and start making compromises for the sake of a better education for the children.

Summary

Power is the ability to influence the attitudes and behaviors of others. Issues of power and influence are always present in group settings as members strive to influence the decisions, direction, and performance of the group. Members gain power through a number of sources and use various strategies to influence others and garner support for their ideas. While groups exert pressure on members to conform to group norms, members will resist if the pressure is perceived as coercive or punitive. Influential members who are effective at persuading colleagues establish credibility, find common ground with others, provide compelling evidence for their position, and connect emotionally with the group.

 CONCLUDING CASE ────────────────────────────────

Dealing with a Resistant Group Member

Brenda Jones is an enthusiastic and gifted seventh-grade math teacher. She expects a lot out of her students and has high standards. But she also treats her students with respect and is very encouraging. Brenda has a very positive reputation in the school and is respected by both her students and peers alike. As a result, she has been asked by the principal, Mrs. Green, to lead a group of middle school teachers in evaluating and redesigning the math curriculum to better prepare students for annual standardized tests. At the end of one of the task force meetings, Brenda asked John, an administrative assistant assigned to support the task force, to type up some notes she wrote and distribute them to the rest of the members by the end of the week. He responded by saying that he is too busy that week and that the request was outside the bounds of his responsibility anyway.

Discussion Questions

1. How would you respond if you were in Brenda's shoes?
2. Everyone is looking at you. What do you say? Your authority is being challenged.
3. Why might you react in anger to John's resistance?
4. How might gender be playing a role in this scenario?
5. What kind of power does Brenda have?
6. What influence tactics might she use to get John's commitment to the goals of the task force?
7. Construct some statements that she could use to respond to and influence John.

References

Ansbacher, H. L., & Ansbacher, R. R. (Eds.). (1956). *The individual psychology of Alfred Adler*. New York: Harper & Row.

Argyris, C. (1994). Good communication that blocks learning. *Harvard Business Review*, July-Aug., 77–85.

Ashforth, B. E., & Mael, F. A. (1998). The power of resistance: Sustaining valued identities. In R. M. Kramer & M. A. Neale (Eds.), *Power and influence in organizations* (pp. 89–119). Thousand Oaks, CA: Sage.

Barker, L. L., Wahlers, K. J., & Watson, K. W. (2001). *Groups in process: An introduction to small group communication* (6th ed.). Boston: Allyn and Bacon.

Bolman, L. G., & Deal, R. E. (2003). Reframing *organizations: Artistry, choice, and leadership* (3rd ed.). San Francisco: Jossey-Bass.

Bond, R., & Smith, P. B. (1996). Culture and conformity: A meta-analysis of studies using Asch's (1952b, 1956) line judgment task. *Psychological Bulletin, 119*, 111–137.

Cialdini, R. B., & Goldstein, N. J. (2004). Social influence: Compliance and conformity. *Annual Review of Psychology, 55*, 591–621.

Conger, J. (1998). The necessary art of persuasion. *Harvard Business Review*, May-June, 85–95.

Craig, J. H., & Craig, M. (1979). *Synergic power beyond domination, beyond permissiveness* (2nd ed.). Berkeley, CA: Proactive Press.

Falbe, C. M., & Yukl, G. (1992). Consequences for managers of using single influence tactics and combinations of tactics. *Academy of Management Journal, 35*, 638–652.

French, Jr., J. R. P., & Raven, B. (1959). The bases of social power. In D. Cartwright (Ed.), *Studies in social power* (pp. 150–167). Ann Arbor, MI: Institute for Social Research.

Friedman, M. I., & Lackey, Jr., G. H., (1991). *The psychology of human control: A general theory of purposeful behavior*. New York: Praeger.

Griffith, B. A. (2004). The structure and development of internal working models: An integrated framework for understanding clients and promoting wellness. *Journal of Humanistic Counseling. Education, and Development, 43*, 163–177.

Griffith, B. A., & Duesterhaus, M. (2000). Integrating a moral conversation: A framework for counselors. *Journal of Humanistic Counseling, Education, and Development, 39*, 47–55.

Guillen, M. F. (1994). *Models of management: Work, authority, and organization in a comparative perspective*. Chicago: University of Chicago.

Haney, C., & Zimbardo, P. (1998). The past and future of U.S. prison policy: Twenty-five years after the Stanford Prison Experiment. *American Psychologist, 53*, 709–727.

Johnson, D. W., & Johnson, F. P. (2006). *Joining together: Group theory and group skills*. Boston: Allyn and Bacon.

Kayser, T. A. (1994). *Building team power: How to unleash the collaborative genius of work teams*. New York: Irwin Professional Publishing.

Kotter, J. P. (1998). Winning at change. *Leader to Leader, 10,* 27–33.

McClellan, D. C. (1975). *Power: The inner experience.* New York: Irvington.

Milgram, S. (1974). *Obedience to authority.* New York: Harper & Row.

Osland, J. S., Kolb, D. A., & Rubin, I. M. (2001). *The organizational behavior reader* (7th ed.). Upper Saddle River, NJ: Prentice Hall.

Pfeffer, J. (1992). *Managing with power: Politics and influence in organizations.* Boston: Harvard Business School Press.

Schutz, W. C. (1958). *FIRO: A three-dimensional theory of interpersonal behavior.* New York: Rinehart.

Seifert, C. F., Yukl, G., & McDonald, R. A. (2003). Effects of multisource feedback and a feedback facilitator on the influence behavior of managers towards subordinates. *Journal of Applied Psychology, 88,* 561–569.

Senate Intelligence Committee. (2004). *Report on the U.S. Intelligence Community's Prewar Intelligence Assessments on Iraq.* Retrieved March 4, 2006, from http://intelligence.senate.gov/conclusions. pdf.

Senge, P. M. (1990). *The fifth discipline: The art and practice of the learning organization.* New York: Doubleday.

Shannon, W. T. (1996). *The power struggle: How it enhances or destroys our lives.* New York: Plenum Press.

Stiles, W. B., Lyall, L. M., Knight, D. P., Ickes, W., Waung, M., Hall, C. L., & Primeau, B. E. (1997). Gender differences in verbal presumptuousness and attentiveness. *Personality and Social Psychology Bulletin, 23,* 759–772.

Trompenaars, F., & Hampden-Turner, C. (1998). *Riding the waves of culture: Understanding cultural diversity in global business* (2nd ed.). New York: McGraw Hill.

Valley, K. L., & Thompson, T. A. (1998). Sticky ties and bad attitudes: Relational and individual bases of resistance to change in organizational structure. In R. M. Kramer & M. A. Neale (Eds.), *Power and influence in organizations* (pp. 39–66). Thousand Oaks, CA: Sage.

Wageman, R., & Mannix, E. A. (1998). Uses and misuses of power in task-performing teams. In R. M. Kramer & M. A. Neale (Eds.), *Power and influence in organizations* (pp. 261–285). Thousand Oaks, CA: Sage.

Yukl, G., Chavez, C., & Seifert, C. F. (2005). Assessing the construct validity and utility of two new influence tactics. *Journal of Organizational Behavior, 26,* 705–725.

Yukl, G., & Falbe, C. M. (1990). Influence tactics and objectives in upward, downward, and lateral influence attempts. *Journal of Applied Psychology, 75,* 132–140.

Yukl, G., & Falbe, C. M. (1991). Importance of different power sources in downward and lateral relations. *Journal of Applied Psychology, 76,* 416–423.

Yukl, G., Kim, H., & Falbe, C. M. (1996). Antecedents of influence outcomes. *Journal of Applied Psychology, 81,* 309–317.

Yukl, G., & Tracey, J. B. (1992). Consequences of influence tactics used with subordinates, peers, and the boss. *Journal of Applied Psychology, 77,* 525–535.

CHAPTER SEVEN

Decision Making

▓ INTRODUCTION

One of the key reasons for relying on groups is that they offer unique assets for solving problems and making decisions. Although groups are capable of making decisions that are superior to those made by individuals, groups are also vulnerable to a variety of biases and limitations that can impede this ability. This chapter examines group vulnerabilities and provides recommendations for how groups can make better decisions.

LEARNING OBJECTIVES

After reading this chapter, you should be able to

- Recognize the assets that groups bring to the decision-making process.
- Understand the potential liabilities that groups bring to the decision-making process.
- Recognize what members can do to assist the group in the decision-making process and avoid these liabilities.
- Understand Vroom's theory of group decision making and how to use it.

 OPENING CASE

Deciding Asset Allocation at Montgomery Life

John Bates, President of Montgomery Life, a large insurance company, had just read the book *The Wisdom of Crowds* (Surowiecki, 2004), and he was fascinated by it. He could see an immediate use for it in his business. The author pointed out that by asking a large number of people their best estimate about an uncertain quantity or future event, one can average their estimations and derive a reasoned projection of the true quantity or outcome of a future event. He could see how this could be useful to asset-allocation decisions in his own company.

An important facet of the insurance business is investing the cash from the business wisely; but most investments involve risk, and determining where to invest always involves some element of research, forecasting, wisdom of experience, and a fair amount of guesswork and luck. Paul Crayton was the chief investment strategist at Montgomery Life and was responsible for determining asset allocation. He had to decide what percentage of the investment portfolio to allocate to stock, bonds, and cash. Choosing the wrong asset allocation could be costly to the firm. Crayton would listen to what his staff of analysts thought would be the right allocation and why, but he would make the decision himself as to what allocation to choose for the near term.

In checking his voice messages, Crayton noticed he had a voice mail from Bates. Bates was talking in an excited voice about *The Wisdom of Crowds* and how Crayton could use it to enhance his ability to determine the best asset allocation. Bates thought that Crayton and his analysts should each privately record their estimate of what they thought the best near-term asset allocation percentages should be, and then they could average them and use that as their asset allocation. Crayton was irritated by this suggestion and felt that it devalued his expertise and wisdom. Although he did not like the idea, Bates was the president, and Crayton had to be respectful of Bates's perspective.

Discussion Questions

1. How do you think Crayton and Bates should proceed?
2. What are some other ways Crayton could decide on how to invest the company's money?

▓ INTRODUCTION TO PROBLEM SOLVING AND DECISION MAKING

A multitude of decisions must be made each day in organizations as employees go about their daily work and as the organization seeks to respond to demands of a constantly changing environment. How effective are these decisions? Unfortunately, research suggests that about half of the decisions made in organizations are failures (Nutt, 1999). Fortunately, not every decision made in organizations is terribly consequential. However, many decisions are crucial, and individuals and groups are often unaware as they are making decisions just how crucial a certain decision might become (Beech & Connolly, 2005; Weick, 2001).

Consider the example of Nick Leeson, a 28-year-old who was having an incredible run of success as a foreign currency trader stationed in the Singapore office of Barrings Bank. The management team that oversaw Nick Leeson's trading had allowed him simultaneously to be chief trader and to be responsible for the settling of his own trades. A corporate internal memo warned the management team that this practice was unwise because it meant that there would be no check on his activities. However, the management team decided to take no action as a result of this memo, and this turned out to be a fatal error. After a long run of success, Leeson made several bad calls in a row and ran up huge losses that he concealed from the executive team. In an effort to regain the lost money, he took another set of risky trades and bet wrong again. In all, he racked up $1.3 billion in losses and thereby bankrupted and destroyed the 233-year-old bank that had at one time financed the Napoleonic wars. He left a note on his desk that said "I'm sorry" and fled the country. He was later apprehended and sentenced to prison in Singapore. Some time later, ING assumed most of the debts of the bankrupt bank and purchased the company for a mere one pound sterling.

It seems unlikely that the team managing Leeson ever imagined that they were risking the entire company through the way they managed him. Nonetheless, the decisions to structure his role as they did and to take no action in response to the internal memo led to the demise of a company that had lasted well over two centuries.

It is often only after the fact and with the remarkably accurate benefit of hindsight that we recognize where we were limited, biased, or vulnerable in our decision making.

The human mind has both significant assets and significant liabilities when it comes to decision making. On one hand, the brain is an incredibly powerful entity that is fully capable of making superb decisions and creating clever innovations and solutions to problems. However, the mind is also vulnerable to a variety of limitations, biases, and traps (Bazerman, 2006). In addition, it is difficult to see what we are missing or where we are biased when making decisions. For example, President Kennedy questioned "How could we have been so stupid?" after the ill-fated Bay of Pigs invasion—a question you do not often hear presidents ask.

ASSETS ASSOCIATED WITH GROUP DECISION MAKING

A group should have advantages over an individual in making decisions. In a study of decision making in organizations, groups outperformed their best member the vast majority of the time (Michaelson, Watson, & Black, 1989). Thus, groups typically have more assets to bring to bear than their best individual. This chapter initially describes advantages groups have over individuals in decision making. Then, there is the exploration of a variety of issues that produce potential vulnerabilities in group decision making. Despite their assets, groups often make disastrous decisions (Plous, 1993). Group members who understand these vulnerabilities and are proactive in helping the group manage them effectively increase the probability that a group will make effective decisions. We will first look at the advantages associated with group decision making.

Information and Memory

If we consider the assets of a group versus an individual in making a decision, the group can draw on more information given the collective memory of the group—each member has had different educational and life experiences. As the decision process unfolds, each member may have some unique bit of information that enlightens the process and makes for a better decision.

Another benefit that can emerge when groups work together over a period of time is *transactive memory* (Moreland & Argote, 2003). This refers to the finding that, over time, group members understand each other's areas of knowledge and expertise. With transactive memory, they are able to address problems more quickly because they know which member is the best source of information on a particular topic. For example, a consulting team may know that Jerry is a wizard with Excel, Lane is fast and skilled with PowerPoint, and Judy is a great writer and editor. With this knowledge, they can quickly allocate responsibilities for analyzing data, writing a report, and designing a client presentation. They can work much more quickly and effectively than if they were unaware of the unique talents within the group.

Variety of Perspectives

Beyond information, group members often have different perspectives or ways of looking at a problem based on unique ways that they perceive the world as a result of their upbringing, cultural heritage, and so on. A diverse group at Geneva Steel, a steel-producing company, provides an example of how the group relied on different perspectives and different information held by members, collectively, to solve a problem. Geneva Steel had been closed down by its original owner but was later purchased and reopened by a set of entrepreneurs. They rehired some of the former steel workers as well as workers who were completely new to the steel-making process. Early in the days after being reopened, for no apparent reason, one of the furnaces overheated and threatened a melt down. Having been accustomed to a certain way of doing things, the former workers had a more narrow perspective on the range of options for addressing the crisis. By contrast, the new workers had a fresh perspective on how to resolve the crisis and had numerous creative ideas. Many of these ideas were impractical, but the new workers did not have the experience to know which were practical and which were impractical. The former workers had the information and memory to sort out the practical from the impractical, and together they combined the new perspectives with the wisdom of experience and resolved the crisis.

Thus, groups bring more assets to the table, yet the research shows that groups vary significantly in the extent to which they do or do not utilize assets available to them (Allen & Hecht, 2004). Effective decision making requires that group members be vigilant and proactive in helping the group make the most of its potential. An education in the issues that can hinder group decision making, and what can be done about them, can also be helpful. Thus, we next examine a number of issues that affect the quality of decision making and often contribute to less-effective decisions. We will also provide some options for strategies that group members can use to limit the possibility that these will hinder the decision process. These options are labeled *Member Intervention*. Each of these apply to the steps involved in the problem-solving process in Chapter 3: define, analyze, plan, execute, and evaluate (DAPEE). Groups that understand and proactively manage the issues described below will be more effective in each of the DAPEE problem-solving steps.

▪ VULNERABILITIES IN GROUP DECISION MAKING

Overconfidence

Overconfidence refers to the finding in the psychological literature that people tend to have greater certainty about the quality and accuracy of their perceptions and decisions than is justified by objective reality (Juslin, Winman, & Olsson, 2000). Examples of overconfidence in decision making are readily available. Consider the decision to marry. The divorce rate in the United States varies, but generally the percentage of marriages that end in divorce is 40 to 50%. Now, consider how often you have encountered someone who is getting married who considers this base rate to apply to him or herself. How often have you heard someone say something like: "Well, I am feeling fine about the prospect for this marriage, I think it has at least a 50% chance of lasting." Although engaged people may often have some doubts, most have a great deal of overconfidence as they enter into marriage.

Overconfidence is evident in individual stock picking. Mutual funds can be actively managed or can simply be pegged to an index (e.g., the Dow Jones Industrial Average or the Russel 2000). The actively managed funds hire professionals to use their expertise to choose the stocks that have the best prospects for rising in value. Once again, significant overconfidence appears to exist among these professionals. On average, the index funds (which make no effort to distinguish between the best and the worst stocks) consistently beat the actively managed funds performance when the costs of management are included (McGuigan, 2006). Of course, there are notable exceptions such as Warren Buffet of Berkshire Hathaway, who has delivered exceptional performance for years, but such individuals are indeed the rare exception.

A final example of overconfidence can be found among entrepreneurs. One study estimated that about 50,000 new businesses are started each year within the United States alone, and that these entrepreneurs put an average of about $20,000 of their own money into the business (Cooper, Woo, & Dunkleberg, 1988). Unfortunately, most of these businesses fail within the first few years. Another unfortunate fact is that entrepreneurs tend to be grossly overconfident in their prospects for success. A full 33% of those questioned in the study said that their new venture was a "sure thing" with no chance of failure.

Overconfidence can be unusually harmful to the decision-making process. In addition, there is evidence that groups can exacerbate overconfidence (Kerr & Tindale, 2004). Overconfidence may lead a group to commit to actions and ideas that they cannot successfully accomplish and to which they should not commit. It can also hinder the quality of decision making because the group is likely to think that the quality of their decision is better than it really is. Thus, they may prematurely stop their search for better solutions. They may also be closed to the possibility that they may be missing something, and thus they do not recognize the need to recheck their work, assumptions, or completeness of their information.

Member Intervention: Group members can use their knowledge of overconfidence to play a constructive role in keeping it in check. Group members can question assumptions and provide objective evidence of base rates. For example, a group member might remark:

> It looks like our group of engineers is about ready to commit to designing this new product in six months. I checked into this and the fastest time frame any similar group has achieved is a full year. So, I am wondering how realistic we are being about how long this will take. Before we make that commitment I would like for us to make a critical examination of what evidence we have that suggests this is realistic and what liabilities and potential problems we might have that could keep us from making that deadline.

Undersampling of Unique Information

One of the key benefits of using a group to make a decision, as mentioned at the start of the chapter, is that each member has different educational and life experiences and can potentially contribute unique information (not held by other members of the group) to the process. When individual members share this information, it enhances the decision-making process. Unfortunately, the way group discussions naturally evolve, the unique information that individual members have often does not get shared with the rest of the group. Even if it does get shared, it often is underweighted in the groups' consideration (Medvec, Berger, Liljenquiest, & Neale, 2004).

Stasser and Titus (1985) manipulated the information given to group members who were working on a decision-making task, such that some of the crucial information was shared by all team members, but some individuals had unique information. Unique information is some bit of crucial information that only one individual has and is not known by anyone else in the group. When the group went to work to make the decision, the discussion was dominated by the shared information, and the crucial information that was held by single individuals either did not get into the discussion, or it was underdiscussed and underweighted in the decision-making process by the group. Consequently, groups made poor decisions because they did not surface (get individuals to disclose) and take into account all the information that was available within the group. If leaders and members are to make the most of the information within their group, they should be aware of this pitfall and proactively draw out unique information.

Member Intervention: Sometimes just asking a question to address an issue can be helpful. A group member might ask: "Does anyone have any relevant information about this problem that they have not voiced or that has not been given a fair hearing in this discussion?" A question like that may be all that is needed because group members are rarely hiding their information, they just need a nudge to disclose it.

Framing

A *frame* is a set of assumptions or a perspective that an individual or group holds that influences the approach they take to solving problems and making decisions. Frames often hinder problem solving because they are too narrow. Furthermore, because people tend to be unaware of their own frames, they have a difficult time reframing (Bolman & Deal, 2003). We define *reframing* as bringing a different, creative, more appropriate perspective or set of assumptions to understanding and acting on the problem.

Because the concept of framing is somewhat abstract, we often use the following exercise, contributed by Philip McArthur of Action Design, to illustrate a frame and its effects. We ask students to find a partner and to thumb wrestle for 30 seconds. Students are told to get as many wins as possible in their 30 seconds. A win occurs when one individual has the other individual's thumb firmly pinned down. After the students have finished their 30 seconds we ask how many wins they achieved. Then we explain that the most wins we have had in 30 seconds is 33. Students typically explain this as the result of one party giving up or perhaps one party simply has a massive, bone-crushing thumb. Eventually it occurs to someone that the pair who achieved 33 *collaborated* rather than *competed*. Sometimes students will say that collaborating is cheating, but someone usually explains that this is an issue of framing. Specifically, the traditional frame for this game is a competitive frame rather than a collaborative frame—get more wins than your opponent, versus get as many wins as possible. So, when given different criteria for success that are more amenable to collaboration, few of us think to reframe—select a different frame that is more appropriate for what we are trying to accomplish. The same thing happens in group problem solving. Specifically, groups often adopt a frame that is limiting in some way.

Sometimes a frame can be too narrowly focused on a solution. For example, one group wanted to improve the quality of tomatoes available for sale by reducing damage occurring in the picking process. Therefore, they set out to determine how to design better machines for picking tomatoes to reduce the damage that often resulted from harvesting. The initial effort met with little success. It was only after they reframed the problem more broadly that a solution was developed. They had initially framed the problem too narrowly in terms of a particular solution (improving machinery) when the real goal was to reduce damage to tomatoes. A broader framing of the problem enabled them to search more widely for solutions and they found more success with a completely different idea. They realized that another way to solve the problem would be to breed tomatoes with characteristics that were less vulnerable to damage during picking. This solution proved more successful, though it also produced tomatoes that are more square than round.

Member Intervention: Members can assist the group by working to retain a big-picture perspective. A good question to ask oneself is What are we really trying to accomplish here? Group members should keep this question in mind and apply their thinking in a way that addresses the particular issue that the group is working on. In the tomato case, a member could say: "Is our goal to improve picking machinery, or is our goal to get tomatoes to market in better condition? If our goal is the latter, we might want to consider whether there are better options than tinkering with machinery."

Group members can also help by keeping in mind what is fact and what is assumption and by periodically bringing that to the group's attention. For example, the group member might say, "If I understand correctly, we are basing the entire solution on the assumption that_____, and I am wondering how confident we should be that this assumption is correct."

Framing and Risk

Framing can also affect the way we feel about risk. Take a look at the following examples, and you will see that two objectively equal situations can be described (framed) in slightly different ways. This simple difference in framing can have a significant impact on how decisions makers feel about the decision and how they deal with risk (Kahneman & Tversky, 2000). In this case, it is because humans are especially sensitive to loss.

Scenario
A farmer is facing the possibility that a terrible storm could wipe out her crops if it gets to her geographical area. Her options are to harvest the crops now before they have reached maturity, or to wait and take the chance that all the crops will be destroyed. The best estimates are that the storm has a 50% chance of reaching her farm. If she harvests today, the best estimate is that she would retain half the value of what she would get if the storm does not hit and she waits for her crops to reach maturity. Consider the following two alternative ways of framing the decision. Should she:

A. Harvest the crops now to have a sure *savings* of half the value of the crops.
B. Wait and take a 50% chance of *saving* the full value of her crops.

or

C. Harvest the crops now and take a sure *loss* of half their potential value
D. Wait and take a 50% chance of *losing* the full value of her crops.

The options A and B and the options C and D reflect the same objective situations, but C and D are framed in terms of loss while A and B are framed in terms of savings or gain. Logically, there is no reason why people should respond differently to A and B than to C and D, but in fact they do. When decisions such as this are framed in terms of saving, most people (about 80%) choose option A, the sure thing. By sharp contrast, when the options are framed in terms of loss, the preferences reverse and most people (about 80%) choose option D in which they expose themselves to an all-or-nothing kind of risk or gamble (Tversky & Kahneman, 1981).

Daniel Kahneman and Amos Tversky (1979) developed an explanation for this finding in their work on prospect theory. This theory developed from the observation that people have a far more extreme emotional reaction to loss than they do to gain. For example, consider an individual who is given the following offer: You can flip a coin and call it either heads or tales, and if you call it correctly, I will give you $10.00. However, if you call it incorrectly, you will give me $10.00. The individual has a 50% chance of wining $10.00 and a 50% chance of losing $10.00, and the expected value of this bet is zero. Even though the expected value is zero, most people avoid this wager. People tend to recognize that the pain that comes from the loss of $10.00 will not be offset by the pleasure of winning $10.00. In fact, most people require that the deal be sweetened considerably before they are willing to accept the gamble. From a purely rational, economic standpoint, people should be willing to accept a bet that has a positive expected value and thus should get into the gamble as soon as the bet is sweetened at all (e.g., you can win $10.00 if you are right, but you will only lose $9.00 if you are wrong). However, most people do not accept the gamble because of the "loss aversion" that they experience.

Prospect theory explains why most people's preferences reverse across the option pairs A and B and C and D. People tend to avoid risk when the options are framed in terms of gain or savings (options A and B) and thus they take the sure bet (option A). However, when the decision is framed in terms of loss (options C and D), their loss aversion instinct is triggered, and they feel a high motivation to avoid loss. So, as they look at the options, they ask themselves if there is some way to avoid loss altogether. They realize that taking the risk of losing everything also provides them with the possibility of not losing anything at all. Because loss is so bitter, most people decide to take the option that involves risk with the hope that they will be able to eliminate the loss altogether. They consider it worth taking the risk of twice the amount of loss if it frees them from any loss altogether.

This is the kind of dynamic that can get gamblers into trouble as they go "double-or-nothing" (Bazerman, 2006). In hope of wiping out their losses, they expose themselves to greater risk. This is the logic that hedge fund specialist Nick Leesom used at Barrings bank, as described at the beginning of the chapter. Rather than accept a survivable level of loss, he tried desperately to eliminate the loss altogether by making additional risky bets. He dug himself deeper and deeper until he had bankrupted his firm and ruined his personal life.

Member Intervention: There is not an objectively right or wrong way to frame a problem when it comes to loss or gain. However, a group member could at least call attention to whether the group is framing the problem in terms of loss or gain and point out how that might be affecting the group's attitude toward risk. A group member might also explore whether the group would think differently about the issue if it were framed in a different way and then state the alternative way of framing the problem.

Confirmation Bias

When analyzing different possible courses of action, people are vulnerable to the confirmation bias. *Confirmation bias* refers to people's tendency to seek data that confirms what they want to believe or think they already know (Wason, 1960). What people should do instead is seek objective data that would provide a fair "test" of their thinking and that could either validate or invalidate their preconceptions (Einhorn & Hogarth, 1978).

Inventor Example. Consider the scenario depicted in Figure 7.1. An inventor has developed a sophisticated new technology to predict weather. He claims that every time the device has predicted rain, it has rained within 12 hours. Your assignment is to test this claim. Below are weather predictions and outcomes. Each sheet has a prediction on one side and the corresponding outcome on the other side. You are to test the claim that the inventor has made. Which sheets would you most like to turn over in order to test this claim? Please make a decision before reading further (adapted from Einhorn and Hogarth, 1978).

People tend to recognize correctly that Sheet 3 is valuable in testing the claim. If they turn Sheet 3 over and the outcome is that it did not rain, they have invalidated the claim merely by turning over one sheet, and their task is completed. They would now know that the claim that "every time the device has predicted rain, it has rained within 12 hours" is false. The prediction on Sheet 4 "Rain will not fall" is irrelevant to the claim that you have been asked to test, so Sheet 4 is of no value to your task.

People also often think that Sheet 1 has valuable information on the other side. However, it actually is of very little value, and this selection is consistent with idea of the confirmation bias. At best, the reverse side of Sheet 1 will produce one data point of confirming

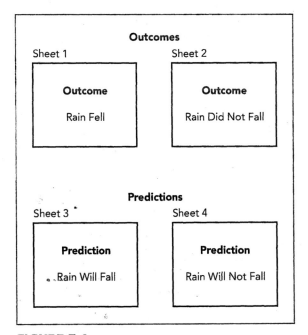

FIGURE 7.1

Source: Adapted from Wason, P. (1960). On the failure to eliminate hypotheses in a conceptual task. *Quarterly Journal of Experimental Psychology*, A12, 129–140.

evidence. Finally, people often do not realize that Sheet 2 is highly valuable. Both Sheet 2 and Sheet 3 have the potential to invalidate the claim and thus complete your task by merely turning over one sheet. If the other side of Sheet 2 has the prediction "rain will fall," then the claim has been invalidated. This example illustrates the confirmation bias.

The confirmation bias is common in the workplace (Bazerman, 2006). For example, a group leader may have an idea that she thinks is good and that she hopes the group will like. Thus, she may say "I think this is a pretty good idea, don't you?" If a few heads nod, she feels free to move forward with it. This behavior may intentionally or unintentionally enact the confirmation bias. An alternative approach that would not enact the confirmation bias would be to ask: "What, if any, reservations does anyone have about this idea?" Similarly, a teacher may hope that he has explained a concept clearly and may enact the confirmation bias by saying to the class: "I think that is clear, isn't it?" If a few heads nod, the teacher may move on. An alternative that would not enact the confirmation bias would be to say: "Is there anyone in class who would like further clarification?"

Member Intervention: Members may assist by reminding the group that the purpose of gathering information is to give a fair test to an idea or solution. This means making sure that the group is open not only to validating their beliefs but also to deliberately uncover any information that would invalidate their beliefs. When someone suggests a way of testing the idea, a group member could ask: "Would that data also tell us if we were wrong?"

Group Polarization

Ideally, group discussion should not create a bias toward taking risks or avoiding risks. Instead, participants should simply use resources available to the group to provide an accurate assessment of risks and liabilities associated with a scenario and make a sensible decision as to how much risk to take. In 1961, James Stoner was conducting research on group decision making at Massachusetts Institute of Technology and discovered that the groups he studied seemed to have a bias toward risk taking. Stoner provided a scenario in which an individual was considering whether to take a new job with attractive possibilities, but a much-less-certain future than his current job. Stoner had participants read a description of the individual and the jobs and then had participants select an option. He compared the options that individuals selected after just reading the scenario with those that were selected after group discussion and found that group discussion led toward greater risk taking. He termed this finding *risky shift*. Below is an example of the kind of approach that Stoner used in setting up this problem. Stoner developed what came to be known as "choice dilemmas" that are illustrated below.

Example

Ms. Sheila Rein is a successful accountant in a large firm. Her job is stable and secure, but it provides little personal or professional satisfaction. She has just been offered a position as Chief Financial Officer of a start-up company that her former college roommate has established. Ms. Rein would have stock options and an opportunity to become rich if the company succeeds. She would also like the excitement of being part of a new venture. However, she is also aware that most new companies fail. If the company fails, she would likely have to give up her home because she does not have enough cash in the bank to keep up the payments based on her savings for much more than about a year. On the other hand, this experience would provide her with an opportunity to learn some new skills that might help her make a bridge to a more engaging job, even if it were not at this company.

You have been requested to advise her on how to proceed. Below is a list of probabilities for success for her new organization. Select the lowest probability for success for the company at which you believe she should take the new position.

- ☐ The chances are 1 in 10 that the company will prove financially sound
- ☐ The chances are 3 in 10 that the company will prove financially sound
- ☐ The chances are 5 in 10 that the company will prove financially sound
- ☐ The chances are 7 in 10 that the company will prove financially sound
- ☐ The chances are 9 in 10 that the company will prove financially sound
- ☐ Place a check here if you believe that Ms. Rein should not take the job no matter what the probabilities for success. (Adapted from Pruitt, 1971)

Further research on group decision making and its effect on risk demonstrated that group discussion does indeed appear to have an effect on the preference for risk taking. However, after conducting a variety of experiments, researchers determined that the shift in preference for risk is not always in the more risky direction. Sometimes discussion leads a group toward greater caution, and sometimes toward greater risk. Thus, the label *group polarization* was developed to identify the finding that, after discussion, group member preferences typically shift more strongly in either a more cautious or more risky direction from where they were prior to the discussion.

What Causes Group Polarization?   Several explanations have been given for group polarization. Some researchers have argued that the phenomenon is driven by the desire to create a positive impression of oneself (Isenberg, 1986). Group members neither want to appear foolhardy nor do they want to appear overly timid. As the group discussion unfolds, the group tends to congeal around a particular level of risk taking, and it becomes more obvious what the appropriate responses are. As the group members who are on the extremes realize that they do not appear to be in the respectable position, they shift away from their initial position toward whatever position the group is leaning in order to appear reasonable.

Other researchers constructed an alternative explanation: the persuasive arguments hypothesis (Lamm, 1988). This hypothesis explains that as the discussion evolves some particularly persuasive arguments or insights emerge and these attractive arguments lead group members to change their mind about their original assessment. They think, *in light of that information, I can see that it is more reasonable to take a more cautious/risky approach.* Both of these explanations have some validity (Isenberg, 1986).

Member Intervention: Group polarization is neither right nor wrong. It is important to consider the breadth of ideas and quality of thought that went into the decision. If the shift occurs for good reasons, it can be fine. Group members may just want to note that the group shifted and assess whether they have good reason for making that shift.

Brainstorming

When a creative solution is desired, brainstorming is often used by groups to enhance the process of developing novel ideas. During brainstorming, group members are supposed to develop as many wild, off-the-wall ideas as they can and are encouraged to build on each other's ideas and not to critique any ideas until the brainstorming process is over (Osborn, 1957). How effective is brainstorming? As we mentioned in Chapter 1, brainstorming tends not to be very effective for generating creative ideas.

According to the theory, a group of four individuals that brainstorms should come up with more creative solutions to a problem than if those four individuals were simply to sit in isolation and write down their most creative ideas. This hypothesis has been tested many times and the individuals that work in isolation and do not brainstorm come up with more creative solutions than the groups that brainstorm (Rietzschel, Nijstad, & Stroebe, 2006).

Why do brainstorming groups fail to generate more creative ideas? There are several reasons. First, brainstorming groups often do not follow the rules for brainstorming. For example, people are supposed to share unconventional, even bizarre ideas; but people tend not to share these ideas due to apprehensiveness about how they might be evaluated (Diehl & Stroebe, 1987). In addition, people are instructed to refrain from criticizing ideas; but they tend to break this rule, and this can increase the apprehensiveness of others in the group.

Another complication has to do with the limited efficiency with which group members can share their ideas verbally without interrupting each other (Deihl & Stroebe, 1991). Fortunately, recent studies have shown that using computers in the brainstorming process helps in overcoming these complications (Paulus & Yang, 2000). When people are online, they can share their thoughts anonymously, which helps to reduce their apprehensiveness. They can also share their ideas more efficiently.

Member Intervention: Members may benefit by using computer technology in the brainstorming process and by creating a sense of acceptance among group members so that they are not apprehensive about sharing their more unusual ideas.

Attribution Error

Decision making often involves some element of diagnosing, evaluating, or explaining the behavior of another person or people. Attribution theory seeks to explain how people make sense of each other's behavior. The theory suggests that people are subject to attributional biases or errors (Kunda, 1999). The fundamental attributional error refers to the finding that, when making sense of other people's behavior, we tend to put too much emphasis on their dispositions or personalities as the explanation of their behavior and not enough attention on the situational factors that may be impacting them (Ross, 1977).

A common task for groups is to decide who should be hired to fill a crucial role in the organization. Naturally, the group will consider the qualities of each candidate and how well the candidate performs in his or her current job. In addition, if the group is to avoid making the fundamental attributional error, they should also consider carefully the context in which the candidate is currently succeeding and the extent to which that context matches the context into which he or she is being hired to work. As an example, Michael Jordan had phenomenal athletic ability that he applied to basketball to become one of the world's greatest players. He and many others thought he could take this athletic ability and apply it with success to baseball. However, they failed to understand that, even though these are both sports, the context is different enough that even with the great athletic ability and motivation of Michael Jordan, it is difficult to transfer ability across contexts. Similarly, just because someone is a great teacher does not mean that he or she will also be a great principal, because the roles call for different sets of skills. Another example is provided by research on stock market analysts who move from one firm to another. Even though the work is similar, it can take analysts years to gain the level of performance within the new firm that they had in their previous firm (Marktino, Douglas, & Harvey, 2006).

Attribution complications appear to affect not only the sense making that groups perform in understanding the behavior of outsiders, but also in understanding the performance of their own group. One study showed that when asked to explain the reasons for effective or ineffective group performance, group members were often not able accurately to diagnose whether the causes were internal (resulting from the group members or leader) or external (resulting from the favorability or unfavorability of the context in which they were operating) (Corn, 2000).

Member Intervention: The key action members can take to avoid the fundamental attributional error is to be highly aware of the context or situation and how that is impacting a person's behavior and performance. A member might say something like: "We seem to be in agreement that Jack is very successful in his current role. Let's compare the similarities and differences between his current role and the role for which we are considering him to determine the extent to which it is a good match for his demonstrated talents."

Groupthink

The topic of groupthink has been frequently written about and discussed. Irving Janis (1972) invented the term to describe a destructive decision-making phenomenon that he observed among high-level political leaders. *Groupthink* is defined as the tendency within a cohesive group to let pressure for building or maintaining consensus block critical thinking and analysis. Janis observed that despite the great amount of resources available to high-level leaders, their decisions have often been of very poor quality. According to Janis, one illustration of groupthink is President Kennedy's participation in planning the Bay of Pigs invasion of Cuba. Kennedy's team grossly overestimated the quality of their decision, and the invasion turned out to be a disaster. Janis also attributed the unproductive escalation of the Viet Nam War and the failure to give adequate attention to protecting American ships in Pearl Harbor to groupthink.

In an effort to understand why these decisions turned out so badly, Janis studied the context in which these decisions occurred and observed a number of contextual characteristics that were shared across these situations. Janis, identified: (1) a number of antecedent conditions that appear to lead to groupthink, (2) a set of symptoms associated with groupthink, and (3) a set of recommendations for avoiding groupthink.

Antecedent Conditions. Janis noted a set of conditions that appeared to contribute to groupthink, including: cohesiveness, insulation, directive leadership, and decisional stress. Group members tend to value the feeling of closeness and unity that they experience when a group becomes cohesive. Thus, members of cohesive groups can become averse to sharing discordant information or publicly disagreeing with the rest of the group. Group members may not openly share criticisms or disagreements for fear of being expelled from groups whose membership they value. For example, being a member of a president's, CEO's, or superintendent's cabinet is prestigious, and members typically do not want to be perceived as unsupportive and thereby risk being pushed out the next time the cabinet is reshuffled. Therefore, they may keep their questions and criticisms to themselves.

The groups that experienced groupthink also tended to be somewhat insulated. They were able to make their decisions without a lot of interference from, or interaction with, outsiders who might bring up different points of view. Janis also noted groups suffering from groupthink often had strong, directive leaders who openly revealed their personal points of view. Rather than act as facilitators who structured their role in a way that encouraged the very best thinking, these leaders let their personal preferences be known. Thus, group members were often stuck in the dilemma of having to choose between being supportive of the leader or engaging in a process of critical thinking and debate. One other characteristic of these groups is that they were typically operating under stressful circumstances. They were making potentially high-stakes decisions, often under time pressure, and these stressful circumstances appear to have contributed to the formation of groupthink.

Symptoms of Groupthink. Janis also observed the following qualities that he described as symptoms of groupthink:

> **Illusion of Invulnerability:** The group develops a sense of invulnerability—that it can do no wrong and that it can vanquish any foe.
> **Inflated Sense of Morality:** The group perceives itself as morally superior to any opponents and to other individuals who are not members of the group.
> **Rationalization:** The group rationalizes or discounts in some way any information that would suggest that it may be wrong.
> **Stereotyping Opponents:** Group members view opponents stereotypically and as inferior morally and otherwise.
> **Self-Censorship:** The group polices itself from getting into controversial topics that could arouse disagreement or contention within the group.
> **Pressure to Conform:** Pressure is exerted on anyone who appears to be straying from the party line.
> **Illusion of Unanimity:** Group members perceive the group to be in greater agreement than they really are.
> **Mindguards:** Individuals within the group take it on themselves to shield the group from information that would disrupt the flow and from individuals who might challenge the thinking of the group or publicly state a dissenting opinion. (Janis, 1972)

Recommendations. Janis identified a set of antecedent conditions that contribute to groupthink, and he identified eight symptoms of groupthink. Given the destructiveness of groupthink, he also wanted to go beyond just identifying and describing this problematic phenomenon. So, he also constructed a set of recommendations that groups and their leaders could put into place in order to avoid groupthink:

> **The Role of Critical Evaluator:** Each member of the group should be assigned the role of critical evaluator. In other words, each member should be informed that the quality of the decision is dependent on each member taking a proactive role in speaking up, sharing concerns, and helping the group face the truth objectively.
> **Impartial Leadership:** Leaders should not reveal their preferences or opinions. Instead, the leader should be impartial and should work to bring out the best thinking and arguments on each side of the issue.
> **Independent Policy-Planning and Evaluation Groups:** Groups that work independently on similar issues should be set up to counterbalance what the focal group is perceiving.

Meet Separately as Subgroups: Periodically, the group should divide into subgroups and meet separately to discuss important issues and form their own opinions. Later the groups can reunite and critically evaluate each other's perspectives.

Report Back to Own Units: Occasionally, team members should report back to their own units on how the group is understanding the situation.

Outside Expert Critique: Experts, or others who can play the role of critical evaluator who are not members of the group, should be invited in.

Devil's Advocate: Someone in the group should be assigned the role of devil's advocate. Devil's advocates are to make the most potent critique of the decision process they can, even if they agree with the decision.

Construct Alternative Scenarios/Interpretations: Especially when dealing with foreign nations or others who might be viewed as enemies, the group should explore alternative explanations or interpretations for what appear to be hostile actions from these others.

Second-Chance Meeting: Even after the group has come to a tentative decision, they should have a second-chance meeting in which they rigorously question and challenge the decision and assumptions they have made before making a final decision to move forward. (Janis, 1972)

In sum, Janis observed that intelligent, hard-working groups at high levels in government sometimes made very poor decisions. He labeled this phenomenon groupthink and made an effort to explain it. He identified several antecedent conditions that appear to contribute to groupthink, and he listed the symptoms associated with it. He also provided an extensive list of actions that policy makers could implement in order to reduce their chances of falling victim to groupthink.

Does the research support Janis's model of groupthink? Although the model seems to have great intuitive appeal and captures a number of potential problems with group decision making, the research has not generally supported the model (Baron, 2005). In short, many of the groups that were subject to the conditions that were proposed to lead to groupthink do not fall prey to it, and many groups that are not subject to those conditions appear to make similarly bad decisions. For example, many highly cohesive groups make excellent decisions despite their cohesiveness. Actually, cohesiveness appears to help when it relates to the task rather than to interpersonal relationships. In other words, groups can be cohesive because they share a desire to accomplish something even if they are not close in terms of personal relationships.

Despite the fact that Janis's model does not consistently predict the emergence of groupthink, he has nonetheless given us helpful concepts to think about and a number of suggestions and potentially useful recommendations for improving decision making.

■ WHO SHOULD MAKE THE DECISION?

So far, we have focused mostly on how the quality of decision making is influenced by the way that group members handle their contribution. Vroom and Yetton (1973) recognized that decision quality is not the only important factor in determining who should make the decision. They argue that both the costs and benefits of involving others should be recognized and that involvement in the decision-making process can also affect other important variables, such as the quality of implementation. Vroom and Yetton developed a framework that uses these variables for determining who should be involved in the decision-making process and what their involvement should be. Thus, this is a normative model—a model that prescribes how managers *should* make decisions.

Importance of Decision Quality

The volume of decisions that need to be made just to keep organizations going is large, and many of them are relatively unimportant and their impact is relatively trivial. So, although no one wants to make even unimportant decisions badly, the relative importance of decisions varies widely and thus the importance of decision quality varies widely. An example of a relatively unimportant decision might be whether to order yellow, green, or blue Post-It notes for the office this month. An example of a more important decision would be whether a private school should take on additional debt in order to develop a new building that might payoff handsomely or flop in terms of attracting additional students.

The more significant the decision, the more important it is to consider what is required to ensure the quality of the decision. Ensuring quality often means making sure that those employees with relevant information provide input. Vroom and Yetton argue that the manager should assess the decision's significance and the importance of decision quality in determining who should be involved in making the decision.

Costs of Collaborative Decision Making

Time is a scarce resource, and professionals typically feel a constant pressure to accomplish more in less time. Addressing a decision as a group means that all those who are involved are allocating time toward a decision at the expense of allocating that time toward doing other things the organization values. In addition, collaborative decision making typically takes longer than having a single manager make the decision. Thus, it prolongs the decision making process. For example, if a manager has a good intuitive sense of what the group wants, and the decision is not likely to have a significant impact on the group, then the manager can resolve things more quickly just by making the decision alone. The alternative might be waiting several weeks until the next monthly meeting before the issue can be discussed by the team and resolved. Or, it might mean taking the time and effort to check everyone's calendar to try to find a convenient meeting time to discuss the issue.

Leaders in organizations often feel immense pressure to push projects forward with speed in order to be effective in today's hypercompetitive market place. Thus, there is no reason to take the extra time to have a group make the decision unless the merits of having their involvement outweigh the costs. Unless something is lost by the manager making the decision alone, the manager should do so. Thus, managers should assess whether valuable information will be lost if members do not participate. Another important consideration is that commitment to the decision and its implementation may be lost if members do not participate in the process.

Commitment

Vroom and Yetton suggest that the manager assess the extent to which the group is likely to feel commitment to the decision. They argue that participation in the decision-making process tends to breed more commitment to the decision. For example, companies occasionally reconfigure the production work space, to make the process more efficient. One way to go about this is to have industrial engineers study the work space, design a new work space, and then reconfigure the workspace while the organization is shut down. Workers come in the next day to a completely new configuration without a clear sense of why it has been laid out this way. An alterative approach would be to have the workers and industrial engineers discuss the options together, each understanding and exploring each other's ideas and then working together to redesign the space and make the changes. As you can imagine, workers in the latter situation are much less likely to resist the changes because they understand them and have participated in their design. Instead, they are more likely to be committed to making the new design work effectively.

Depending on the particular decision, commitment may or may not be a key factor. Sometimes it does not matter whether the group members are committed or not. Consider the decision as to what kind of lighting to have in an office area. The workers may be affected by the alternative that is chosen, but the lighting can be purchased, installed, and function properly whether they feel committed to it or not. Alternatively, consider a situation in which people have a habit of not cleaning up after themselves in the lunchroom. A leader might decide that each employee will be responsible for cleaning up after him- or herself and for washing and stacking any cups and plates that are used, immediately on completing a meal. However, if the employees do not feel committed to the decision, they are likely to ignore it and not comply with the decree. On the other hand, if they are involved in deciding how the problem should be dealt with, they are more likely to be committed to implementing the solution.

Circumstances may also exist under which managers do not need to worry about commitment. For example, if the group has complete trust in its manager, it may be committed even without being involved because it trusts that the manager has taken their interests into account and has done whatever is required to make a high-quality decision. Under other circumstances commitment may be ensured by the organizational circumstances. For example, in the military, a loyal soldier might not feel committed to an order but will execute the order nonetheless because she is a loyal soldier and understands that doing so is her duty.

In sum, involving others in the decision-making process has both costs and benefits. The question of whether the benefits outweigh the costs depends somewhat on the importance of the decision quality, the importance of commitment, and whether commitment is likely to emerge even if the group is not involved in the decision. At the same time, managers have multiple options for involving others or not involving them. Vroom and Yetton developed a continuum of involvement (see Figure 7.2) which has five basic styles for making decisions, each having a different level and method of involving, or not involving, group members.

On the far left in Figure 7.2 is *decide* in which the manager simply makes the decision him- or herself without consulting anyone. This is the most autocratic option. The next two options are consultative, in which the manager seeks input from others but still makes the decision alone. The main difference between *consult individually* and *consult group* is the format for exploring the issue. The former involves the manager exploring the issue with each person individually, whereas the later involves presenting the issue to the group as a whole. The final two options are distinctive in that the group, rather than the manager, makes the decision. In the *facilitator* role, the manager is responsible for defining the decision to be made, structuring a process for making the decision, and for making sure that

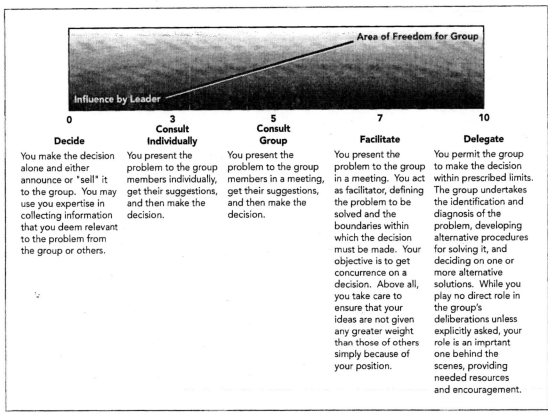

FIGURE 7.2   Levels of Group Participation

Source: Vroom, V. H. (2000). Leadership and the decision making process. *Organizational Dynamics 28*(4), 82–94.

individuals are heard and that their input is given appropriate weight. If the manager *delegates*, he or she passes the full responsibility for structuring the decision-making process and for making the decision to the group.

To help managers sort out how they should decide which style to use, Vroom and Yetton put all the variables together and identified various questions that managers should ask as they work through the various contingencies. Figure 7.3 shows the order in which managers should address the variables. The following lists the variables and the questions that managers should ask as they address each variable. By starting at the left and working toward the right, Figure 7.3 works sort of like a funnel that enables managers to narrow the range of options until they have identified a good fit between the decision styles and the unique circumstances that they face.

Variables and Questions to Ask

Decision significance: To what extent is the quality of the decision highly important to the organization or group?

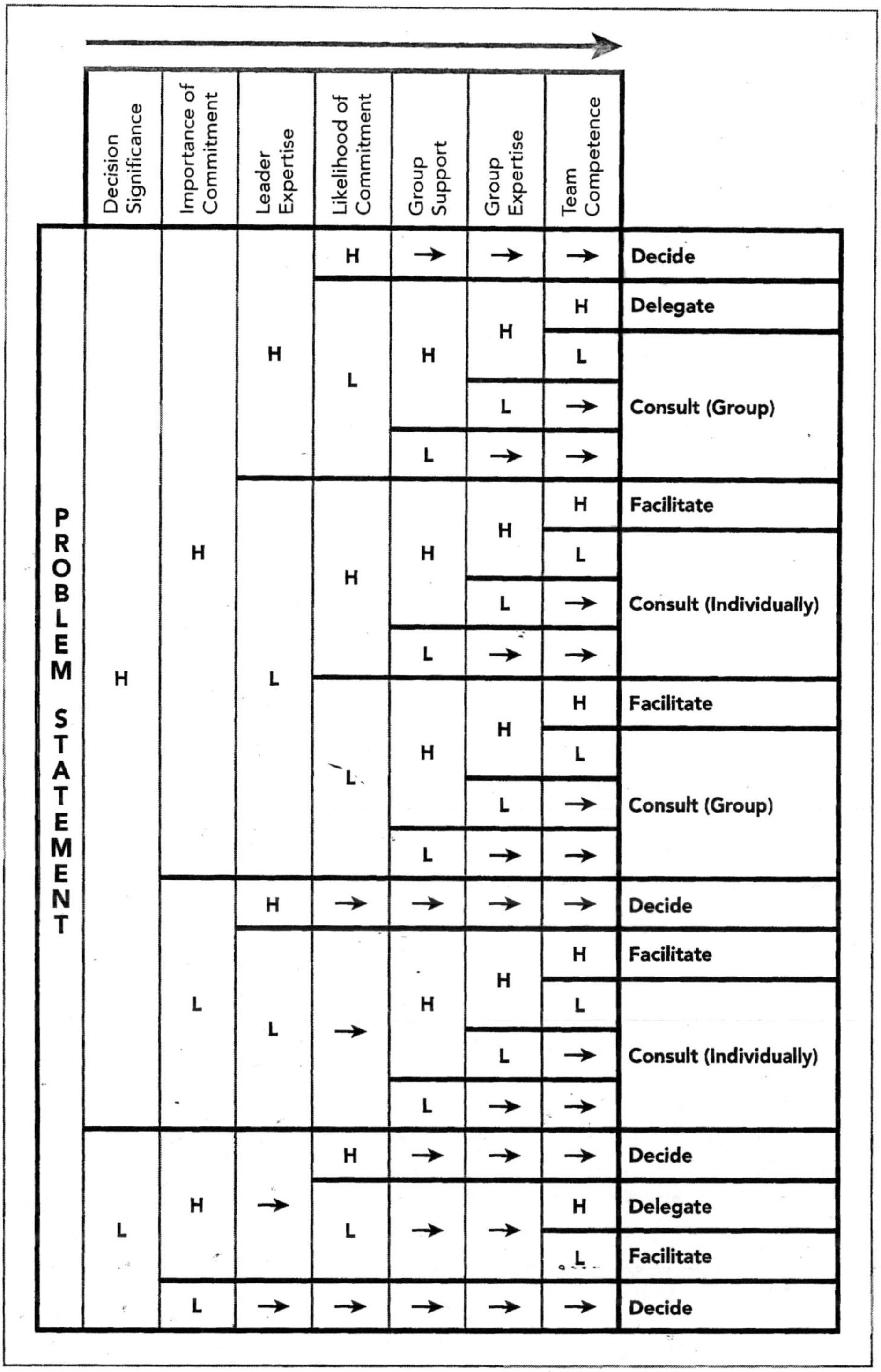

Decision Significance	Importance of Commitment	Leader Expertise	Likelihood of Commitment	Group Support	Group Expertise	Team Competence	
P R O B L E M S T A T E M E N T							
H	H	H	H	→	→	→	Decide
			L	H	H	H	Delegate
						L	Consult (Group)
					L	→	Consult (Group)
				L	→	→	Consult (Group)
		L	H	H	H	H	Facilitate
						L	Consult (Individually)
					L	→	Consult (Individually)
				L	→	→	Consult (Individually)
			L	H	H	H	Facilitate
						L	Consult (Group)
					L	→	Consult (Group)
				L	→	→	Consult (Group)
	L	H	→	→	→	→	Decide
		L	→	H	H	H	Facilitate
						L	Consult (Individually)
					L	→	Consult (Individually)
				L	→	→	Consult (Individually)
L	H	→	H	→	→	→	Decide
			L	→	→	H	Delegate
						L	Facilitate
	L	→	→	→	→	→	Decide

FIGURE 7.3 Vroom and Yetton's Decision-Making Model

Source: Vroom, V. H. (2000). Leadership and the decision making process. Organizational Dynamics 28(4), 82–94.

Importance of commitment: How crucial it is to have the support of the group in implementing this decision?

Leader's expertise: Does the leader have the knowledge and expertise to make the decision effectively by him or herself?

Likelihood of commitment: Is the group likely to support a decision that the manager makes without their involvement?

Group support for objectives: Does the group support the objectives and goals of the group and organization?

Group expertise: Does the group have relevant knowledge or expertise to bring to decision-making process?

Team competence: Is the group able to collaborate effectively in working toward an intelligent decision? (Vroom, 2000)

In sum, Vroom wrestled broadly with the costs and benefits associated with different approaches to decision making. He addressed not only issues of quality, but also questions associated with the time it takes to make a decision and the costs and benefits of having group members participate in the decision-making process. Is Vroom and Yetton's normative model a good source of advice for managers to follow? The research evidence is reasonably supportive of their assertion that using this model will produce better outcomes than deviating from its suggestions (Vroom, 2000).

 OPENING CASE REVISITED

Deciding Asset Allocation at Montgomery Life

Crayton and Bates agreed to experiment with the idea. Prior to the next meeting of Crayton and his staff, each of them recorded their estimates in writing. At the meeting, everyone was given a printout of what each individual had estimated and what the average of all the estimates was. Crayton retained his authority to make the final decision as to what the asset allocation would be. However, there was now objective data being collected over a period of time. Each individual, including Crayton, would come to the next meeting and have a written report that showed their previous estimates and the gap between what they estimated and what would have been ideal. Thus, there was a new form of accountability, and feedback was provided to each individual that had not been collected before. They were now in a better position to reflect on why they may have been right or wrong in their previous estimates, and this provided them with a new opportunity to learning that had not been in place before.

Summary

This chapter examines the assets and liabilities associated with group problem solving and decision making. Groups have greater assets to draw on, such as greater information, memory, and variety of perspectives. However, groups are subject to a number of vulnerabilities. More specifically, groups may suffer from overconfidence, undersampling of unique information, framing, confirmation bias, group polarization, brainstorming limitations, attributional error, group polarization, and groupthink. We have provided a number of suggestions in the *Member Intervention* sections about what group members can do to improve decision making.

We also summarized Vroom and Yetton's framework for deciding who should participate in the decision-making process and what role they should play. Vroom and Yetton introduce a number of considerations, including the importance of decision quality, costs of collaborative decision making, and importance of commitment.

 CONCLUDING CASE

Racial Tensions at Jefferson High

Jefferson High School is an urban high school with over 4,000 students. The principal, Jim Thompson, is a white administrator who has been in the school district for over 25 years and was known as a strict disciplinarian. The majority of teachers and students were white but with significant African American and Hispanic populations. The school had a racial incident earlier in the week when an after school program, the Hip Hop Club, was discontinued. Mr. Thompson thought that the students were engaging in inappropriate discussions about sex and drugs and ended the program.

Parents were extremely upset and demanded an explanation. The program was popular among students and kept them in a safe environment after school. Principal Thompson defended his decision and suggested that hip hop music promoted sexually suggestive behavior. Parents confronted him and accused him of being a racist. They demanded to know why he was so judgmental about rap music and whether or not he had any concrete evidence that teens were engaging in sexual behavior. Had he attended the club? Had he talked to students about the music? Did he really understand the slang and culture of rap music? They were adamant that he reconsider his decision until he had more facts.

As the week progressed, students and faculty became more divided along racial lines. Tensions were rising and the district office was brought in to resolve the problem. A district administrator, Sandy Coleman, convened a meeting with the principal, assistant principal, three outspoken parents, and three faculty members to discuss the issue. This group had to decide what to do about the future of the Hip Hop Club and, more importantly, what to do about the racial tensions in the school.

Discussion Questions

1. If you were Sandy Coleman, how would you open up the meeting under these conditions?
2. Speculate on how the school became so polarized on this issue.
3. Who should make the decision about the status of the Hip Hop Club?
4. How can the group help resolve the tensions at Jefferson High?

Exercise   Who Gets Laid Off?

Form groups of four to six students for the following task. You are a group of middle managers in an electrical wholesale company that sells electrical equipment to contractors and electricians. You inventory most of what you sell and have a retail counter to handle walk-in customers in addition to an outside sales force. Sales have been declining since a national competitor moved into the area two years ago and it requires you to lay off at least two employees. Rank the following employees in the order in which you would lay them off.

Bob is a new salesperson that has been with the company for only six months. He was hired from a competitor but feels the company has not made good on the promises that were made to him. He has been very outspoken and frequently complains about management. While he seems to bring in a significant amount of new business, he is having a negative effect on morale among the other outside salespeople. He is arrogant and treats other employees poorly.

Julio has been working in the warehouse for 15 years. He never complains, is always on time, and works hard. But he has just turned 55 and is not able to keep up the pace he used to due to increasing physical limitations. There isn't another place in the company where his skills could be used due to his limited English proficiency. He smiles a lot and seems to be liked by everyone.

Mary is the receptionist who has been handling the fairly significant phone traffic for nine years. While other administrative assistants cover for her when she goes to lunch or takes a day off, she is the primary person who answers the phone. She is a single mom who misses about one day a week due to issues with her children, one of whom is a special needs child with a physical disability. The company has been exploring the possibility of purchasing an automated phone answering system that would make her job obsolete.

Pete works at the counter and has a good relationship with many of the contractors who come in. He spends a lot of time socializing with them but doesn't do a lot of work. The customers seem to like him and even talk about going fishing together on the weekends. He has worked as an electrician and knows the business extremely well and does some moonlighting on the side. But he doesn't work very hard and has a habit of telling other employees what to do.

Pam is another worker at the counter. She doesn't know the electrical business as well as Pete, but is one of the hardest-working people in the company. Whenever there are no customers, she is busy cleaning up the warehouse shelves or organizing the counter area. She only has a few years with the company but rumor has it that she's been dating the president of the company. Pam is a team player but with limited skills.

References

Allen, N. J., & Hecht, T. D. (2004). The "romance of teams": Toward an understanding of its psychological underpinnings and implications. *Journal of Occupational and Organizational Psychology, 77,* 439–461.

Baron, R. S. (2005). So right it's wrong: Groupthink and the ubiquitous nature of polarized group decision making. In M. P. Zanna (Ed.), *Advances in experimental social psychology, Volume 37* (pp. 219–253). San Diego, CA: Elsevier Academic Press.

Bazerman, M. (2006). *Judgment in managerial decision making* (6th ed.). Hoboken, NJ: John Wiley & Sons.

Beach, L. R., & Connolly, T. (2005). *The psychology of decision making.* Thousand Oaks, CA: Sage.

Bolman, L. G., & Deal, T. E. (2003). *Reframing organizations: Artistry, choice and leadership* (3rd ed.). San Francisco: Jossey Bass.

Cooper, A. C., Woo, C. Y., & Dunkelberg, W. C. (1988). Entrepreneurs' perceived chances for success. *Journal of Business Venturing, 3,* 97–108.

Corn, R. (2000). *Why poor teams get poorer: The influence of team effectiveness and design quality on the quality of group diagnostic processes.* Unpublished doctoral dissertation, Harvard University.

Diehl, M., & Stroebe, W. (1987). Productivity loss in brainstorming groups: Toward the solution of a riddle. *Journal of Personality and Social Psychology, 53,* 497–509.

Diehl, M., & Stroebe, W. (1991). Productivity loss in idea-generating groups: Tracking down the blocking effect. *Journal of Personality and Social Psychology, 61,* 392–403.

Einhorn, H. J., & Hogarth, R. M. (1978). Confidence in judgment: Persistence in the illusion of validity. *Psychological Review, 85,* 395–416.

Isenberg, D. (1986). Group polarization: A critical review and meta-analysis. *Journal of personality and social psychology, 50*(6), 1141–1151.

Janis, I. L. (1972). *Victims of groupthink: A psychological study of foreign-policy decisions and fiascoes.* Boston: Houghton Mifflin.

Juslin, P., Winman, A., & Olsson, H. (2000). Naïve empiricism and dogmatism in confidence research: A critical examination of the hard-easy effect. *Psychology Review, 107,* 384–396.

Kahneman, D., & Tversky, A. (1979). Prospect theory: An analysis of decision under risk. *Econometrica, 47,* 263–291.

Kahneman, D., & Tversky, A. (Eds.). (2000). *Choices, values, and frames.* Cambridge, England: Cambridge University Press.

Kerr, N. L., & Tindale, R. S. (2004). Group performance and decision making. *Annual Review of Psychology, 55,* 623–655.

Kunda, Z. (1999). *Social cognition: Making sense of people.* Cambridge, MA: MIT Press.

Lamm, H. (1988). A review of our research on group polarization: Eleven experiments on the effects of group discussion on risk acceptance, probability estimation, and negotiation positions. *Psychological Reports, 62,* 807–813.

Martinko, M. J., Douglas, S. C., & Harvey, P. (2006). Attribution theory in industrial and organizational psychology: A review. In G. P. Hodgkinson & J. K. Ford (Eds.), *International review of industrial and organizational psychology 2006, Volume 21* (pp. 171–175). Chichester, England: John Wiley & Sons.

McGuigan, T. (2006). The difficulty of selecting superior mutual fund performance. *Journal of Financial Planning, 19,* 50–56.

Medvec, V. H., Berger, G., Liljenquist, K., & Neale, M. A. (2004). Is a meeting worth the time? Barriers to effective group decision-making in organizations. In S. Blount (Ed.) *Research on managing groups and teams volume 6: Time in groups* (pp. 213–233). Oxford, England: Elsevier.

Michaelson, L. K., Watson, W. E., & Black, R. H. (1989). A realistic test of individual versus group consensus decision making. *Journal of Applied Psychology, 74,* 834–839.

Moreland, R. L., & Argote, L. (2003). Transactive memory in dynamic organizations. In R. Peterson & E. Mannix (Eds.), *Understanding the dynamic organizations* (pp. 135–162). Mahwah, NJ: Erlbaum.

Nutt, P. C. (1999). Surprising but true: Half of the decisions in organizations fail. *Academy of Management Executive, 13*(4), 75–90.

Osborn, A. F. (1957). *Applied imagination.* New York: Scribner.

Paulus, P., & Yang, H. (2000). Idea generation in groups: A bias for creativity in organizations. *Organizational Behavior and Human Decision Processes, 82,* 76–87.

Plous, S. (1993). *The psychology of judgment and decision making.* New York: McGraw Hill.

Pruitt, D. G. (1971). Choice shifts in group discussion: An introductory review. *Journal of Personality and Social Psychology, 20,* 339–360.

Stasser, G., & Titus, W. (1985). Pooling of unshared information in group decision making: Biased information sampling during discussion. *Journal of Personality and Social Psychology, 48,* 1467–1478.

Suroweicki, J. (2004). *The wisdom of crowds: Why the many are smarter than the few and how collective wisdom shapes business, economies, societies, and nations.* New York: Double Day.

Rietzschel, E. F., Nijstad, B. A., & Stroebe, W. (2006). Productivity is not enough: A comparison of interactive and nominal brainstorming groups on idea generation and selection. *Journal of Experimental Social Psychology, 42,* 244–251.

Ross, L. (1977). The intuitive psychologist and his shortcomings: Distortions in the attribution process. In L. Berkowitz (Ed.), *Advances in experimental social psychology* (Vol. 10, pp. 174–214). New York: Academic Press.

Tversky, A., & Kahneman, D. (1981). The framing of decisions and the psychology of choice. *Science 211,* 453–463.

Vroom, V. H. (2000). Leadership and the decision-making process. *Organizational Dynamics, 28,* 82–94.

Vroom, V. H., & Yetton, P. W. (1973). *Leadership and decision-making.* Pittsburg, PA: University of Pittsburg Press.

Wason, P. (1960). On the failure to eliminate hypotheses in a conceptual task. *Quarterly Journal of Experimental Psychology, A12,* 129–140.

Weick, K. (2001). *Making sense of the organization.* Oxford, England: Blackwell Publishers.

CHAPTER EIGHT

Diversity in Groups

▓ INTRODUCTION

Effective group problem solving requires creativity in identifying, describing, and proposing possible solutions to complex and often ill-defined problems. Groups that value and promote diversity of thought, experience, and knowledge can be more effective at accomplishing goals when members feel free to offer divergent perspectives and ideas. Unfortunately, many groups are reluctant to enter into controversy and prefer to stay within the safe zone of conformity. This chapter describes characteristics of healthy group dynamics where differences are valued and creativity is nurtured.

LEARNING OBJECTIVES

After reading this chapter, you should be able to

- Describe various types of diversity in groups.
- Detail three perspectives on diversity within organizations.
- Describe the positive and negative effects of diversity on group performance.
- Recognize and overcome the five typical dysfunctions of groups and teams.

 OPENING CASE

Team Tensions at Summer School

Debangshu spent a summer at a community organization designed to provide inner-city public middle school students with an academically rich experience that will prepare them for success. The organization was relatively small (30 staff members), relatively new (begun in 1999), and quite complex. They not only provided children with extra classes in humanities, math, and science, but they also provided volunteers with real-world teaching experience. Most of the volunteer teachers were college students who were interested in the fields of education or community activism.

Debangshu's particular situation revolved around himself, his teaching partner, Laura, and their team leader, Eddie. Debangshu and Laura were team teaching a civil-rights curriculum. Laura was a white female who had gone to private school. Her background made it difficult for her to approach students comfortably. Because most of the students were public school students of color, she claimed that she felt misjudged by them.

Communication between Debangshu and Laura was strained at best. They would frequently argue about philosophical pedagogy issues. Interpersonal conflicts made it difficult for them to approach the students as a unified team. In addition, both of them were new to teaching and neither had prior experience with lesson planning or disciplining children. As a result, the summer campers were confused by the inconsistent responses they received, and they reacted by misbehaving. Their misbehavior caught Eddie's attention to the point that he had to call a meeting to address the issue.

In the meeting with Debangshu and Laura, Eddie asked how they thought things were going. They both agreed that things were not going well. Debangshu described their communication as inefficient and awkward. He told Eddie that he felt uncomfortable being direct and honest with Laura because of how she might take it. Debangshu asked Eddie if he would be willing to facilitate a conversation between them to which he agreed. In the mediated conversation, Debangshu told Laura that although he respected her positions on education, she did not need to be so domineering in order to get her ideas across. Debangshu also told Laura that he did not feel respected by her. He even had a hard time looking directly into her eyes when he made that comment. Debangshu then asked Eddie if he could propose a solution to their interpersonal dilemma.

Eddie asked Laura how she felt about what Debangshu had said. She began to cry. She said that she felt uncomfortable around the camp participants because she was white. She also said this was her first experience being the minority. Eddie responded by giving her a box of tissues and being very supportive. He said that a good educator must acknowledge his or her own privileges and asked both Laura and Debangshu to do the same. Both of them agreed to do this and spoke briefly about their backgrounds and educational experiences. At the end of the session, Laura and Debangshu hugged and seemed to establish a new level of trust and understanding.

Discussion Questions

1. What are your reactions to this case?
2. What issues of diversity and group dynamics are salient?
3. In what specific ways do you think the interpersonal problems between Debangshu and Laura affected their performance?
4. If you were the team leader, how would you handle this situation?

With changing demographics in the United States, organizations are becoming more diverse (Hays-Thomas, 2004). In addition to this trend, members of organizations are working closer together in teams and work groups. The confluence of these demographic and organizational trends presents both a challenge and an opportunity as people work with others who may be different from themselves. Increased diversity in work teams creates the possibility of increased productivity due to the benefit of multiple perspectives and skill sets. However, it can also lead to difficulty fostering trust, cohesion, and a shared identity. Group researchers have long observed that member similarity, or homogeneity, produces higher levels of cohesion (Mannix & Neale, 2005). Individual differences, or heterogeneity, make it more difficult to create a sense of commitment and trust in the group. To realize the benefits of diversity, groups must overcome an initial tendency for differences to divide. A whole industry of training professionals and consultants has emerged in the last two decades to help organizations minimize problems and maximize potential benefits of a diverse workforce. This chapter will examine the benefits, as well as the challenges, of diversity in work teams. And because this book is targeted toward practitioners, we will also provide strategies and suggestions to reap the rewards of diversity.

Although there has been a wealth of research conducted on diversity and its effects on the workforce, the results have been inconsistent (Jackson, Joshi, & Erhard, 2003). Some studies have shown that certain types of diversity reduce performance even when implemented properly. Other studies have shown that both personal motivation and group performance increase due to diversity. Diversity is a complex issue that affects organizations in various ways, both positive and negative. Not all forms of diversity foster positive relationships or organizational effectiveness. Yet diversity has the potential to bring innovative and fresh perspectives to complex problems and stagnant systems.

For the purpose of this text, *diversity* will mean difference or variety. According to Milliken and Martins (1996), organizations are operating in a more multicultural and multinational context where differences and variety are commonplace. Due to the global marketplace, the frequency with which employees will interact with persons of diverse backgrounds will inevitably increase (Milliken & Martins, 1996). For these reasons, it is particularly important to understand how diversity affects organizations.

Recent trends have shown that work teams have become popular within many successful organizations (Milliken & Martins, 1996). Cross-functional work teams coordinate and manage tasks and projects in organizations by increasing the amount of time employees spend with people outside of their particular product group (Milliken & Martins, 1996). These functionally diverse groups have an ability to generate a wider range of perspectives and come up with higher-quality solutions than nondiverse groups (O'Reilly, Caldwell, & Barnett, 1989). This same study also showed that greater diversity is linked to less integrated workgroups and higher levels of member dissatisfaction.

■ TYPES OF DIVERSITY

Visible Demographic Differences

On one level, all human beings are unique and, therefore, diverse or different from each other. In order to identify general differences between people, diversity researchers have classified these differences as visible and nonvisible (Milliken & Martins, 1996). Visible forms of diversity include characteristics such as race, age, and gender, while nonvisible differences include individual differences such as education, socioeconomic background, personality, and values. The distinction is important because different types of diversity affect groups differently. Thus, a mixed gender group from different nationalities and languages will experience diversity differently than a group of middle class, white, male executives with backgrounds in engineering, marketing, accounting, and human resources. Visible differences tend to have less favorable group outcomes than nonvisible differences (Mannix & Neale, 2005). Yet, those outcomes are moderated by the work environment within which the groups operate (Jehn & Bezrukova, 2004). For example, virtual groups can minimize the negative effects of diversity since members might not see each other and make assumptions based on visible differences. In some virtual groups, all that is observed about others is a name and the quality of their work.

Nonvisible differences can be further divided into characteristics that are more psychological in nature and functional differences related to work and occupation (Jackson & Ruderman, 1995). Table 8.1 describes three types of diversity that can exist within organizations.

Personality Differences

Personality differences include those psychological traits and characteristics that make people unique. Much of the research on personality characteristics uses the big five model of personality. The big five model is a well-established conceptual framework for psychological research that measures individuals on five dimensions: conscientiousness, agreeableness, openness, neuroticism, and extroversion (Halfhill, Sundstrom, Lahner, Calderone, & Nielson, 2005). All the variables except neuroticism are positively correlated to group effectiveness. Neuroticism, or emotional instability, is negatively correlated to group effectiveness.

Occupational/Functional Differences

Functional differences are often used to influence the composition of work groups. For example, a team leader might want someone on the team who is technologically savvy if she wants to utilize regular virtual meetings. That specialized training and knowledge fills a need for the group. Furthermore, there has been a trend toward cross-functional or vertical work groups because of the varied perspectives members bring to groups. Within schools, vertical teams often include administrators, teachers, and staff members.

Visible demographic differences have been the most difficult issues to deal with in organizational life. With the diversification of the workforce over the last few decades, demographic changes have been challenging for organizations. People are generally more comfortable with those who are similar to them (Mannix & Neale, 2005). This being the

TABLE 8.1   Types of Diversity in Organizations

Types of Diversity	Examples
Demographic differences	Race, ethnicity, gender, age
Personality differences	Personal beliefs, goals, past experiences, personality, interpersonal style, attitudes
Functional differences	Training, work experience, education, knowledge, skills

case, those similarities that are observed on the surface can either give a person a sense of security or a cause for concern. Internal working models, those perceptual frameworks that interpret incoming data, contain core beliefs about self and others that include characteristics or schemas that define general categories of people. Internal representations have been formed from past experiences and sociocultural forces. Categories that are most visible (race, gender, age, and ethnicity) are associated with specific characteristics that are projected onto others who are perceived to belong to that category. Exercise 8.1 helps uncover the many assumptions we make about various categories of people.

Exercise 8.1   **Uncovering Assumptions**

Write down the first two or three characteristics that come to mind when you look at the following categories of people. There are no right or wrong answers. Please do not censor or screen your responses. Write down the first things that come to your mind.

Characteristics of people in the following occupations:

Teachers	Janitors
Accountants	Secretaries
Lawyers	Nurses
Salespeople	

Characteristics of the following types of people:

Extroverts	Depressed
Open-minded	Ambitious

Characteristics of the following groups of people:

Men	Hispanics
Women	Blacks
Japanese	Whites
French	Asians
British	

There is really no way to escape the classification of others based on certain perceived characteristics or labels. This is how people quickly assess incoming data and make sense of life experiences. Based on personal experiences, the perspectives of friends and family, or images from the media, people construct beliefs about specific groups of people that tend to be overly simplistic and over generalized. When people are categorized by visible characteristics, judgments can be unconscious and unfair. For this reason, demographic differences regarding race, ethnicity, and gender can be the most challenging for teams to overcome.

Cultural Differences

Certain groups of people may, indeed, have similar characteristics. Members of various familial, geographic, or professional cultures share similar values, beliefs, and attitudes. Not everyone in a cultural group holds to the exact same beliefs in a consistent manner, but a common worldview helps maintain a sense of community and facilitates mutual understanding and communication. Trompenaars and Hampden-Turner (1998) identify a number of cultural differences in the way business is conducted. A survey of over 15,000 participants in 30 companies spanning 50 different countries yielded different approaches toward relationships, attitudes about time, and perceptions of the environment. The way members of a certain culture engage in business relationships can be described in terms of universalism versus particularism, individualism versus collectivism, neutral versus emotional, specific versus diffuse, and achievement versus ascription.

Universalism versus *particularism* describes the degree to which members adhere to societal norms and values. A universalist believes in absolute and universal rules, while a particularist is more contextual and willing to bend rules and give special treatment. *Individualism* versus *communitarianism* describes whether people define themselves primarily as individuals or members of a group. Individualists give priority to the individual, while communitarians regard the community as more important than any one person. Cultures define the appropriate level of emotion in normal interpersonal transactions in the dimension of *neutral* versus *emotional*. *Specific* versus *diffuse* describes the degree to which members include their personal lives in business relationships. Some cultures are task oriented (specific) and require little in the way of relationship building while others (diffuse) require people to share their lives with each other and welcome social connectedness. Finally, *achievement* versus *ascription* defines the criteria for status. Achieved status focuses on doing (specific achievements) whereas ascribed status is afforded on the basis of being (age, education, profession).

Attitudes toward time and environment are additional dimensions that differentiate cultural influences on individual worldviews. Cultures with a past orientation value tradition and time-tested institutions and procedures. In contrast, a future orientation attempts to create a more desirable future by being progressive, innovative, and idealistic. Present oriented cultures tend to minimize the value of tradition and do not necessarily strive to improve the future but, instead, focus on current activities and enjoyments. In addition to these general orientations to time are norms regarding the role that time plays in daily life. In some cultures, for example, a 3:00 appointment should start exactly on time, while in other cultures it might mean anytime between 3:00 and 3:30.

Finally, cultures have different attitudes toward the environment or natural world. Some cultures attempt to control the environment, while others view it as something with which to live in harmony. Cultures with a controlling orientation tend to be domineering and feel they have the power to influence the events of life. Cultures with a cooperative orientation understand events to be the product of powerful natural or supernatural forces worthy of our respect. Plausibility structures exist to explain good and bad events such as a booming economy or a catastrophic earthquake. Certain explanations place the locus within human control related to effort and ability, while others attribute the locus of control to external forces such as fate, luck, or a divine force.

People from diverse cultures and backgrounds have different ways of seeing the world, making sense out of life experiences, and solving problems. These differences can be beneficial to group performance. However, members of certain groups may be negatively evaluated and devalued based on visible characteristics. According to Mannix and Neale (2005), people have a greater tendency to attribute positive characteristics toward their own group and associate negative characteristics toward other groups. Over time, minority-group members might learn to distrust majority-group members creating a less than optimal working environment. As a result, diversity can have a significant effect on a number of group processes including communication, member satisfaction, cohesion, commitment, and decision making (Milliken & Martins, 1996).

▓ PERSPECTIVES ON DIVERSITY

With today's workforce becoming increasingly diverse, employees are finding themselves working with people who are different. This can be an asset to work groups or a liability depending on the perspectives of members themselves. Ely and Thomas (2001) studied three culturally diverse, professional-services firms and identified three perspectives that members held toward diversity: (1) an integration-and-learning perspective, (2) an access-and-legitimacy perspective, or (3) a discrimination-and-fairness perspective. They also found that the specific perspective or justification for embracing diversity had a significant effect on individual and group functioning.

Organizations pursue the diversification of their workforce for a number of reasons. These reasons may be explicitly stated publicly or demonstrated tacitly through work processes and human-resource practices. The integration-and-learning perspective maintains that the insights, skills, and experiences of employees from different cultural groups are valuable resources (Ely & Thomas, 2001). These resources allow work groups to re-think their markets, products, and strategies and improve their effectiveness. Essentially, diversity creates adaptive change and is a resource for learning.

According to the access-and-legitimacy perspective, diversity is based on the initial recognition that an organization's markets and customers are diverse. Therefore, it is a good marketing decision to hire minority employees to gain legitimacy and insight into those markets. For example, automobile manufacturers have benefited from putting women on design teams for products targeted toward women (Jackson & Ruderman, 1995). Work groups that adopt the access-and-legitimacy perspective use diversity to more effectively understand and appeal to specific market segments (Ely & Thomas, 2001).

The discrimination-and-fairness perspective espouses the belief that diversity in the workforce is a moral necessity. A diverse workforce ensures that there is fair treatment for underrepresented minorities; diversification initiatives provide opportunities in hiring and promotion. Organizations are obviously concerned about the legal ramifications of discrimination and the effects of negative public press (Jackson & Ruderman, 1995). In this perspective, diversification plays a proactive role in overcoming prejudice and stopping discrimination. A diverse work force serves as evidence of just and fair treatment of employees (Ely & Thomas, 2001). As a result, programs such as affirmative action and hiring quotas attempt to bring demographic parity to employee composition.

Interestingly, only the integration-and-learning perspective was found to have positive effects on both the work group as a whole and minority members in particular (Ely & Thomas, 2001). As a result of adopting the integration-and-learning perspective in a small, well-diversified law firm, employees of color felt valued and were treated with respect. Almost everyone in the firm commented on the personal and professional growth they felt because of their approach to diversity. In addition, the organization changed their work practices. They chose to staff law cases with two attorneys, one of whom was a person of color, in order to garner a better perspective on the case. Such action enabled people to engage in various forms of cross-cultural discourse. In fact, cultural discourse had become a central competence to how the organization operated (Ely & Thomas, 2001).

Ely and Thomas (2001) found the access-and-legitimacy perspective at work in a financial services firm that contained two departments in its sales division. One department, retail operations, serviced the banking needs of a predominantly black, working-class, urban clientele in the local surrounding neighborhood. The other department, external deposits, serviced the banking needs of a predominantly white, affluent, national clientele. The staffs of the two departments from the lowest- to the highest-ranking employees mirrored the clientele they serviced. And just like the clientele they served, the two departments were fairly segregated themselves. Managers of both departments felt it was legitimate to have their staffing reflect the racial composition of their customers. It would be inappropriate for a predominantly white bank to service a black neighborhood. Similarly, minority-owned banks have not faired well with a predominantly white clientele and are not perceived favorably (Ely & Thomas, 2001).

Unfortunately, blacks felt limited in terms of their role and influence in the organization. Outside of retail sales, the organization was guided by a predominantly white cultural identity in which people of color had limited access and ability to contribute. Since whites retained positions of influence in the larger organization, the culture of the firm did not change and remained consistent with the previous dominant culture. In fact, most workers believed that upper- and middle-class white culture dictated how they were supposed to do their work. Specifically, the access-and-legitimacy perspective did not work to empower minorities because it only focused on placing minorities in strategic positions that established credibility with a specified customer base. Minority perspectives were not represented in the larger organization beyond retail sales (Ely & Thomas, 2001).

The discrimination-and-fairness perspective was identified by Ely and Thomas (2001) in a nonprofit, international planning and consulting firm that focused on urban economic development. Traditionally, the organization was predominantly white, but for the 15 years prior to the study, they had embarked on an aggressive affirmative action plan designed to increase the number of women and people of color employed at the firm. At the time of the study, 63% of the support staff, 42% of middle managers/professionals, and 31% of the senior managers were people of color. The firm was committed to eliminate discrimination and establish equality and measured success through recruitment and retention goals. Committees were established to police the firm for sexism and racism and to advocate for minorities but had little to do with the actual work of the firm.

With its emphasis on equality, the consulting firm developed two norms. First, employees were encouraged to be color blind and suppress any differences that may exist. This norm created an aversion to differences and potential conflict. Employees received clear messages from management that conflict was potentially dangerous and should be avoided. In turn, minorities were forced to assimilate to white cultural standards. Unfortunately, minority staff members who believed their ideas were important could not openly espouse their views due to the norms and values related to the discrimination-and-fairness perspective (Ely & Thomas, 2001). Furthermore, employees were nearly unanimous in their negative assessment of race relations in the firm. People of all races described relations between whites and African American employees, specifically, as tense, cynical, hostile, and distrustful and their own feelings as disappointed and hopeless. Part of the underlying tension revolved around the fear of being accused of being racist in any decision or confrontation. This created a superficial and precarious situation in which honest feedback and meaningful communication could not take place. Consequently, minority employees were left without adequate supervision or coaching. When underperforming employees were disciplined or fired, fears were confirmed and the system was reinforced.

These findings suggest that the integration-and-learning perspective is the most effective in enhancing group dynamics and ensuring that minority individuals feel empowered (Ely & Thomas, 2001). Employees who were part of an organization that held the integration-and-learning perspective reported feeling valued and respected by their colleagues in addition to being able to espouse their opinions without the threat of being silenced. Overall, there were general feelings of well-being among all employees within the organization.

Organizations that do try to diversify may fail because they create a culture that is not optimally conducive to group effectiveness (Mannix & Neale, 2005). Hiring and retaining minority employees is an honorable goal for organizations who want to eradicate racism and discrimination. But an unintended consequence of this philosophy is to create an environment of distrust and compliance with legal mandates and company policies. Similarly, when organizations employ minorities to symbolically legitimize diverse markets, there is little room for genuine minority involvement and for the appreciation of differences. Other organizations go further by hiring minorities because they can provide insight into the buying habits and interests of diverse customers. However, such a perspective segregates minorities to only a few departments within a company for a specific purpose. The most progressive reason for diversity is the integration-and-learning perspective whereby insights, skills, and opinions of diverse employees are shared among the organization so that work groups can change their primary way of thinking. Such a perspective provides both dominant members and minorities with a chance to learn from each other and makes diversity a resource for growth and adaptive change (Ely & Thomas, 2001).

Even with the right perspective, strategic implementation of diversity policy and practice is imperative for ongoing learning and group effectiveness (Whitt, Edison, Pascarella, Terenzini, & Amuray, 2001). According to Whitt, et al. (2001), efforts to promote diversity should be varied and encompass all facets of organizational life. Furthermore, a developmental approach that promotes trust and openness can help members of the organization talk openly about the difficulties of a diverse workplace. A safe and supportive context will allow members to express their frustrations and personal opinions. Finally, organizations must continuously assess and improve on their commitment to fostering a climate of diversity.

OUTCOMES OF GROUP DIVERSITY

The research is mixed as to the effects of diversity on group effectiveness (Ely & Thomas, 2001; Mannix & Neale, 2005; van Knippenberg, De Dreu, & Homan, 2004). In an attempt to synthesize the research on this topic, Milliken and Martins (1996) surveyed the literature in 13 leading management journals between 1989 and 1994 and found 34 studies related to diversity in organizational settings. Most of the studies looked at the influence of visible demographic characteristics (race, ethnicity, gender, and age) and functional differences (educational background, occupational history, job-related knowledge and skills) on group performance. Very few studies have focused on the effects of personality differences within organizational groups. In general, the majority of results indicate that diversity at all levels has the potential to increase the effectiveness of work groups, but also poses a threat to the relational connectedness and satisfaction of group members. People tend to be more comfortable and enjoy being with those who are most similar to them. But groups that are diverse have a greater potential for success especially with tasks that require innovation and creativity.

Cognitive Outcomes and Task Performance

Diversity has been linked to a number of positive advantages within organizations (Milliken & Martins, 1996). Ethnicity and nationality have been shown to improve the quality of ideas and the amount of group cooperation on complex tasks. It is assumed that these positive outcomes emerge from the fact that heterogeneous groups will be able to offer a greater variety of perspectives, eventually leading to more realistic and sophisticated ways to analyze issues, make decisions, and solve problems. Ethnic diversity initially has negative effects on group outcomes due to the lower levels of initial attraction. However, after an initial stage of conflict through which the group achieves integration, ethnic diversity can garner a plethora of perspectives among the group (O'Reilly, et al., 1989).

Gender diversity has been linked to higher personal productivity for women when there are high-level female executives present in the organization. Gender diversity produces a positive effect due to the symbolic significance of that diversity for stakeholders. If women perceive that career advancement is a realistic goal as evidenced by the success of other women, they will work harder to obtain it if that is of personal interest.

In relation to communication, studies suggest that diverse groups communicate more formally and more frequently with members outside of their work group (Milliken & Martins, 1996). Although decreased communication within their own group may be a slight drawback, the entire group ultimately benefits from the communication with non-group members. The entire group gains valuable information and resources from people both within and outside the organization. This increases the range of perspectives and the number and quality of ideas. There were not many significant results found regarding age diversity and its effects on group performance other than age was negatively related to the frequency of communications that occurred (Milliken & Martins, 1996).

Results for both functional and educational diversity are not consistent across various work contexts. Studies show some benefits at the board, top management, and organizational task-group levels. Groups that are more functionally diverse have better links to external networks, thereby allowing them to have greater access to outside information. But cross-functional teams also have greater process losses because of different ways of approaching tasks and projects. These groups need more communication and coordination of efforts to work collaboratively. For example, engineers might have a very different way of working in comparison to advertising professionals. They may be working on the same project but coming from very different professional cultures. In general, though, occupational and industry diversity produces more varied perspectives that are used to make decisions and solve problems (Milliken & Martins, 1996).

Affective Outcomes and Relational Connection

In general, members who are different from their work groups in terms of race and ethnicity were found to be less committed to their organizations, less inclined to stay there, and more likely to be absent (Milliken & Martins, 1996). Furthermore, minority members have lower levels of group identification, lower levels of member satisfaction, and are more likely to be evaluated negatively by their supervisors. Results on racial diversity indicate that minorities within organizations experience less positive emotional responses from their organizations as compared to their white colleagues. In addition, they are more likely to be negatively reviewed by superiors. Lower attachment rates and lower performance ratings lead to an increase in turnover among minority workers.

Clear evidence also shows that skill-based diversity incurs more coordination costs than skill-based homogeny (Milliken & Martins, 1996). It takes more effort to coordinate the work of members who have different skill sets and functional backgrounds. Consequently, functional diversity has been linked to higher turnover rates and lower social integration within organizations. Members from different functional backgrounds have a more difficult time fitting into groups comprised of members who are not of their specialty.

The most consistent finding in the meta-analysis done by Milliken and Martins (1996) is that groups have a systematic tendency to homogenize all forms of diversity. Diverse groups have lower levels of member satisfaction and higher rates of turnover than homogenous groups. These results apply to multiple types of diversity including race, ethnicity, age, and gender. In particular, minority members are less satisfied with the group than other members. But if groups can overcome the initial difficulties and predisposition toward conformity and learn to value differences, then they can experience the benefits of diversity (Watson, Johnson, & Zgourides, 2002).

Contextual Conditions for Success .

Clearly, organizations can benefit from a diverse work force. However, some organizations are either not convinced of the benefits of diversity or do not know how to utilize its advantage. Organizations that are either faced with a diverse workforce or are deliberately trying to embrace diversity will have a greater chance for success if (a) the organizational or workgroup context is supportive, (b) if the influence of the minority is enhanced, and (c) if the group tasks require creativity and a variety of perspectives. These three conditions are related to positive outcomes of diverse groups.

First, organizational and workgroup cultures that value the provided diversity and cooperation are better suited to capitalize on the power of diversity. As Ely and Thomas (2001) found, organizations that view diversity as an asset will most likely benefit from it. Jehn and Bezrukova (2004) studied 10,717 members of 1,528 work groups in a Fortune 500 company to evaluate the effects of diversity on performance. In this case, performance was measured by merit-based performance reviews, bonuses, and stock options at both the individual and group levels. Members of functionally diverse groups had higher bonuses in departments that cultivated a people-oriented, cooperative environment. Educationally diverse groups received higher bonuses in environments that emphasized customer service and building customer relationships. Interestingly, in this study, exposure to diversity training and other diversity-oriented HR practices had no effect on helping groups perform better. Jehn and Bezrukova (2004) speculate that those groups that had diversity training were either selected for training because of existing problems within the group or because they had higher expectations placed on them. Clearly, researchers need a better understanding of how to create organizational cultures conducive to diversity.

Second, due to the tendency of groups to encourage cohesion and conformity, divergent perspectives can too easily be silenced, especially when members are in the minority.

Groups that have more than just nominal representation by minority members are better positioned to succeed. Kanter's (1977) theory on the proportion of minority to majority members suggests that "skewed" groups, where minority members constitute from between 1% to 15% of the group, are the most problematic for diverse members. Without a significant proportion of minority perspectives, minority members are more likely to be marginalized and subject to stereotyping. Yet, balanced groups where minority proportions range from 35% to 65% can create hostility and resentment among majority members (Mannix & Neale, 2005). Thus, creating a diverse group can be a bit tricky. Demographic diversity such as race, ethnicity, and gender are especially sensitive and require more than token representation, but can create negative feelings if percentages get too large. Knouse and Dansby (1999) found that optimal diversity levels are obtained when the diversity subgroup comprises between 11 and 30% of the total workgroup.

Finally, certain tasks might be better suited to benefit from a diverse group membership. Diversity can help groups perform better within an organization by introducing different perspectives and generating new, innovative ideas. Thus, diverse groups may be more salient for complex tasks that require innovation, creativity, and change. Those work groups that manage existing processes and practices may not benefit as much from a diverse membership (Mannix & Neale, 2005). But even in groups that manage existing day-to-day operations, team leaders can utilize the power of diversity to improve group functioning by eliciting divergent perspectives on how the group is performing and how it could improve. Over time groups can become blind to their own deficiencies and weaknesses. Diverse perspectives can help groups accurately evaluate performance and often improve functioning.

▓ OVERCOMING THE CHALLENGES OF DIVERSITY

Even if the organizational conditions, proportional composition, and type of tasks are conducive to a diverse membership, diverse groups must still overcome relational, affective, and typical group development obstacles. Lencioni's (2002; 2005) identification of five common challenges or dysfunctions of groups certainly applies to diverse groups. In his work with organizations, he has often seen these obstacles prevent groups from realizing their potential. Furthermore, diversity has the potential to magnify all of these dysfunctions. Each of the challenges is interrelated and begins with the *absence of trust*. Without trust, groups are reluctant to engage in conflict and, as a result, develop a *fear of conflict*. A reluctance to speak up and voice individual and diverse perspectives will often produce a *lack of commitment* to the group. A lack of commitment and buy-in will mean that members are not giving their best effort to the group which leads to an *avoidance of accountability*. People do not want to be held accountable and will not hold their fellow group members accountable to the goals of the group. Finally, without mutual commitment and accountability, group members will often put their own agendas before that of the group and become *inattentive to results* regarding the main tasks of the group. These dysfunctions are described below, along with practical suggestions to address them and improve group functioning.

Absence of Trust

Researchers have long recognized the importance of trust in group and organizational performance (Costa, Roe, & Taillieu, 2001; Kramer, 1999; Mayer, Davis, & Schoorman, 1995).

Trust requires member vulnerability and the willingness to share weaknesses and admit mistakes. If this type of group culture is developed, members will be willing to take risks. Furthermore, trust is developed when members believe that others are competent, respectful, and dependable. Distrustful group members might be convinced of the competence of their peers, but might question their level of respect for others and their dependability. An absence of trust creates a tentative environment where members are reluctant to engage in collaborative relationships and genuine communication.

In diverse groups, minority members might not trust the majority. Whether a member is the only female in an all-male group, or the only engineer in a group of marketing professionals, minority members tend to have a lower level of group satisfaction and are more reluctant to talk. Minority members can feel marginalized and disrespected by the group. Group members in the majority might believe that minority members are not really committed to the group and, therefore, not dependable enough to be given major roles on a project. In addition, if there is a large percentage of minority members in the composition of a group, majority members can become suspicious and feel "outnumbered," thus, inhibiting trust (Mannix & Neale, 2005). Trust is a major issue facing all groups but especially those with a diverse membership.

Lencioni (2002; 2005) makes a number of practical suggestions for building trust in teams. Groups can engage in a personal histories exercise, whereby members share basic background information about themselves. It is difficult to stereotype when members begin to see others as human beings with similar life experiences. These icebreakers can go a long way in establishing a shared identity and building bridges between members (Mannix & Neale, 2005). Other ways to share information about group members include personality profiles such as the DISC, Myers-Briggs Temperament Indicator (MBTI), or Learning Styles Inventory. These profiles give members an opportunity to understand each other better and to value individual differences.

Members can also describe the single most important contribution they perceive that others bring to the group. This allows members to recognize strengths and generate goodwill between members. Consequently, members will begin to feel valued and appreciated. Finally, team leaders can be influential in building trust as they model vulnerability and initiate the willingness to critique one's own mistakes or weaknesses. This can establish group norms that value honesty, learning, and respectful feedback.

Fear of Conflict

For most people, conflict can be uncomfortable even when it is healthy and productive. Conflict can easily provoke a "fight or flight" response, both of which are detrimental to group functioning. The biological human response to perceived danger is to fight or flee to safety. For some, conflict provokes an aggressive response, while others retreat into a passive or defensive posture. As a result, groups can establish an artificial harmony to avoid conflict and the corresponding emotional reactions. Even when a group develops trust and engages in healthy conflict, there is still a tendency over time to avoid conflict and encourage conformity, a concept called groupthink.

Counterproductive attitudes about conflict include the attempt to win arguments and convince others of a certain way of doing things. Conflict that turns personal and bitter can sabotage the work of any group and is often the most distasteful part of group life. Conflict that exists but is not adequately addressed can to go underground and resurface in the impromptu meetings after the official group meeting. In contrast, healthy conflict exists when members can vigorously debate and challenge each other without personally attacking others and without the fear of being personally attacked.

Minority members may experience a reluctance to disagree with the majority in order to maintain stability, avoid provocation, and gain acceptance. Especially in racially diverse groups, there can be an underlying tension about race that creates tentativeness in group discussions. As previously described in the outcome research, diverse groups communicate more formally and less frequently. Part of this diminished communication can be due to not wanting to offend others who are of a different race, nationality, gender, age, personality type, or functional background. Even well-meaning people may avoid vigorous discussion so as not to create any misunderstandings or conflicts. Diversity, by definition, increases the possibility of misunderstanding and miscommunication because members have a different way of seeing and interpreting the world. Thus, avoiding conflict diminishes the benefits of diversity.

On one end of the conflict spectrum is avoidance of conflict and an overemphasis on cohesion and conformity. On the other end of the spectrum is conflict that is personal and aggressive. Even the most effective groups will have difficulty finding the right balance. For example, Lencioni (2005) suggests a forum for group members to discuss their own comfort level and experiences with conflict. Tools such as the Thomas-Kilmann Conflict Mode Instrument allow members to identify and describe their style of conflict. Discussing various conflict styles allows groups to create norms that value and define productive conflict. Another strategy is to assign the role of "miner of conflict" to a group member who will identify and call attention to potential conflicts that are not being addressed in group discussions. Finally, group leaders can model healthy conflict-resolution skills by not avoiding issues and encouraging group members to engage in vigorous discussion.

Lack of Commitment

Commitment is similar to the concept of shared vision. Group members must have a clear understanding of the task, goal, or vision of the group in order to commit to it. Effective teams have clearly defined goals and commitment from all members to achieve those goals. A lack of commitment on the part of any member weakens the whole group. Ironically, when members have concerns that are not expressed through productive conflict, they will only be marginally committed to the group or even work against the goals of the group. Lencioni (2005) has consistently found that members will buy into group decisions, even when their ideas are not adopted, as long as their ideas have been heard. The Intel Corporation describes this as the ability of team members to "disagree and commit."

Lack of commitment can be a problem for minority members, especially demographically diverse members, because they tend to have lower levels of social identification and satisfaction with work groups. Minority members who feel devalued and unwelcome to share their perspective will be less committed to the tasks and success of the group. Greater levels of diversity make it more difficult for group members to identify with a unified vision and purpose. In addition, a diversity of perspectives makes it more difficult for groups to come to consensus on any given decision or plan.

A lack of commitment can occur at the group level when groups are indecisive and reluctant to make a decision or choose a course of action. While consensus is an admirable goal in group decision making, it is not always possible or even advisable. A lack of commitment can occur at the individual level when a member is not personally committed to the group's goals and direction. To assess and overcome issues related to commitment, the leader can ask for a *commitment clarification* at the end of meetings so members can summarize what was decided and to review individual commitments (with deadlines) for each of the members. This simple practice removes uncertainty and reinforces responsibility. In addition, a regular assessment of group goals and progress toward those goals helps keep the group motivated and focused. Leaders can help engender commitment by clarifying the decisions of the group, pushing for action on open issues, and adhering to agreed on schedules and deadlines.

Avoidance of Accountability

Lencioni (2002; 2005) has noticed that group members have a hard time holding each other accountable to performance standards. Many group members assume that it is the leader's job to hold members accountable; but groups reach a higher level of effectiveness when members hold each other accountable. Peer accountability is effective because committed members do not want to let their team members down. Thus, positive peer pressure can be an effective tool for maintaining high standards of performance and accountability.

Members who have low status due to issues of diversity will be reluctant to confront a colleague. For example, a young Hispanic woman in a predominantly white, male dominated group might be chastised for asking another member why he had not completed his portion of the project by the deadline. Unfortunately, when certain members are silenced it sends a powerful message and creates norms whereby minority members learn to avoid taking risks and speaking out. Similarly, majority group members may be reluctant to challenge a minority group member for fear of being labeled a racist or sexist. When there is a lack of trust, an avoidance of conflict and a lack of commitment in diverse groups, there will be a reluctance to hold each other accountable. Yet, when group members perceive that others are not pulling their fair share of the work load, resentments and hostility can build.

A helpful way to encourage members to hold each other accountable is to publish the group's goals and work plan for all to see. If everyone is clear about the tasks of the group and the contribution of each member, then there is a standard against which individual performance can be measured. Members can give regular progress or status reports to update the group. If a member is not performing, the leader could ask the group what needs to be done. This empowers the group to take responsibility for its own maintenance and deal with the underperforming member. At times, the leader will fail as well. Similarly, the leader should be willing to be held accountable to the group and model gracious acceptance of constructive feedback. Another way to increase the likelihood of peer accountability is to use team performance incentives. If the team, as opposed to the individual, is rewarded for performance, members will be more inclined to hold each other to higher standards.

Inattention to Results

Effective groups have clearly defined goals and regularly evaluate their progress toward those goals. Measurable goals and regular assessment provides continuous feedback that keeps groups focused and on task. Over time, though, members can lose sight of the group's success and become more concerned with their own advancement. Lencioni (2005) makes the point that groups can get distracted by a number of issues including individual egos, career development, money, and the importance of competing loyalties. Members can let their own agendas and loyalties to other groups deter them from focusing on the success of the work group.

Diverse groups are especially prone to this tendency of losing sight of the goal. Understandably, minority members might be more concerned with professional survival and may not be as invested in the success of the group. If a group member is just trying to make it through uncomfortable meetings, he or she is not going to be eager to regularly evaluate the performance of the group. In addition, the advancement and protection of fellow minority group members might be more of a priority than the overall success of the team. In this way, personal or coalition goals might dilute the importance of the larger group goals. If group goals are not as important to members, they will be less inclined to regularly evaluate progress and results.

To overcome these tendencies, Lencioni (2002; 2005) encourages use of a scoreboard or dashboard that gauges group performance. Various quantitative metrics can be charted such as student achievement scores, drop out rates, or deadlines in a graphically appealing fashion. In addition, those results can be made available to the larger organization in the same way that box scores document the performance of baseball players and teams the day after a ballgame. Public accountability ensures that members will pay more attention to their own performance. Finally, reward systems that are tied to team performance remind members to pay attention to team metrics. Bonuses and promotions that are related to team results reinforce the importance of team success.

📁 OPENING CASE REVISITED

Team Tensions at Summer School

Debangshu was happy after his meeting with Laura because he felt Eddie framed the situation in a very positive way. But later on when he was alone, Eddie asked Debangshu to help Laura with her situation. Eddie knew that Debangshu grew up around lots of ethnic, cultural, socioeconomic, and educational diversity. He wanted Debangshu to support Laura in her cross-cultural experience. Reluctantly, he agreed to do so. However, Laura's controlling and domineering behavior continued. For example, she would tell Debangshu to "sshh" when he tried to discuss the pedagogy of grammar. It was then that he realized that Eddie entirely ignored his request for help and was only supporting Laura.

Debangshu felt disrespected and marginalized by Laura, but still felt pressure to support her because he agreed to do so. Therefore, even though her negative behavior continued, Debangshu felt obligated to allow her to continue as a means of support. He also felt that she was being quite selfish to cry because of her first experience as a minority. Debangshu was a minority every day and did not receive special attention or support when he cried. The tension in the relationship was never addressed again; other meetings focused on education issues. By the end of the summer, Debangshu felt very uncomfortable around Laura and was eager to finish his commitment, even though he cared deeply for the students and the work of the organization.

Ironically, this diverse team was never able to overcome its own issues to more effectively help their diverse group of students. The team leader,

Eddie, seemed unaware of Debangshu's needs and frustrations. Laura was ill prepared to understand the students she taught and had a difficult time with her own experience as a minority. Furthermore, she never understood how her interpersonal style was offensive to Debangshu. Unresolved conflict created an absence of trust and a further avoidance of conflict. The potential for success was compromised as the team hobbled toward the end of summer. Instead of having a clear understanding of their goal and a commitment to achieve that goal, team members resigned themselves to just enduring the situation until it was over.

Summary

Issues of diversity can be difficult to resolve. Group members often find it easier to work with people who are similar to them. Group members who are in the minority tend to be less committed to their work groups and are less satisfied with group experiences. However, diversity can be a major asset to groups and organizations if initial obstacles can be overcome. Organizations that value diversity and see it as an advantage create the conditions within which diversity can produce positive outcomes. Diverse groups that value different perspectives and encourage the influence of the minority have great potential for innovation and creative problem-solving.

Diversity in the workplace is no longer optional and can most assuredly be an asset. But diversity tends to magnify the typical challenges present within all groups. Thus, group leaders must pay closer attention to issues of trust, conflict, commitment, mutual accountability, and attention to results.

 CONCLUDING CASE

Changing of the Guard

Clovis Prep is a highly regarded public preparatory school located in the midst of one of the nation's premier agricultural areas. The school once was an elite educational institution. Now, it is rapidly becoming a comprehensive high school, enrolling both middle-class and farm-worker children.

The community has a mixed demographic. On one hand, many residents are upper-middle-class professionals and managers responsible for the operation of the agribusinesses that form the spine of the area's economy. This comfortable group also includes many of the families who settled the area more than a century ago and who still often own controlling interests in the land and agricultural companies attached to the land. On balance, these individuals, and the professionals working for them, comprise a privileged class.

But, increasingly, the area has also become home to hundreds of new families, Hispanic and Asian immigrants, who perform the hard manual labor that result in bountiful harvests and plentiful profits. Their children now comprise half of Clovis Prep.

James "Doc" Donaldson is the superintendent of schools. He has held his position for 20 years, far longer than the mean for other school superintendents in the nation and in his area. He is proud of what he had constructed, both by way of culture and facilities. His schools were known for their academic and athletic prowess, and their intense community engagement.

Clovis Prep now needed a new principal. The headmaster had announced his retirement. Doc was eager to identify a new leader quickly. He did not want any lapse in the school's smooth operation or lose the civic elite's confidence.

The district was famous for attracting and grooming leadership. Young teachers often came to the district because of the administrative opportunities its fast growth afforded. The district had such a wealth of talent that it almost always promoted administrators from within its own ranks. The procedure ensured a steady stream of talent; and the practice had long served the district admirably. Clovis's elite residents had come to expect this pattern of capable leadership.

However, in this instance, Doc did not have any talent in the pipeline that was not Caucasian. There were very few teachers and school administrators who were not white. Also, there were few women in positions of leadership. He felt trapped. On one hand he had more talent available to him to consider for promotion than almost any superintendent in his area, perhaps the nation. He had candidates who had been loyal to the district, to students, and to him. They were good. He knew it, they knew it, and the district elite knew it.

On the other hand, Doc had a growing community segment that wanted to ensure that their needs were met, both operationally and symbolically. They had a point too. Perhaps he should abandon the past and pursue a new strategy presently. Then again, past practice had proven productive. Talent, loyalty, and tradition versus social change and legitimate needs.

Discussion Questions

1. How should he proceed?
2. Provide a short-term and a long-term strategy for addressing these issues.

References

Costa, A. C., Roe, R. A., & Taillieu, T. (2001). Trust within teams: The relation with performance effectiveness. *European Journal of Work and Organizational Psychology, 10*, 225–244.

Ely, R. J., & Thomas, D. A. (2001). Cultural diversity at work: The effects of diversity perspectives on work group processes and outcomes. *Administrative Science Quarterly, 46*, 229–273.

Halfhill, T., Sundstrom, E., Lahner, J., Calderone, W., & Nielson, T. M. (2005). Group personality composition and group effectiveness: An integrative review of empirical research. *Small Group Research, 36*, 83–105.

Hannan, M. T. (1988). Organizational population dynamics and social change. *European Sociological Review, 4*, 95–109.

Hays-Thomas, R. (2004). Why now? The contemporary focus on managing diversity. In M. S. Stockdale & F. J. Crosby (Eds.), *The psychology and management of workplace diversity* (pp. 3–30). Malden, MA: Blackwell Publishing.

Helms, J. E. (1993). *Black and white racial identity: Theory, research, and practice.* Westport, CT: Praeger.

Jackson, S. E., Joshi, A., & Erhard, N. L. (2003). Recent research on team and organizational diversity: SWOT analysis and implications. *Journal of Management, 29,* 801–830.

Jackson, S. E., & Ruderman, M. N. (1995). Introduction: Perspectives for understanding diverse work teams. In S. E. Jackson & M. N. Ruderman (Eds.), *Diversity in work teams: Research paradigms for a changing workplace* (pp. 1–13). Washington, DC: American Psychological Association.

Jehn, K. A., & Bezrukova, K. (2004). A field study of group diversity, workgroup context, and performance. *Journal of Organizational Behavior, 25,* 703–729.

Kanter, R. (1977). *Men and women of the organization.* New York: Basic Books.

Karen, A. J., Northcraft, B., & Neale, M. A. (1999). Why differences make a difference: A field study of diversity, conflict and performance in work groups. *Administrative Science Quarterly, 44,* 741–763.

Knouse, S. B., & Dansby, M. R. (1999). Percentage of work-group diversity and work-group effectiveness. *Journal of Psychology, 133,* 486–494.

Kramer, R. M. (1999). Trust and distrust in organizations: Emerging perspectives, enduring questions. *Annual Review of Psychology, 50,* 569–598.

Lencioni, P. (2002). *The five dysfunctions of a team: A leadership fable.* San Franscisco: Jossey-Bass.

Lencioni, P. (2005). *Overcoming the five dysfunctions of a team: A field guide for leaders, managers, and facilitators.* San Francisco: Jossey-Bass.

Mannix, E., & Neale, M. A. (2005). What differences make a difference? The promise and reality of diverse teams in organizations. *Psychological Science in the Public Interest, 6,* 31–55.

Mayer, R. C., Davis, J. H., & Schoorman, F. D. (1995). An integrative model of organizational trust. *Academy of Management Review, 20,* 709–734.

Milliken, F. J., & Martins, L. L. (1996). Searching for common threads: Understanding the multiple effects of diversity in organizational groups. *The Academy of Management Review, 21,* 402–433.

O'Reilly, C. A., Caldwell, D. F., & Barnett, W. P. (1989). Work group demography, social integration and turnover. *Administrative Science Quarterly, 34,* 21–37.

Simons, T., Pelled, L. H., & Smith, K. A. (1999). Making use of difference: Diversity, debate and discussion in top management teams. *The Academy of Management Review, 42,* 662–673.

Trompenaars, F., & Hampden-Turner, C. (1998). *Riding the waves of culture: Understanding cultural diversity in global business.* New York: McGraw Hill.

van Knippenberg, D., De Dreu, C. K. W., & Homan, A. C. (2004). Work group diversity and group performance: An integrative model and research agenda. *Journal of Applied Psychology, 89,* 1008–1022.

Watson, W. E., Johnson, L., & Zgourides, G. D. (2002). The influence of ethnic diversity on leadership, group process, and performance: An examination of learning teams. *International Journal of Intercultural Relations, 26,* 1–16.

Whitt, E. J., Edison, M. I., Pascarella, E. J., Terenzini, P. T., & Amuray, N. (2001). Influences on students' openness to diversity and challenge in the second and third years of college. *The Journal of Higher Education, 72,* 172–204.

CHAPTER NINE

Managing Conflict

▦ INTRODUCTION

Some degree of conflict is inevitable both within and between groups. This chapter examines the sources and consequences of different types of conflict. It describes the ways conflict can be constructive or destructive and how conflict can be managed most effectively. This chapter explains negotiation and illustrates, how negotiation skills can be used successfully to address conflict.

LEARNING OBJECTIVES

After reading this chapter, you should be able to

- Understand why conflict is a natural part of group and organizational life and how it can be either constructive or destructive, depending on the circumstances.
- Understand the different types of conflict in groups and the five styles of dealing with conflict.
- Identify the basic methods of resolving conflict.
- Comprehend the principles of effective negotiation and understand how to use them.

 OPENING CASE

Organizational Change at Tremont

Fred Sands was an organizational development consultant who specialized in organizational change. He was working with Carla Prince, Vice President of Human Resources at Tremont on a major effort to change her organization's culture. Sands was pleased that the entire top-management team had agreed to attend the full two-day retreat that would be dedicated to the topic of change at Tremont. He believed that top-management support was essential to show that the organization was serious about change. He continued to feel optimistic until he received a call from Prince saying that the team needed to change their plan and only come for the afternoon of the second day.

Sands felt devastated. He came back at her with an uncharacteristically strong reaction. He said, "Look, you have to get them there for the full two days. That is the only way we can show that top management is really serious about change, and that is the only way that the rest of the employees would really commit to change." She agreed that she would do her best to get them there. He said, "I am counting on you to get them there. You've got to make it happen." This was the first unpleasant conversation he had had with Prince. He was uncomfortable about being pushy, but he thought it was important enough to be worth pushing hard.

Discussion Questions

1. What do you think of Sands's handling of the situation?
2. Would you have handled it differently? Why or why not?

■ INTRODUCTION TO CONFLICT

Conflict occurs when two or more parties perceive their interests, behaviors, or attitudes as mutually incompatible and disagreements or disputes result. One only has to look through the pages of history to see that human interaction has been rife with conflict. Warfare and sometimes even attempts at genocide have characterized world history. Short of war, people have a variety of other conflicts at the borders of nations, but also within nations, states, cities, and communities as people divide themselves up along racial, ethnic, religious, political, socioeconomic lines, and so on. Groups regularly form negative, often inaccurate, stereotypes of each other, hold hostile feelings, and engage in a variety of aggressive and sometimes even violent acts.

Although one might imagine that people would put away their differences for the purpose of the shared goal of maintaining their employing organization, conflict is nonetheless common in organizations, between and even within teams. As one costly example, consider the experience of Michael Ovitz at Disney. Michael Eisner, Chief Executive Officer of Disney, brought Ovitz in as President in 1995. Wall Street analysts thought this was a smart move and the value of Disney stock jumped 4.4% in one day, increasing the market capitalization of the company by one billion dollars. Unfortunately, Eisner and Ovitz were not able to find a way to work together constructively. After fourteen months, Eisner pushed Ovitz out of the company. Disney had to pay 140 million dollars to get rid of Ovitz because he had negotiated a lump sum payment of that amount in the event that he was fired. Not only did Disney lose the 140 million, but then they also faced a second conflict with their shareholders who filed a derivative action against Disney directors for their ineffective handling of the situation.

Even though individuals vary in their level of comfort with conflict, people tend to be uncomfortable with it and prefer less conflict in their lives and workplaces. Conflict in the workplace can be costly in a variety of ways and has been associated with emotional fatigue, absenteeism, and turnover intentions (Giebels & Janssen, 2005). Another study revealed that interpersonal conflict had a negative impact on job satisfaction and overall well-being (Guerra, Martinez, Munduate, & Medina, 2005). One of the potential hazards associated with conflict is the unpredictable way in which it can play itself out. It can quickly escalate from something minor into something extremely unpleasant and even unsafe. Threats of violence, violent acts, and even homicides occur in the workplace from time to time.

Given the problems associated with conflict, one might conclude that conflict should be avoided. Because people tend to be uncomfortable with conflict, some believe that individuals should strive to eliminate conflict. By contrast, many scholars believe that eliminating conflict is not possible and is not even desirable because the absence of conflict can also be harmful (Tjosvold, 1997). Chapter 7 explored how the suppression of conflict could lead to a lack of critical thinking, groupthink, and poor decision making. Scholars have also argued that some degree of conflict is essential for effective problem solving and innovation (Leonard, 1995). In fact, some effective organizations deliberately select individuals who will clash with each other to work together in teams (Leonard, 1995). When team members with different personalities, cognitive styles, preferences, and perspectives come together, they have the potential for enhanced creative thinking. When these individuals are able to work through their differences toward a common end, a creative tension is produced that can be immensely valuable in developing new products or coming up with creative solutions to problems.

Thus, there appear to be both potential assets and liabilities associated with conflict. Scholars suggest that conflict is inevitable and that employees should seek to understand and manage contention rather than strive to eliminate it (Tjosvold, 1993). Managing conflict means maintaining reasonable levels and having the skill to make the conflict as constructive as possible. In this chapter, we explore some of the sources of conflict, types of conflict, consequences of conflict, styles for handling conflict, and methods of managing conflict constructively.

▇ SOURCES OF CONFLICT

One of the reasons that conflict is pervasive is that there are so many sources of disagreement. Common sources of conflict include allocation of scarce resources, functional differences, personality clashes, structural and role complications, communication and perception challenges, value differences, demographic differences, power and control issues, competition and the desire to win, and social identity and self-esteem.

Scarce Resources

Conflict often springs from a basic economic dilemma that people have unlimited wants but limited resources to satisfy those wants. In other words, there are never enough of the things that people desire in life to satisfy them completely. Consider some of the things that people want in careers such as salary, bonuses, stock options, vacation time, benefits, office size, and equipment. People tend to disagree about how resources should be allocated, so they end up both competing for and quarrelling over them.

For example, in an episode of Donald Trump's *The Apprentice*, the two competing teams each independently decided that they could be more effective in accomplishing their task if they had bullhorns to distribute to their workers. The first team reserved bullhorns at Radio Shack which they planned to pick up the morning of the task. When the second team went to reserve bullhorns at Radio Shack, they found that the first team had already reserved all the available bullhorns. Rather than lose this scarce resource, the second team decided that they should rush immediately to the Radio Shack store, pretend to be members of the first team, and collect the bullhorns that the other team had reserved. They were successful in their ruse, and when the first team went to pick up their bullhorns just before beginning the task, they were horrified to find that they had been sabotaged by the second team. They were unable to recover and to find an alternative supply of bullhorns. Thus, the second team successfully obtained the scarce resource while simultaneously undermining their rival, and ended up winning the competition. When the first team complained to Donald Trump of foul play, rather than admonish the second team, he congratulated them on their cleverness in obtaining the scarce resource and succeeding in the task.

Similarly, in hospital emergency rooms, different shifts of nursing staff have been known to hoard equipment so that it will be available for their shift. In management teams, different functions and divisions compete over how the organization's resources should be allocated.

Functional Differences

Functional differences, discussed in Chapter 8, including training, work experience, education, knowledge, and skill sets can be a source of conflict. Professional training (e.g., engineering, accounting, law, and management) is in some ways designed to socialize students into having a particular set of beliefs and approaches to problem solving. These can affect how people view the world and how they prioritize which can lead to conflicting approaches and interpretations. In addition, organizations often structure themselves according to function. This can put those functions into conflict with each other as they compete with each other for organizational resources.

Personality Clashes

Often from the first meeting members find themselves liking some colleagues and disliking others. People are placed in teams in organizations based on the needs of the organization rather than on the basis of whether they like the other members. People who would prefer not to work together are sometimes required to work together nonetheless. Sometimes these conflicts are unable to be resolved, as was the exorbitant case with Disney. There were immediate personality clashes between Ovitz and a number of his subordinates, and these persisted throughout his stay at Disney.

Structural and Role Complications

Organizational structures and the roles in which people are placed often contribute to conflict. Compliance officers are responsible for making sure that rules are not being broken and may see themselves as preserving the integrity of the organization. By contrast, those they audit are often under pressure to increase the volume or speed of their work, and thus see these officers as slowing things down with their excessive checking, nitpicking, or fault finding. The compliance officers see those they audit as needing to be reminded to be efficient without being reckless. The audited often feel the organization should support them by cutting them some slack. The people in each of these roles often feel a frustration with those in the other role. Regardless of personality, their roles alone potentially put them in conflict.

Another structural issue that can cause conflict is a lack of clarity in goals or objectives. As we discussed in Chapter 5, effective leaders clarify the objectives, and a lack of clear objectives gives group members another issue to fight about. Without clear objectives, group members may have different perceptions about what the goal or objective is or should be and may disagree over how to focus their work.

Reward systems are sometimes structured in ways that encourage competition rather than cooperation among team members or among teams, and this can cause conflict as well. If individuals see themselves as being able to profit by undermining their colleagues, they may engage in conflict-oriented behavior for their own benefit at the expense of team or organizational performance.

Communication and Perception Challenges

People have an imperfect ability to interpret each other's behavior and often misperceive each other's intentions (Kunda, 1999). There are multiple ways that this can happen. People can get angry if they believe others are not keeping them informed. They may also take offense at the way things are communicated (Hinds & Mortensen, 2005). Then, they may misperceive meanings and attribute bad intentions to others (Musch & Klauer, 2003). For example, consider a teacher who explains to his colleagues how he arranged a special field trip for his students and what a great experience they had. The teacher might simply be sharing an idea that might benefit his colleagues. However, his colleagues could interpret this announcement as boasting or trying to "one up" them.

Similarly, if an action accidentally inconveniences or harms another person, the other may perceive the harm as intentional rather than accidental. For example, one child might bump another on the playground without meaning to do so. However, the bumped child might take it as an intentional hostile act and strike back.

Value Differences

Value differences are also a cause of conflict and are particularly apparent in the political arena. Consider the wide variety of interest groups and political action committees that seek to influence voters and legislation toward their valued ends. Values have to do with strong commitments and feelings individuals have about issues and agendas. Value differences are apparent when determining an outcome for a problem with no objectively right or wrong solution. An example of a value difference would be people disagreeing over how much of the federal budget should be allocated toward programs for the elderly versus for education. Both sides have merit, and many arguments can be made for each side, but there is not an objectively right or wrong way to determine the exact allocation. Thus, two well-meaning individuals can disagree based on their feelings about an issue, and people are often willing to fight great battles in order push their valued agendas forward.

Demographic Differences

Demographic differences, discussed in Chapter 8, include differences such as race, ethnicity, gender, and age. History is replete with accounts of conflict, often violent, between different demographics. Racial and ethnic boundaries and conflicts are often apparent within schools and on the borders of neighborhoods and communities.

Power and Control Issues

Throughout history, whether in nations, states, cities, or towns, groups have status and power differences. As individuals and groups vie for power, they come into conflict with each other. As President of Disney, the Chief Financial Officer and the General Counsel would naturally both report to the newly appointed Ovitz. However, Chief Financial Officer Bollenbach and General Counsel Litvack apparently resented having someone between them and CEO Eisner, so they immediately announced to Ovitz that they refused to report to him.

In organizations, lower-level employees often form unions to address power imbalances. Many people also simply resent authority figures and come into natural conflict with them. Consider how conflict tends to emerge in families as children enter the teenage years and disagree with parents over who should make what decisions. Conflicts can be severe and long lasting.

Competition and the Desire to Win

Although organizations often try to encourage cooperation, many people are competitively oriented or perceive situations competitively and thus try to win (beat others) rather than find ways to cooperate and collaborate. Variations of the prisoner's dilemma game bear this out. The game's idea is that two alleged criminals are captured and temporarily imprisoned. They are separated by authorities who encourage each prisoner independently to confess. If neither prisoner confesses, then they both go free. However, if one prisoner confesses and the other does not, the confessor will receive a short sentence and the one who does not confess will receive a long sentence. Thus, each prisoner must guess whether the other will confess under pressure. If they could trust each other to cooperate, they could both go free. However, rather than cooperate, they have a tendency to turn on each other in order to "win," or more accurately, to keep from "losing."

Similarly, organizations often realize that they could restrict output, charge higher prices, and make more profit if they could count on their competitors to simultaneously restrict output and not undercut their prices. Although price fixing is illegal, there is a natural incentive for organizations to collude either explicitly or implicitly. However, they are rarely able to sustain this kind of collaboration because the propensity to cheat is so strong. Specifically, what organizational leaders often do is undercut their competitor's prices slightly to capture both market share and profits. However, that leads others to cut prices and the system or agreement breaks down—and the consumers benefit from the competition. The Organization of Petroleum Exporting Countries (OPEC) stands as a rare exception that has been able successfully to restrict production to keep prices up over periods of years. However, during certain time periods, cheating was so rampant that oil prices plunged.

Social Identity and Self-Esteem

Scholars argue that there is motivation to maintain positive self-esteem (Baumeister, 1993). Self-esteem is the affective component of our evaluation of our self-worth and is based on how capable, likeable, and valuable we perceive ourselves to be. The ability to think well of ourselves and believe that others think well of us is a fundamentally powerful human desire, and group membership plays an important role in the maintenance of self-esteem (Tajfel & Turner, 1979). Part of a person's self-esteem comes from groups in which that person is a member. Thus, the more positively people feel about the groups in which they hold membership, the better able they are to maintain their self-esteem. Consequently, there is a natural tendency for people to try to build their self-esteem by seeing their own groups as superior to others and to show in-group favoritism (Hewstone, Rubin, & Willis, 2002).

■ TYPES OF GROUP CONFLICT

As stated in the chapter introduction, both conflict and the lack of conflict are potentially problematic. One way to conceptualize this might be to say that a group should try to achieve the right balance between conflict and harmony and to avoid having too much or too little of either one (Robbins, 2003). This is illustrated in Figure 9.1. At one extreme, a group that does not exhibit any overt conflict may be problematic because of issues like groupthink, but too much conflict would be problematic because it might get in the way of achieving sufficient agreement to work collaboratively.

Although the idea of avoiding extremes might have some intuitive appeal, researchers also discovered that conflict could be categorized into different types, and that these types might differ in how they impact group effectiveness. Next, we examine the research on different types of conflict and how they affect groups.

Even though conflict in groups can emanate from many sources, it was categorized by early researchers into two main types—task and interpersonal (Pinkley, 1990), with the possibility of a third type. First, *task conflict* has to do with disagreements over how the group should go about accomplishing the task. For example, a group of teachers may agree that their students need to better understand fractions, but each teacher may have a different idea about which approach to teaching fractions would be most suitable to achieve this goal. Thus, they might have task conflict as they disagree over how to address the problem.

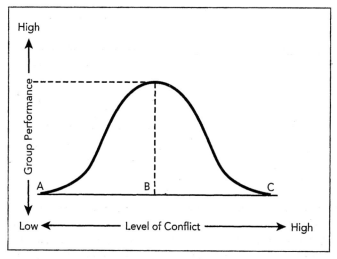

FIGURE 9.1   Conflict and Performance

Second, relationship or *interpersonal conflict* has to do with the extent to which group members like or dislike each other. People vary in the extent to which they like each other, and often individuals rub each other the wrong way. This can be due to any number of differences including racial, ethnic, political, religious, cultural, value, and personality differences.

Personality clashes commonly take place among people who present with different categories on the Myers-Briggs Type Inventory. For example, a highly extroverted person and a highly introverted person might be working together. Because extroverts tend to like a lot of social interaction and introverts prefer time alone, the introvert may be thinking *Why can't he close his mouth and let me think through this problem?* By contrast, the extrovert may experience the introvert as cold, aloof, or not much fun. Those who score as judgers and perceivers on the Myers-Briggs also often clash. Judgers tend to like order, structure, definitive schedules, and organization. Perceivers like to keep their options open, take a wait-and-see approach, and change course as they feel necessary. They see structure as interfering with the ability to take advantage of opportunities that present themselves in the moment. These two often clash. The judgers see the perceivers as maddeningly disorganized, unreliable, and unpredictable. Perceivers often find judgers to be too rigid, controlling, obsessive, or "anal."

Third, one study of conflict in teams concludes that another type of conflict, *process conflict*, could be considered an additional category (Jehn, 1995). Process conflict has to do with disagreements over who should be doing what within the group. For example, all teachers in a school might agree that the cafeteria needs to be monitored and might agree on what the role and responsibilities of a monitor should be. However, they may disagree about whose turn it is to monitor the cafeteria. Similarly, members of a group might agree that group meetings run better when someone in the group manages the process, but disagree over who should manage the process. When an office purchases new equipment, group members may disagree over who gets to use the new equipment, how often, and when.

Thus, groups engage in at least three different types of conflict. Early researchers hypothesized that interpersonal conflict was likely to be harmful because it would cause trouble without any compensating benefit. On the other hand, they hypothesized that task conflict could be beneficial because exploring different perspectives on how to approach the task might lead to critical and innovative thinking about smarter ways of working.

What is the impact of these types of conflict? Group members tend to dislike conflict, and both task and relationship conflict have consistently been associated with lower group member satisfaction (De Dreu & Weingart, 2003). Relationship conflict has also consistently been shown to hinder performance. However, the relationship between task conflict and performance has been less clear.

The popular Harvard Business Review article "How Management Teams Can Have a Good Fight" (Eisenhardt, Kahwajy, & Bourgeois, 1997b) argues that a lack of task conflict in a management team should actually be a warning sign. Having a good fight means getting the relevant issues and ideas on the table and working though the differences in an open manner. They argue that conflict is natural, even necessary, in this process.

Jehn (1995) studied the impact of different types of conflict on team performance and discovered that the impact of task conflict varied depending on the type of task. Task conflict was harmful to groups working on routine tasks, but this harmful effect was not found when groups were working on complex tasks. In fact, task conflict was sometimes helpful when groups were working on complex tasks.

Another study demonstrated that in a decision-making task, groups that engaged in more task conflict made better decisions (De Dreu & West, 2001). However, this was influenced by the level of participation. In other words, a significant amount of group participation is necessary in order for the benefits of task conflict to be realized.

Jehn and Mannix (2001) examined the impact of conflict on team effectiveness among MBA students. They found that high-performing teams generally have lower levels of conflict than teams that do not perform as well, with one major exception. The high-performing teams experienced a spike in task conflict at the midpoint in the project timeline. This is consistent with Gersick's (1988, 1989) punctuated equilibrium model, introduced in Chapter 3. This model suggests that teams tend to evaluate and rethink their strategies and effectiveness about midway between their inception and the project deadline. This midway evaluation enables them to identify problems and make helpful adjustments to achieve success by the deadline. The work of Jen and Mannix leads people to the general conclusion that relationship conflict is harmful to performance, but task conflict may be helpful. Many textbooks reflect this underlying assumption (See De Dreu & Weingart, 2003 for examples).

De Dreu and Weingart's (2003) research reopens the question of what impact task and relationship conflicts have on groups. Based on their knowledge of existing research, they were concerned that the extent to which task conflict is beneficial to performance was being overestimated. To clarify the impact of task conflict on performance and satisfaction, they conducted a meta-analysis of the literature on conflict in groups and discovered that both task and relationship conflict had a consistent negative effect on both member satisfaction and group performance.

Why the mixed perceptions on this topic? Task conflict appears to have a complicated relationship with performance. It appears to impact performance in at least two distinct ways. First, it does appear to have the potential benefit of stimulating depth and diversity of thinking when it comes to problem solving and making decisions. At the same time, task conflict can cause problems through its impact on cognitive load (Carnevale & Probst, 1998). This may not be a problem when task conflict is low; but as conflict grows, it begins to overload the cognitive system (intellectual resources are consumed dealing with the conflict rather than the task) and effective information processing is inhibited. In sum, it appears that some degree of task conflict can be helpful in encouraging critical thinking; but at higher levels, it interferes with cognitive processing so much that performance is damaged (De Dreu & Weingart, 2003). As conflict increases, attention that might otherwise be directed toward accomplishing the task is distracted by the conflict.

One other interesting point from this research is that task conflict had a less negative impact on group performance when it was not correlated with relationship conflict and when groups had higher levels of psychological safety (De Dreu & Weingart, 2003). In other words, a positive interpersonal climate appears to help protect or buffer the group from the potentially harmful effects of task conflict.

In reflecting back on Figure 9.1, this conceptualization appears to be inadequate in some ways. Relationship conflict is consistently detrimental to performance; thus, performance is best when relationship conflict is as low as possible. Task conflict is also largely detrimental to performance. However, its impact is more complicated. It appears to have potential benefits at low levels, but these benefits are overwhelmed by the damaging effect that task conflict has on cognitive activity as the conflict increases. Thus, minimizing relationship conflict and keeping task conflict at reasonable levels appears to be beneficial to group functioning.

One other important point is that relationship conflict and task conflict are not necessarily independent of each other. Consider a group that is facing task conflict but does not have relationship conflict. If the group is able to resolve its task conflict, it may proceed to perform smoothly without task or relationship conflict. However, if the group is unable to resolve its task conflict, frustrations may build and disagreements may become personal. Thus, hostility may emerge toward other group members. The unresolved task conflict has now generated relationship conflict, and the group must now struggle with both types of conflict. Given the potential for unresolved task conflict to result in relationship conflict, groups would be well advised to resolve their task conflicts in a timely manner. Next, we look at different styles for handling conflict.

■ CONFLICT MANAGEMENT STYLES

Conflict can be handled in different ways, and people tend to be most comfortable with one or two styles that may become default styles; they are implemented automatically in most situations (Thomas, 1976). Each style has its own strengths and weaknesses and can be more or less appropriate, depending on the particular situation. At the end of this chapter, there is an assessment that will help you identify your most natural styles. Here are the five basic styles for handling conflict—*avoiding, accommodating, competing, compromising,* and *collaborating*—and we will examine their assets and liabilities for different situations.

As Figure 9.2 illustrates, these styles are distinguished by the extent to which they are assertive (focusing on one's own interests or agenda) versus cooperative (focusing on the interests or agenda of others). The *compromising* and *collaborating* options involve both assertiveness and cooperation. By contrast, when parties are a*voiding, accommodating,* and *competing,* they are not integrating the interests of both parties.

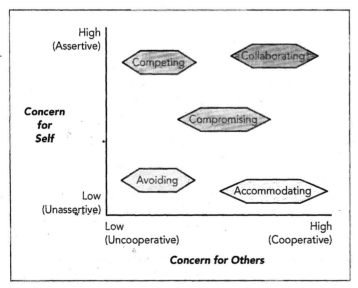

FIGURE 9.2   Styles for Handling Conflict

Source: Thomas, K. W. (1976). Conflict and conflict management. In M. D. Dunnette (Ed.), *Handbook of industrial organizational psychology* (p. 900). Chicago: Rand McNally.

Avoiding means the conflict is not verbalized nor addressed. At least one party simply disengages from the conflict and is thus low in both assertiveness and cooperativeness. *Accommodating* means that one party foregoes its own interests or agenda in order to let the other party have its way. This style is high on cooperation and low on assertiveness. *Competing* means that one party is pressing its own agenda at the expense or exclusion of the other and is thus high on assertiveness and low on cooperation. The statement "It's my way or the highway" characterizes the *competing* style. By contrast, *compromising* and *collaborating* both involve some recognition and integration of both parties' interests and agendas. *Compromising* involves a moderate amount of cooperativeness and assertiveness, and *collaborating* involves a high degree of both.

One major disadvantage associated with *avoiding*, *accommodating*, and *competing* is that none of these styles make productive use of the informational and intellectual assets of both parties. Thus, the potential for creative thinking and problem solving that might enable a solution that is appealing to all parties is lost.

At the same time, there are conditions under which these styles are viable. What might make these noncollaborative styles appropriate? First, a potential asset associated with these strategies is that they can be efficient because parties do not spend their time trying to collaborate or work out a compromise. In emergency situations, time may be so crucial, that it is more important to act on an adequate solution than it is to invest the time into trying to determine the optimal solution. For example, two emergency room physicians might have different ideas about the best approach to stop profuse bleeding from a gunshot wound. However, provided that each has a reasonable solution, fast action on either solution might be more important for saving the patient than taking time to debate the possible merits of each approach and arrive at a mutual decision on how to proceed.

Second, sometimes the potential benefit of searching for a higher-quality solution or decision is not worth the effort. This may be the case for any of the following reasons. The alternatives may not be different enough such that one is much better or worse than another. Regulations or task structure may be so strict that there is little freedom to implement a creative, collaborative solution. Parties may not have strong feelings or preferences about the alternatives. For example, if a group is deciding where to go to dinner, and there are several restaurants that are very appealing, any will do. In other circumstances, there may be so much unpredictability that the outcome of either approach is difficult to estimate, and everyone is equally ignorant about what solution is best.

In the section Integrative versus Distributive Framing later in this chapter, we show that there is immense benefit from finding collaborative, integrative solutions. However, for the moment, we will examine the costs and benefits of each style in more detail, examining their assets and liabilities and the conditions under which they are more and less functional. One question that should be asked is not only how these styles will influence the way in which a particular conflict is addressed, but how the way that the conflict is resolved might affect the future for both parties.

Avoiding

Avoiding may be most appropriate when the dispute can work itself out on its own, or when the prospects for resolving the situation are not positive, are too costly, or too risky. For example, a team has a leader who occasionally gets in a bad mood and goes to his or her office and closes the door. With a little alone time he or she is back to normal and things are back on course. The team simply learns to give the leader space by temporarily using the avoiding style. Similarly, in relationships outside of work, sometimes one party briefly needs a little space to sort out thoughts and feelings. If others continue to pursue the party that needs space, the conflict often grows rather than dissipates.

One study examined the impact of various styles on dealing with relationship conflict in groups (De Dreu & Van Vianen, 2001). The groups that used the avoiding style when relationship conflict emerged performed better than those that tried to work through the conflict. This was because relationship conflict is sufficiently difficult to work out, and the groups did not get sufficient benefit from working on the conflict to justify the cost of taking time away from working on the task. Does this mean that groups should not work on their relationship conflicts? No, it simply means that groups should be realistic about the fact that relationship conflicts can be complicated and will not necessarily be resolved quickly. Groups should simply be intelligent in considering when to spend time working on relationship conflict versus maintaining focus on the task.

From a political perspective, opportunities to confront others often present themselves in organizations, but not all of these battles are worth fighting. Some are insufficiently important to be worth the effort. Others can be costly and are not likely to be won, so people may be just as well off to avoid them or accommodate, and save their time and energy for a more worthy cause.

Although avoiding can sometimes be the most reasonable style to use, it certainly has a number of potential disadvantages. The obvious disadvantage of avoiding is that it does not proactively resolve the conflict or address the issue. It can be problematic if the situation will not get better on its own, and especially if the situation is likely to deteriorate without action. One disadvantage of avoiding is that it may be perceived by others as a sign of weakness and a willingness to be victimized without responding or retaliating. If a victimized party does not stand up for itself in some way, the aggressor may feel free to continue to take advantage of that party and may even intensify the mistreatment.

Avoiding also tends to be looked down on, especially in Western cultures, and can have a negative effect on a manager's reputation (Pfeffer, 1992). The ability to be forceful and face conflict with confidence is a managerial and executive competency, and employees do not like to be led by someone who does not seem willing to fight for their interests (Kanter, 1977).

Accommodating

Accommodating may be beneficial under similar circumstances to avoiding. One potential advantage of accommodating is that accommodating can be taken by the other party as having done a favor for them, and they may be inclined to return the favor at some point. This style can be appropriate in the area of customer service. The statement "The customer is always right" reflects the idea that the organization may be wisest to accommodate at times to retain good relationships with customers. At the same time, if an accommodating style becomes a pattern, others may get a sense of entitlement and may take advantage of the accommodating party. Also, the accommodating party may not get its own needs met and may lose motivation or become worn out or resentful. The accommodating party may become a doormat if it does not use other styles at times.

Competing

Like avoiding and accommodating, competing is unlikely to take advantage of potentially valuable input from other parties. However, competing can be useful when moving the group forward is most important. It may be helpful in an emergency situation, and it can be helpful when a leader uses it to put an end to quarreling. As a professor mentioned to one of the authors, "Our former dean would take a competing stance at times, but sometimes we found that very helpful because he would resolve issues that faculty members would have otherwise continued to squabble over unproductively."

A competing stance can be essential when a party knows it is right and taking a more cooperative strategy would allow harm to be done. For example, when the Space Shuttle *Challenger* was launched, the engineers who worked on the O-rings knew that it was not safe to launch. However, rather than hold firm to their competing stance and blocking the launch, they succumbed to pressure from management and NASA and allowed the launch to go forward, causing the death of all the passengers and the loss of the shuttle.

The potential disadvantage of a competing style is that it sometimes provokes the other to respond with a competing style; then the conflict escalates, and parties become deadlocked. Alternatively, the other party might comply and go along with the competing party, but never really becomes committed to the new course of action. The other party might harbor a grudge against the competing party and become passive-aggressive, sabotage the project, or wait for an opportunity to get back at the competing party.

Compromising

In contrast to the previous styles, compromising blends assertiveness and cooperation and thus addresses each party's interests, at least to some degree. Therefore, compromising avoids some of the disadvantages of the other styles just described. The main difference between compromising and collaborating is the extent to which efforts are made to find solutions that will be satisfying or even beneficial to both parties. For example, a team might get a new machine that works faster and with better quality than the others that they typically use. Each group member wants to use the machine. So there is conflict about how the scarce resource should be allocated. A compromise might be to just divide the time equally, and let each group member use the machine for one hour a day. This is a quick solution that seems fair.

In contrast, a collaborating solution might involve a greater investment of time in determining how best to allocate the scarce resource. For example, they might consider the flow of work and figure out who is busiest at what time during the week and then make a schedule that provides the greatest relief from stress by enabling each team member to have more time on the machine when they are under the greatest pressure.

Collaborating

Collaborating involves the greatest degree of consideration for both parties' interests. With a little effort to understand what each party wants and what solutions might suit each party, creative solutions that may make life better for all parties can often be discovered. Although finding a clever solution may take some time, the benefits are often well worth the costs. We will explore steps for achieving effective collaborations and negotiations in the section Integrative versus Distributive Framing.

Another benefit of working toward collaboration is that doing so can help create a general climate in which collaboration and teamwork is appreciated. This can reduce the propensity for unproductive conflict and escalation of conflict in the future.

■ ESCALATION OF CONFLICT

One problem with conflict is that it can escalate from something minor and mundane into something serious and damaging. Individuals can easily become fixated on defeating the other party at the expense of other more important things. Consider the following example of the dollar auction and how it illustrates how conflict can spiral irrationally out of control.

The professor begins the process by saying:

> I am about to auction off a dollar to the highest bidder. Everyone in the class is welcome to participate in the auction, but no one is required to bid. I will sell the dollar at any price no matter how low. One condition of this auction is that the highest bidder pays for and receives the dollar, but the second highest bidder is also required to pay. Let's begin the auction.

The bidding usually starts out below a dollar and when it reaches a dollar, bidders begin to consider their bids more carefully. With each successive bid, the professor asks if anyone would like to outbid the previous bid. Bidders become hesitant as the bids approach a dollar, but the professor reminds the participants of the rule stating that the second highest bidder is also required to pay. Rather than come away from this process having paid and received nothing, the second highest bidder usually continues to bid and a competitive battle ensues between the highest and second highest bidder. As the two alternate between the highest and second highest bidder, the amount they have bid continues to increase. Fairly quickly the bidding can exceed $10.00, all for the sake of winning one dollar. Professor Max Bazerman of Harvard Business School reports that he has earned over $30,000 using this exercise in his classes (Bazerman, 2006). However, in recent years, he has started with $20.00 rather than $1.00. He also reports that all proceeds are either given to charity or used for a class party.

One of the lessons from the dollar auction is that some situations are worth avoiding because they naturally lead to escalation of conflict. The rule that both the highest and second highest bidders must pay creates a structure that is likely to result in escalation at the expense of both bidders. A more common arena where conflict often escalates is in divorce proceedings. Rather than preserve assets to be divided amongst the former spouses, individuals often use lawyers to fight with the intent of punishing the other or getting a relatively larger settlement for oneself. Legal fees associated with such wrangling can quickly eat up marital assets, leaving less to be divided between former spouses. Sometimes mediation can be useful in divorce and in other conflicts to keep the conflict from escalating and to work to find mutually agreeable solutions.

People in conflict tend to underestimate the likelihood of being able to develop mutually beneficial solutions. Instead, they tend to see themselves as fighting over a pie with a fixed size. Having an integrative perspective, explored in the next section, can be helpful.

■ INTEGRATIVE VERSUS DISTRIBUTIVE FRAMING

One barrier to resolving conflict is that people often have a tendency to view their own interests as diametrically opposed to the interests of others with whom they are in conflict (De Dreu, Koole, & Steinel, 2000). In fact, this conclusion is overly pessimistic. There tend to be multiple possibilities for identifying mutually acceptable, even mutually beneficial, agreements or negotiations. The way that people think under conditions of conflict has been labeled *fixed-pie perceptions*—they view whatever they are fighting over as a pie of fixed size in which a larger slice of the pie for one party means a smaller slice of pie for the other party, a zero-sum game. Negotiations that take place under this framework are referred to as distributive. The focus of the negotiation is how scarce resources will be divided up or distributed.

By contrast, integrative bargaining holds the perspective that there may actually be ways of enabling all parties to have more of what they want if they are clever in how they approach the negotiation. Holding a distributive mindset discourages parties in the negotiation from discovering opportunities for integrative bargaining. The elements of principled negotiation can assist parties in finding ways to engage in integrative negotiations (Thompson & Leonardelli, 2004). Fisher and Ury (1996) developed four key elements of principled negotiation: (1) separate people from the problem, (2) focus on interests, not positions, (3) invent options for mutual gain, and (4) insist on objective criteria.

Separate People from the Problem

Strong unpleasant emotions often develop among parties involved in a conflict. Each party becomes frustrated with the other and emotions can grow more intense and bitter as conflict escalates. Another complicating factor is that people tend to develop inaccurately negative perceptions about each other during conflict (London, 2001). They infer malice and evil intent that may not really be present. These factors tend to have a negative effect on prospects for resolving differences. In fact, parties sometimes get so angry at each other that punishing the other party becomes more important than reaching a rational solution (Fisher & Ury, 1996).

Getting people to defer judgment and focus on mutual interests rather than exclusively on their own interests can be helpful in deescalating conflict and moving toward cooperative solutions.

Focus on Interests, Not Positions

Understanding the difference between interests and positions can be extremely helpful in resolving disagreements or in opening up blocked negotiations. A *position* is a specific proposal, request, offer, or demand. For example, a roommate might say "I just have to borrow your new coat tonight." An *interest* reflects the underlying need or desire that the position is designed to satisfy. Interests are somewhat like ends, and positions are possible means for achieving those ends. The interest of the roommate who is demanding the coat might be to look and feel good for a special date that evening. Borrowing the coat is one way for the roommate to achieve this end, but there might be other ways to achieve this same end.

When people are in conflict, they tend to focus narrowly on positions rather than more flexibly and creatively on their interests (what it is they are really trying to accomplish). The key point here is that there may be many ways to satisfy a particular interest, and the initial position that a person articulates is merely one possible way of satisfying an interest. There may be many other ways that might be equally good or even superior to their initial position; but when they focus rigidly on the position, they lose sight of creative alternatives for resolving their disagreement. To provide a simple example, a story is told of two children fighting over an orange (West, 2004, p. 173). Each held the position "I need that orange." With each child fixating on her position, there was no apparent solution that would completely satisfy each child. As it turned out, each child's interests could have been satisfied if only they had articulated them rather than focusing on positions. One child wanted the orange so she could scrape fragments of the peel for a cake. The other child wanted to drink the juice. Each child could have had what she wanted, but without knowing the interests, the parent sliced the orange in half and each child had only half of what she wanted.

When parties in conflict focus on their interest (what they are really trying to accomplish) and realize that their initial position is only one of many possible ways to satisfy that interest, they have set the stage for generating options for mutual gain.

Invent Options for Mutual Gain

As mentioned earlier, one issue that keeps parties stuck in conflict is thinking of bargaining and negotiations as distributive rather than integrative. People tend to underestimate the extent to which they could invent options for mutual gain that benefit each of the parties.

Consider the military conflict between Egypt and Israel. Egypt attacked Israel in 1973, but Israel was successful in fending off Egyptian forces and even pushed Egypt back and took over Egyptian land—the Sinai Peninsula. After the war was over, Egypt held the position that they should have their land back; and Israel took the position that they would keep the land. The conflict appeared irreconcilable until they were able to focus on interests and invent options for mutual gain. Egypt's interest was sovereignty (they wanted to possess the land that had been theirs since the time of the Pharaohs). Israel's interest was security (they did not want tanks parked up against their border and feel the constant threat of attack). Eventually, they were able to focus on these interests and invent an option for mutual gain. Specifically, they created a demilitarized zone that was a creative way of addressing each party's interest. Israel would have security because they would not have a military presence along their border, and Egypt would have control over their land with the one caveat that they would not be able to put military forces on that land.

People have a natural tendency to become rigidly focused on their position and to ignore other possibilities to achieve their interest that are at least as good as if not superior to their original position.

Insist on Objective Criteria

The ambiguity surrounding what is fair can also be a sticking point that perpetuates disagreement. When parties see each others' positions as unreasonable, they are inclined to make negative inferences about the other party and to assume that the other is not acting in good faith, is excessively self-interested, or is trying to cheat them. One way to reduce this problem is to focus on objective criteria. Each party may mistrust what the other party says is fair, and each party may have some bias in making its own determination of what is fair. The idea of focusing on objective criteria is to provide some reasonable, concrete standard to be used as a point of comparison. Objective criteria provide a benchmark against which parties can compare and adjust their own subjective interpretations of value or fairness.

Objective standards are commonly used in a variety of negotiations. For example, when buying or selling a used car, people can look at blue book values, which can provide a sense of what a reasonable price range for the car might be. Similarly, when buying a home, people can refer to the prices that comparable homes in the area have sold for to make an estimate of the value of a particular home. In trying to determine what a fair work load or division of labor is for a group and the roles within the group, the team might examine how other groups doing similar work in similar organizations arrange conditions and use that as a template to provide an estimate of what is reasonable.

▮ CLEAR GOALS AND SUPERORDINATE GOALS

One way that organizational leaders can keep from inadvertently contributing to conflict within and between groups is to set clear objectives for groups and to emphasize superordinate goals. As discussed in Chapter 5, an excellent way to make the best of a group's potential to perform is to specify a clear, compelling direction but to let the group members use their own creative thinking in deciding how to achieve the objective that they have been given. If both ends and means are specified, the group does not take advantage of the member's ideas. However, if the end is not specified, then the group has the potential to spend most of its time arguing about what it should be doing. A lack of clarity about the group's objective paves the road for unproductive conflict. Thus, making sure that all group members have a clear, shared objective is an excellent way to avoid unproductive conflict.

The Robbers Cave Experiment and Use of Superordinate Goals

One of the historical developments in the study of conflict between groups was the Robbers Cave field experiment conducted by Muzafer Sherif and colleagues (Sherif, Harvey, White, Hood, & Sherif, 1961). He and other psychologists wanted to understand conflict between groups and what could be done to reduce it. He decided use a boys' camp, located at Robbers' Cave, Oklahoma, as a field experiment for the opportunity to examine the nature of intergroup conflict and the best ways to intervene.

The experimenters selected 22 11-year-old boys for the study and divided them up into two camps—the Rattlers and the Eagles. At first, each camp was unaware that the other camp existed. Slowly, the experimenters brought the boys into contact with each other under conditions that were designed to lead to competition. Within groups, loyalties formed quickly, and the boys in each camp came to see their own camp as superior, to like members of their camp better and to dislike and to develop negative stereotypes about members of the other camp. It was not long before boys were raiding and vandalizing each others' camps; fighting was breaking out, and violence was escalating to a level at which the experimenters had to intervene for the boys' safety.

Having established intergroup conflict, the researchers were in a position to experiment with interventions for reducing conflict between the camps. Other psychologists had hypothesized that the following could reduce intergroup conflict: (1) placing group members into noncompetitive contact with each other in neutral settings in which they had equal power and status, and (2) developing commitment to a superordinate goal that could only be accomplished if the groups were able to collaborate with each other (Deutch, 1973; Allport, 1954).

The experimenters placed the groups into neutral contact with each other but found that this did little to resolve the conflict. Conflict was not reduced until the experimenters were able to introduce superordinate goals, and even then, it took some time before the conflict was resolved.

The first superordinate goal had to do with a threat to the camp's water supply. The boys had to work collaboratively to resolve the problem. The second superordinate goal had to do with working together to raise money so that they could all see a movie that was of interest to everyone. The final superordinate goal had to do with working together to make possible a trip to go camping at Cedar Lake and continue their journey across state lines. For example, one of the trucks for the trip was ailing, and they had to work together to get it started. They also had to cooperate in preparing meals and making camp.

Some conclusions from the Robbers Cave experiment are that intergroup conflict can be precipitated fairly easily. Once such conflict is in place, it can be difficult to undo. Neutral contact alone did little to resolve the conflict. Commitment to superordinate goals was most helpful but still required some time to take effect.

OPENING CASE REVISITED

Organizational Change at Tremont

Despite Sands's insistence that Prince deliver the top-management team for the full two days, the top team only came for part of the second day of the program. Unfortunately, Sands's relationship with Prince and Tremont deteriorated over time, and the change program was not very successful. Sands placed the blame mostly on Prince, but partly on the top-management team as well.

Some years later, in a seminar on conflict management and negotiation, Sands shared this experience and gained some insight into his own contribution to the deterioration of the relationship and the project. He came to realize that, although at that time he was doing his best to be helpful, there were some ways in which he could have been undermining his own efforts. Specifically, he realized that he had adopted a competitive stance with Prince rather than a collaborative stance and that he had been very positional with her. He was pushing his agenda and his position—that the team must get to the program for the full two days. But his real interest was in getting commitment to the change program. Getting the top team to the program was only one of the ways that commitment to change might be built, but he had focused narrowly on that issue and had failed to think more broadly about how to accomplish the overall objective of commitment.

In addition, he realized that he had been pushy with Prince, rather than supporting her and collaborating with her. For example, he never inquired as to her thinking about the situation or what pressures may have been on her or on the top team. He did not know whether she understood the importance of the team's attendance, and he did not explain it. Although his job was to assist the organization, he never inquired into what would keep the team from attending. He assumed a lack of commitment rather than finding out if there were troubles brewing that required their attention. Being effective in his role would have required probing for such information. After all, how could he assist the organization if he did not try to understand the stresses they were experiencing?

Assuming there was no crisis, he also did not check to see whether he could have assisted her in some way to persuade them to come. He also did not check into whether she was having doubts of any kind about the program. He did not consider what the impact would be on her if the program did not meet the top team's expectations, and whether they were irritated with her for convincing them to come for the whole time. He also could have inquired as to whether she had any doubts about the program and then figured out either how to reassure her or how to alter the program to ensure its success. In retrospect, he wished he had taken a cooperative stance rather than a competitive stance.

Summary

Conflict stems from many sources, including scarce resources, functional differences, personality clashes, structural and role complications, communication and perception challenges, demographic differences, power and control, competition and the desire to win, and social identity and self-esteem. Conflict is common both within and between teams. Groups typically find both relationship and task conflict unpleasant. Relationship conflict undermines performance. Task conflict has both potentially positive and negative effects on performance. As task conflict grows, its negative effects tend to predominate.

People have different preferred styles for handling conflict, and these include: avoiding, accommodating, competing, compromising, and collaborating. Each of these has potential assets and liabilities depending on the circumstances. Only compromising and collaborating attempt to integrate both parties' interests. Conflict can often be ameliorated if parties frame it as integrative rather than distributive.

One of the dangers of conflict is that it can escalate fairly easily. Skills for negotiation and addressing conflict successfully include separating people from the problem, focusing on interests rather than positions, inventing options for mutual gain, and insisting on objective criteria. Conflict between groups can develop easily and is difficult to reduce. However, the development of superordinate goals has been used effectively to reduce such conflict.

 CONCLUDING CASE

Hidalgo Demarest's Dilemma

Hidalgo Demarest was the superintendent of schools in a medium-size school district near the Mexican border. All his life he had been enamored with education, from the time he was a schoolboy in a poor city in Bolivia, through his difficult migration to the United States, until he took his first teaching job as an elementary teacher in a suburb of Los Angles. Now, two graduate degrees and twenty years later, he was a superintendent of an elementary district in Texas.

Hidalgo still remembered a great deal about his South American boyhood. One of the enduring features of his early life was violent, seemingly sustained rioting as land and factory owners continually attempted to deprive workers of a fair wage, and then used the police to quell revolt. The resulting strikes and riots seared themselves deeply into his memory. He took a boyhood and adolescent vow to be a professional, to rise above such conflicts. He wanted to educate all students so that there never again would be food riots or civil strife.

On assuming his superintendency, Hidalgo set about making allies. He made a point of getting to know the city's mayor and all members of the city council. He worked as cooperatively as he possibly could with teacher's union leaders. He sought and made alliances with representatives of the town's minority associations and various civic clubs. He was popular with town officials, with his school board, and with his teachers, and he still always had time for students.

Hidalgo was surprised one morning to have a phone call from his school board president saying that he had decided to challenge the incumbent mayor in the upcoming municipal election. The school board president said he assumed that the superintendent would endorse his candidacy as repayment for hiring Hidalgo in the first place and for providing him with political and personal support, as well as a good salary the entire time Hidalgo had been superintendent.

The school board president reminded Superintendent Demarest that his contract extension was now before the board and would certainly be looked upon more favorably with Hidalgo's endorsement than without it. What the board president did not say, but what Hidalgo knew without any mention, was that the board majority was likely to support the board president's mayoralty bid.

As luck would have it, Hidalgo was scheduled to have lunch with the mayor that very day, and he was reasonably sure the mayor would announce that he was running for re-election and would expect Hidalgo to endorse his candidacy. After all, as he would be quick to remind Hidalgo, it was the mayor's connections with the city's business leaders, large manufacturers, and big agricultural employers and property owners that ensured the school district had steady increases in its revenues. Hidalgo also remembered the mayor's extensive reputation for aligning himself with shady figures, some of whom were known to use violence to enforce real, or imagined, personal commitments.

He listened to the phone call, but his mind flamed with the pain of his boyhood.

Discussion Questions

1. What sources of conflict do you see playing themselves out in this case?
2. What are some of his options?
3. What should Hidalgo do?

Exercise   Salary Negotiation

You will need a partner for this exercise. One of you will play the role of the employer and the other will play the role of job applicant. Your task is to negotiate an annual salary. The absolute maximum that the employer is allowed to pay is $50,000. However, the employing organization is undergoing financial distress, so the employer is under extreme pressure to keep salary expenses as low as possible in the immediate term. The absolute minimum the applicant should take is $40,000. As you begin the process, consider the elements of principled negotiation: (1) separate people from the problem, (2) focus on interests, not positions, (3) invent options for mutual gain, and (4) insist on objective criteria.

After you complete the negotiation, give your partner some feedback on how he or she handled the negotiation. Then address each of the following questions:

1. Did you separate people from the problem?
2. What were the interests of each party? How well did you do with considering each party's interests?
3. Were you able to invent any options for mutual gain? If this had been a real negotiation, what opportunities might have been available for satisfying each party's interests by inventing options for mutual gain?
4. What would constitute "objective criteria" for this type of negotiation? Did you refer to any objective criteria in your negotiation?

Exercise   How Do You Handle Conflict?

Research suggests that each individual has their own unique style for dealing with conflict and that we tend to use the same approach every time we are in the face of adversity. Answer each of the 15 questions listed below depending on how you would handle that specific conflict situation. After you complete the survey the scoring key will help you identify your conflict-management style.

	Rarely				Always
1. When dealing with a problem, I hold onto my position firmly.	1	2	3	4	5
2. I believe in the principles of negotiation and compromise.	1	2	3	4	5
3. I go along with coworkers' ideas to avoid problems.	1	2	3	4	5
4. I believe it is important to find mutually acceptable solutions to problems.	1	2	3	4	5
5. I am firm in pursuing my side of an issue.	1	2	3	4	5
6. I don't like to disagree with coworkers.	1	2	3	4	5
7. I can stand up for my position when debating an issue with coworkers.	1	2	3	4	5
8. If I find myself in a stalemate with a coworker, I propose a middle ground to resolve the issue.	1	2	3	4	5
9. I believe that the free exchange of ideas is essential to successful problem solving.	1	2	3	4	5
10. If I'm frustrated with my coworkers, I will keep it to myself.	1	2	3	4	5
11. I accommodate the wishes of my coworkers.	1	2	3	4	5
12. I encourage my coworkers to openly discuss all sides of an issue to find the best possible solution to a problem.	1	2	3	4	5
13. I think that compromise is one of the most important virtues in working with others.	1	2	3	4	5

	Rarely			Always	
14. I try to live up to others' expectations of me.	1	2	3	4	5
15. I try not to have disagreements with my coworkers so there are no hard feelings between us.	1	2	3	4	5

Scoring Key

Avoiding	Accommodating	Compromising	Collaborating	Competing
Question: 6. _____	Question: 3. _____	Question: 2. _____	Question: 4. _____	Question : 1. _____
10. _____	11. _____	8. _____	9. _____	5. _____
15. _____	14. _____	13. _____	12. _____	7. _____
Total = _____	Total = _____	Total = _____	Total = _____	Total = _____

Your primary conflict-management style is: _____
(Category with the highest total.)

Your backup conflict-management style is: _____
(Category with the second highest total.)

Source: Adapted in part from Rahim, M. Afzalur (1983, June), A measure of styles of handling interpersonal conflict. *Academy of Management Journal,* 368–376.

References

Allport, G. W. (1954). Relative deprivation, rising expectations, and black militancy. *Journal of Social Issues, 3,* 119–137.

Baumeister, R. F. (1993). *Self-esteem: The puzzle of low self-regard.* New York: Plenum Press.

Bazerman, M. (2006). *Judgment in managerial decision making* (6th ed.). New York: John Wiley & Sons.

Carnevale, P., & Probst, T. (1998). Social values and social conflict in creative problem solving and categorization: Personality process and individual differences. *Journal of Applied Psychology, 74*(5), 1300–1309.

De Dreu, C. K. W., & Beersma, B. (2005). Conflict in organizations: Beyond effectiveness and performance. *European Journal of Work and Organizational Psychology, 14*(2), 105–117.

De Dreu, C. K. W., Koole, S., & Steinel, W. (2000). Unfixing the fixed pie: A motivated information-processing approach to integrative negotiation. *Journal of Personality and Social Psychology, 79*(6), 975–987.

De Dreu, C. K. W., & Weingart, L. R. (2003). Task versus relationship conflict, team performance and team member satisfaction: A meta-analysis. *Journal of Applied Psychology, 88*(4), 741–749.

De Dreu, C. K. W., & West, M. A. (2001). Minority dissent and team innovation: The importance of participation in decision making. *Journal of Applied Psychology, 86*(6), 1191–1201.

De Dreu, C. K. W., & Van Vianen, A. E. M. (2001). Managing relationship conflict and the effectiveness of organizational teams. *Journal of Organizational Behavior, 22,* 309–328.

Deutsch, M. (1973). *The resolution of conflict.* New Haven: Yale University Press.

Eisenhardt, K., Kahwajy, J., & Bourgeois III, L. (1997a). Conflict and strategic choice: How top management teams disagree. *California Management Review, 39*(2), 42–62.

Eisenhardt, K., Kahwajy, J., & Bourgeois III, L. (1997b). How management teams can have a good fight. *Harvard Business Review, 75*(4), 77–86.

Fisher, R., & Ury, W. (1996). *Getting to Yes*. New York: Penguin Books.

Gersick, C. J. G. (1988). Time and transition in work teams: Toward a new model of group development. *Academy of Management Journal, 31,* 9–41.

Gersick, C. J. G. (1989). Marking time: Predictable transitions in task groups. *Academy of Management Journal, 32,* 274–309.

Giebels, E., & Janssen, O. (2005). Conflict stress and reduced well-being at work: The buffering effect of third-party help. *European Journal of Work & Organizational Psychology, 14*(2), 137–155.

Guerra, J., Martinez, I., Munduate, L., & Medina, F. (2005). A contingency perspective on the study of the consequences of conflict types: The role of organizational culture. *European Journal of Work & Organizational Psychology, 14*(2), 156–176.

Hewstone, M., Rubin, M., & Willis, H. (2002). Intergroup bias. *Annual Review of Psychology, 53,* 575–604.

Hinds, P., & Mortensen, M. (2005). Understanding conflict in geographically distributed teams: The moderating effects of shared identity, shared context, and spontaneous communication. *Organization Science: A Journal of the Institute of Management Sciences, 16*(3), 290–307.

Jehn, K. (1995). A mulitmethod experimentation of the benefits and detriments of intragroup conflict. *Administrative Sciences Quarterly, 40*(2), 256–282.

Jehn, K., & Mannix, E. (2001). The dynamic nature of conflict: A longitudinal study of intragroup conflict and group performance. *Academy of Management Journal, 44*(2), 238–251.

Kanter, R. (1977). *Men and women of the corporation*. New York: Basic Books.

Kunda, Z. (1999). *Social cognition: Making sense of people*. Cambridge: MIT Press.

Leonard, D. (1995). *Wellsprings of knowledge: Building and sustaining and sources of innovation*. Boston: Harvard Business School Press.

Lewicki, R., Saunders, D., & Minton, J. (Eds.). (1999). *Negotiations* (3rd ed.). Boston: McGraw-Hill.

Li, J., & Hambrick, D. (2005). Functional groups: A new vantage on demographic faultlines, conflict, and disintegration in work teams. *Academy of Management Journal, 48*(5), 794–813.

London, M. (Ed.). (2001). *How people evaluate others in organizations*. Mahwah, NJ: Lawrence Erlbaum Associates.

Musch, J., & Klauer, C. (Eds.). (2003). *The psychology of evaluation: Affective processes in cognition and emotion*. Mahwah, NJ: Lawrence Erlbaum Associates.

Pfeffer, J. (1992). *Managing with power: Politics and influence in organizations*. Boston: Harvard Business School Press.

Pinkley, R. L. (1990). Dimensions of conflict frame: Disputant interpretations of conflict. *Journal of Applied Psychology, 75,* 117–126.

Rau, D. (2005). The influence of relationship conflict and trust on the transactive memory: Performance relation in top management teams. *Small Group Research, 36*(6), 746–771.

Richter, A., Scully, J., & West, M. (2005). Intergroup conflict and intergroup effectiveness in organizations: Theory and scale development. *European Journal of Work and Organizational Psychology, 14*(2), 177–203.

Robbins, S. P. (2003). *Organizational behavior* (10th ed.). Upper Saddle River, NJ: Prentice Hall.

Sherif, M. (1966). *Group conflict and cooperation: Their social psychology*. London: Routledge & Kegan Paul.

Sherif, M., Harvey, O. J., White, B. J., Hood, W. R., & Sherif, C. W. (1961). *Intergroup conflict and cooperation: The robbers cave experiment*. Norman: University of Oklahoma Book Exchange.

Tajfel, H., & Turner, J. C. (1979). An integrative theory of social conflict. In W. Austin & S. Worchel (Eds.), *The social psychology of intergroup relations* (pp. 33–47). Monterey, CA: Brooks/Cole.

Thomas, K. W. (1976). Conflict and conflict management. In M. D. Dunnette (Ed.), *Handbook of industrial organizational psychology* (p. 900). Chicago: Rand McNally.

Thompson, L., & Leonardelli, G. (2004). The big bang: The evolution of negotiation research. *Academy of Management Executive, 18*(3), 113–117.

Tindale, R., Dykema-Engblade, A., & Wittkowski, E. (2005). Conflict within and between groups. In S. Wheelan (Ed.), *The handbook of group research and practice* (pp. 313–328). Thousand Oaks, CA: Sage Publications.

Tjosvold, D. (1993). *Learning to manage conflict: Getting people to work together productively*. New York: Lexington Books.

Tjosvold, D. (1997). Conflict with interdependence: Its value for productivity and individuality. In C. De Dreu & E. Van de Vliert (Eds.), *Using conflict in organizations* (pp. 23–37). Thousand Oaks, CA: Sage Publications.

West, M. A. (2004). *Effective teamwork: Practical lessons from organizational research* (2nd ed.). Oxford, UK: BPS Blackwell.

CHAPTER TEN

Team Development and Training

▨ INTRODUCTION

This chapter draws a distinction between groups and teams, and illustrates what is required to build an effective team. Various methods of developing knowledge, skills, and abilities that are relevant to team effectiveness are examined. We describe interventions for improving team performance and note the limited utility of many current interventions. We also focus on conditions that organizations should put in place in order to enhance the chances that teams will thrive.

LEARNING OBJECTIVES

After reading this chapter, you should be able to

- Understand how professionals develop in the workplace.
- Identify the key knowledge skills and abilities that are associated with effective teamwork.
- Understand how training can be improved.
- Recognize the value of feedback, coaching, mentoring, and job assignments in professional development.
- Understand the key components of effective coaching.
- Know the common mistakes organizations make when implementing teams.

 OPENING CASE

Building a Team to Upgrade Security at Ellington

Not long after September 11, 2001, the senior leadership of Ellington thought that they would be wise to upgrade the management of their security. They decided to create a new position—Chief Security Officer. The Chief Security Officer would be responsible for leading a team that would comprise a top executive from each of the organization's divisions. Each individual would be responsible for bringing security issues to the table from his or her own division. Team members were then expected to put their heads together to construct ideas about new initiatives that the organization should undertake to better manage its security, and the means for implementing them.

Senior leadership decided that Kate Stein, an extremely smart, dedicated employee with a reputation for technical excellence in her role in corporate finance would be a good choice for this position. It would provide her with an opportunity to lead a team and to gain exposure to each of the divisions. Stein was delighted with her promotion, and, true to form, got to work immediately to get the team organized and moving forward. Fred Daniels, Stein's boss, assumed things would be going fine, but he soon started hearing grumblings from the team. When Daniels checked with Stein, she did not seem concerned about how things were going, other than perceiving that sometimes the other team members were not making the security team's efforts as high a priority as they should. Daniels thought that things would probably work themselves out until he started to hear reports of growing frustration within the team. Still, although Stein was not highly satisfied with the team's performance, she did not seem to share the same level of concern as Daniels. Furthermore, she did not have any clear sense of what would make the team work better. Daniels pondered what he should do to address the situation.

Discussion Questions

1. What are some options for Daniels?
2. What do you think he should do?

■ INTRODUCTION TO TEAM AND DEVELOPMENT TRAINING

Chapter 1 mentioned that the terms *group* and *team* are often used somewhat synonymously, but *teams* are actually defined more specifically. The term *group* refers to a general category of which a *team* is a subset. Thus, all teams are groups, but not all groups should be considered teams. One general difference is that teams typically have more specific, demanding performance expectations. Teams have the following four characteristics (Alderfer, 1977; Hackman, 1990):

1. They are designed with the purpose of accomplishing at least *one or two specific goals or objectives.*
2. At least some degree of *interdependence* must exist such that team members depend on each other in order to accomplish the outcome.
3. For the purpose of accomplishing the task, team members adopt or are assigned one or more *specific roles* that they are responsible to enact.
4. Teams are *bounded* social systems with a relatively stable, intact structure. Membership may vary over time, but team members need clarity as to who is or is not on the team and what their roles are in order to function effectively as a team.

Because teams are designed specifically for the purpose of accomplishing one or more tasks effectively, this chapter focuses on various methods of developing teams and enhancing their performance. We noted in Chapter 1 that groups have great potential, but often fail to achieve their potential. Thus, organizational leaders must ask what can be done to enable teams to achieve more of their potential. The purpose of this chapter is to illustrate various methods for developing teams and to examine their effectiveness.

▌ HOW DO PROFESSIONALS DEVELOP IN THE WORKPLACE?

Several leaders at McKinsey & Co., one of the world's most prestigious consulting firms, observed that competition among organizations to attract and retain the most talented employees was intensifying. They labeled this the *war for talent* and decided to study what organizations were doing to attract, develop, and retain the most talented people (Michaels, Handfield-Jones & Axelrod, 2001). To do so, they conducted an extensive survey of middle and senior managers throughout the world. They found that many successful organizations were using developmental opportunities as a means of attracting the best employees. They also learned that organizations used multiple methods for developing their people, and they decided to examine how employees evaluated these various methods of their employers. Specifically, they asked respondents to rate how important these methods were to their development and how good a job their organizations were doing of providing these developmental opportunities in a competent manner. Figure 10.1 shows a summary of how respondents rated these methods on these two dimensions.

Although training may be one of the most common ways that professionals develop, these results illustrate that it is only one means through which individuals can learn and grow. Also, these methods of developing employees are not mutually exclusive; they can and should be used in conjunction to reinforce one another. For example, when training has been used in conjunction with coaching, it has more impact than training alone (Dixon & Young, 1997).

Traditional classroom training was ranked as the least-important method of development and the most poorly executed. Another interesting finding is that these professionals did not consider many of the other methods of developing employees as very well done by their organizations. This suggests that there is considerable room for improvement in current people-development practices in organizations. Next, we describe a number of methods for developing people and examine their strengths and weaknesses.

▌ TRAINING

Human resource professionals in organizations recognize that new employees often do not have the knowledge, skills, or abilities to perform tasks and jobs effectively. Thus, organizations spend an immense amount of money on training. Estimates of private sector annual training expenditures range from $55 to $200 billion (Salas & Cannon-Bowers, 2001). For example, America's 14,000 local public school districts spend, depending on how the calculations are made, between $10 and $100 billion on employee training (Guthrie, et al., 2007). Training is important not only for new employees, but also for keeping current employees informed regarding new developments in their area of work and for preparing them to assume greater responsibility or to be promoted to new assignments.

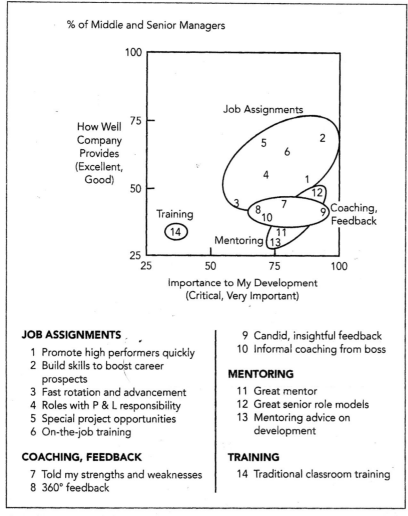

% of Middle and Senior Managers

FIGURE 10.1   Managerial Evaluation of Management Development Practices

Source: Michaels, E., Handfield-Jones, H., & Axelrod, B. (2001). *The war for talent.* Boston: Harvard Business School Press.

Thus, current technical knowledge, skills, and abilities are important for any jobs that require technical ability. The ability to work effectively in a team often requires that certain individuals on the team have the right technical knowledge and skills. However, relevant technical skills alone are not enough to ensure that individuals will be able to work effectively together as a team. Team members also need knowledge, skills, and abilities specifically about teamwork. Organizations often make the mistake of simply assuming that "everyone knows how to work in a team" (Stewart, Manz, & Sims, 1999). Unfortunately, employees are often lacking in the knowledge, skills, and abilities that are essential for enabling the individuals within a team to operate in a way that really takes advantage of the individual efforts and talents within the group. Organizational decision makers tend to give too much emphasis to technical skills and place insufficient emphasis on skills related to working in a team (Hollenbeck, DeRue, & Guzzo, 2004).

Stewart, Manz, and Sims examined the implementation of teams in a variety of organizations and concluded that "training requirements for teams cannot be overestimated" (1999, p. 159). But what kind of training is necessary? What does it take to work effectively in a team? To address these questions, Stevens and Campion (1994) reviewed the literature on team effectiveness in order to identify what knowledge, skills, and abilities are necessary for effective teamwork. Their research uncovered two major dimensions, each with important subcategories. The two major dimensions are: First, *interpersonal*, having to do with the ability to work effectively with other people, and second, *self-management*, having to do with the ability to manage the task effectively. Their interpersonal knowledge, skills, and abilities have been evaluated and appear to be good measures of the ability to work effectively in a team (Hollenbeck, DeRue, & Guzzo, 2004). Research shows that their two categories have been associated with higher team performance (McClough & Rogelberg, 2003).

▓ INTERPERSONAL KNOWLEDGE, SKILLS, AND ABILITIES

Interpersonal knowledge, skills, and abilities involve the ability to work collaboratively with others and include *conflict resolution*, *collaborative problem solving*, and *communication*.

Conflict Resolution

As described in Chapter 9, at least some degree of conflict or disagreement occurs in most teams. Team members should recognize that conflict is natural but that it can be destructive. Thus, team members need skills for making the best of their differences and for keeping disagreements from getting out of hand. Integrative negotiation skills can be helpful in this regard.

Collaborative Problem Solving

Team members should have the knowledge to discriminate which problems are appropriate for bringing to the team for collaborative problem solving. Team members should also have the ability to use the team effectively for this purpose. This may require encouraging input from all team members, understanding different perspectives, working through differences of opinion, and assisting the team in coming to a decision that takes advantage of all the knowledge within the team.

Communication

As mentioned in earlier chapters, communication breakdowns are a frequent culprit in leading to deteriorating team performance. Communication skills include an ability to listen, willingness to speak up about concerns, ability to get one's message across, and an ability to facilitate constructive dialogue. This may also extend outside the team to having the ability to network and communicate effectively with outsiders who have relevant information or input for the team.

■ SELF-MANAGEMENT KNOWLEDGE, SKILLS, AND ABILITIES

Self-management knowledge, skills, and abilities include *goal setting and performance management*, and *planning and task coordination.*

Goal Setting and Performance Management

As discussed in Chapter 2, effective goal setting is associated with higher performance. Effective goals are Specific, Measurable, Attainable, Relevant, and Time-bounded (SMART). Team members need the ability to develop SMART goals and build team commitment to these goals. Performance management involves understanding that work is a process that unfolds over time and being able to assess whether performance is on target at any particular point in the process. This also involves having the ability to address any problems in the performance process and make corrections.

Planning and Task Coordination

By themselves, well-constructed goals are insufficient. Once goals are in place, team members need to establish effective plans to accomplish their goals. Effective plans include concrete steps with timelines, deadlines, and clear performance expectations. In a team structure, this also involves determining how to divide up the tasks among individual team members and then making sure that their individual roles and responsibilities are coordinated and that individuals are held accountable.

■ HOW EFFECTIVE IS TRAINING?

Studies suggest that training tends to be an effective means of educating employees and enhancing their knowledge, skills, and abilities (Arthur, Bennett, Edens, & Bell, 2003). Organizations have been growing more sophisticated in their use of training, and training programs can be improved over time (Salas & Cannon-Bowers, 2001). For example, crew management training was originally developed several decades ago for aviators after researchers observed that most plane crashes are a result of human error. Over the past decades, crew management training has evolved and become more effective. Today, it is used not only among commercial airlines and the military, but also in a range of other work environments from hospitals to oil rigs, and it appears to have a positive impact on team functioning.

Although traditional classroom training received a low ranking in the McKinsey & Co. survey, research suggests that it may be more effective than it is perceived to be (Ellis, Bell, Ployhart, Hollenback, & Ilgen, 2005). Classroom and other forms of training can be more effective when augmented by other approaches to development, such as coaching, mentoring, feedback, and job assignments.

Organizational leaders might also consider more cross training within teams. Cross training involves teaching members of a team how to perform each other's jobs. This knowledge may facilitate greater coordination and adaptability within the team. By learning each other's jobs, team members gain a greater understanding of how the team as a whole operates, and are better positioned to assist each other and coordinate efforts. Cross training also facilitates sustained performance in an emergency, when one or more members of a team are injured or unavailable for their tasks. Research has reported that cross training has led to improvements of between 14 and 40% (Sims, Salas, & Burke, 2005).

▪ HOW CAN TRAINING BE IMPROVED?

The fact that training appears to produce considerable benefits does not mean that it does not have significant room for improvement. Specifically, training that is conducted in many organizations might be enhanced by better utilizing general principles of training effectiveness, conducting a needs analysis, systematically evaluating training effectiveness, and improving the transfer of training.

General Principles of Training Effectiveness

The following are general principles that contribute to training effectiveness (Salas & Cannon-Bowers, 2001). Trainers may at times neglect one of more of these, so we provide this as a checklist of items that trainers and training designers should consider.

1. The informational and conceptual content of the program should be relevant and useful to trainees, and trainees need to perceive it as such.
2. The knowledge, skills, and abilities that trainees are supposed to learn should be demonstrated clearly.
3. Trainees should be given opportunities to practice using the knowledge, skills, and abilities that they are learning.
4. Developmental feedback should be given to trainees both during and after the training.

Needs Analysis

Experts contend that the design of effective training should start with a needs analysis. A needs analysis is an assessment of what knowledge, skills, and abilities employees have and what they need in order to undertake their work effectively. With this information, those who design the training can ensure that the training suits the trainee's needs. One review of training programs revealed that only 6% of those studied clearly indicated that they had conducted a needs analysis prior to designing and delivering the training programs (Arthur, Bennett, Edens, & Bell, 2003). Foregoing the needs analysis is not necessarily wrong. The key question is whether something is missed as the training designer makes assumptions about what trainees need. A designer who has a good understanding of trainees and what they do is less likely to miss something by forgoing a needs analysis than one who is less familiar. Nonetheless, training is more likely to be designed effectively if a needs analysis is conducted.

Evaluation

With a needs analysis, training can be targeted and designed more effectively. However, being well informed and well intentioned in designing the training does not necessarily guarantee that the training will produce desired results. Thus, training should also be evaluated to determine its effectiveness, and evaluation results should be used further to develop the training to build its effectiveness over time. Also, given the cost of training, organizations are experiencing greater pressures to evaluate and quantify the costs and financial payoffs that are expected to result from training (Phillips, 2003), and this should involve evaluation. Human resources practitioners may be less likely to receive an adequate budget for training if they cannot demonstrate its value.

Transfer of Training

Effective trainers try to make training as realistic as possible, but training is often conducted in a classroom; thus, trainees therefore are learning in a context that is different from the work context in which they are expected to implement what they have learned. Skills and abilities can vary dramatically with respect to the relative difficulty of implementation outside the classroom. Learning can be fairly technical or formulaic, such as how to read a gauge on a machine or how to follow a procedure for changing a part. Other skills and abilities are more difficult to put into practice. For example, employees may learn conflict management skills in a classroom, but their need to enact them may erupt unexpectedly while the team is struggling to meet an important deadline. Team members may be tired, with emotions running high, making it difficult to know what to say to dampen conflict. The training and role-playing that went on in a classroom may not be easy to put into practice in the heat of the moment.

One solution is training conducted on the job. Thus, the individual is simultaneously learning and engaging in the work. In the McKinsey & Co. survey, on-the-job training was ranked as being more important to employee development and was being done better than traditional classroom training. Organizations may be able to make training more effective by integrating training with the actual work that an employee is doing on the job.

Thus, one potential limitation of traditional classroom training is that the learning that takes place solely in the classroom may not translate well into the workplace. The effectiveness of classroom training can often be augmented by coaching that assists trainees in bridging the gap between conceptual knowledge and an ability to act effectively on that knowledge. Coaching will be addressed later in this chapter.

■ GROUPS AS THE UNIT OF TRAINING

Educators and trainers often organize students or trainees into groups in order to facilitate development (Michaelsen, Knight, & Fink, 2004). Groups may be used for training whether the training involves competencies related to teamwork or not. Hollenbeck, DeRue, and Guzzo (2004) documented that training that occurs within complete work teams has multiple positive benefits. For example, those trained in groups remembered more and were better able to transfer training to their work performance; and the team's overall performance improved when training was conducted within their work teams.

Both the interactions among team members as they learn, as well as the impact of the team leader, appear to have been significant factors in achieving these results. Unfortunately, these researchers also reported that managers have a tendency to think that individuals must be trained to a level of individual capability before training should be conducted within a team. Thus, teams may be missing some of the benefits that they could accrue if their members had been able to be trained in a team earlier.

■ MULTISOURCE FEEDBACK

Psychologists have understood the importance of feedback for learning and performance improvement for many decades (Locke & Latham, 1990). Unfortunately, people are often inaccurate in how they perceive their own performance; in particular, they have inaccurately positive views of themselves and their performance (London, 1997). Thus, they may have difficulty understanding both the need to improve and the behaviors and communications that they need to improve unless they are given feedback. Over the past several decades, multisource feedback (sometimes called 360-degree feedback) has become a popular means of providing feedback that is useful to employee development. London (1997) reported that all of the Fortune 500 companies are making some use of multisource feedback or are at least planning to do so.

What is multisource feedback, and what makes it useful? Multisource feedback simply means that performance feedback comes from multiple people. In a team, the feedback might come from each peer within the team, the team leader, the team leader's boss, the individual's subordinates (if any), and even the team's customers and members of other teams with whom a team member interacts.

To understand how such feedback is useful, we should first examine traditional practices for performance appraisal and giving feedback. Most commonly, the boss or team leader would be responsible for providing feedback and appraising performance. Employees would confer with their boss or team leader once a year and the boss would share his or her performance ratings and discuss the employee's performance. These meetings were often uncomfortable for both the boss and the employee because both giving and receiving feedback, especially negative feedback, can be an unpleasant process. Because people tend to hold unrealistically positive views of themselves and their performance (Taylor & Brown, 1988), accurate feedback may be disappointing and disconcerting to receive. Bosses typically do not want to upset employees or to hurt their feelings, so they sometimes pull their punches and are not sufficiently detailed or clear when giving negative feedback (Cannon & Witherspoon, 2005). Thus, employees often do not receive an accurate picture of their shortcomings and developmental needs. Because of the interpersonal tensions that are sometimes associated with these meetings, bosses have been known simply to procrastinate on scheduling an annual performance appraisal and employees sometimes go for years without a performance appraisal, which can exacerbate existing problems. Thus, the quality of feedback can be disrupted because the boss does not want to face the interpersonal discomfort associated with being completely open and honest.

The quality of feedback is further limited by other factors. Bosses may have limited information, especially if they do not spend much of their time observing or interacting with a particular subordinate. In addition, subordinates often try to deliberately manage the impression that the boss has of them to create an inaccurately rosy picture in the boss's mind in order to get a good evaluation. Thus, efforts at impressing management may hurt the quality of feedback that employees receive.

Not only does the boss have limited or even deliberately distorted information, but humans are also vulnerable to a number of biases as they make assessments of others. This may also interfere with the quality of feedback (Cannon & Witherspoon, 2005).

Multisource feedback can ameliorate many of these problems. Typically, raters go on-line and give the individual numerical ratings on multiple performance dimensions that are most relevant to the job. Many multisource feedback systems also enable raters to provide open-ended feedback in which they may write comments or suggestions. The source of the feedback is usually kept anonymous, and this eliminates the major disincentive for people to be honest in their evaluations. Without anonymity, raters may be worried that the feedback receiver will "shoot the messenger," holding it against him or her, possibly retaliating in some way, withdrawing friendship, or becoming unpleasant to work with.

Anonymity shields raters from some of these repercussions and encourages them to be honest.

By including multiple individuals in the process, the feedback can provide a more well-rounded view of the person, diluting any bias. Employees who might have some success managing impressions in front of the boss usually have more difficulty managing impressions among all team members. In addition, feedback that comes from many individuals is more difficult to dismiss than feedback that comes from a single source.

Research demonstrates that multisource feedback can produce helpful information for learning and development (Smither, London, & Reilly, 2005). Do employees use this feedback to improve their performance? Overall, multisource feedback has been associated with modest performance improvement; however, individuals vary significantly in the extent to which they dedicated themselves to improving after receiving feedback (Smither & Walker, 2004). Employees had more success in improving when they were able to translate their feedback into specific goals for improvement, developing and following effective action plans, and maintaining a sense of optimism about their prospects for making successful changes (Smither, London, & Reilly, 2005). Optimism, effective goals, and action planning often do not emerge spontaneously from this medium, so multisource feedback does not inevitably lead to improvement. Coaching is a helpful way to facilitate the developmental process and assist individuals in achieving more progress more quickly than they could on their own.

■ COACHING

The use of coaching (sometimes called executive coaching) has grown dramatically in recent years (Bacon & Speer, 2003). Figure 10.1 shows that managers find coaching useful to their development. Coaching is discussed in Chapter 5, but we provide more detail of what coaching is here.

Coaching is rooted in the word *coach* which involves transporting an individual from one destination to another. In contrast to the original meaning of coaching, we refer to the providing of assistance to an individual in transcending from a lower level of competence and ability to a higher level. Coaching can be focused on almost any knowledge, skill, ability, or attitude that affects job performance. Thus, coaching is not limited exclusively to work within teams, but there are many ways in which coaching can be used to promote team effectiveness. Coaching may be given to an individual, a subgroup within a team, or the team as a whole, though most of the writing on coaching focuses on coaching individuals. Coaching can promote team effectiveness either by focusing on enhancing individual, technical skills of team members, or by fostering a better ability to work effectively within a team. For example, the focus could be on any of the interpersonal or task-knowledge skills and abilities discussed above (conflict resolution, collaborative problem solving, communication, goal setting and performance management, and planning and task coordination).

Focusing coaching on the team leader can also be a helpful way of enhancing team effectiveness. Just as organizational leaders may assume that everyone knows how to work in a team, they may also believe that anyone can manage people, or anyone can run a team. Thus, individuals who do not have good skills for leading teams are sometimes placed in team-leadership roles without even realizing what the role requires or what their strengths and weaknesses are for handling this role (Hill, 1992). This can be costly because poor leadership can hinder all members of a team. This was one of the issues that complicated Kate Stein's ability to move smoothly into her security team leadership role.

Key Components of Effective Coaching

The GROW model by Sir John Whitmore (1996) captures the basic components that are helpful to employee development. Effective coaching facilitates clarity about each of the following:

Goal: What is my goal for performance or development?
Reality: Where do I stand now?
Options: What are my options for achieving the goal?
Will: How will I maintain the will or motivation to succeed?

If any one of these elements is missing, prospects for effective development are diminished considerably. So, how does one develop all four of these? A number of key skills and elements in the coaching relationship are useful here. At this point, we make a distinction between formal and informal coaching. Much of the coaching that goes on in teams is conducted informally. Informal coaching is more spontaneous and less structured than formal coaching, and may be done as needs or opportunities present themselves in the moment.

Formal coaching is often done by professional coaches from outside the organization or by specialists within the organization. However, managers or team leaders may also conduct formal coaching with team members or subordinates if they can find time and if they have the skills and inclination. Formal coaching is distinguished from informal coaching in that it is more structured and planned and is usually characterized by greater investment of time and effort. Sometimes organizations provide formal coaching to a level, or a set of levels, of management within the organizational hierarchy. Managers may get one or two coaching sessions per month that may last from one to several hours to focus on one specific issue that the individual is striving to develop. What we describe below are the components that constitute effective formal coaching. Each of these elements is also helpful in informal coaching, and those engaging in informal coaching can benefit from polishing as many of these elements as they have time to develop.

Because of the cost of formal coaching, organizations vary significantly in the extent to which they offer this developmental opportunity to employees. More often, employees are likely to receive informal coaching to the extent that they receive any coaching at all. Informal coaching may be done by anyone, but is often done by managers or team leaders. Informal coaching is understood in many organizations to be a managerial or leadership responsibility, but given the many demands on these individuals' time, there is little opportunity to fully engage in all the elements of formal coaching. Instead, managers or team leaders take opportunities to conduct informal coaching on an ad hoc basis as opportunities present themselves. They pick and choose what elements of formal coaching to use depending on the situation and the time they have available to them. In a survey of professionals from Fortune 500 companies, 57% of respondents indicated that they would like to receive more coaching than they are currently getting, and 60% of respondents indicated that they would like to receive higher-quality coaching than they are currently receiving (Bacon & Spear, 2003).

Next, we describe the elements that contribute to effective formal coaching. Though these work best when used in conjunction with each other, each is potentially of value on its own. Elements that contribute to an effective coaching relationship include:

- Relationship
- Listening
- Assessment
- Feedback
- Goal Setting
- Action Planning
- Ongoing Follow-Up

Relationship. Coaching is different from psychotherapy, but it has some overlapping aspects. For example, an effective working relationship is important for success in each (Costa & Garmston, 1994). Decades of research have shown how important the therapeutic relationship is to success in psychotherapy (Corsini & Wedding, 2005). Coaching differs from psychotherapy in focusing primarily on the present and future, rather than on the past, and in focusing on developing more effective ways of approaching work, rather than on exploring feelings and resolving psychological issues. Nonetheless, as in psychotherapy, the person being coached is in a potentially vulnerable position of acknowledging some area of weakness that needs to be faced and addressed. So, having a relationship in which the coached person feels safe and supported, though also challenged and confronted at times, is helpful to achieving success in the coaching process. A good relationship sends a signal that someone cares about the person being coached and his or her development, and this should provide support for the *will* to change.

Listening. Listening is an immensely helpful part of coaching (Schein, 1999). First, listening is an effective way for coaches to illustrate that they are sincerely interested in the person coached, which helps to build the coaching relationship. Second, listening enables the coach to better understand the problem and therefore be more useful. Third, listening, rather than immediately telling the other person what to do, assists the coached person in taking personal responsibility for the problem and in developing the motivation to work on the problem—another component of the will to change. Employee internal commitment to a change process typically grows with greater personal involvement in the process. Offering advice is a natural human reaction to hearing another person's problem (Schein, 1999). If the problem is simply a lack of technical knowledge, advice might be useful. However, if the performance issue is at all complicated or multidimensional, unsolicited advice may be worth just what the receiver paid for it.

Assessment. Assessments may include any activities that capture information on personality, interests, abilities, styles, and so on. This includes written tests or inventories, such as the Myers-Briggs Type Inventory (MBTI), the Thomas-Kilmann Conflict Mode Instrument (TKI), and the Fundamental Interpersonal Orientations-Behavior (FIRO-B). Multisource feedback can also be considered an assessment. Assessment can also be conducted by having a skilled observer examine how an individual or team approaches their work. Assessments can be particularly helpful in enabling individuals to understand how they are similar to or different from other people with whom they work. With this understanding, they are better able to realize why others perceive them the way they do and what they can do to be more effective.

Feedback. Coaches are often designated to collect and deliver multisource feedback. The coach can help to make sense of the feedback and use the feedback as the basis for establishing goals and an action plan. Both feedback and assessments help the coached person clarify current reality (Where do I stand right now?). Also, because some organizations do a poor job of giving feedback, the coach may need to initiate the feedback-gathering process.

Goal Setting. Once coached people understand current reality, coaches can assist them in developing SMART (specific, measurable, attainable, relevant, and time-bounded) objectives. Without the support and assistance of coaches, people often do not develop effective, actionable goals.

Action Planning. Effective development requires more than just a goal; it also requires an intelligent plan of action. Big goals must be disaggregated into a set of concrete steps that can be followed. Goal setting and action planning have to do with the options part of the GROW model.

Ongoing Follow-Up. Knowing that someone will be following up is motivating and supportive. Following-up can also enable any necessary adjustments to be made. For example, the coach and the coached may need to do some problem solving to address a difficulty that the coached person is encountering. Goals may need to be adjusted if they were set too high or too low. If the person being coached has already achieved a goal, the coach may want to have a discussion about how to make sure the goal continues to be met and then offer encouragement to take on another issue that came out of the multisource feedback.

An Illustration of Formal Coaching

Kate Stein's boss, who had benefited personally from coaching he had received from Robert Witherspoon (a seasoned executive coach), decided that coaching might help Kate. Witherspoon developed a relationship with Kate in which she felt safe to explore the problem. He listened to her talk about her background and her experience with this team and learned that she had received very little of the kinds of coaching, feedback, or other developmental experiences that other leaders might have received prior to taking on her current assignment. He gave her the Myers-Briggs Type Inventory and collected multi-source feedback on her from her team.

He learned that the team members were extremely low in their opinions of her and were intensely frustrated. He also obtained detailed feedback about the specific things they did not like. Together, Witherspoon and Stein used the feedback and assessments to understand why things were going poorly and to develop goals and action plans to rescue the situation. For example, one criticism was that meetings were run ineffectively. Specifically, she was criticized for talking too much and not listening sufficiently, for getting mired in minutia and losing focus on the big picture, and for not bringing the team to closure on issues in a timely manner. Witherspoon noticed that all of these had potential connections to her Myers-Briggs Type Inventory results. She was extroverted, sensing, thinking, and perceiving. Given that she was highly extroverted, and extroverts like to talk and often have difficulty finding the patience to listen, her extroversion appeared to contribute to her tendency in meetings to do too much talking and not enough listening. Sensors tend to like concrete details, specifics, and procedures, whereas intuitives gravitate toward seeing the big picture and broader vision. Sensors focus on the trees while intuitives focus on the forest. In her previous financial role, this focus on the details was helpful, but in a leadership position in which she needed to understand and integrate the needs of various parts of the organization, a big picture perspective was imperative. Finally, perceivers have a tendency not to tie up loose ends in a timely manner. As a perceiver, she frustrated other members of the team who wanted to achieve clarity and closure on how the team was going to proceed.

She was fascinated to learn about this. With her new understanding of the Myers-Briggs, she now had a much clearer grasp on how and why she was coming across as ineffective. Stein and Witherspoon worked together to establish SMART goals and a concrete action plan for improvement. In sum, she now had *Goals*, and understanding of her current *Reality*, a set of *Options* for going forward, and the *Will* to make changes. These all contributed to a significant performance improvement.

An Illustration of Informal Coaching

In contrast to the previous illustration of formal coaching focused on an individual, we provide an example of informal coaching focused on a team. The informal leader of a self-managing team might say, "I know I am not the only one who has noticed that we get sidetracked in this team a number of times in each of our weekly meetings. It's not a big deal, but I wonder if we should examine that and see whether we could reduce its occurrences so that we could get through the meetings a little quicker." After the team agrees that the idea is worth exploring, the leader says: "OK, what if I visit a meeting of the Stanton team? They are known for being efficient, and I would be curious as to what they do differently." After visiting the Stanton team, the leader reports back: "They cover the same material we do in about an hour, whereas we take around two hours. One thing they do differently is to have the role of 'process checker'—an individual whose job it is to point it out when the team appears to be getting sidetracked and redirects the conversation to keep things on course. Each member rotates through this role such that everyone takes a turn, and a different person plays that role each meeting. I wonder if we should experiment today with having someone play that role and see if it helps. I would like to see whether we could complete our meeting today in an hour and a half or less." After experimenting successfully with this role, they made their goal of keeping the meeting to less than an hour and the team decided to continue using the role.

■ COACHING VERSUS DESIGN INTERVENTIONS

Wageman (2001) sought to understand the impact of informal coaching on self-management and performance in teams. She observed that teams commonly do not achieve their potential, and this raised the question of what team leaders can do to be most effective in enhancing team performance. Drawing on Hackman's theory of team leadership (described in Chapter 5), she noted that the variables in his model could be divided into *design* and *coaching* categories, and she set out to explore how coaching versus design interventions would influence team self-management and performance. As a brief review, Hackman's theory suggests that teams will perform effectively when the following conditions are in place:

- A real team
- A compelling direction
- An enabling structure
- A supportive organizational context
- Expert coaching

Wageman categorized the first four of these as having to do with the *design* of the team, and the final condition constitutes the nondesign intervention *coaching*. Drawing on data from teams at Xerox, she looked at how these variables affected team self-management and performance. Overall, she found that the quality of team design had far more impact on self-management and performance than did coaching (Wageman, 2001). Coaching affected self-management, but had little impact on performance. Her study also demonstrated that the ability of coaching to affect team self-management was significantly affected by how well teams were designed (see Figure 10.2). Specifically, well-designed teams experienced more benefits from effective coaching. She also noted that coaching was sometimes conducted in an ineffective manner and that such coaching could actually have a negative impact on a team. The quality of team design also affected the extent to which ineffective coaching influenced self-management. Effective design appears to act as a buffer that protects the team from the potentially damaging effects of ineffective coaching. Thus, well-designed teams were damaged less by ineffective coaching than were less well-designed teams. The fact that design was a much more potent variable than coaching in influencing the effectiveness of the team suggests that team leaders would be well advised to focus their efforts first on making sure that teams are well designed. In other words, an excellent starting place for creating effective teams is to develop real teams with a compelling direction, an enabling structure, and a supportive organizational context.

The fact that informal coaching did not have a strong impact on self-management and had a rather weak impact on performance may appear to suggest that coaching is not

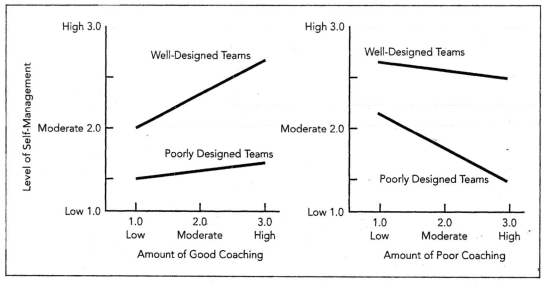

FIGURE 10.2 How Team Design and Leader Coaching Jointly Affect Team Self-Management

Source: Wageman, R. (2001). How leaders foster self-managing team effectiveness: Design choices versus hands-on coaching. *Organization Science, 12*(5), 559–577.

worthwhile. However, Hackman and Wageman (2005) examined the evidence and concluded that coaching can indeed have a significant helpful impact on teams, but the conditions for teams to be able to realize benefits from coaching must be in place first. In particular, they identified the following as conditions that would enable coaching to have a positive valuable impact (Hackman & Wageman, 2005, p. 283):

1. The group performance processes that are key to performance effectiveness (i.e., effort, strategy, and knowledge and skill) are relatively unconstrained by the tasks of organizational requirements.
2. The team is well-designed and the organizational context within which it operates supports rather than impedes teamwork.
3. Coaching behavior focuses on salient task performance process rather than on members' interpersonal relationships or on processes that are not under the team's control.
4. Coaching interventions are made at times when the team is ready for them and able to deal with them—that is, at the beginning for effort-related (motivational) interventions, near the midpoint for strategy-related (consultative) interventions, and at the end of a task cycle for (educational) interventions that address knowledge and skill.

The first two points involve implementing the organizational conditions that are prerequisites for coaching to have an impact. Naturally, if the task or organizational constraints are so tight that there is no freedom to act on what the team learns from coaching, the team will not be able to put its learning into practice, and performance will not improve. Thus, in order for coaching to have an impact, task and organizational structure need to be sufficiently flexible to give team members the autonomy they need to act on what they learn.

The second point reflects the conclusions of Wageman's (2001) research—that having a well-designed team is extremely important. Unless the team is well designed, the necessary prerequisites will not be in place to enable the team to benefit from coaching.

The third point addresses the target of coaching. Coaching interventions that focus on interpersonal relationships have shown minimal results (Salas, Rozell, Mullen, & Driskell, 1999). In addition, interventions that focus on issues that are not under the team's control will not translate into better performance. Thus, coaching should be targeted strategically at salient task-performance processes that team members can readily put into practice.

Finally, a team's openness and readiness to receive coaching is influenced by where it is in its task cycle (Hackman & Wageman, 2005). Teams tend to be most open to coaching at specific intervals during the beginning, middle, and end of a task cycle. In addition, the type of coaching that will be most useful also varies according to whether the team is at the beginning, middle, or endpoint in its task cycle.

At their inception, team members are typically open to coaching. At this point, the most helpful kind of intervention is for the team to have a *motivational* intervention that focuses them on the task and raises their commitment to accomplishing the task and to working together for this purpose. Once the team is launched and on its way, members tend to become engrossed in performing the task, and coaching interventions may be more distracting than useful.

At the midpoint in the task cycle, teams typically pause to assess their progress, reassess their strategies, and make any adjustments necessary to move toward completion of the task. Thus, the team is once again open to coaching for a brief period. At this point, *consultative* coaching is most appropriate because team members are open to rethinking their approach to the task and to trying new ideas to assure a successful result.

Once the team passes the midpoint in its task cycle, they tend once again to become task focused and prepare to sprint toward the finish line. Thus, between the midpoint and endpoint, coaching can be more of a distraction than an asset. Finally, after the task is completed, the team becomes open again to coaching. At this point, *educational* coaching that focuses on knowledge and skill is most helpful. Team members can reflect on what they have learned in the process of accomplishing this task. They can inquire into how well they used the knowledge, skill, and ability within the team; they can consider whether there is additional knowledge, skill, and ability that they have yet to acquire that would be beneficial to future performance.

In sum, Hackman and Wageman contend that informal coaching can be useful to teams. However, appropriate conditions need to be in place such that the team is able to utilize the coaching, and the coaching needs to have both the right focus and the occurrence at the right interval. Their research reemphasizes the importance of the design variables described previously. Thus, a managerial implication is to start with effective design. Getting a team started on the right foot and then providing appropriate support is the best way to ensure effectiveness. Teams that do not get started on the right foot are often unable to recover. Instead, they often enter a downward spiral of deteriorating performance (Ericksen & Dyer, 2004).

▓ MENTORING

Mentoring can serve many of the functions of coaching, but it is usually less formal and less structured. It may occur independent of roles and be based upon intangibles of personalities, interests, or other commonalities. Mentors often provide information, advice, and support. Mentors choose those that they mentor, whereas coaching often is associated with a particular role or function. For example, a senior person in another part of the organization might strike up a friendship with a new employee in the company gym while they are working out. The senior person may share his or her greater knowledge about how the organization operates, where there are good developmental opportunities, how to deal with difficult people in the organization, and so on. This forms the mentoring relationship. A team leader may mentor team members, and sometimes senior members of a team will mentor junior members on their own initiative. For example, principals mentor assistant principals and teachers, and experienced teachers often mentor teachers with less experience (Young, Sheets, & Knight, 2005).

▓ JOB ASSIGNMENTS

Researchers have discovered that many of the key ways in which leaders learn is from the experience of doing their jobs (McCall, Lombardo, & Morrison, 1988). Thus, receiving a challenging new assignment can be a great developmental opportunity. Still, developmental opportunities are more likely to be beneficial if they are designed intelligently and if they are accompanied by other forms of development, such as those described above.

▧ TEAM-BUILDING INTERVENTIONS

Because the McKinsey & Co. study was not about teams in particular, it did not inquire about team-building interventions. However, we mention these interventions because they have been popular for several decades. At one time, team building was reportedly the most popular organizational development intervention (Porras & Berg, 1978). Such interventions are designed to improve the ability of the individuals to cooperate effectively as a team and thereby enhance performance. Team building can be done in various ways. Many team-building interventions involve some kind of physical or outdoor challenge. Group members sometimes do tasks individually, such as climb an extremely tall structure with various barriers to overcome. As they climb, other group members cheer them on, provide encouragement, and make suggestions as to how to get over the obstacles. Alternatively, they may all work together on a team task such as white-water rafting in which they have to rely on each other. Sometimes activities are designed to build trust and sense of group safety. For example, individuals are asked to climb a structure and then allow themselves to drop off the structure backwards and blindfolded, safely falling into the arms of their teammates. If their teammates were to fail to catch them, they could be seriously injured. Thus, trust can develop as individuals fall, taking the risk that their teammates will catch them and are rewarded for their trust as they are safely caught.

Other tasks involved requiring the team to solve some kind of dilemma or problem together. They may have to find their way out of a wilderness situation, or they may be given an organizational problem to solve. Tasks may also involve the need to make plans and set goals.

Teammates tend to like these activities and often feel exhilarated and good about themselves and optimistic about their team after these trainings. These good feelings may account for much of the popularity of these interventions. Ironically, despite the good feelings and sense of confidence in the team, research on the efficacy of these interventions has had disappointing results. Early studies of team-building interventions failed to show much, if any, benefit (Woodman & Sherwood, 1980). For decades, these interventions have been studied and appear to have almost no impact on team performance.

More recently, Salas, et al. (1999) conducted a meta-analysis of studies on team building that confirmed the finding that it has almost no impact on objective performance. This study differentiated between objective and subjective measures of performance. Subjective ratings are individual opinions of group functioning and performance. These may include assessments from members of the team, or from a manager, boss, or executive. Salas found a small positive relationship between team building and subjective assessments. In other words, people perceived some benefit from the team-building intervention. By contrast, objective measures assess concrete performance outcomes such as how many goods were produced, how many calls were received, or how many problems were solved. Team-building interventions failed to show any impact on objective measures of performance. The one possible exception was with respect to team-building interventions that focused on clarifying roles and structure within the team; these appeared to show some benefit. In conclusion, although teams tend to like team building and may experience an improvement in subjective measures of performance, one should not expect team building to make a difference in objective measures of performance.

▓ FREQUENT MISTAKES ORGANIZATIONS MAKE IN USING TEAMS

In addition to the variety of topics addressed in this chapter, organizational leaders can also benefit by understanding and avoiding the costly mistakes that organizations frequently make when using teams. By studying teams in a variety of organizations over a period of decades, Hackman (1992) observed that organizational leaders make a number of common mistakes when implementing teams, and that these mistakes can keep teams from achieving their potential.

Frequent mistakes organizations make in using teams:

1. Use a team for work that is better done by individuals
2. Call the performing unit a team but really managing members as individuals
3. Fall off the authority balance beam
4. Dismantle existing organizational structures so that teams will be fully "empowered" to accomplish the work
5. Specify challenging team objectives, but skimping on organizational supports
6. Assume that members already have all the skills they need to work well as a team

Use a Team for Work That Is Better Done by Individuals. Because teams have become so popular, managers do not always carefully consider whether the tasks they are assigning teams to do are really best performed by teams. Some tasks are better performed by individuals, and assigning them to a team simply produces inefficiency and frustration.

Call the Performing Unit a Team but Really Manage Members as Individuals. Because of the popularity of teams, managers are sometimes inclined to group people into teams with the hope of gaining the benefits of teams but without making the changes necessary to manage them as a team. For example, an organization may choose to use a team structure, but retain its individualistic incentive system rather than adapting it to reward collaboration and thus support teamwork. This undermines team effectiveness.

Fall Off the Authority Balance Beam. One of the keys to achieving the potential benefits of teams is striking the right balance between delegating too much versus too little authority to the team. Teams need enough authority over their work and autonomy so that they are free enough to develop team synergies by enabling each member to make the best use of his or her unique talents. However, a team that is given too much autonomy may find that it loses its focus and begins to work on things that are outside of its purpose and that are not important priorities for the organization. Thus, organizational leaders in charge of teams need to provide the right balance of autonomy and direction.

Dismantle Existing Organizational Structures So That Teams Will Be Fully "Empowered" to Accomplish the Work. Because teams have a looser structure than traditional methods of organizing work, managers may inadvertently go too far in dismantling organizational structures in order to give a team sufficient freedom in order to unleash its full potential. The important thing is that teams do not need an absence of structure, they need different structures that support a different way of working. Structures may need to be altered, but not eliminated.

Specify Challenging Team Objectives, But Skimp on Organizational Supports.
Competitive pressures result in a consistent drive in organizations to do more with less.
Thus, there is sometimes a tendency to provide insufficient support for teams doing challenging work. This lack of support can undermine all that might otherwise be accomplished by a team.

*Assume That Members Already Have All the Skills They Need to Work Well as
a Team.* This observation provides additional confirmation of what was stressed at the
beginning of the chapter. Effective teamwork requires a variety of skills in both interpersonal and task arenas, and many individuals need training in order to acquire these skills. If
effective training is not available, managers may consider not assigning an individual without good team skills to a team.

 OPENING CASE REVISITED

Building a Team to Upgrade Security at Ellington

This case provides an example of how an individual (Kate Stein) can be placed
in leadership position within a team for which he or she has not been well prepared. Furthermore, such individuals may be unaware of what team leadership capabilities they lack, and may not know what to do when the team is not
performing effectively. In this case, Stein's boss recognized that coaching
could be a helpful way to accelerate her learning. Stein's coach provided her
with multisource feedback that enabled her to understand her performance
gaps and what she was doing that was leading to poor performance. They
also developed and executed a plan for enhancing her ability to manage the
team, and this enabled her to be more effective as a leader.

Summary

Multiple options are available for developing teams in the workplace. Training is a common, reasonably effective method of educating employees. However, its effectiveness may
be enhanced by improved usage of general principles of training effectiveness, needs
analysis, more effective design, evaluation, and improving transfer of training. Researchers
have identified both interpersonal (conflict resolution, collaborative problem solving, and
communication) and self-management (goal setting and performance management, planning and task coordination) knowledge, skills, and abilities as helpful to team functioning.
Thus, these are good targets for training.

In addition to training, multisource feedback, coaching, improved design, mentoring, job assignments, and teambuilding have been proposed as methods for improving
teams. Effective design has emerged in the research as one of the best ways to promote effective teams. Effective coaching has more positive impact when teams are
well-designed than when they are poorly designed. Despite its popularity, team building has not demonstrated much ability to enhance performance. Finally, organizational

leaders should also take care to avoid the common mistakes that leaders make when implementing teams.

 CONCLUDING CASE

Challenges for Mike Burns's "Traditional" Approach

Mike Burns was a newly appointed deputy superintendent for instruction in a mid-size school district. He had taught and been an administrator in the district for 20 years. He knew everyone, from the mayor to the maintenance men. He was affable, tall, handsome, outgoing, and politically savvy. He had been an unusually talented high school and college athlete. There were still not many who could keep up with him on the basketball court or the golf course.

Mike had operated his former middle school with an iron hand. He not only tolerated little by way of horseplay from students, he also kept a tight leash on teachers. There were timecard clocks for all employees to punch. Lesson plans, reports, and grades were due on time. He knew discipline paid off on the playing field, and he was sure it would pay off in the classroom. Modern day "constructivist pedagogy," "critical theory," and "social justice" were but empty slogans that had little application and operational meaning to Mike.

Things were going well for Mike in his new position. Then he got blindsided by a federal mandate and a lawsuit. First, the recently enacted No Child Left Behind Act began to be taken seriously both by state officials and his district superintendent and board. Suddenly, student discipline was insufficient as a district focus. Now someone was serious about student learning also. Second, a group advocating added instructional services for disabled students took the district to court.

The confluence of these events placed a new set of responsibilities on Mike's shoulders, and he was well outside his comfort zone. New terms such as *Adequate Yearly Progress (AYP)*, *Individualized Educational Programs (IEP)*, *Value Added Tests (VAT)*, pay for performance, and *defining student subgroups for purposes of determining AYP* were intruding on the reality of his job description and consciousness with an obsessive drumbeat that threatened his piece of mind. After all, he had never claimed to be an expert about pedagogy, reading and mathematics instruction, testing, and special education.

One group in town was even planning a "charter school," whatever that was.

Mike knew how to keep the buses running on time, the corridors waxed, and parents and upperlings happy. Now an entirely new educational management world was unfolding, and he felt left out.

Mike noted that other school districts were adjusting to the new expectations in a variety of ways. Some had begun to outsource some of their testing and even some of their instruction and counseling functions. Others were forming and joining county consortia from which they could acquire expertise and specialized consultants. Some districts were hiring assistant superintendents for instruction who had advanced degrees in cognitive studies.

Mike knew something had to change. He just was not sure what.

Exercise   Practicing Your Informal Coaching Skills

Part 1: Assignment

You will work with another class member on this exercise. Each of you will take a turn playing the role of coach and the coached. Once you have a partner, you will need to decide on some area on which you would be willing to be coached. Choosing one of the areas of knowledge, skill, and ability associated with effective teamwork might be of particular interest for this course (interpersonal: conflict resolution, collaborative problem solving, and communication; self-management: goal setting and performance management, planning and task coordination). However, you should feel free to choose some other topic on which you would like to be coached.

When you are in the coaching role, consider how you might use the GROW model:

Goal: What is my goal for performance or development?
Reality: Where do I stand now?
Options: What are my options for achieving the goal?
Will: How I will maintain the will or motivation to succeed?

Do your best in the limited time that your instructor gives you to cover as many of the coaching steps as possible:

- Relationship
- Listening
- Assessment
- Feedback
- Goal Setting
- Action Planning
- Ongoing Follow-Up

We suggest that you first work on your listening and relationship development by listening to the person being coached for at least two minutes without giving any advice. You may find that you are tempted to rush in with a solution before you have a complete understanding of what he or she is trying to work on. Try to take a "facilitation" stance (rather than a "directive" stance) in which you ask questions and get your partner to take the initiative on developing a program of change and on motivating him- or herself to make the change.

Part 2: Feedback

After each of you has had an opportunity to be in both the coach role and the coached role, give your coach some feedback on the process. What was most helpful? What was least helpful? What would you advise your coach to do differently the next time he or she has an opportunity to coach someone?

Part 3: Reflection

Please consider the following questions:

- What did it feel like to be a coach?
  What was the most enjoyable part?
  What was the most difficult part?
  Was it difficult to listen without interrupting or giving advice? If so, what made it difficult?
- How did it feel to be coached?
- What did you learn from this experience?

References

Alderfer, C. P. (1977). Group and intergroup relations. In J. R. Hackman, J. L. Suttle (Ed.), *Improving life at work* (pp. 227–296). Santa Monica, CA: Goodyear.

Arthur, Jr., W., Bennett, Jr., W., Edens, P., & Bell, S. (2003). Effectiveness of training in organizations: A meta-analysis of design and evaluation features. *Journal of Applied Psychology, 88*(2), 234–245.

Beer, M., & Cannon, M. (2004). Promise and peril in implementing pay-for-performance. *Human Resource Management,43*(1), 3–20.

Bacon, T. R., & Spear, K. I. (2003). *Adaptive coaching: The art and practice of a client-centered approach to performance improvement.* Palo Alto, CA: Davies-Black Publishing.

Campbell, J., & Kuncel, N. (2001). Individual and team training. In N. Anderson, D. Ones, H. Sinangil, & C. Viswesvaran (Ed.), *The handbook of industrial, work and organizational psychology* (pp. 278–312). Thousand Oaks, CA: Sage Publications.

Cannon, M. D., & Witherspoon, R. (2005). Actionable feedback: Unlocking the power of learning and development. *Academy of Management Executive, 19*, 120–134.

Chen, G., Donahue, L., & Klimoski, R. (2004). Training undergraduates to work in organizational teams. *Academy of Management Learning and Education, 3*(1), 27–40.

Corsini, R. J., & Wedding, D. (Eds.). (2005). *Current psychotherapies* (7th ed.). Belmont, CA: Thomson, Brooks, Cole.

Costa, A. L., & Garmston, R. J. (1994). *Cognitive coaching: A foundation for renaissance schools.* Norwood, MA: Christopher-Gordon.

Devine, D., Clayton, L., Philips, J., Dunford, B., & Melner, S. (1999). Teams in organizations: Prevalence, characteristics, and effectiveness. *Small Group Research, 30*(6), 678–711.

Dixon, N., & Young, D. (1997). *Helping leaders take effective action: Program evaluation.* Greensboro, NC: The Center for Creative Leadership.

Ellis, A., Bell, B., Ployhart, R., Hollenback, J., & Ilgen, D. (2005). An evaluation of generic teamwork skills training with action teams: Effects on cognitive and skill-based outcomes. *Personnel Psychology, 58*, 641–672.

Ericksen, J., & Dyer, L. (2004). Right from the start: Exploring the effect of early team events on subsequent project team development and performance. *Administrative Science Quarterly, 49*, 438–471.

Goldsmith, M., Lyons, L., & Freas, A. (Eds.). (2000). *Coaching for leadership: How the world's greatest coaches help leaders learn.* San Francisco: Jossey-Bass/Pfeiffer.

Guthrie, J. W., Springer, M. G. R., Rolle, A., & Houck, E. A. (2007). *Modern education finance and policy.* Boston: Allyn & Bacon.

Guzzo, R., & Dickson, M. (1996). Teams in organizations: Recent research on performance and effectiveness. *Annual Review of Psychology, 47*, 307–338.

Hackman, J. R. (1998). Why teams don't work. In R. S. Tindale (Ed.), *Theory and research on small groups*. New York: Plenum Press.

Hackman, J. R. (2002). *Leading Teams: Setting the stage for great performances*. Boston: Harvard Business School Press.

Hackman, J. R., & Wageman, R. (2005). A theory of team coaching. *Academy of Management Review, 30*(2), 269–287.

Hill, L. A. (1992). *Becoming a manager: Mastery of a new identity*. Boston: Harvard Business School Press.

Hollenbeck, J., DeRue, D., & Guzzo, R. (2004). Bridge the gap between 1/0 research and HR practice: Improving team composition, team training, and team task design. *Human Resources Management, 43*(4), 353–366.

Hunt, J. M., & Weintraub, J. R. (2002). *The coaching manager: Developing top talent in business*. Thousand Oaks, CA: Sage Publications.

Ketter, P. (2006, January). Soaring to new safety heights. *Training & Development*, 51–54.

Konrad, A., & Decktop, J. (2001). Human resources management trends in the USA: Challenges in the midst of prosperity. *International Journal of Manpower, 22*(3), 269–278.

Kroeger, O., Thuesen, J. M., & Rutledge, H. (2002). *Type talk at work: How the sixteen personality types determine your success on the job*. New York: Dell Publishing.

Krueger, J. (1998). Enhancement bias in descriptions of self and others. *Personal and Social Psychology Bulletin, 24*(5), 505–516.

Locke, E. A., & Latham, G. P. (1990). *A theory of goal setting and task performance*. Englewood Cliffs, NJ: Prentice-Hall.

London, M. (Ed.). (2001). *How people evaluate others in organizations*. Mahwah, NJ: Lawrence Erlbaum Associates.

London, M. (Ed.). (1997). *Job feedback: Giving, seeking, and using feedback for performance improvement*. Mahwah, NJ: Lawrence Erlbaum Associates.

McCall, M. W., Lombardo, M. M., & Morrison, A. M. (1988). *The lessons of experience: How successful executives develop on the job*. Lexington: Lexington Books.

McClough, A. C., & Rogelberg, S. G. (2003). Selection in teams: An exploration of the teamwork knowledge, skills, and ability to test. *International Journal of Selection and Assessment, 11*(1), 55–66.

Michaels, E., Handfield-Jones, H., & Axelrod, B. (2001). *The war for talent*. Boston: Harvard Business School Press.

Michaelsen, L. K., Knight, A. B., & Fink, L. D. (Eds.) (2004). *Team-based learning*. Sterling, VA: Stylus Publishing.

Musch, J., & Klauer, C. (Eds.). (2003). *The psychology of evaluation: Affective processes in cognition and emotion*. Mahwah, NJ: Lawrence Erlbaum Associates.

Phillips, J. (1991). *Handbook of training evaluation and measurement methods* (3rd ed.). Boston: Butterworth-Heinemann.

Phillips, J. (2003). *Return on investment in training and performance improvement programs* (2nd ed.). Boston: Butterworth-Heinemann.

Porras, J. I. (1979). The impact of organization development. *Academy of Management Review, 3*, 249–266.

Porras, J. I., & Berg, P. O. (1978). The impact of organizational development. *Academy of Management Review, 3*, 249–266.

Prien, E., Schippmann, J., & Prien, K. (2003). *Individual assessment: As practiced in industry and consulting*. Mahwah, NJ: Lawrence Erlbaum Associates.

Rynes, S., Gerhart, B., & Parks, L. (2005). Personnel psychology: Performance evaluation and pay for performance. *Annual Review of Psychology, 56*, 571–600.

Salas, E., Burke, C., Bowers, C., & Wilson, K. (2001). Team training in the skies: Does crew resource management (CRM) training work? *Human Factors, 43*(4), 641–675.

Salas, E., & Cannon-Bowers, J. (2001). The science of training: A decade of progress. *Annual Review of Psychology, 52*, 471–499.

Salas, E., Rozell, D., Mullen, B., & Driskell, J. (1999). The effect of team building on performance: An integration. *Small Group Research, 30*(3), 309–329.

Salas, E., Sims, D., & Burke, C. (2005). Is there a "big five" in teamwork? *Small Group Research, 36*(5), 555–559.

Schein, E. H. (1999). *Process consultation revisited: Building the helping relationship.* Reading, MA: Addison Wesley Publishers.

Sims, D., Salas, E., & Burke, C. (2005). Promoting effective team performance through training. In S. Wheelan (Ed.), *The Handbook of Group Research and Practice*, (pp. 407–425). Thousand Oaks, CA: Sage Publications.

Smither, J., London, M., & Reilly, R. (2005). Does performance improve following a multisource feedback? A theoretical model, meta-analysis, and review of empirical findings. *Personnel Psychology, 58*(1), 33–66.

Smither, J., & Walker, A. (2004). Are the characteristics of narrative comments related to improvement in multirater feedback ratings over time? *Journal of Applied Psychology, 89*(3), 575–581.

Stern, D., Song, Y., & O'Brien, B. (2004). Company training in the United States 1970–2000: What have been the trends over time? *International Journal of Training and Development, 8*(3), 191–209.

Stevens, M., & Campion, M. (1994). The knowledge, skill, and ability requirements for teamwork: Implications for human resource management. *Journal of Management, 20*(2), 503–530.

Stevens, M., & Campion, M. (1999). Staffing work teams: Development and validation of a selection test for teamwork settings. *Journal of Management, 25*(2), 207–228.

Stewart, G., Manz, C., & Sims, H. (1999). *Team work and group dynamics.* New York: John Wiley & Sons.

Stout, R., Salas, E., & Fowlkes, J. (1997). Enhancing teamwork in complex environments through team training. *Group Dynamics: Theory, Research, and Practice, 1*(2), 169–182.

Taylor, S. E., & Brown, J. D. (1988). Illusion and well-being: A social psychological perspective on mental health. *Psychological Bulletin, 103*, 193–210.

Tilin, F., & Sumerson, J. (2005). Team consultation. In S. Wheelan (Ed.), *The handbook of group research and practice* (pp. 427–438). Thousand Oaks, CA: Sage Publications.

Wageman, R. (2001). How leaders foster self-managing team effectiveness: Design choices versus hands-on coaching. *Organization Science, 12*(5), 559–577.

West, M. (2001). The human team: Basic motivations and innovations, Individual and team training. In N. Anderson, D. Ones, H. Sinangil, C. Viswesvaran (Eds.), *The handbook of industrial, work and organizational psychology* (pp. 270–288). Thousand Oaks, CA: Sage Publications.

Whitmore, J. (1996). *Coaching for performance.* London: Nicholas Brealey Publishing.

Witherspoon, R., & Cannon, M. D. (2004). Coaching leaders in transition: Lessons from the field. In A. F. Abuono (Ed.), *Creative Consulting: Innovative Perspectives on Management Consulting, Vol. 4* (pp. 201–228) Greenwich, CT: Information Age Publishing.

Woodman, R. W., & Sherwood, J. J. (1980). The role of team development in organizational effectiveness: A critical review. *Psychological Bulletin, 88*, 166–186.

Young, P. G., Sheets, J. M., & Knight, D. D. (2005). *Mentoring principals: Frameworks, agendas, tips, and case stories for mentors and mentees.* Thousand Oaks, CA: Corwin Press.

CHAPTER ELEVEN

Team Learning

■ INTRODUCTION

The ability to learn and adapt has become critically important in today's highly competitive and achievement-oriented environment. Many organizations and teams attempt to improve their learning capacity, and generally they find this aspiration difficult. Numerous barriers hamper the ability of teams and organizations to learn. This chapter explores what inhibits team learning and what can be done to enhance learning.

LEARNING OBJECTIVES

After reading this chapter, you should be able to

- Understand the importance of continual learning in teams and organizations.
- Recognize the key barriers to learning in groups and organizations and how the barriers operate.
- Know what can be done to overcome barriers to learning.
- Understand why people give poor-quality feedback and what can be done to improve the quality of feedback.
- Understand how framing influences the quality of communication.
- Recognize the impediments to learning from failure and how these impediments can be overcome.

 OPENING CASE

Shedding Losses at International Harvester

International Harvester, one of the world's leading producers of farm and heavy construction equipment, had fallen on hard times. They were in debt and had a desperate need to cut costs. In an effort to save the company, they were looking to sell off expendable assets. One of the operations of which they decided to divest themselves was an engine remanufacturing plant in Springfield, Missouri. The work of this plant was to take old truck engines, burn the grime off them, and then rebuild them. The plant had been producing at a loss. One of the concerns of the community was that the plant was a major employer, and community members were worried about what might happen if the plant were sold to a new owner. One of the options considered in order to retain local control over the operation was for employees to find a way to raise money, purchase the plant, and operate it themselves.

Discussion Questions

1. What do you see as the strengths and weaknesses of this idea?
2. If they were to purchase the plant, what might they consider doing to make the plant profitable?

▮ INTRODUCTION TO TEAM LEARNING

Today's organizations, public and private, face a fiercely competitive marketplace with intense pressures to perform. To optimize performance, they need the ability to respond rapidly to change. As pressures on organizations have increased, many have come to question the traditional command-and-control approach to arranging the traditional forms of organization structure. The private sector is known for rapid adaptation. Even the American military has demonstrated a remarkable ability to reinvent itself (Garvin, 2000). Unfortunately, school systems often hang on to ineffective or outdated operating modes (Fullan, 2003; Ouchi, 2003). However, enactment of the No Child Left Behind Act, with its emphasis on student achievement and higher levels of performance, may be motivating school systems to re-examine their operational procedures.

Organizations are perceived as needing to become more agile and able to learn. Teams have been one of the components that many organizations have employed to enhance capability and competitiveness. Many of the organizational leaders and scholars who have focused on learning in organizations have also proposed teams as mechanisms through which organizational learning might be enhanced (Argote, Gruenfeld, & Naquin, 2001).

The term *learning organization* became popular in the 1990s, and many entities sought to enhance their learning capacity (Easterby-Smith, Araujo, & Burgoyne, 1999). We define *learning* as the ability to acquire, assimilate, and act appropriately on new information. A *learning organization* is an organization in which employees are adept at learning collaboratively. Both scholars and a number of organizational leaders recognized that most employees, especially at lower levels within organizations, were not given many opportunities to think for themselves and take initiative (Senge, 1990). The changing demands of the marketplace have pressed organizations to utilize the full capacity of their people. Work has been redesigned to be more decentralized and to empower (give more authority and autonomy to) employees even at the lower ranks of the organization. School districts vary significantly in the extent to which they empower principals by giving them discretion over how to spend the money that is allocated to their schools. Ouchi (2003) found that the amount of the entire budget controlled by local schools in traditional districts in New York City averaged only 6.1% and in Los Angeles only 6.7%. By contrast, local schools in

Houston and Seattle are given control over how they spend 58.6% and 79.7% of their respective budgets. Ouchi argues that most principals use this autonomy wisely and proactively to make sure the school gets optimal value out of each dollar spent, and this empowerment has contributed to impressive academic performance in Houston and Seattle.

During the 1990s, many organizations invested vast sums of money and effort to transform themselves into learning organizations (Senge, 1999). A number of organizations had reasonable success in adopting learning capacities. However, despite effort and money spent on the development of learning organizations, few have had long-term success in constructing and sustaining learning organization capabilities (Senge, 1999). This may seem ironic given the benefits of learning capabilities. Unfortunately, initiating enduring learning capacity turns out to be much more complicated and difficult than anticipated. The following sections illustrate why such a goal is challenging.

■ COMPONENTS OF LEARNING

Effective experiential learning involves various facets of the following: *concrete experience, reflective observation, abstract conceptualization,* and *active experimentation* (Kolb, 1984). People have different preferences for such features, but each contributes something to learning, and together they facilitate learning.

Concrete experience provides input that can be analyzed. *Reflective observation* provides an opportunity to review, experience, and consider what the meanings might be. *Abstract conceptualization* involves building the reflections into a theoretical model to explain or predict. *Active experimentation* utilizes a hands-on involvement in trying various alternatives to achieve an end and focuses on doing whatever works.

Although all of these are valuable to the learning process, organizations tend not to provide sufficient opportunity and encouragement to get employees to participate regularly in these activities (Argote, 1999). In particular, organizations typically have a bias toward being efficient by staying focused on current practices. Thus, they do not make time for reflective observation, abstract conceptualization, or active experimentation. Also, experimentation involves trying multiple approaches with the hope of finding one that works. There is an inherent uncertainty as to which will or will not work. Thus, experiments often fail to produce desired results, and many managers see these failed experiments as wasteful and unnecessary.

An individual can engage in any of these elements—concrete experience, reflective observation, abstract conceptualization, and active experimentation—alone or in conjunction with other people. An additional set of dynamics affects the process in a social or team context. For example, if reflection and conceptualization occur in a dialogue with others rather than in the privacy of an individual's head, there may well be disagreements over interpretations and meanings. These disagreements can be useful in bringing different perspectives to bear on the issue; however, they can also be the source of conflict, which could become problematic if it escalates.

Another important difference between a team and an individual learning effort is that team members can observe and reflect on each other's behavior and can provide each other feedback. This can be extremely beneficial for learning. At the same time, feedback giving has the potential to bring about conflict as members share criticisms of each other.

Despite the desirability of enhanced learning capabilities, organizational learning efforts have been hampered by a number of challenges or barriers. We discuss several of these challenges including psychological and instrumental threats, gaps in knowledge and skills, and structural barriers.

▓ PSYCHOLOGICAL AND INSTRUMENTAL THREAT

Employees face a variety of potential threats when they engage in learning-oriented activities. Below we explain two primary categories of threat—psychological and instrumental. *Psychological threat* involves the discomfort that people feel as a result of engaging in learning activities. These are automatic internal reactions. By contrast, *instrumental threat* is produced by the perception that engaging in learning activities may adversely affect one's prospects for achieving organizational rewards or receiving some kind of organizational sanction or punishment. Thus, an individual who tries an experiment in an organization that values experimentation would not experience instrumental threat, but might experience instrumental threat in an organization that sees experimentation as a waste of time.

Psychological Threat

For a variety of reasons, learning can be psychologically threatening. Psychological threat involves emotional discomfort such as fear, anxiety, discouragement, disappointment, and embarrassment. Sometimes learning involves discovering unflattering things about ourselves, our team, or our organization. Such learning can be threatening and unpleasant. People tend to see themselves more positively than others see them or than is justified by objective standards (Cannon & Witherspoon, 2005). Thus, receiving accurate feedback can threaten people's self-esteem (our perceived self-worth) and self-efficacy (our perceptions of our capabilities and prospects for success). Taylor and Brown (1988) argue that people have positive illusions (unrealistically positive views of themselves) and that these illusions are helpful for maintaining energy, productivity, self-esteem, happiness, mental health, and for avoiding depression. Similarly, Bandura (1986) has demonstrated that performance is influenced not only by ability but also by self-efficacy. He has also argued that a somewhat unrealistically positive view of one's self-efficacy is more performance enhancing than viewing one's self-efficacy accurately. Thus, receiving accurate feedback can be deflating and discouraging.

Consider the following two examples that illustrate how painful feedback can be. At a top-management retreat, each executive received balanced feedback on his or her performance with the goal of helping each to learn and improve. Despite the positive things that were said, one executive said: "I was so disturbed by the feedback that I went back to my hotel room and wrote out a formal resignation." After a night's sleep, he realized that this was too extreme a response, and he committed to using the feedback to improve himself. In a different organization, the president went home and went to bed in the middle of the afternoon after seeing a newspaper article that critiqued his performance. In both cases, these individuals soon found constructive ways to use the feedback, but their initial reaction was one of discouragement and intense emotional pain.

As Jim Collins notes in *Good to Great* (2001), one of the key features of organizations that were able to become great is their ability to "confront the brutal facts." Collins provides a number of contrasting examples of organizations in which the leaders refused to confront reality. They were unwilling to endure the discomfort of looking at themselves and their organization rationally. Thus, people often find ways to avoid learning, and especially, situations likely to produce negative feedback. They sometimes also distort or deny feedback or rationalize about its implications (Argyris, 1990). When this happens, learning is hindered.

Instrumental Threat

Whereas psychological threat involves emotional reactions to the learning activities themselves, instrumental threats involve undesirable consequences that are byproducts or results of engaging in learning. For example, a scientist in a lab might start tinkering with an experiment that is not immediately related to the current assignment. The scientist might enjoy the experiment and learn something useful but might risk the instrumental threat of being reprimanded for taking longer than necessary to complete the main project.

Similarly, some leaders are known to "shoot the messenger" after receiving bad news or negative feedback. In other words, although feedback givers are providing a service that is necessary for learning, leaders sometimes retaliate against those who deliver feedback or bad news even when those individuals are not at fault. For example, in one school district, a principal who pointed out some flaws in the superintendent's plan was shortly thereafter transferred from his desirable school to one that was considered very undesirable. The other principals took this as a message not to give feedback to the superintendent. Thus, employees learn to avoid providing feedback or delivering bad news in order to avoid the instrumental threat of having the leader hold a grudge against them (Tyan, 2005).

Similarly, learning is often a process of trial and error. Thus, some errors (unsuccessful experiments) are natural (Cannon & Edmondson, 2005). Other employees may benefit from hearing about an error or an unsuccessful experiment so that they can learn from it. However, by disclosing the mistake, employees risk the prospect that others will think negatively of them for making the mistake in the first place. This may hurt their reputation, reduce their chances for promotion, or invite ridicule.

KNOWLEDGE AND SKILL

Since learning has not historically been as high a priority as it is today, many jobs have not required continual learning. Thus, many employees do not have the knowledge nor the skills necessary to engage effectively in learning activities (Sessa, & London, 2006). In particular, employees often lack skills for effectively giving and receiving feedback and engaging in learning dialogue. Most employees also lack technical knowledge related to designing experiments and analyzing results.

Giving and Receiving Feedback

As was discussed in the last chapter, employees often avoid giving each other feedback. One of the benefits of multisource feedback is that anonymity encourages employees to be more frank with each other. Nonetheless, the quality of feedback that people naturally produce, whether in anonymous multisource feedback, or in face-to-face situations, is of poor quality (Argyris, 1993). Thus, it may contribute more to defensiveness than to learning. Without an understanding of how to provide feedback effectively, employees may give feedback that does not produce learning or they may simply avoid giving feedback.

Learning Dialogue

A diversity of perspectives on how to handle a task or how to solve a problem can be helpful to team learning. However, sometimes teams struggle to have a constructive dialogue and work through the different perspectives toward greater insight. Sometimes discussing different perspectives leads to harmful conflict because team members do not have adequate skills for talking though disagreements constructively.

Technical Knowledge

At times, effective team learning requires technical knowledge. For example, some variation in the quality of goods produced and services rendered is natural, but too much variation may mean that something is wrong with the system which needs to be addressed (Argote, 1999). The ability to interpret the meaning of variation may require knowledge of statistical process controls or other technical methods. Statistical process controls enable people to detect when a machine or system needs adjustment. Detecting the need for adjustment is difficult because there is a natural variation within any system, and people can have difficulty determining whether performance that is outside the norm means that the system needs to be adjusted or is just random variation that will self-correct. Similarly, a school district would want to know whether test results that were not as expected were the result of random variation or the result of specific activities within the classroom.

In addition, individuals and teams learn by experimenting, but employees may not know how to design an experiment that produces useful knowledge. Some technical knowledge may also be required in order for a team to interpret experimental results. Similarly, employees are encouraged to learn from failure, but discovering the root cause of a particular failure also sometimes requires technical knowledge (Cutcher-Gershenfeld & Ford, 2005).

▪ STRUCTURAL BARRIERS

Structural barriers arise from the characteristics of roles, rules, policies, and procedures. These may be designed such that learning-oriented behavior is enabled and rewarded—or constrained and punished. Commonly, they are structured to maintain control, predictability, and efficiency (Dierkes, Antal, Child, & Nonaka, 2001). Thus, they are sometimes at odds with learning activities, because learning takes time, and the outcome of learning experiments is often uncertain. In the long run, the benefits of learning may lead to greater control, predictability, and efficiency, but in the short run they take time away from accomplishing current assignments. Leaders often succumb to short-term performance pressures and do not make time and resources available for employee learning.

Organizations have learned to maintain predictability and efficiency through specialization and coordination (Scott, 2003). For example, the invention of the assembly line vastly increased productivity, predictability, and standardization. Workers were assigned highly specialized tasks that they could learn to conduct efficiently. Their work was designed by managers and engineers who coordinated each small piece of the process. This arrangement was efficient in stable environments, but it is often not very adaptable and does not encourage learning throughout an organization. Employees might learn how to do only one task and do that repetitively throughout the workday. They would then learn nothing else about other functions within the organization and how all the functions all fit together. Self-managing teams have been proposed as an alternative that provides greater autonomy, flexibility, and learning; but traditional managers are often uncomfortable with ceding control to teams. Even when teams are working well, managers have sometimes disbanded them because of their discomfort with the structure (Hackman, 2002).

Furthermore, organizational leaders are particularly likely to demand more control in the face of challenges or when they feel threatened (Staw, Sandlands, & Sutton, 1981). This is one reason that organizational learning initiatives have stalled in many organizations (Senge, 1999). Leaders are comfortable delegating and providing autonomy when things are going smoothly, but when new challenges emerge in a competitive environment, they are often inclined to retrench, and this retreat may harm learning initiatives.

Another structural barrier is that leaders often do not take the time or make the investment necessary to develop information systems that will enable learning. By contrast, eBay has invested a great deal of money and effort into developing information systems that are constantly tracking transactions throughout the world. This enables them quickly to detect any problems so that they can be promptly addressed. Similarly, a school or school district needs to have good data in order to assess how it is doing and make intelligent decisions as to what parts of the educational system need attention and what type of attention and resources are needed.

The following sections explore some of the actions that organizations can undertake to reduce learning barriers or manage them more effectively. Specifically, we will examine psychological safety, skills for giving feedback and facilitating learning dialogue, and structural innovations.

■ PSYCHOLOGICAL SAFETY

Given that learning can be discouraged by psychological and instrumental threats, one way to look at encouraging learning is to examine how to make learning less threatening. One way to encourage learning is to educate and train employees on the benefits of learning and work to build a learning culture within the organization. Such efforts can be helpful but are not necessarily sufficient to reduce threats of organizational learning.

For example, some organizations have invested time and money into becoming a learning organization. However, despite receiving similar levels of training, and existing within the same supportive organization, teams vary significantly in the extent to which they engage in team learning (Cannon & Edmondson, 2001). Edmondson (1999) investigated team learning with a goal of understanding what enabled some teams to be so much more effective at learning than others. She found significant variance in the extent to which team members believed that their teams were psychologically safe. Furthermore, psychological safety predicted learning behavior.

Psychological safety refers to the extent to which group members believe that well-intentioned actions that result in mistakes or errors will not be punished. Psychological safety should not be confused with having lax standards or accepting haphazard results. These teams recognize that learning involves experimentation and trial-and-error approaches, so some new ideas or experiments will inevitably fail. Thus, these teams do not punish mistakes if they are well intentioned. They simply try to learn from mistakes and failed experiments, and strive to do better next time. This applies not only to technical experimentation but also to interpersonal actions such as giving feedback or raising threatening issues for discussion. If the critical feedback is given or threatening issues are raised for the purpose of facilitating performance, team members agree not to hold a grudge or retaliate against those who initiated the communication.

Edmondson's research suggests that employees are sufficiently sensitive to psychological and instrumental threat that they are reluctant to engage in learning behaviors unless they feel that their local environment or team is secure. The behavior of the team leader is a significant factor in predicting the development of psychological safety. Since Edmondson's original study, the role of psychological safety has been examined in a number of contexts including mountain climbing (Roberto, 2002). Roberto found that the lack of psychological safety contributed to the death of two of the world's most experienced and skilled high-altitude climbers and three other members of the climbing team in an expedition to climb Mount Everest in 1996.

The psychological climate that develops around team leaders can vary significantly from team to team (Edmondson, 1999). For example, nurses' attitudes about reporting errors varied significantly depending on their team leader. Some nurses reported that the natural thing to do when one makes an error was to disclose it to others on the team immediately. This may be important so that they know what happened with a patient and can have an informed perspective on treating that patient. It can also help team members learn about types of errors to which team members are vulnerable so that they do not make the same mistake. Other nurses in the same hospital reported that that the natural thing to do would be to keep the error to yourself because of the unpleasant consequences that result when errors are disclosed (Mann, 2004).

Leaders can encourage psychological safety by modeling good learning behavior. Leaders who seek feedback send a message that giving feedback is helpful and should be encouraged. By disclosing their own mistakes, leaders can send a message that there is no shame in making a well-intentioned mistake and that the appropriate thing to do is learn from it. Leaders can also encourage team members to give feedback and discuss mistakes for the sake of learning. By contrast, leaders who publicly ridicule those who make mistakes and who are defensive when given feedback are not likely to develop a climate of psychological safety.

▌ KNOWLEDGE AND SKILLS FOR GIVING FEEDBACK

Although psychological safety may encourage team members to give each other feedback and discuss differences, psychological safety alone does not guarantee learning. One reason is that people have a tendency to produce feedback that contributes to defensiveness rather than learning because they lack skills for producing high-quality feedback.

Consider the following examples of feedback given for the purpose of providing an accurate description of each individual's performance:

- Jean is divisive and tries to make us look bad.
- Fred does not stand firm.

- Ben is a poor administrator.
- Larry is an ineffective teacher.
- Paula is unprofessional.
- Tina is not committed.

This feedback lacks some of the characteristics that would facilitate learning, and it contains a number of characteristics that could contribute to defensiveness. In particular, it has the following attributes (Cannon & Witherspoon, 2005, pp. 123–124):

- Attacks the individual rather than the person's behavior
- Assertions are vague or abstract rather than concrete and specific
- Does not provide illustrations or examples
- Has an ill-defined range of application
- Is not clear about the impact of the behavior and the implications for action

This feedback may provoke defensiveness because it comes across as a personal attack. It seems to condemn the person rather than the action that the person took. Vague, abstract, negative labels also provoke defensiveness. Because no concrete examples or illustrations are given, understanding the feedback and what specifically is problematic may be difficult to ascertain. The range of application is not specified, so we do not know whether the problem occurs in all situations, just with new clients, only in social settings, and so on. The impact of the behavior and the implications for action are also not specified, so the receiver does not get a clear sense of why the behavior is problematic and what should be done about it. All these factors heighten the chances that the feedback will provoke a defensive response and reduce the chances that feedback will be received well and will lead to learning and appropriate change.

Why Do People Give Poor-Quality Feedback?

Why do people produce feedback that has so many harmful characteristics? A major complication with producing feedback is caused by the way the mind operates. Argyris (1985) developed the *ladder of inference* concept to describe how people draw conclusions about each other. Philip McArthur, Robert Putnam, and Diana Smith of Action Design further embellished the concept (see Figure 11.1). When people make sense of each other's behavior, they begin with fairly directly observable data—watching people's actions and listening to what they are saying. Next, they select and focus on a particular behavior or statement. They paraphrase the data (state the meaning in their own words). They name or label what is going on, and then evaluate and explain what is happening. Finally, they decide what to do in response. This whole process can take place in a second or less, and it happens continuously as people are communicating.

This process can be useful as long as people are interpreting each other accurately. However, this process also suffers from a number of potential limitations (Argyris, 1999). First, because the process is so automatic, people are often somewhat unaware that they are making interpretations of each others' behavior. Second, instead of remembering their inferences about others as tentative hypotheses, people tend to remember them as cold, hard facts. Thus, people are overconfident in the accuracy of their conclusions. Third, people tend to remember their conclusions about the other person but forget how the sense-making process unfolded. In other words, they may forget what the other person said or did that led them to make an inference about them in the first

FIGURE 11.1   Ladder of Inference

Source: Adapted from Cannon, M. D., & Witherspoon, R. (2005).
Actionable feedback: Unlocking the power of learning and performance
improvement. *Academy of Management Executive, 19,* 120–134.

place. Thus, they do not have readily in mind examples to share that would help the
feedback receiver understand why the feedback giver came to a particular conclusion in
the first place.

Fourth, people sometimes misinterpret each other's behaviors without realizing that
they have done so. Figure 11.2 illustrates how a teacher can hear a statement from her
principal and come to completely different conclusions as to what the statement means,
depending on how she travels up the ladder of inference.

In addition, people tend to be unaware of the ways in which attributional biases and
strong emotions can interfere with accurate sense making (Kunda, 1999). Thus, people are
overconfident that their conclusions are correct. They also overestimate the likelihood
that others will see things the same way. Thus, when people give each other feedback, they
tend to think that the accuracy of their conclusions is self-evident. This leads to the kind
of ineffective feedback illustrated earlier (Cannon & Witherspoon, 2005).

Fortunately, an understanding of the ladder of inference and the sense-making
process can be used to produce more effective feedback. People can either walk themselves
down the ladder of inference, or a coach or facilitator can help them in the process. The
following are examples of a coach assisting feedback givers in going down ladders of inference in order to clarify their conclusions.

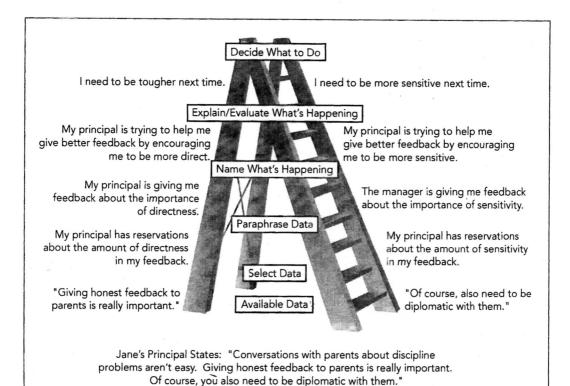

I need to be tougher next time.   ·Decide What to Do·   I need to be more sensitive next time.

Explain/Evaluate What's Happening

My principal is trying to help me give better feedback by encouraging me to be more direct.

My principal is trying to help me give better feedback by encouraging me to be more sensitive.

Name What's Happening

My principal is giving me feedback about the importance of directness.

The manager is giving me feedback about the importance of sensitivity.

Paraphrase Data

My principal has reservations about the amount of directness in my feedback.

My principal has reservations about the amount of sensitivity in my feedback.

Select Data

"Giving honest feedback to parents is really important."

Available Data

"Of course, also need to be diplomatic with them."

Jane's Principal States: "Conversations with parents about discipline problems aren't easy. Giving honest feedback to parents is really important. Of course, you also need to be diplomatic with them."

FIGURE 11.2   Ladder of Inference Example: Jane's Feedback

Source: Adapted from Cannon, M. D., & Witherspoon, R. (2005). Actionable feedback: Unlocking the power of learning and performance improvement. *Academy of Management Executive, 19,* 120–134.

 CASE 1 ───────────────────────────────

"Jean Is Divisive and Tries to Make Us Look Bad"

An angry, frustrated teacher went to the principal's office and declared: "Jean is competitive and tries to make us look bad." She wanted Jean to be disciplined for her misbehavior.

Dialogue

Teacher: Jean is divisive and tries to make us look-bad, and I want you to address this.

Principal: Can you give me an example of what she does that leads you to see her this way?

Teacher: Well, she does things that make her look better than the rest of us.

Principal: What would be an example of that?

Teacher: She initiates field trips that the kids really like, and she does not ask whether the rest of us would also like to be part of the field trip.

Principal: Are there other examples?

Teacher: Well, I guess not, but these field trips make a big impression on kids and parents, and they make the rest of us look bad and make her look like the star.

Principal: If, in the future, she were to invite you and others to come along, would that resolve the issue for you?

Teacher: Yes, it would.

Principal: Could you say to her: "Jean, you put together some impressive field trips, and when you do not invite our classes to participate, we feel excluded. In the future, would you be willing to offer us an opportunity to participate?"

Teacher: OK, I suppose I could do that.

By asking a few simple questions, the principal was able to lead the teacher down her ladder of inference, identify the source of her concern and design a statement that did not provoke defensiveness in Jean and that resolved the teacher's concern.

 CASE 2 —————————————————————————————————

"Fred Does Not Stand Firm"

Fred, a senior vice president and the director of financial reporting in a Fortune 50 company, had been successful but had not advanced recently, and it did not appear that he was being groomed for further advancement. In short, his career seems stalled. Therefore, he initiated the 360-degree evaluation in order to explore what might be blocking his advancement and what, if anything, he could do about it. The pivotal key-person interview took place with the corporate vice chairman, who oversaw the finance and risk management function and served as Fred's 3-up boss (Fred reported to the comptroller, who reported to the CFO, who reported to the Vice Chairman).

Dialogue

Vice Chairman: Fred does not stand firm.

Coach: I get the general idea. What would be an example of not standing firm?

Vice Chairman: Well, that is hard to say, but let me illustrate. When Fred's boss comes in to review our 4th quarter earnings release, we may have ideas about how to goose up the numbers a little and make things look a little better for the quarter. Many of these ideas might be perfectly fine, but if any of them were ever to stretch into a grey area, we would have to count on the comptroller to say, "That is going too far, and I will not sign that." I fear that Fred would not stand firm against the ideas of top management the way his boss does.

Coach: What leads you to see him this way?

Vice Chairman: Well, he is affable, amiable, anxious to please, and does not have sharp elbows.

Coach: OK, I can see how you would wonder about him. However, I still am not getting a clear picture. Is this a demonstrated weakness or just an untested skill? Can you think of anything Fred has done that leads you to conclude that this is a demonstrated weakness?

Vice Chairman: (Pauses to contemplate for moment, then shakes his head no.) That is a good distinction. I think it is an untested skill.

Coach: OK, so you believe it is an untested skill. Do you have ideas about how you could test it?

Vice Chairman: No, not for now.

Coach: OK, let's continue the interview . . .

Vice Chairman: (About five minutes later he interrupts his own train of thought) Wait, I have an idea how we can test it. We will give Fred a job which demands that he demonstrate those skills!

Coach: Great, what job would that be?

Vice Chairman: Well, I'm not sure specifically now, but we should probably shift Fred to a CFO function for one of our big businesses to create a fair test.

Source: Case 2 reprinted by permission of *Academy of Management Executive*. From Cannon, M. D., & Witherspoon, R. Actionable feedback: Unlocking the power of learning and performance improvement (May 2005). Copyright © 2005 Academy of Management Executive.

The coach used a set of questions to guide the vice chairman down his ladder of inference. This process was revealing for the vice chairman because it helped him to learn that he actually did not have good evidence for his evaluation of Fred. In fact, he had not given Fred an opportunity to demonstrate whether or not he would stand firm under pressure. Several months later, the vice chairman promoted Fred into a new position that required him to stand firm, and Fred proved to be successful in this new role (Witherspoon & Cannon, 2004).

These cases illustrate how a leader or coach can assist in this process, but team members can also assist themselves in crafting more effective feedback by asking themselves the following questions (Cannon & Witherspoon, 2005, p. 131):

- How did I arrive at this conclusion?
- What illustrations or examples would I need to share with the other person in order for him or her to understand why I see it this way?
- Under what conditions have I observed this behavior?
- What do I see as the specific, undesirable consequences of this behavior?
- What would be the most constructive way to help this person achieve better results?
- How might my emotions be affecting my evaluation and intentions?

By understanding the ladder of inference and the sense-making process and by addressing these questions, team members can increase the chances that their feedback will facilitate learning and reduce the chances that it will produce significant defensiveness.

▪ KNOWLEDGE AND SKILLS FOR FACILITATING LEARNING DIALOGUE

Differences of opinion in a team have the potential to produce learning and insight or to produce unproductive or even damaging conflict. One of the reasons that disagreements often result in conflict is that team members lack skills for producing learning dialogues. The issues discussed in the last section apply here as well. One difference is that those inferences had to do with interpersonal feedback, and this section deals with solutions to problems rather than with conclusions about people's behavior. People are vulnerable to error in leaping up the ladder of inference when considering solutions to problems just as they are when making inferences about another person's behavior.

Having observed conflictual conversations for decades, Argyris noted that team members rarely ask each other sincere questions that would lead to learning (Argyris, 1985, 1990). They may ask each other questions, but they are often leading questions. For example, a person might say: "I think we can all agree on that, can't we?" or "I think you can see that, can't you?" Rather than trying to elicit information that could be enlightening, these questions are designed to encourage others to agree.

Argyris explains that one of the reasons people do not ask each other sincere questions is that they are overly confident in the accuracy of their own views. They also have frames that are dominated by control rather than by learning. As was discussed in Chapter 7 on decision making, a frame is a persistent assumption or set of assumptions that influences individual actions. One of the hazards associated with frames is that individuals are often unaware of how they are routinely influenced by them. We provided an example in Chapter 7 of thumb wrestling in which students were unaware that they could have framed their task either competitively or cooperatively. As Argyris (1990) explains, in tense situations, people tend to have control frames about themselves, the other and their task as follows:

Control Frame

Self: I am right, and that should be obvious.

Other: You are wrong, and you should see it my way.

Task: Convince the other to see it my way.

The following is an example of the kind of dialogue that results when the control frame dominates an interaction:

Control Frame Dialogue

George: I've had enough; we need to boot Paula off the committee right now.

Jennifer: No way, we have not really given her a chance.

George: That's ridiculous. You are being too soft.

Jennifer: You're the one who is being ridiculous. You're not being fair.

Argyris inferred the presence of these frames based on what people said and did. In other words, people appear to be driven by the control assumptions, but they may be unaware that these assumptions are propelling them. Instead, they simply see themselves as "obviously right"; they are trying to be constructive. Next, we examine how frames encourage this kind of dialogue, and how the dialogue might look different if a learning frame were applied.

By examining the statements, we can see that both George and Jennifer state their conclusions as though they were obviously correct, and they expect that the other should agree with them. In other words, their statements are high on the ladder of inference. They do not share the reasoning behind their conclusions or any of the examples on which their conclusions are based. This makes it difficult for them to learn from each other. In addition, neither of them asks the other any clarifying questions; and neither inquires of each other why they have arrived at their particular conclusions. Finally, when the other does not agree, each individual attacks the other.

Argyris points out that engaging in learning dialogue requires a different frame and a different set of strategies from those most people use in difficult conversations. A learning frame would look something like the following:

Learning Frame

Self: I have an informed perspective, but I could also be missing something.

Other: You may have things to learn from me, and I may have things to learn from you.

Task: Have an informed discussion in which we learn from each other.

In addition to adopting a learning frame, Argyris recommends using high-quality advocacy, inquiry, and testing. High-quality advocacy means stating not only our conclusions but also sharing the reasoning behind our perspective and providing examples and illustrations that would enable the other person to understand why we see things the way we do. High-quality inquiry means asking sincere questions of others in order to understand their perspectives and encouraging them to raise any unresolved concerns so that we can work them through. Finally, high-quality testing means seeking additional information that might resolve our disagreement.

Both George and Jennifer used poor-quality advocacy, inquiry, and testing; this limits their ability to learn from each other. If they had been using a learning frame, the conversation would have looked different. Using high-quality advocacy, each would have provided a clearer picture of the reasoning and examples behind their conclusions. George would have said what made him think that firing Paula was the appropriate response. Jennifer would have explained why she felt that they had not really given her a chance. They could also have engaged in high-quality inquiry. Specifically, George could have asked whether others shared his thinking or whether they thought differently. Jennifer could have asked George to explain why he had come to his conclusion. Each of them might have tested their conclusions against others in the group to find out whether they felt the same or different.

By understanding the concept of the control frame, the learning frame, high-quality inquiry, high-quality advocacy, and testing, team members are better positioned to communicate with each other constructively and maintain a learning-oriented dialogue.

▮ STRUCTURAL INNOVATION

Organizational leaders are responsible for striking a balance between the response to short-term pressures and momentary needs versus the long-term goals of building an organization that learns, renews itself, and is able to grow and adapt to meet future challenges (Sessa & London, 2006). This means that leaders must carefully consider the consequences of their actions and how they affect not only efficiency and predictability but also learning. Although leaders may feel inclined to retaliate against those who deliver bad news or give unpleasant feedback, they should consider the consequences of such behavior on learning. Similarly, they may feel angry when errors are made, even when they are in the service of learning and may be inclined to punish the perpetrators of those errors. They may restrict the time and resources available for learning and they may define roles and responsibilities so narrowly and specifically that minimal learning occurs. Although these approaches are common in organizations, they have a negative impact on learning. Organizational leaders may also need to invest in systems that gather information to be used in learning.

General lessons about team learning and examples of how to enact what we have described can be found in the literature on learning from failure. Next, we explain a generic set of steps that organizations can use to learn from failure and how the elements described can be helpful to this process.

▮ LEARNING FROM FAILURE

Cannon and Edmondson (2005) noted that the importance of learning from failure is often acknowledged in the literature on organizational effectiveness and practicing managers, but learning from failure tends to be rare in practice. They identified three steps required to enact an effective process of learning from failure: timely identification of failure, effective analysis of failure, and deliberate experimentation.

To learn from failure, failures first need to be identified. However, for several reasons, failures are often not identified in a timely manner in most organizations. Employees often deliberately hide their failures or may at least not take the initiative to share them. Also, in complex systems, failures can be difficult to detect.

Learning from failure requires not only identifying failures but also analyzing them. Simply experiencing a failure and acknowledging it does not mean that the lessons from the failure have been successfully extracted. Determining why something went wrong and what can be learned from it often requires rigorous thinking and analysis.

Finally, an effective process of learning from failure also involves deliberate experimentation. Effective organizations encourage small, thoughtful experiments so that they can learn more quickly. If experiments do not turn out as desired, these organizations analyze and learn from them and continue to experiment until they achieve the desired results. They understand that small experiments that fail are a natural by-product of a healthy learning process. Next, we examine each of these steps in more detail and will provide illustrations of how to assist in enabling teams and organizations to learn from failure.

Identifying Failure

Building psychological safety that reduces threat is an excellent way to encourage identification of failure. As mentioned previously with examples of the nurses, those whose team leader encouraged an atmosphere of psychological safety were inclined to report errors. By contrast, nurses whose team leader did not encourage psychological safety were more inclined to hide errors or at least not report them willingly.

Team leaders can encourage psychological safety by modeling learning behaviors themselves. Katie Delaney, founder of the Delaney Group, has established formal sessions through which employees examine failures in order to learn from them. She takes the lead in reporting her own failures and modeling a nondefensive discussion in which she takes in feedback, learns from her mistakes, and helps others to do the same.

Another way to reduce threat is with blameless reporting systems. Airline administrators have such a system for reporting near misses. Identifying errors is essential for passenger safety, so the administrators have instituted blameless reporting systems that do not punish participants so long as they voluntarily report near misses in a timely manner.

A different way to assist in the identification of failure is to train employees with a knowledge of statistical process controls. Without such systems, it is often difficult to tell whether something is really wrong, or whether apparent anomalies are merely the product of natural variation within a system.

Providing timely feedback is another way to help employees identify error. For example, reading x-rays for mammograms is an inherently imperfect process, so some level of error is expected. Thus, doctors are not necessarily expected to study their errors. However, Dr. Kim Adcock of Kaiser Permanente noted that without a system to keep records and report feedback, doctors would not have the data they needed to determine whether they were making more than the average number of errors in reading x-rays. So, he designed a system through which doctors' error records would be tracked and monitored. Doctors on his team are now expected to re-examine x-rays that they had misread in order to learn to make fewer errors.

Finally, organizations can infuse into their operation methods of identifying failure in complex systems. For example, Electricitie De France operates nuclear power plants at multiple sites in France. Because of the potential danger associated with failure, they have a complex information-technology system that monitors all operations and immediately reports any anomalies throughout the system so that they can be investigated right away.

Analyzing Failure

Simply identifying failure does not guarantee that learning will occur. Often, failure must be analyzed in order for the lessons from failure to be distilled. Consider for example, the painstaking analysis that goes into learning from the failure of an airline crash. Thousands of hours can go into identifying and documenting exactly what transpired and why. This kind of process stands in sharp contrast to the type of analysis that is typically associated with organizational failures.

The U.S. military recognized the need to better learn from their failures and successes from operations and exercises and thus developed the after action review. The review is deliberately structured to produce learning. Participants conduct a detailed review of what happened, what was done well, what was not done well, and what can be learned. Participants are instructed to speak frankly with each other about shortcomings. There is an understanding that what is said during these reviews will not be held against the provider of feedback. There is also an understanding that withholding negative feedback is grounds for punishment. The military schedules time for these reviews into their regimen. They also enforce rules that provide psychological safety for participants.

In addition to making an effort to provide psychological safety, providing team members with skills for giving feedback and facilitating learning dialogue is also important. Analyzing failure often puts team members in a potentially defensive position because of the possibility of being blamed, so having the skills to minimize communication difficulties is important.

Technical knowledge can also be important for analyzing failure. For example, a team that needs to make sense out of a complex set of data may need a knowledge of statistics and computer software in order to make sense out of what happened and why (Argote, 1999). Team members may be given this knowledge through training, but an organization might also simply make specialists available if the need for such expertise is only sporadic.

Deliberate Experimentation

IDEO, one of the world's leading design firms has a saying: "Fail often, in order to succeed sooner" (Kelley & Littman, 2001). They recognize that learning and innovation happen faster and more successfully when employees experiment frequently.

Similarly, Bank of America decided that finding the best ways to satisfy customers would require deliberate experimentation. So, they set up 24 branches as "laboratories" for trying out experimental products and services. They even set a target failure rate for experiments at 30% (Thomke & Nimgade, 2002). Their reasoning was that significant innovation would be more likely if their employees experimented with unconventional ideas. The cost of finding a few unconventional ideas that worked well would probably be experimenting with a large number of unconventional ideas, and many of them would turn out to be impractical and would be failed experiments. Thus, when the branch that was given responsibility for experimentation came back with a low failure rate, their managers suggested that they might not be trying enough really novel ideas. So, the managers encouraged them to experiment with more unconventional ideas.

Minnesota Mining and Manufacturing (3M) also has policies that encourage experimentation and innovation. For example, they have a policy that scientists spend a portion of their time working solely on new, innovative products that are outside the mainstream of their current projects. They also have a requirement that 25% of division revenues come from products developed within the last five years.

Threat and knowledge are also relevant to deliberate experimentation. Organizations should ensure that employees are not punished for intelligent experiments that do not turn out as hoped. Also, designing effective experiments sometimes requires technical knowledge. Team members can either be trained in such methods, or organizations can make experts available to them. For example, in the Bank of America example above, leaders created an innovation and development team and staffed it with people knowledgeable in research methodologies (Thomke & Nimgade, 2002).

 OPENING CASE REVISITED

Shedding Losses at International Harvester

Under the leadership of President Jack Stack, the workers raised money and bought their plant from International Harvester. Stack had an idea about how they could turn around their performance—he called it the "great game of business" (Stack & Burlingham, 1992). The basic idea was that Americans love sports and could also love business if they could think of it as a sport. Three key elements seemed crucial to Stack. Employees needed to: (1) understand the rules of the game, (2) know how to keep score, and (3) have a stake in the outcome. Stack inferred that if blue-collar workers were smart enough to understand sports statistics, they could also understand financial statements and accounting. Thus, everyone in the organization was trained to understand financial statements and accounting, and regular reports on organizational performance were given to all employees. All members of the company also became stock owners so that they had a stake in the outcome. Decision-making authority was delegated down to low levels in the organization, and workers on the floor were encouraged to innovate to make the organization more effective.

With these changes, they quickly went from losing money to turning a profit, and the company became a great success. Despite the fact that American industries like this have been downsized and shipped overseas in recent years, this company (now known as Springfield Remanufacturing) continues to grow and succeed.

Summary

The idea of developing learning teams and learning organizations has great appeal and has been pursued by many organizations. Such efforts have the potential both to increase organizational effectiveness and to make work more interesting and engaging for employees. However, a number of barriers have made learning initiatives difficult to enact. Specifically, psychological and instrumental threats, gaps in knowledge and skill, and structural barriers often interfere. Psychological safety, training in skills for giving feedback, and training to facilitate learning dialogues can help. In addition, employees may need technical knowledge about how to acquire or interpret data on relevant systems. In addition, organizations may need to alter the structure, roles, rules, policies, and procedures to eliminate or change those that discourage learning and institute more that reward learning. Finally, the research on learning from failure is also relevant to enhancing organizational and team learning. Organizations that learn effectively put in place conditions through which they can identify failure, analyze it, and engage in deliberate experimentation.

 CONCLUDING CASE ───────────────────────────

Susan's "New Team" and a Tight Time Line

Susan Guinn had just moved to the central office of her 50,000-student school district. She had been a successful principal, and she had both knowledge of instruction and people skills. Her newly appointed superintendent, in whom she had great confidence, had permitted her to pick a team of professionals to come into the central office with her. She now had three new directors, one to supervise each set of schools: elementary, middle, and high. She also had reporting to her a testing director, a recruitment director, and so on. In effect, there now was a whole new team in place.

Well, at least on paper, there was a whole new team. In fact, the newly appointed superintendent had brought some of the team with him, and Susan had had to accept a few of them. It was not exactly a "cramdown," but she did not know several of the new directors well and had never worked with them. Her new team was a mix of those in whom she had confidence from past experience and about half she had simply had to accept because they were part of the superintendent's prior district team.

Susan was confident from her past experiences that she could mold her new employees into a productive team. After all, as a principal, she was quite used to inducting several new teachers and staff each year into her school and arranging for them to enter into her school's culture graciously. This would be a similar challenge. She would make her expectations clear. She would be fair in her judgments, and she would tailor assignments to the strengths of individuals. It might take a few months, but it could be done.

Susan did not have a few months. The new superintendent had arranged for a management and performance audit of the district on assumption of his duties. The outside consulting firm undertook a quick appraisal and gave its initial report. It could hardly have been a more disastrous evening. The board and the community were alarmed and the headlines looked like World War III. Achievement was documented as terrible. Dropout rates were far higher than previously reported. District spending was out of control. Nepotism, at lower levels, was rampant. Worse yet, the collective district culture was found to be one of mediocrity, not excellence.

The day following the consulting report release, the superintendent asked Susan and others in his cabinet to meet with him. He did not seek suggestions. He gave orders. He needed detailed plans for confronting the district's problems on his desk within a week. Every part of the district had to be turned upside down in a search for solutions, and it had to be documented to a high standard. He reminded them that all of them had much professionally and personally to lose.

As she walked back to her office to assemble her new team, Susan speculated about their collective ability to coalesce quickly, cooperate, and seek solutions to problems that a day before they did not even know existed. She wondered about her ability to lead this team. She braced herself for a period of rapid learning.

Discussion Questions

1. What is your assessment of the learning climate Susan is facing?
2. As you consider the concepts in this chapter, how would you advise her to go forward?

Exercise Team Learning in Practice

Consider a group or organization that is familiar to you. In what ways does it act consistently with the learning organization or learning team principles discussed in this chapter? Could it benefit by adopting more of the practices described here? What specific things would it need to do to enhance its learning capacity?

References

Alge, B., Wiethoff, C., & Klein, H. (2003). When does the medium matter? Knowledge-building experiences and opportunities in decision-making teams. *Organizational Behavior and Human Decision Processes, 91*(1), 26–37.

Argote, L. (1999). *Organizational learning: Creating, retaining, and transferring knowledge.* Boston: Kluwer Academic Publishers.

Argote, L., Gruenfeld, D., & Naquin, C. (2001). Group learning in organizations. In M. Turner (Ed.), *Groups at work: Theory and research* (pp. 369–411). Mahwah, NJ: Lawrence Erlbaum Associates.

Argyris, C. (1985). *Strategy, change and defensive routines.* Boston: Pitman.

Argyris, C. (1990). *Overcoming organizational defenses: Facilitating organizational learning.* Boston: Allyn & Bacon.

Argyris, C. (1993). *Learning for action.* San Francisco: Jossey-Bass.

Argyris, C. (1999). *On organizational learning* (2nd ed.). Malden, MA: Blackwell Publishing.

Baer, M., & Frese, M. (2003). Innovation is not enough: Climates for initiative and psychological safety, process innovations, and firm performance. *Journal of Organizational Behavior, 24*(1), 45.

Bandura, A. (1986). *Social foundations of thought and action: A social cognitive theory.* Englewood Cliffs, NJ: Prentice-Hall.

Bandura, A., & Wood, R. E. (1989). Effect of perceived controllability and performance standards on self-regulation of complex decision-making. *Journal of Personality and Social Psychology, 56,* 805–814.

Beer, M., & Cannon, M. (2004). Promise and peril in implementing pay-for-performance. *Human Resource Management, 43*(1). 3–20.

Bogenrieder, I., & Nooteboom, B. (2004). Learning groups: What types are there? A theoretical analysis and an empirical study in a consultancy firm. *Organizational Studies, 25*(2), 287–313.

Cannon, M. D., & Edmondson, A. C. (2001). Confronting failure: Antecedents and consequences of shared beliefs about failure in organizational work groups. *Journal of Organizational Behavior 22,* 161–177.

Cannon, M. D., & Edmondson, A. C. (2005). Failing to learn and learning to fail (intelligently): How great organizations put failure to work to innovate and improve. *Long-Range Planning, 38,* 299–319.

Cannon, M. D., & Witherspoon, R. (2005). Actionable feedback: Unlocking the power of learning and development. *Academy of Management Executive, 19,* 120–134.

Collins, J. (2001). *From good to great: Why some companies make the leap . . . and others don't.* New York: HarperCollins.

Cutcher-Gershenfeld, J., & Ford, J. (2005). *Valuable disconnects in organizational learning systems: Integrating bold visions and harsh realities.* New York: Oxford University Press.

Dierkes, M., Antal, A., Child, J., & Nonaka, I. (2001). *Handbook of organizational learning and knowledge.* New York: Oxford.

Dusya, V., & Crossan, M. (2005). Improvisation and innovative performance in teams. *Organization Science: A journal of the Institute of Management Sciences, 16*(3), 203–224.

Easterby-Smith, M., Araujo, L., & Burgoyne, J. (Eds.). (1999). *Organizational learning and the learning organization.* Thousand Oaks, CA: Sage Publications.

Edmondson, A. (1999). Psychological safety and learning behavior in work teams. *Administrative Science Quarterly, 44,* 350–383.

Edmondson, A. C. (2003). Speaking up in the operating room: How team leaders promote learning in interdisciplinary action teams. *Journal of Management Studies, 40*(6), 1419–1452.

Fullan, M. (2003). *Change forces with a vengeance.* New York: RoutledgeFalmer.

Garvin, D. A. (2000). *Learning in action: A guide to putting the learning organization to work.* Boston: Harvard Business School Press.

Hackman, J. R. (2002). *Leading Teams: Setting the stage for great performances.* Boston: Harvard Business School Press.

Kelley, T., & Littman, J. (2001). *The art of innovation: Lessons in creativity from IDEO, America's leading design firm.* New York: Currency Books.

Kolb, D. (1984). *Experimental learning: Source of learning.* Upper Saddle River, NJ: Prentice Hall.

Krueger, J. (1998). Enhancement bias in descriptions of self and others. *Personal and Social Psychology Bulletin, 24(5),* 505–516.

Kunda, Z. (1999). *Social cognition: Making sense of people.* Cambridge, MA: MIT Press.

Langfred, C. (2004). Too much of a good thing? Negative effect of high trust and individual autonomy in self-managing teams. *Academy of Management Journal, 47(3),* 385.

Mann, C. (2004). Safety culture? What safety culture? *Nursing Management, 11(7),*10.

Michaelsen, L., Knight, A., & Fink, L. (Ed.). (2004). *Team-based learning.* Sterling, VA: Stylus Publishing.

Ouchi, W. (2003). *Making schools work.* New York: Simon & Schuster.

Roberto, M. (2002) Lesson from Everest: The interaction of cognitive bias, psychological safety, and system complexity. *California Management Review, 45*(1), 136–158.

Scott, R. W. (2003). Organizations: Rational, natural, and open systems (5th ed.). Upper Saddle River, NJ: Prentice Hall.

Senge, P. (1990). *The fifth discipline: The art and practice of the learning organization.* New York: Currency Doubleday.

Senge, P. M. (1999). *The dance of change: The challenges to sustaining momentum in the learning organization.* New York: Currency/Doubleday.

Senge, P., Cambron-McCabe, N., Lucas, T., Smith, B., Dutton, J., & Kleiner, A. (2000). *Schools that learn.* New York: Currency Doubleday.

Senge, P., Kleiner, A., Roberts, C., Ross, R., Roth, G., & Smith, B. (1999). *The dance of change: The challenges to sustaining momentum in learning organizations.* New York: Currency/Doubleday.

Sessa, V. I., & London, M. (2006). *Continuous learning in organizations.* Mahwah, NJ: Lawrence Erlbaum Associates.

Stack, J., & Burlingham, B. (1992) *The great game of business.* New York: Currency/Doubleday.

Staw, B., Sandelands, L., & Dutton, J. (1981). Threat-rigidity effects in organizational behavior: A multilevel analysis. *Administrative Science Quarterly, 26*(4), 501–524.

Stone, D., Patton, B., & Heen, S. (1999). *Difficult conversations: How to discuss what matters most.* New York: Penguin.

Taylor, S. E., & Brown, J. (1988). Illusions and well being: A social psychological perspective on mental health. *Psychological Bulletin, 103,* 193–210.

Thomke, S., & Nimgade, A. (2002). *Bank of America.* Harvard Business School Case, 9-603-022.

Tyan, R. (2005). The effects of threat sensitivity and face giving on dyadic psychological safety and upward communication. *Journal of Applied Psychology, 35*(2), 223–247.

Von Krogh, G., & Roos, J. (Eds.). (1996). *Managing knowledge: Perspectives on cooperation and completion.* Thousand Oaks, CA: Sage Publications.

Witherspoon, R., & Cannon, M. D. (2004). Coaching leaders in transition: Lessons from the field. In A. F. Abuono (Ed.), *Creative Consulting: Innovative Persepctives on Management Consulting, Vol. 4* (pp. 201–228). Greenwich, CT: Information Age Publishing.

Wenger, E., McDermott, R., & Snyder, W. (2002). *A guide to managing knowledge: Cultivating communities of practice.* Boston: Harvard Business School Press.

CHAPTER TWELVE

Virtual Teams

▓ INTRODUCTION

Advances in technology have produced a new context within which members of groups interact. There is no shortage of computer-savvy individuals who are well acquainted with email, instant messaging, and chat rooms. As a result, organizations are increasingly using technology to form virtual teams that perform various tasks and solve complex problems. This new technology-driven medium offers promise, but also presents unique challenges to group functioning. Instead of focusing on instructional technology or distance learning, this chapter will explore the possibility of building virtual teams among teachers, administrators, and stakeholders in schools.

LEARNING OBJECTIVES

After reading this chapter, you should be able to

- Describe the potential benefits of virtual teams.
- Describe the challenges of working in a virtual or computer-mediated environment.
- Understand the conditions necessary for group success in a virtual environment.
- Describe the five developmental phases of a virtual team.

 OPENING CASE

Quality Comes Last at Quality First

Quality First, Inc. is a dot-com company providing consulting services for retail companies desiring to improve customer service. The company recently landed a new account with a high-end men and women's clothing retailer that needs a computer-based training program for new employees. Program requirements are that the training program be web-based (accessible by any computer on the internet) and include text, graphics, audio, and video. Susan Johnson, managing director of

Quality First, assembled a virtual team of employees from across the United States and made them responsible for development, design, and implementation of the online training program.

The client's goal for the training system is to improve sales and to shrink the time it takes for new employees to become productive. The project manager met face-to-face with both the client and the account executive a number of times to understand the client's exact needs and expectations for the six-month timeline. Susan assigned Joe Dillard to manage the project and build a team comprising two training specialists, two curriculum designers, a graphic designer, a programmer (familiar with the authoring software that would deliver the training), and a technician to shoot video. All team members were freelance workers who were contracted specifically for this project.

The team used a collaborative website that included features such as online chat, threaded discussions, shared file space, and email. Team members were all comfortable using this technology and most had done contract work for Quality First in the past. Joe, the project leader, emailed team members and scheduled the first meeting. Each member was given the URL (web address) and password to access the project website. During the first meeting, team members were asked to introduce themselves using the online chat forum and to describe their role as a team member. After 30 minutes, Bob gave a brief overview of the project and told them he would email everyone a detailed work plan and task assignments.

Although there was some initial excitement about the project, by the time the task and role descriptions arrived a week later, enthusiasm had waned. Bob suggested that members meet online every week for people to give a report outlining the status of their project component. After six weeks, the project seemed to be stalled. Deadlines were missed and certain members such as the videographer and programmer were waiting on content and direction from the curriculum designers and trainers, who were still not exactly clear on client expectations. To find out what was going wrong, Bob set up a conference call. During the call, members complained that there was no clear plan on how to go about the project. Members were giving priority to other projects where there were clearer expectations and task assignments.

Discussion Questions

1. Why was the project failing?
2. What areas contributed to the failure of this project?
3. How did technology contribute to the failure?
4. What effect did leadership have on the project?
5. What effect did group process have on the project?

Technology has the potential to help individuals, groups, and organizations improve productivity and efficiency. As Collins (2001) suggests, great companies are not driven by technology, yet they do utilize it in effective ways to increase productivity and obtain better results. One of the benefits of technology and the internet is that they have made the world a smaller place (Friedman, 2006). National and multinational organizations no longer have to rely on travel and transportation systems to unite geographically distant members. Groups of people are now able to connect "virtually" through technology. Organizations are able to coordinate and strategically allocate human capital in the most effective ways by creating work teams that transcend geographic location or time zones. Since administrative groups in school systems are often located in the same building, virtual teams have not been used extensively in educational settings apart from distance education. But virtual teams have the potential to link administrators across schools and enable them to work more closely with district offices.

There is an abundance of emerging research on the characteristics and functioning of virtual teams (Hertel, Geister, & Konradt, 2005; Martins, Gilson, & Maynard, 2004; Riskell, Radtke, & Salas, 2003). Because this is a relatively recent organizational trend, researchers are still defining basic terms and studying relevant topics. Technology is ever changing, and there will continue to be a significant amount of fluidity in our understanding of concepts related to virtual teams. However, this chapter defines virtual teams as workgroups in which the majority of interaction between members occurs through electronic rather than face-to-face (F2F) communication.

In a study of 293 members of 54 virtual teams in 26 companies representing a wide variety of industries, Majchrzak, Malhotra, Stamps, and Lipnack (2004) found the following characteristics:

- Fewer than 17% of team members had ever met another team member in person
- More than three-fourths of the teams had members from more than one nation
- Almost two-thirds of teams had members from three or more time zones
- Almost half (48%) had members from more than one company

These teams were found in companies such as EDS, IBM, Emery, Kraft, Motorola, and Shell Chemicals where members were distributed across geographic, temporal, and organizational boundaries.

Virtual teams utilize various technologies including videoconferencing, email, telephone, threaded discussions (where users post comments to a continuous online discussion), instant messaging or online chats, file sharing, knowledge bases, and application sharing. Researchers describe virtual teams in terms of their degree of "virtualness" or amount of communication richness available to participants. Some teams meet exclusively in a virtual environment, while others meet periodically in person. For those groups that are operating in a primarily virtual environment, team members are dependent on technology for success. While synchronous communication such as net meetings and conference calls require all members to be present at the same time, asynchronous tools such as email and threaded discussions allow members to make contributions to a project at any time (see Table 12.1).

TABLE 12.1   Communication Mediums

	Synchronous (Instantaneous)	Asynchronous (Delayed Interaction)
Video	Video conferencing or webcam	Video files
Audio	Phone conferencing	Voicemail
Text	Online chat	Email
	Electronic whiteboard	Knowledge bases
		Threaded discussions

Groupware or collaborative software applications are web-based tools that include multiple communication mediums depending on the product. For example, one might find all of the communication mediums listed in Table 12.1 in one package. This area of technological development holds promise for the future efficiency of virtual teams. Collaborative software applications allow teams to share files, manage projects, and track processes from different locations at different times. Malhotra and Majchrzak (2005) have identified a number of various components of new and emerging virtual workspaces that include:

- electronic whiteboards and collaborative document editors that enable members to see where others are pointing and gesturing;
- instant poll capabilities to gauge member opinions on issues under discussion;
- instant messaging for quick, pointed personal and back-channel communication;
- electronic calendars for joint scheduling;
- a common electronic repository for sharing documents (which can be organized by the team's processes and/or their task assignments to facilitate document retrieval);
- discussion threads for conflict identification and resolution;
- links within discussion threads to facilitate document retrieval;
- annotations within documents to identify owners of particular perspectives; and
- version control and change tracking capability to trace evolution of a document. (p. 12, bullets added)

These workspaces can include both synchronous and asynchronous communication tools and offer a single place from which all of the work of the group can be performed and monitored.

Technology-based communication can be extremely effective and even enjoyable. Email, online chats, text messaging, facebook, and Myspace have become an integral part of popular culture and have insinuated themselves into organizational settings as well. While these tools can improve productivity, they can also be a distraction. In addition, people can inadvertently commit an electronic *faux pas*. During a summer internship in London, a student sent an email to her supervisor complaining about difficulties she was having with another department. Her supervisor replied to her email by saying members of the other department were "getting their knickers in a twist." The student mistakenly forwarded this email to the very individuals with whom she was having problems. Obviously, this caused quite a stir but in the end provided a good laugh and lesson for all.

Many of us have sent emails or posted comments that we wished we could retrieve. Electronic communication can be embarrassing. Once the enter key is clicked, emails or text messages are sent and become part of an archive somewhere. Reflect on some of the most embarrassing emails or instant messages you have experienced. Careful consideration is warranted in electronic communication.

▓ BENEFITS OF VIRTUAL TEAMS

The purpose of workgroups and teams is to accomplish organizational goals in ways that are more effective than by individual efforts. However, groups can lose productivity due to coordination costs and communication problems inherent in group work. Scheduling meetings and managing deadlines can be challenging facets of directing teams, and these issues have only increased with the escalating complexity of today's workplace. Technology has become an integral tool of commerce to deal with this complexity. It is difficult, for example, to imagine organizational life without voicemail or email. Electronic tools such as these increase organizational efficiency and productivity. Other communication technologies, both present and future, offer the same kind of benefits to organizations. Virtual teams and the technology that drives them offer the following benefits: (a) team compositions that increase quality and outcomes, (b) efficiency of communication, and (c) the development of intellectual capital.

Groups have the potential to increase productivity and efficiency within organizations. Putting the right mix of people together without regard to geographic location allows managers to maximize knowledge, skills, and abilities (Blackburn, Furst, & Rosen, 2003). These types of diverse and specialized teams are especially necessary to solve complex organizational problems and tasks. For instance, a team of school principals and district administrators working on educational reform might be able to benefit from the experience and knowledge of a parallel team in another state. The team might also benefit from the perspective of a curriculum specialist at a university in a third state who consults with school districts. Administrators can be involved on multiple virtual projects and participate on various teams.

Virtual teams allow team members in various locations to interact without the need for F2F meetings which can be time consuming and prohibitive. Cross-functional teams are composed of members from different educational and disciplinary backgrounds and include a mix of skill sets and experiences to tackle problems and achieve common goals. Vertical teams include faculty and administration from K-12 to align curriculum and instruction to meet educational objectives. Virtual teaming allows diverse members to collaborate in ways that were heretofore difficult if not impossible. While some of the obstacles have been removed, there are other details that need to be considered when creating and managing a virtual team.

Coordinating the work of groups requires communication. Scheduling and attending meetings may be easier when workers can stay at their own desk (wherever that may be) and participate in virtual meetings. Since physical spaces and other arrangements such as travel and accommodations are not necessary, organizations can save both time and money. While virtual meetings may not be as efficient as F2F meetings (Levenson & Cohen, 2003), the financial and logistical benefits are attractive. Without the benefit of nonverbal clues, though, group communication can be ambiguous and cohesion difficult to build. Yet these obstacles can be overcome by effective leadership.

Knowledge sharing links team members together through a virtual repository of expertise. Knowledge-management systems assist members in capturing, storing, and cataloging what they know so that others can access that knowledge and experience. For example, Proctor and Gamble has an electronic network that links 900 factories and 17 product development centers in 73 countries. In the past, it was difficult to know what new products were being developed in different locations, centers, and departments. To address this issue, Proctor and Gamble purchased collaborative knowledge-sharing software that permits product developers to search a database of 200,000 existing product designs to see if a similar design or process already exists in another part of the company. As a result, the time it takes to develop new products has been reduced by 50% (Ante, 2001).

Buckman Labs, a chemical manufacturing company, has effectively pooled the expertise of 1,400 employees in over 90 nations through a global strategy of knowledge sharing

(Buckman, 2004). For example, if a paper mill in Brazil has an outbreak of a bacterial contamination that threatens production, they can call on the local Buckman associate for a solution. The situation demands an immediate response. The Buckman employee can access the company knowledge base for information about paper, bacteria, and possible solutions based on the knowledge and experiences of other employees. In addition, the local associate can place an electronic call for help. In this way, solutions can be accessed quicker and problems solved more effectively than when field offices operate independently. This type of quality customer service earned Buckman Labs the 2005 MAKE Award (Most Admired Knowledge Enterprise) from a panel of leading knowledge-management experts.

Schools can also benefit by sharing knowledge among its professionals. For example, school counselors, psychologists, and social workers face challenging situations every day. At times, these service providers are without the necessary support and resources to handle the problems presented to them. Furthermore, legal and ethical issues can be complex and confusing. Often, teachers and school administrators do not have the level of training and expertise to help. One solution to this common problem is to create a virtual team of service professionals from different schools to provide expertise, consultation, and support. Over time, a knowledge base can be built that includes information such as local resources, treatment plans, and legal guidelines. In this way, service providers no longer operate in isolation, but they are connected to a network of resources and information. This model can be applied to any school specialty such as principals, librarians, reading specialists, special education teachers, advanced placement teachers, and so on.

▮ CHALLENGES OF VIRTUAL TEAMS

Virtual teams are abstract and ambiguous, and by their nature are challenging to manage. Davis (2004) found that problems take longer to identify and solutions longer to implement. There is less clarity about group dynamics within a team and the status of progress toward goals. Thus, Davis (2004) suggests that the distance inherent in virtual teams (a) amplifies dysfunction, (b) dilutes leadership, and (c) weakens human relations and team processes. Virtual groups can be especially challenging in the areas of goal definition, task distribution, coordination, and member motivation.

Teamwork requires interdependence and the belief that others are equally committed to the task and will competently do their part (Aubert & Kelsey, 2003). By far, the greatest challenge for virtual teams is developing this kind of trust. In organizational contexts, levels of trust are determined by assessing the ability, benevolence, and integrity of other group members (Mayer, Davis, & Schoorman, 1995). In virtual groups the lack of F2F interaction makes it difficult to carry out this assessment. Therefore, virtual teams struggle to gain a level of trust that maximizes group potential. Buckman (2004) emphasizes that the success of a virtual organization is built on a foundation of trust.

When group members interact in person, they are able to observe each other and draw conclusions about a number of variables including intellectual ability, past experiences, interpersonal style, and personality type which leads to the development or absence of trust. For example, in a F2F meeting, Bob might observe Suzy speak with great insight and experience about directing a peer-mentoring program for middle school children. In addition, she speaks in a manner that demonstrates her passion to help children. Bob also notices how willing Suzy is to make copies of her program manual to share with the group and the respect with which she interacts with office secretaries. All of these observations lead Bob to believe that Suzy is, indeed, a team player with ability, benevolence, and integrity. In a virtual environment, Bob might not be able to come to the same conclusions. Virtual members have less information from which to make assessments. Thus, virtual environments can be more tenuous and less trusting (Gibson & Manuel, 2003).

In addition to developing trust, virtual groups may also have a difficult time creating a shared vision. Shared vision, as described in Chapter 2, includes an understanding of the group's goal and member commitment to that goal. But in a virtual environment, it can be difficult to assess the level of importance and commitment that members have toward the team. Because virtual members typically interact less frequently and with less perceptual richness, they do not have the opportunity to observe interpersonal characteristics such as vocal tone, body language, and facial expressions. In contrast, an administrative team that meets every morning with established rituals and behaviors from which to derive a shared identity will have an easier time gaining member commitment to a shared vision. A virtual team that includes eight superintendents across any given state and two administrators from the state board of education that is pursuing educational reform will likely have a more difficult time creating the urgency, synergy, and commitment necessary to produce change.

Communication is more of a challenge in virtual teams than in F2F teams (Martins, Gilson, & Maynard, 2004). Since trust is difficult to achieve, members are more reluctant to express their opinions in virtual discussions (Baltes, Dickson, Sherman, Bauer, & LaGanke, 2002). Contributions in a virtual environment lack the nonverbal and social context to understand others accurately and to be understood. Teams take longer to make decisions and arrive at a shared understanding. In a F2F meeting, an idea can be acknowledged and agreed on through nods, smiles, or verbal responses. Puzzled looks, shrugs, raised eyebrows, and the like signal a lack of understanding or nonverbal requests for more information. Virtual environments lack these rich social and visual cues.

Even the most sophisticated computer-mediated communication channels are not able to capture the richness of F2F exchanges (Driskell, Radtke, & Salas, 2003). It is certainly more difficult to communicate complex information over the phone or through email than in person. Even video conferencing has its limitations. For example, consider the experience of going to a college football game or hearing a symphony perform. Live action includes the sights, smells, sounds, and various intangibles that cannot easily be put into words. Even watching a game or musical performance on TV does not capture all the details of the experience. Listening on the radio or reading a review does even less to convey the nuances of a live performance. Likewise, virtual environments are limited in capturing all the detail and "feel" of F2F meetings.

Virtual teams, by there nature, tend to be more diverse than F2F teams since they often span multiple geographic locations. Greater geographical distances can translate into differences in regional, national, and organizational cultures. Diversity posseses the potential for increased creativity and problem solving, but it also creates a context for miscommunication and misunderstanding. So, in addition to the challenges already noted, virtual teams also have to contend with the lack of a common set of assumptions and social norms that facilitate effective communication (Hinds & Weisband, 2003). Members might not even be communicating in their native language. Yet even with a common language, different words and phrases have different meanings from culture to culture. The potential for communication problems is great.

▓ CONDITIONS FOR SUCCESS

Organizations are interested in virtual teams because of their potential to maximize resources (human and intellectual capital) and reduce costs. But, as noted before, there are significant hurdles to overcome before those rewards can be realized. Virtual teams are not always the best strategy to accomplish organizational goals. Organizations need to evaluate group resources and consider whether there is a good fit between group tasks and the type of technology that is available (Maruping & Agarwal, 2004). Regardless of the type of technology employed, organizations can increase their chances of success by fostering the following conditions in the virtual team environment: (a) trust, (b) shared vision, and (c) effective communication.

Trust

Trust is an important variable in group work and is strongly related to performance outcomes, satisfaction with the group experience, and member commitment (Costa & Taillieu, 2001; Duarte & Snyder, 2001; Kanawattanachai & Yoo, 2002). Researchers studying companies such as IBM, Sun Microsystems, and Motorola attribute the success or failure of virtual teams primarily to the establishment of trust (Lipnack & Stamps, 1997). Yet virtual groups can have an especially difficult time establishing trust due to a lack of data that is used to assess the ability, benevolence, and integrity of other group members. Group members want to know if others are competent, respectful, and dependable. Trust takes time to develop and is established by observing what people say and how they interact with others. Initial or periodic F2F meetings can be helpful to jump start the trust-building process by providing richer data from which team members can make assessments of others (Martins, Gilson, & Maynard, 2004). Some researchers suggest that it is extremely difficult to establish trust in virtual teams without some F2F interaction (DeRosa, Hantula, Kock, & D'Arcy, 2004).

When teams are formed at Buckman labs, members are formally introduced to each other and leaders specifically explain why each person was chosen for the team (Buckman, 2004). Members are invited to describe their personal and professional backgrounds so that they can begin to get to know each other. Members need to know with whom they are working and what each member brings to the team in order to develop trust. One particularly successful team-building strategy at Buckman has been to have members post digital pictures of themselves on a team map that shows geographical locations and time zones. In addition, team roles and responsibilities are described so that members can see the "big picture" of how the team fits together. Members also list their knowledge, skills, and abilities in order to gain the confidence of others. In this way, members have a visual representation of the team and a description of each member to compensate for the lack of richness that is present in F2F meetings.

Dealing with conflict is another, albeit counterintuitive, strategy for developing trust in groups. Instead of trying to minimize or avoid conflict, effective leaders identify and confront potential problems. When intermember conflicts, frustration, and even hostility are openly discussed and successfully resolved, trust is developed. Because there is less data available to virtual teams from which to make judgments about other members, there is a greater potential to misunderstand and incorrectly attribute motives to others. A mistrusting environment can develop quickly and needs to be identified and addressed by the group before those behaviors become a norm. In virtual teams, trust can be developed through open communication, acknowledgment of underlying tensions, appropriate emotional expression, and self-disclosure (DeRosa, Hantula, Kock, & D'Arcy, 2004). When conflict has damaged trust between specific members, leaders will need to facilitate intensive and supportive interactions to rebuild trust (Zaccaro & Bader, 2003). This may be done in the larger group or privately between specific members. As a general rule, if an interpersonal problem occurs in the group context, it should be dealt with in the larger group context. In this way norms can be demonstrated and established.

While virtual teams tend to be "flatter" with less of an authority structure than other groups, members will still challenge the leadership. This is a normal part of group development and actually helps to establish boundaries, rules (norms), and roles of individual members. When leaders are confronted with passive, aggressive, or passive-aggressive behavior, they have an opportunity to model appropriate interpersonal strategies that respect and value others. Benevolence as one of the three antecedents of trust can be expressed when it is needed most—in the midst of interpersonal tension and conflict. Leaders can demonstrate their good faith in others while still confronting inappropriate behaviors that are potentially damaging to the group.

Shared Vision

As with F2F groups, virtual team success depends on a clear understanding of the group's goal and member commitment to that goal. Because members of virtual teams typically have more autonomy than F2F teams, it can be difficult to assess their commitment to shared goals. Leaders have less power and influence over the way members work and carry out their tasks. As a result, choosing the right people for the team is important. Virtual team members should be self-motivated and able to work on their own with minimal input and direction from superiors.

Buckman labs considers the development of a shared vision as a necessary component of success and strives to achieve at least 90% consensus on the group's goals (Buckman, 2004). Threaded discussions (asynchronous postings of text-based comments) have been used at Buckman to achieve this level of consensus. In this way, members can build on each others' comments until agreement is reached and coordinated group efforts can begin. The following is an example of how a threaded discussion might be used to define the shared vision of a virtual human resources team assessing the issue of alcoholism within a large manufacturing company.

John: Operations has requested a set of policies for handling drinking on the job.

> **Suzy:** I understand that front line managers are concerned about the increase in alcohol-related injuries.

>> **Stan:** How do managers find out that workers are getting drunk? And how are we defining "alcohol related injury"?

>>> **Sara:** Obviously, an "alcohol related injury" is an injury that happens while an employee is under the influence of alcohol.

>>> **Bob:** I think we need to understand the big picture first before we start defining specific terms and issues.

>> **Jane:** I've heard that one of our workers almost lost an arm because he was intoxicated so this is a pretty important issue.

> **Sara:** Ok, so we need to create some policies for alcohol abuse. Is the goal to identify this kind of behavior and get rid of those employees, or do we want to create programs to help them?

> **Stan:** What, exactly, is our timeframe here and what, specifically, do we need to deliver to operations?

This type of online discussion can be held on a password-protected website to ensure confidentiality and security. Comments can be posted asynchronously at any time of the day. Members can then respond to a specific comment (or *post*) and it will appear in the threaded discussion as indented and below the post to which it is related. Threaded discussions have the added benefit of keeping a running record of the groups' discussion and decisions. Conversations can continue for days. Another forum for this type of discussion is online chat. When discussions are held in a chat environment, comments are posted in real time (synchronous text-based communication) which can make it difficult to know who is responding to whom. For example, all of the comments above would appear along the left hand margin and happen at approximately the same time which can get quite confusing.

A shared vision requires a shared understanding of the group goal and buy-in from group members. Arriving at a mutually supported description of the group's goal is the first step in developing a shared identity. When goals are written down and archived such as in the threaded discussion example above, members can refer to them periodically for guidance in future decisions and direction. Whereas team leaders in F2F meetings can assess nonverbal assent through facial expressions and gestures, virtual team leaders have to specifically ask members to state their commitment. For example, a leader might ask "Are we all agreed that this is the goal of the group?" and then "Is everyone committed to this goal?" If there is either a lack of consensus or lack of commitment, more discussion is needed. Objections and resistance will need to be identified and processed before the group can effectively devise a strategy to achieve their goals.

Effective Communication

Effective communication helps enhance the previous two conditions for success. Communication builds trust and helps to establish a shared vision. When members communicate in a supportive and optimistic way, groups develop the good faith necessary for effective functioning. Supportive messages go a long way toward helping the group develop cohesion and can be as simple as "Bob, I like the way you see this problem and think we should take your perspective into account," or "Sarah is really working hard and making a significant contribution to this project." It takes relatively little effort to make comments like these but they create trust and develop positive norms.

In order to overcome the increased ambiguity in virtual communication, active listening can be used to clarify and better understand the comments of others (Gibson & Manuel, 2003). Especially when members are from different cultures, teams will have to work harder to understand the messages that others are communicating. Assumptions that are made in normal F2F communication within a common culture cannot be made in a virtual environment. Things normally taken for granted in F2F teams must be carefully considered and explicitly stated in virtual teams which often span multiple cultures, time zones, measurement systems and worldviews. Communication skills such as paraphrasing and probing questions can be helpful in alleviating potential misunderstandings as demonstrated in this online chat:

John: We need more resources to achieve our goals.

Janet: Help me understand how you arrived at that conclusion, John. [probing question]

John: Given our current deadline, I just don't see how we can deliver.

Janet: So you think that there are no other options for us, such as revising our strategy or asking for an extension, and think we just need more people on the team? [paraphrase]

John: No, actually, I don't think we need more people, just more funds to meet F2F as a team over the next few months.

Janet: How does the rest of the team feel about calling a few F2F meetings? [probing question]

An additional challenge for virtual teams is the sharing of information and knowledge. While members may have a wealth of knowledge and expertise, virtual meetings may not be the best place for that knowledge to be shared among the team. For this reason, organizations create knowledge bases or online databases that contain the collective wisdom and expertise of their employees. Knowledge management systems capture, organize, and disseminate this wealth of information. Because knowledge can be seen as proprietary and beneficial to one's own advancement, employees typically need to be rewarded for their contribution to a common database of information. When reward systems reinforce the sharing of information and a commitment to collective success, cohesion increases and positive organizational norms are strengthened.

Coordinating efforts is an especially important part of virtual-team effectiveness. Because it is not as easy to stop by a team member's office, check in with a quick phone call, or obtain the benefits of regularly scheduled status meetings, virtual teams must create other ways to coordinate and collaborate. Zaccaro and Bader (2003) suggest the following specific strategies to increase positive communication among team members:

- Establish task norms and standard operating procedures
- Provide clear task roles and expectations
- Create a structure for routine updates and reports by members
- Maintain an electronic archive of team actions and decisions
- Convey a clear sense of direction and purpose for the team

Again, what can be taken for granted in F2F teams must be made more explicit in virtual teams. Even a video conference which most closely emulates the richness of an F2F meeting can benefit from the guidelines suggested in Appendix A at the end of this chapter.

When this textbook was being written, the second author was teaching a class in London, England. With the help of two inexpensive webcams, the authors met regularly to talk to each other and discuss our progress. This medium was richer than email, and allowed us to coordinate efforts more effectively. But when more people are involved and tasks are complex, virtual communication can be confusing and produce frustration. Exercise 12.2 was given to one of our classes and generated strong feelings of frustration and anger.

Exercise 12.1   Virtual Team Simulation

Your task is to create an e-learning organization that will provide continuing-education opportunities for teachers and administrators. Each member of the simulation will be assigned to one of the virtual teams listed below. Members of the teams will interact with each other in an online chat room. Each team also has access to a virtual space to share files and a threaded discussion for use within the team. Please appoint a team leader for the project who can interface with senior management and the operations group. A virtual conference room is available for meetings between members of different groups. You can schedule meetings and request information from other project groups through the group discussion board in the conference room.

Project Groups and Challenges

1. **HR Group:** Create an HR policy that is designed to motivate and retain good talent. In addition, create a compensation plan (salary and benefits) for each of the company's employees based on the project they're working on and whether they are a team leader on that project. The operations group will use these figures for budget allocations.
2. **Marketing Group:** Create a marketing strategy and advertising campaign. How will you get the word out about the organization and find potential customers? You'll need to work with the IT group for the website development as well as the senior management group for direction on how best to describe and portray the company.
3. **Sales Group:** Prepare a PowerPoint presentation that could be presented to faculty and administrators. Describe the sales cycle and forecast sales for the first year. Include a job description of how sales people will spend their time and energy. You'll need to work with the product development group for an understanding of the products and services your company is selling.
4. **IT Group:** Design a company website. You'll need to work with the marketing group and product development group for content. It should reflect the mission statement and core values created by senior management.
5. **Product Development Group:** Create the products and services that the company will market to teachers and administrators. Work with the senior management group to capture their vision for what the company should focus on and the operations group for pricing.
6. **Operations Group:** Create an operations plan from the money you have been allocated for each team by senior management. You'll need to work with the HR group for salary figures and determine a budget for other operating expenses specific to each group. With 36 people in the organization, you'll need to determine what kinds of office space and equipment you'll need.
7. **Graphic Design Group:** Create a name, logo, and tagline for the organization. Work with senior management's mission statement to capture their vision for the company. Many of the other groups will need your design to incorporate into their projects.
8. **Senior Management Group:** Provide oversight and accountability for the organization. This group needs to develop a mission statement, a set of core values, and specific first year goals for the organization. A venture capital firm has invested $3 million for the first year of operations. Allocate a certain percentage of that money to each of the project groups. Give those figures to the operations group to create budgets for each of the teams. Investors are concerned that expenses could easily get out of control and therefore need to be managed closely.

While debriefing Exercise 12.1, students reported being extremely frustrated with the process of trying to coordinate their efforts within and between groups. One student made the comment that she would rather stay in school indefinitely rather than enter the real world of work if that was what it was like. This is a complex assignment that is designed to generate the dynamics that elicit the typical problems of virtual communication. Virtual teams that are just forming might benefit from an exercise like this to raise awareness and identify the challenges of working in a virtual environment. Once the various issues are on the table, the team can proactively create norms and operating procedures (structure) that address potential problems.

▓ BUILDING AND MAINTAINING EFFECTIVE VIRTUAL TEAMS

Designing and launching a virtual team requires planning and forethought. Based on empirical data, Hertel, Geister, & Konradt (2005) have created a model of team effectiveness that considers the unique needs of virtual groups at different stages of development. They have identified five key activities in the life of a virtual group each with unique tasks and challenges that need to be addressed. Groups have different characteristics and needs at different times in their existence. Effective leaders are aware of these developmental needs and provide appropriate structuring and guidance (see Figure 12.1).

Preparations

The preparation phase includes those tasks related to the formation of a virtual team. The implementation of a virtual team requires planning to ensure that the conditions for success are met and that an adequate virtual structure is created. First, the purpose of the group has to be clearly defined. In the planning stage, leaders evaluate whether or not a virtual team is the best strategy to accomplish that purpose. The type of tasks that are best suited for virtual teams are (a) information or service based such as R&D, project management, or sales, (b) modular or easily separated into subtasks that can be distributed across different locations and easily coordinated, and (c) have clear metrics that allow members to evaluate progress and the success of the team (Hertel, Geister, & Konradt, 2005). While a purpose of a team is often defined by the organization, it is helpful to give the team some autonomy in elaborating on or operationalizing that purpose.

Based on the purpose and specific tasks that need to be accomplished, the right personnel have to be identified and enlisted. It is helpful if members are given the option to join the team as opposed to being assigned. In selecting members for a virtual team, leaders should consider whether or not potential members have the following competencies:

- Task-related competencies: knowledge, skills, abilities, and experience related to the mission of the group, commitment to the task, and conscientiousness.
- Team-related competencies: cooperativeness, communication skills, benevolence, integrity, and the general ability to trust and work with others.
- Virtual competencies: technological competence and comfort, self-management skills, ability to work in diverse and abstract environments.

Selecting the right members is crucial for a successful team. Some talented and competent people may not be the best choices for inclusion. And in order to motivate potential members to join a virtual team, reward systems should include incentives related to individual *and* group performance.

Based on the group's tasks and the specific membership of the group (skills, experience, and locations), project leaders will decide upon a technology platform. A host of

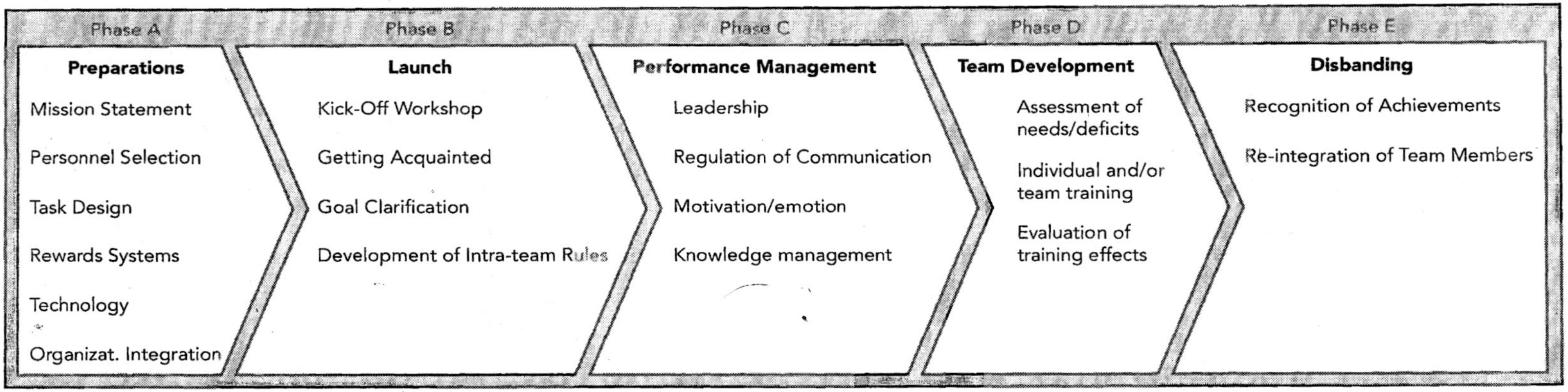

Phase A	Phase B	Phase C	Phase D	Phase E
Preparations	**Launch**	**Performance Management**	**Team Development**	**Disbanding**
Mission Statement	Kick-Off Workshop	Leadership	Assessment of needs/deficits	Recognition of Achievements
Personnel Selection	Getting Acquainted	Regulation of Communication	Individual and/or team training	Re-integration of Team Members
Task Design	Goal Clarification	Motivation/emotion	Evaluation of training effects	
Rewards Systems	Development of Intra-team Rules	Knowledge management		
Technology				
Organizat. Integration				

FIGURE 12.1 Developmental Phases of a Virtual Team

options are available so gaining multiple perspectives both within and outside of the group can be helpful. Leaders can propose a tentative plan to team members and obtain feedback on the strengths and weaknesses of the design. This allows input from members and increases the chances for buy-in. Once a virtual communication medium has been decided, members will need the necessary hardware (computers, cameras, etc.), software (email, online chat, knowledge base systems, groupware, etc.), training, and support to proceed with the interactive system. The training and support plan might include F2F workshops, online tutorials, lists of frequently asked questions (FAQs), online help sessions, or a help center staffed by technology-support personnel. Leaders and members should expect technology problems, especially at the beginning of implementation but also periodically throughout the life of the virtual team. The implementation and use of advanced technology often has many challenges and surprises.

Launch

A concise and well-designed launch can build momentum and cohesion for a new team (Blackburn, Furst, & Rosen, 2003). Because the initial meetings will set a pattern for future interactions, the launch is important. Researchers have consistently found that virtual teams benefit greatly from an initial F2F kick-off meeting or workshop (Hertel, Geister, & Konradt, 2005). Getting members together to jump start the team can save time and unnecessary confusion. An initial F2F meeting helps members get acquainted with each other and begins to build trust and a commitment to shared goals (Warkentin & Beranek, 1999). In addition, members can receive training and define norms and protocols about how they will communicate and work together. These components of group life will eventually emerge in a virtual environment but an initial meeting can be a catalyst for development and productivity.

If group members are not able to meet F2F, team leaders will have to be more creative in launching the beginning of a virtual team. Ideally, members should have information about each other and about the purpose of the group before the first meeting. Written biographies with pictures will help members envision their teammates and begin to build trust. To avoid any technical problems, the communication medium should be tested before the first official meeting and members trained if needed. A successful launch should create an atmosphere of trust, a clear understanding of the group's purpose, and anticipation for success.

Whether a team is using online chat, video conferencing, or groupware, team members must be comfortable operating within that environment. Since virtual communication can be frustrating and lead to misunderstandings, effective leaders understand the limitations of any given medium and are prepared to coach others in its proper usage and begin the group with some structure and a shared understanding of communication norms. For example, in virtual teams that use text-based communication (email or online chat), group members may not be aware that when they use all capital letters they are perceived as "shouting." Members may not know if the use of emoticons to express emotion is appropriate, or what kind of language is considered unprofessional (e.g., profanity or slang). In teams that use video-based communication, members may not know to wait until the camera is focused on them before they speak or how to avoid speaking over someone else. Appendix A identifies a number of suggestions for virtual-communication etiquette, norms, and general operating procedures that can be discussed during the launch phase.

Performance Management

One of the primary roles of team leaders is to monitor progress and motivate members toward task completion. Both of these leadership functions tend to be more difficult in an abstract, virtual context where it is harder to assess both task progress and member commitment. Leaders have less direct control and influence over the functioning of group members. In a study of 13 virtual teams operating in Europe, Mexico, and the United States, Kayworth and Leidner (2001) found that the most effective team leaders acted in a mentoring role that demonstrated a high degree of concern for others, were able to assert their authority without being overbearing, and were effective at providing regular, detailed, and prompt communication about the status of the project.

DAPEE, the task/project management strategy described in Chapter 3, applies to virtual teams as well. After the task, goal, or project is defined and analyzed, the team then creates a plan to achieve the desired results. A detailed work plan defines assignments and schedules for completion. During the execution of a plan, one or more people will need to monitor the progress of individual members and the group as a whole. Some team tasks can be divided, performed separately by group members, and then combined into a finished product. In this case, leaders monitor the progress of individual members and then oversee the integration of each member's contribution. But as tasks become more complex and member responsibilities and roles are increasingly interdependent, monitoring becomes more difficult (Bell & Kozlowski, 2002). Complex tasks require greater levels of synchronous collaboration, communication, and information sharing with the whole team. Progress indicators and feedback should be frequent, concrete, and timely on both the individual and group levels (Hertel, Geister, & Konradt, 2005).

Without formal hierarchies or traditional structures, leaders tend to function more as coaches or trainers, as opposed to traditional managers or supervisors. Among other things, virtual leaders monitor the relational dimension of the team including the motivation and commitment of members, the level of trust and cohesion in the group, and the satisfaction of group members. If interpersonal or communication problems have developed and are not addressed by the group, the leader may need to act as a catalyst to bring issues to the group's attention. Instead of saying "we need to be prompt about deadlines," virtual leaders may need to be more subtle and ask members how they feel about the pattern of missed deadlines in the group. Instead of assigning roles and tasks, effective virtual leaders prompt the group to make those decisions.

Because members are not physically in each other's presence, it may be difficult to develop and maintain motivation (Hertel, Geister, & Konradt, 2005). Leaders and members can increase the individual and collective motivation within the team by being more aware of a number of issues (Hertel, Konradt, & Orlikowski, 2004). First, motivation is related to how members evaluate the team's goals. If members understand the goals and see their importance, they will be more motivated to work toward achieving them. Second, members are more motivated to perform when they believe their contribution to the team is needed. Leaders can regularly communicate the imperative that the team cannot perform up to its capacity unless every member is contributing. Third, members are motivated to work hard when they believe they have the necessary abilities to perform their task. Positive feedback from others can reinforce adequate levels of self-efficacy. Finally, members work hard when they believe others are working hard as well. Therefore, if there is an opportunity for members to stay abreast of the efforts of other team members, they will be more motivated to accomplish their own assigned tasks.

Team Development

Training has been shown to be effective in helping teams overcome the limitations inherent in virtual communication by increasing levels of cohesiveness and team satisfaction (Warkentin & Beranek, 1999). In addition, periodic assessment of both the relational and performance dimensions of virtual teams provides leaders and members with data that can help improve performance. For example, an assessment of 10 virtual procurement teams operating within a large organization found three major areas for improvement: (a) clarification of the team goals, (b) effective use of communication media, and (c) development of group communication norms (Hertel, Geister, & Konradt, 2005). Three months after participating in a two-day training class, members reported improvement in each of these areas as well as overall team effectiveness. Teams grow and change over time. Leaders can facilitate this process by being aware of the needs and deficits of the team and proactively planning individual and team interventions to improve performance.

Teams experience personnel changes as existing members leave and new members are added. When new members join an existing team, they need to be oriented to the goals, strategies, structures, rules, and roles of the group (Bell & Kozlowski, 2002). Team development includes the assimilation and training of new members into the existing structure. Simultaneously, the existing structure may need to adapt as resources are lost or gained. Trainers and team leaders are aware of the need to prepare individuals for the team, and to prepare the team for any changes in personnel.

Disbanding

The end of a group is an opportune time for members to reflect on the successes and failures of the group. The last virtual meeting can include a consolidation of learning, evaluation of performance, assessment of individual contributions, and celebration of successes. This allows members to learn from their experience and take beneficial lessons with them to their next team experience. For example, leaders might ask each member to describe the positive things they experienced as well as what they wish had been different in the group. This encourages members to verbalize their reflections and consolidate learning.

Finally, group members need to say goodbye to each other. They may also choose to resolve any interpersonal issues that may have developed during the course of the experience. If the group has been successful, there may be sadness and promises to stay in touch. Relationships may continue long after the termination of the team. Contributing to the collective success of a team meets the human need for self-transcendence and can be extremely satisfying. In this way, teams are beneficial not only to the organization but to individuals as well.

🗀 OPENING CASE REVISITED

Quality Comes Last at Quality First

Because of the complexity of this project, Bob knew he had to fly all the team members to the headquarters and have a two-day conference to clarify what the client wanted and to devise a plan to meet those goals. After team members spent some time getting to know each other, the client was brought in to explain in detail what they were looking for. Members of the team were able to interact and ask questions that pertained to their individual part of the project. In the afternoon, the curriculum designers gave an overview of the content of the training program that was to be delivered in four "modules." The trainers described the best way to communicate those ideas and the programmer and videographer each got a better idea of his or her assignment. The second day was spent going into greater detail of each component of the project and constructing a detailed work plan that included tasks and deadlines. The team also devised a communication structure whereby people could update others, ask questions, and send information to counterparts who were working on interdependent tasks.

From that point on, members seemed more motivated and invested in the success of the project. They knew where the team was going and understood their part. Online communication was friendlier and included more personal banter. Relationships were being formed and members seemed to be committed to each other and to the project. The team worked extremely hard to get the job done. After the first training module was completed, Bob demonstrated it to Susan Johnson, the managing director, who was satisfied enough to solicit feedback from the client. With only a few minor changes in the design of the product, the project continued and was completed in a total of seven months. With the client pleased and the project finished, Bob rewarded each team member with a $500 gift certificate to the client's clothing stores and included a note expressing his warm appreciation and gratitude for their efforts.

This case shows the importance of getting virtual groups started on the right foot. Without clear goals and a comfort level with other members, virtual teams can quickly stagnate. Bob took the group back to the beginning of team development and re-launched the team. This gave members the opportunity to meet each other, define norms, understand roles and responsibilities, and develop trust. In addition, members were trained on the virtual tools available to the team. With a renewed commitment to the vision of the team and the understanding of their own role, members successfully completed the project and were rewarded accordingly.

Summary

Virtual teams have tremendous potential to assemble the best and brightest members for particular projects that are spread across time zones, geographic areas, and organizations. However, virtual teams also have specific challenges that have to be managed and addressed. This chapter looked at the benefits and drawbacks of virtual teams and proposed a model of virtual-team development that maximizes the potential for success. Specifically, team leaders must be aware of the limitations of computer-based communication and the difficulty of developing trust and commitment in a virtual environment.

📁 CONCLUDING CASE ─────────────────────────────────────

Old Dogs and New Tricks

Dr. Jon Bullard is the superintendent of Folsom County Schools, one of the largest urban districts in the state. Bullard is aggressively addressing the reason for increasing drop-out rates in the four high schools in his district. To do this, he assembled a group of the most successful principals, both current and retired, into an advisory council. The purpose of the council is to develop long-term strategies for improving student attendance and achievement. In addition, Superintendent Bullard would like to create a forum where new or struggling principals can gain access to the advice of seasoned administrators from across the state.

Bullard initially asked his council to participate in a monthly conference call over the phone. But those meetings had low energy with only a few of the ten participants engaging in the conversation. One of those members who said very little was Tyler Morgan. Morgan has been a successful principal for more than 30 years and is well known throughout the state. When Dr. Bullard called him to ask why he was not participating, Morgan said that he thought the phone conferences were a waste of time. Bullard knew Tyler had a wealth of knowledge and experience and asked him if he was willing to have a video camera installed in his office in order to participate in video-based meetings and if he was willing to have other principals email him with questions and to get advice on various topics. Morgan did not use email and wasn't going to learn so that wasn't an option. He was willing, though, for the superintendent to install a video system in his office and participate in a monthly video conference with novice principals.

Discussion Questions

1. How do you envision this project proceeding?
2. How could you help Tyler Morgan to really embrace his role on the council?
3. How would you help him overcome his reluctance to use technology?
4. What are some things to consider in order to launch this project effectively?

References

Ante, S. E. (2001, August 27). Simultaneous software; Tools from a new generation of companies make it easier for employees and business partners to work together. *Business Week*, 46–47.

Aubert, B. A., & Kelsey, B. L. (2003). Further understanding of trust and performance in virtual teams. *Small Group Research, 34*, 575–618.

Baltes, B. B., Dickson, M. W., Sherman, M. P., Bauer, C. C., & LaGanke, J. S. (2002). Computer-mediated communication and group decision making: A meta-analysis. *Organizational Behavior and Human Decision Processes, 87*, 156–179.

Bell, B. S., & Kozlowski, S. W. J. (2002). A typology of virtual teams: Implications for effective leadership. *Group & Organizational Management, 27*, 14–49.

Blackburn, R., Furst, S., & Rosen, B. (2003). Building a winning virtual team: KSAs, selection, training, and evaluation. In C. B. Gibson & S. G. Cohen (Eds.), *Virtual teams that work: Creating conditions for virtual team effectiveness* (pp. 95–120). San Francisco: Jossey-Bass.

Buckman, R. H. (2004). *Building a knowledge-driven organization.* New York: McGraw-Hill.

Collins, J. (2001). *From good to great: Why some companies make the leap . . . and others don't.* New York: HarperCollins.

Costa, A. C., Roe, R. A., & Taillieu, T. (2001). Trust within teams: The relation with performance effectiveness. *European Journal of Work and Organizational Psychology, 10,* 225–244.

Davis, D. D. (2004). The tao of leadership in virtual teams. *Organizational Dynamics, 33,* 47–62.

DeRosa, D. M., Hantula, D. A., Kock, N., & D'Arcy, J. (2004). Trust and leadership in virtual team-work: A media naturalness perspective. *Human Resource Manager, 43,* 219–232.

Driskell, J. E., Radtke, P. H., & Salas, E. (2003). Virtual teams: Effects of technological mediation on team performance. *Group Dynamics: Theory, Research, and Practice, 7,* 297–323.

Duarte, D. L., & Snyder, N. T. (2001). *Mastering virtual teams: Strategies, tools, and techniques that succeed* (2nd ed.). San Francisco: Jossey-Bass.

Friedman, T. L. (2006). *The world is flat: A brief history of the twenty-first century* (1st rev. and expanded ed.). New York: Farrar, Straus and Giroux.

Gibson, C. B., & Manuel, J. A. (2003). Building trust: Effective multicultural communication processes in virtual teams. In C. B. Gibson & S. G. Cohen (Eds.), *Virtual teams that work: Creating conditions for virtual team effectiveness* (pp. 59–86). San Francisco: Jossey-Bass.

Hertel, G., Geister, S., & Konradt, U. (2005). Managing virtual teams: A review of current empirical research. *Human Resource Management Review, 15,* 69–95.

Hertel, G., Konradt, U., & Orlikowski, B. (2004). Managing distance by interdependence: Goal setting, task interdependence and team-based rewards in virtual teams. *European Journal of Work and Organizational Psychology, 13,* 1–28.

Hinds, P. J., & Weisband, S. P. (2003). Knowledge sharing and shared understanding in virtual teams. In C. B. Gibson & S. G. Cohen (Eds.), *Virtual teams that work: Creating conditions for virtual team effectiveness* (pp. 21–36). San Francisco: Jossey-Bass.

Kanawattanachai, P., & Yoo, Y. (2002). Dynamic nature of trust in virtual teams. *Journal of Strategic Information Systems, 11,* 187–213.

Kayworth, T. R., & Leidner, D. E. (2001). Leadership effectiveness in global virtual teams. *Journal of Management Information Systems, 18,* 7–40.

Levenson, A. R., & Cohen, S. G. (2003). Meeting the performance challenge: Calculating return on investment for virtual teams. In C. B. Gibson & S. G. Cohen (Eds.), *Virtual teams that work: Creating conditions for virtual team effectiveness* (pp. 145–174). San Francisco: Jossey-Bass.

Lipnack, J., & Stamps, J. (1997). *Virtual teams: Reaching across space, time and organizations with technology.* New York: Wiley.

Majchrzak, A., Malhotra, A., Stamps, J., & Lipnack, J. (2004). Can absence make a team grow stronger? *Harvard Business Review, 82,* 131–137.

Malhotra, A., & Majchrzak, A. (2005). Virtual workspace technologies. *MIT Sloan Management Review, 46,* 11–14.

Martins, L. L., Gilson, L. L., & Maynard, M. T. (2004). Virtual teams: What do we know and where do we go from here? *Journal of Management, 30,* 805–835.

Maruping, L. M., & Agarwal, R. (2004). Managing team interpersonal processes through technology: A task-technology fit perspective. *Journal of Applied Psychology, 89,* 975–990.

Mayer, R. C., Davis, J. H., & Schoorman, F. D. (1995). An integrative model of organizational trust. *Academy of Management Review, 20,* 709–734.

Riskell, J. E., Radtke, P. H., & Salas, E. (2003). Virtual teams: Effects of technological mediation of team performance. *Group Dynamics: Theory, Research, and Practice, 7,* 297–323.

Tryan, K. L., Tryan, C. K., & Shepherd, M. (2003). Exploring emerging leadership in virtual teams. In C. B. Gibson & S. G. Cohen (Eds.), *Virtual teams that work: Creating conditions for virtual team effectiveness* (pp. 183-195). San Francisco: Jossey-Bass.

Warkentin, M., & Beranek, P. M. (1999). Training to improve virtual team communication. *Information Systems Journal, 9,* 271–289.

Zaccaro, S. J., & Bader, P. (2003). E-leadership and the challenges of leading e-teams: Minimizing the bad and maximizing the good. *Organizational Dynamics, 31,* 377–387.

Appendix A

Tips and etiquette for text-based communication (email, online chats, or threaded discussions):

- Consider opening up your email software at various times during the day. It can be too distracting if you are constantly receiving emails throughout the day.
- Don't overuse email. Be considerate of filling other people's mailboxes with unimportant messages. Don't forward spam (chain mails, cute stories, etc.).
- Wait a few hours or a day before sending an emotional email. You can't get it back once it is sent.
- Be sure the right people are getting your email. Fill out the address field after the email is composed to avoid sending an email prematurely or to the wrong people.
- Consider the size of attachments you might send. If they are too large (greater than 5 or 10 MB), they can shut down another person's mailbox.
- Do not be too casual when writing messages. Use an appropriate style of correspondence for the organizational context.
- Avoid slang, abbreviations, and idioms. Members of other cultures may not understand what might be common knowledge in your culture.
- Avoid personal opinions, profanity, sexually oriented language, gossip, or political views.
- Remember that email is public. There is usually a permanent record somewhere.
- Know when to pick up the phone and call. Some complex issues are best addressed on the phone and not by email or instant messaging.
- Respond to emails within a reasonable timeframe, such as 24 or 48 hours.

Tips and etiquette for video-based communication (video conference or net meeting):

- Videoconferences must be arranged ahead of time. If a bridge is being used, set up the bridging service with a reliable company. Protocols and equipment must be set up in advance (cameras, connections, layout of video, how each site will be viewed, etc.).
- Contact and technical information needs to be exchanged between technical support personnel.
- Set up the date, time, and location of a videoconference at least three days in advance.
- Test the connection between sites 24 hours before the meeting.
- The bridge needs to be scheduled 30 minutes prior to the meeting and 30 minutes after the scheduled meeting.
- Perform an audio check 15 minutes before the scheduled time.
- Encourage attendees to wear appropriate business attire and avoid the use of patterns and stripes which can be hard to see on video.
- Avoid having food which can be noisy and distracting. Drinks are fine.
- Consider using a moderator for the meeting who will confirm connections, check attendance, facilitate conversations, get clarification, acknowledge those who want to talk, and who will generally keep an eye on all sites.
- Files, agendas, biographies, and notes need to be sent to all participants at least 48 hours in advance. Biographies should be organized by site and include a picture or each team member.
- Introductions should be brief, referring participants to more detailed written bios.
- Develop a protocol for how communication is to take place. For example, should participants raise their hand, cough, or announce themselves first?

- Sites should mute their microphone when they are not speaking to avoid extraneous noise and to avoid private comments from being overheard.
- Coordinate PowerPoint presentations. Make sure they are brief (usually less than 20 slides) and concise.
- Consider recording the meeting to have an archive for future reference.
- At the end of the meeting, the moderator should summarize the main ideas and action items, confirm the details of the next meeting, and describe any communication that is to take place before then.

Index

Page numbers followed by f and t represent figures and tables respectively.